ILLMATIC CONSEQUENCES: THE CLAPBACK TO OPPONENTS OF 'CRITICAL RACE THEORY'

Walter Greason, PhD

Danian Darrell Jerry, MFA

ILLMATIC CONSEQUENCES:
THE CLAPBACK TO OPPONENTS OF 'CRITICAL RACE THEORY'

Cover Art by Stacey Robinson
Cover Design by Dave McClinton

Copyright © 2023 Universal Write Publications, LLC
All rights reserved.

Mailing/Submissions:
Universal Write Publications, LLC
421 8th Avenue, Suite 86
New York, NY 10116

Website: UWPBooks.com

ISBN: 978-1-942774-90-7

This book was published with the support of SAGE Publishing.

About the Editors

Walter Greason, Ph.D., DeWitt Wallace Professor and Chair of the Department of History at Macalester College, is the preeminent historian of Afrofuturism, the Black Speculative Arts, and digital economies in the world today. Named one of "Today's Black History Makers" by *The Philadelphia Daily News*, Dr. Greason has written more than 100 academic articles and essays. His work has appeared on *Huffington Post*, *National Public Radio*, and *The Atlantic*, among other popular, professional, and scholarly journals. He is also the author, editor, and contributor to 18 books, including *Suburban Erasure*, *The Land Speaks*, *Cities Imagined*, *Illmatic Consequences*, and *The Black Reparations Project*.

From 2007 to 2012, Dr. Greason served as an advisor to Building One America, the coalition that designed the American Recovery and Reinvestment Act (2009). He was also the founding president of the T. Thomas Fortune Foundation, an organization that saved the National Historic Landmark dedicated to the leading, militant journalist of the nineteenth century. Dr. Greason's digital humanities projects, "The Wakanda Syllabus" and "The Racial Violence Syllabus," have produced global responses in the past six years. His work in historic preservation and virtual reality continues to inspire new research around the world. Dr. Greason currently writes about the racial wealth gap and the patterns of economic globalization.

Danian Darrell Jerry, writer, teacher, and musician, holds a Master of Fine Arts in Creative Writing. He is a VONA (Voices of Our Nation) fellow, a fiction editor of *Obsidian: Literature and Arts in the African Diaspora*, and a 2023 Volcanista of Under the Volcano Writer's Workshop. Danian founded Neighborhood Heroes, a youth arts program that employs comic books and literary arts to educate emerging readers. On stage, he has performed with hip-hop legends KRS-One and DJ Kool Herc, and as a featured guest at the 2019 Mercedes-Benz SXSW MeConvention in Frankfurt, Germany. His work is referenced in *This Ain't Chicago: Race, Class, & Regional Identity in the Post-Soul South*, *Hip Hop in America: A Regional Guide*, *The Commercial Appeal*, *The Memphis Flyer*, and *Southern Soul Magazine*. His writing appears in *Black Panther: Tales of Wakanda*, *Fireside Fiction*, *Cracking the Wire*

During Black Lives Matter, Curating the End of the World: Red Spring, Trouble the Waters: Tales From the Deep Blue, Africa Risen: A New Era of Speculative Fiction, and *The Magazine of Fantasy and Fiction.* Danian resides in Memphis, Tennessee, home of the blues and American soul music.

Table of Contents

Acknowledgments   ix
Preface: Peace God! A Trip Down Memory Lane (A Brief History of the "Critical Race Theory" Controversy)   xi
   Danian Darrell Jerry
Introduction: Straight Up (Sh)It Is Real   xvii
   Walter D. Greason, PhD

Section I: The Crisis   1

Chapter 1: Resistance to Critical Race Theory: Much to Do About Nothing?   3
   Lee E. Ross, PhD

Chapter 2: The Critical Race Theory Legacy of A. Leon Higginbotham's Vision of the Colonial Period   11
   Christel N. Temple, PhD

Chapter 3: Wicked Problems and Illmaticism: A Systems View   17
   LaTanya White, PhD

Chapter 4: The Ubiquity and Formlessness of Hip-Hop and Critical Race Theory: Why Bans Against Critical Race Theory May Be Unconstitutional, as Against the Non-Delegation Doctrine   25
   Andre L. Smith, Esq

Chapter 5: Hip-Hop Represented Long Before Critical Race Theory Became a Conservative Rallying Point   39
   Ronda Racha Penrice

Chapter 6: Rhizomatic   47
   Benjamin P. Levy

Interlude: R-Son the Voice of Reason 65
Gangstagrass, 2022

Chapter 7: Five Mics and Five Tenants: A Content Analysis of
Illmatic to Understand Critical Race Theory 69
Dwayne Matthews

Chapter 8: Represent: Education, Still Groovy but Smoother 83
Walter D. Greason, PhD

Interlude: Systemic Racism: A Theory of Oppression (2006) 87
Joe Feagin, PhD

Section II: The Clapback 89

Chapter 9: Static: The Illmatic Consequences of the
Critical Race Theory Boogeyman 91
Bijoun Eric Jordan

Chapter 10: Decolonizing Public Minds and Public Places:
An Interview With Maurice Broaddus 109
Danian Darrell Jerry

Chapter 11: ANTIBODIES//Shots: Engaging Public Health
Critical Race Praxis to Counter Epistemic Violence in the
Discourse of Dual Pandemics 121
Ryan J. Petteway, DrPH

Interlude: The Sinking White Middle Class A Political History
of Debt, Misery, and the Drift to the Right 133
David R. Roediger, PhD

Chapter 12: Don't Believe the Right: A Message From the Media
Assassin: An Interview With Harry Allen 135
Danian Darrell Jerry

Chapter 13: The Lion Man Project: Creating Critical Comics as
Counterstorying 147
Michael B. Dando, PhD, John Jennings, and David Brame

Interlude: A House Divided and New Abolition 167
Zebulon Vance Miletsky, PhD

Chapter 14: Illmatic Images: A Visual Essay   169
Stacey Robinson

Chapter 15: Christian Nationalism and the Comic: Incognegro   181
Matthew Teutsch, PhD

Chapter 16: Black Noise Whitewash   187
Michael A. Gonzales

Chapter 17: Auto-Ethnographical Notes on Whiteness   195

   I. My Nice White Family   195

   II. Until the Wolf River Howls   209

Kat Moore

Interlude: White Solidarity: A Dangerous Idea   219
Robert Baird, PhD

Section III: The Consequences   221

Chapter 18: Storming the Capitol: An Exercise in the Patriotic Right to Violence   223
Allen Chukwuhdi

Chapter 19: From Visual Representation to Hip-Hop: Using Innovative Sources to Reconcile Hard History and Inspire Young Activism   233
Dory Lerner

Chapter 20: Integrity and Responsible Journalism: Fact Checking False Narratives: An Interview With Jesse J. Holland   251
Danian Darrell Jerry

Interlude: Afrofuturist Design   261
Kurt Wagner and Walter D. Greason, PhD

Chapter 21: Innovating Racism in Digital Detroit   271
Asha E. Criner

Chapter 22: The Dark Green City: The Liminal Space of the
In-Between   279
 C. N. E. Corbin, PhD

Chapter 23: Into the Ether: The Rap Battle as a Parable for
the Slow Burn of Critical Race Theory   285
 Elle L. Littlefield

Chapter 24: Black Zombies   291
 Odell Hall

Conclusion: Afraid Not of None of You, Cowards, But of
My Own Strength   307
 Walter D. Greason, PhD

About the Authors   309

Acknowledgments

Illmatic Consequences: The Clapback to Opponents of 'Critical Race Theory' would not have been possible without UWP Books and its wonderful staff: Dr. Ayo Sekai, Founder and Chief Executive Officer; Geane deLima, SAGE Representative; Marc Medley, Media Specialist; and Dr. Reynaldo Anderson, Editorial Director. Copy editor Shamila Swamy has provided a keen sense of detail that has proven invaluable and indispensable to this project. Thanks to Stacey Robinson for the amazing cover art and visual essay—our team is much obliged. We thank and appreciate the scholars, writers, artists, and community activists who contributed to this volume. We extend our gratitude to legal professionals Derrick Bell and Kimberlé Crenshaw, and the talented cohort who pioneered the discipline of critical race theory through tireless research, courageous courtroom battles, and unparalleled scholarship. To all these legal and education professionals, grassroots organizers in the trenches fighting for social justice, we thank you. Finally, we recognize Nasir bin Olu Dara Jones, Nasty Nas, whose music has inspired and uplifted generations around the world, offering so many of us a depthless insight into the lives of struggling Black people, proving beyond doubt that our time and existence are illmatic.

PREFACE

Peace God! A Trip Down Memory Lane (A Brief History of the "Critical Race Theory" Controversy)

Danian Darrell Jerry

Nas is one of the greatest storytellers that ever lived. His lyrics are relentless, pounding down on the cracked pavements of every disinvested, destabilized community in the country. In 1994, the Queens native knew what we all knew—that irregular garbage pickups, peeling paint and broken-down concrete buildings, starving libraries, and dilapidated playgrounds were not accidents of fate or the result of lazy bootstrap mentalities.

The 20-year-old Nas released his first full-length album, *Illmatic*, on April 19, 1994, to much celebration and astonishment. *The Source* magazine blessed it with a rare 5 Mic rating when it came out, an honor they had only given to 15 other albums at the time of release. Featuring 10 songs, including "Memory Lane (Sittin' in da Park)," the LP was a labor of love and a living testimony, a lyrical assault on deliberate public policy and the prison industrial complex that clotheslined Black men, Black women, and Black families and communities. More than two decades later, the impact of this brave, ingenious work, created in the truth-telling tradition of the blues, is still apparent, and time is still *illmatic*.

Critically acclaimed, the genre-bending album attained commercial success seven years later, when it went platinum. *Seven years.* An interval of time that best fits an Afrofuturist tale, seven years represents epiphanies and transformations as seven is a holy number; even the body's skin resurrects itself every seven years. Perhaps this sacred time was needed for Nas's prophetic words to sink into the consciousness of people, through the blood and tears shed in our communities, the libations and sacrifices of the unwilling casualties. *The most dangerous emcee, coming out of Queensbridge* reminded us to keep our loved ones alive through the stories of their memories.

True in the game, as long as blood is blue in my veins
I pour a Heineken brew to my deceased crew on memory lane.

Illmatic offered listeners a lens into what pioneers Derrick Bell and others theorized as critical race theory. Nas made critical race theory relatable to the younger masses who may never make their way into a law school classroom. His rhymes revealed a truth that needed neither a college degree nor a library card to be understood. *It ain't hard to tell* what forces were being marshalled against Black people all across the United States.

Decades later, on September 2, two months before the 2020 presidential election, when incumbent Donald J. Trump faced Joe Biden, conservative journalist Christopher F. Rufo appeared on the Fox News show *Tucker Carlson Tonight*. During his brief interview, the senior fellow at Manhattan Institute claimed that "critical race theory" had "pervaded every institution" in American government. The infiltrated institutions included the FBI and the Department of Justice. Rufo referred to "critical race theory" as an "existential threat to the United States." He advised Americans to be concerned and distressed. The welfare and safety of the United States hung in the balance.

Rufo called for former president Trump to sign an executive order intended to crush "critical race theory" and remove the dangerous ideology from all government workspaces. Shortly after, Trump responded with an executive order banning diversity training for federal employees. Later, the declaration was abolished by the newly elected president, Biden.

After the Tucker Carlson interview and the Republicans' failed bid for the presidency, Christopher Rufo influenced government officials like former White House chief of staff Mark Meadows and assisted in the composition of legislation aimed at destroying diversity in government work spaces and public school curricula—all of this sheltered under the umbrella term "critical race theory." A calculated move, it echoed the racial animus of President Woodrow Wilson, whose segregationalist policies eroded Black civil service and progress in the early twentieth century.

Our volume, *Illmatic Consequences*, elucidates and demystifies the recent controversy surrounding "critical race theory," a term we place in quotations due to its habitual and strategic misuse by its opponents and by those who fail to recognize this rhetorical tactic. In 2019, many Americans had never heard of the term. Originally, the doctrine was a legal discipline pioneered by Bell, who was a Harvard professor, civil rights attorney, and noted speculative fiction author, in conjunction with a cadre of talented lawyers including Kimberlé Crenshaw, who coined the now familiar phrase in the 1980s. Critical race theory includes a complex methodology and perspective applied by legal professionals seeking to reevaluate and recontextualize racism as it relates to the people in power who create and enforce laws and public policy in the United States.

However, a person today might find themselves confused by the recent vitriol and infamy surrounding "critical race theory." Opponents claim that the discipline introduces left-wing politics into classrooms and that curricula ripe with progressive ideas actually segregate students—reducing African American children to political pawns, lacking the strength needed to pull themselves up "by their bootstraps" from their impoverished condition. They claim that "critical race theory" creates combative learning environments and extreme occasions of discomfort for students of all races, emphasizing the fear that white students might be forced to feel guilt over curricula that discuss racism in America, past and present. For them, the latter concern is placed above any consideration for Black children and other marginalized students discouraged by a lack of representation in a watered-down, sanitized, and censored version of American history.

According to the opponents, "critical race" scholarship trickles down from the heights of higher education and oozes into unsuspecting public K–12 classrooms, where it must be eradicated at all costs. To them, the very minds of America's children are at stake. The opponents have protested vehemently and sometimes violently at school board meetings across the nation, footage widely disseminated on evening news broadcasts. Through distortion and calculated caricature, they ban books and fire educators accused of spreading "divisive" ideas through lesson materials and classroom instruction. They write intentionally vague and overreaching laws designed to erase and regulate American social and political democratic progress, as they campaign for public office to wield more power and reshape society in their image.

Republican and former co-CEO of the Carlyle Group, Glenn Youngkin, won his first gubernatorial seat in Virginia with a campaign platform that openly opposed "critical race theory." Campaigning against the presence of "critical race theory" in public schools, Youngkin conflated the legal perspective with conversations centered on racial identity, discussed in public education and government forums. When Youngkin signed his first executive order into law, banning "critical race theory," he employed vague terms that included ending the use of "inherently divisive concepts," stigmatizing conversations concerning social justice. By signing Executive Order Number One into Virginia law on July 28, 2022, the newly appointed governor set a precedent for other lawmakers across America seeking to rid public schools of socially responsive curricula under the guise of patriotism and conservative values.

Accustomed to oppression, subjugation, and more than 400 years of complex history, African Americans often employ creative, subversive acts, political movements, and theoretical frameworks, such as critical race theory, which includes counter-storytelling, in their search and quest for liberation and full citizenship, recognized, respected, and enforced at every level of American society. From the enslaved bondspeople singing "Swing Low Sweet Chariot" in cotton, sugarcane, rice, and tobacco fields to George Clinton and Parliament-Funkadelic calling down the *Mothership* in *Chocolate City*, Black people in America interrogate and reshape their worlds through art.

In 1994, Nasir bin Olu Dara Jones (Nas) contributed a hip-hop masterpiece that redefined Black art and reflected the oppressive conditions raging in countless ghettos strewn throughout the United States. What Nas and his cohort of music producers accomplished with the iconic, history-making album *Illmatic* was not unlike the pioneering achievements of Bell, Crenshaw, and other activists who were frustrated with the disparity between the American dream, constitutional and civil rights law, and the material conditions and life of Black Americans.

Illmatic's first song, "N.Y. State of Mind," described Queensbridge Houses as a place of incredible danger, constant and pervasive. Nas detailed a landscape circumscribed by the lens of structural racism, mass incarceration, and political violence. Not even children were safe in this perilous world. When Nas rapped about the "black rats trapped" and a packed Riker's Island, he merely described the atmosphere that fostered his growth from a boy to a young man. Through his vivid descriptions of Queensbridge and the underbelly of a 90s-era New York City, Nas tapped into the essential connections between oppression, human suffering, instinctive rebellion, and self-preservation in urban Black America.

Nas applied his own unique perspective to the *Faces at the Bottom of the Well*. As civil rights lawyers during the 1980s reconstructed their legal climates, Nas employed a shrewd outlook, wise beyond his 20 years, sharpened by the lessons of the Nation of Gods and Earths—a cultural movement informed by the teachings of Islam—and his own observations of inner-city life.

Inspired by the creative genius of Bell, Crenshaw, and "Nasty Nas," our volume tethers the creative spirit of artists to academic discourse and scholarship. Like Nas's legendary studio sessions at D&D, Battery, and Chung King Studios, a supergroup of scholars, artists, and activists have assembled to clap back against racial tyranny, political hypocrisy, and social injustice.

The "Crisis" portion of *Illmatic Consequences* sets the stage for the examination of art and social institutions that follows in later chapters. Key terms are defined to demystify the discipline of "critical race theory" and the conflated arguments championed by conservatives who misuse and weaponize the term. These opponents aim to remove materials pertaining to racial injustice from classrooms and the minds of all U.S. citizens. Ironically, they claim to fight censorship and ideology "indoctrination" by censoring the very foundations of American history, whose truths—the good and the bad—are irrefutable. The "Clapback" section of the volume develops perspectives and responses defending the study of race as a social construction. Finally, as the research broadens to analyze the "Consequences" of racism in modern science and technology, the artistic focus transitions to include new analytical tools for discussion and exploration in Afrofuturism, a genre Bell employed brilliantly as a creative continuation of his own scholarly work.

The Black Speculative Arts movement paves the way and claims new territory for the next stages of research and activism established by civil rights scholars and hip-hop practitioners. Adding to his work as an attorney and professor, Bell establishes himself as a celebrated science fiction author with his 1992 collection, *Faces at the Bottom of the Well*, which appeared two years before Nas's *Illmatic*. Bell's short story "The Space Traders" evokes concepts and footnotes drawn directly from his legal scholarship and civic engagement. Using the U.S. government's Japanese internment during World War II as a precedent, Bell's provocative text details the vulnerability of Black people as they become the ultimate bargaining chip for an increasingly callous and desperate U.S. government. His legal writing is an essential cornerstone of academic discourse, while his fiction is a widely celebrated touchstone in the fields of Afrofuturism and Black speculative art.

As a student of the Nation of Gods and Earths, Nas understands the philosophical concept of God manifested in Black men and Black women—resurrected through the births of Black children. His powerful vision of hip-hop as an expression against socioeconomic and political oppression opens the door to new art and modes of research focused on serving Black people on their own terms.

But the opponents of justice and equality and the uncensored critical study of American history and public institutions are increasing the intensity, variety, and sheer number of their attacks. "Critical race theory" has already been weaponized in a successful bid for the governor's seat in Virginia in 2021 and in the national conversation. The fight against "critical race theory" will continue to influence future political discourse and local and national campaigns, including the next presidential election.

In 1992, Nas asked, "Whose world is this?" and *Illmatic* answered, "The world is yours!"

Following "in the God's footsteps," our contributors have provided a resourceful means for twenty-first century educators, creative writers, and liberators to clap back against opponents of social and racial equity, public awareness, educational freedom, and empowerment of marginalized communities across the nation.

Peace, God! Now the shit is explained!

INTRODUCTION

Straight Up (Sh)It is Real

Walter D. Greason

Every day, there is a new massacre in the United States. The cost of the election of Barack Obama as the first Black president of the United States is the complete shredding of the social fabric by socially unstable men as loners and in militias. The daily assault on decency and stability is the price exacted by conservative patriarchs in legislatures, town councils, and school districts nationwide. As their legacy of four centuries of exploitation and abuse comes to an end, their addiction to myths of rugged individualism and militarized defense of private property sparks waves of violence against women, immigrants, Black people, Indigenous people, and the poor. All of these disasters are compounded by climate change, which unleashes fires, tornadoes, hurricanes, and floods, destroying any possibility of social stability between the killings. This book provides the tools to restore peace and civility in the next century.

Hip-hop is, at its roots, the music of the dispossessed. With no instruments, no electricity, no access to authority, street poets crafted lyrics and stories from their imaginations and the surrounding environment to inspire one another. As a praxis, hip-hop culture transformed educational institutions, corporate industries, and spiritual life worldwide. It verbalized the instrumental improvisation that jazz offered to the world. By showcasing dynamic wordplay and unleashing unprecedented forms of sonic force, hip-hop showed how the powerless can reshape every aspect of daily life. The simple aesthetic of adaption and agility bridged hundreds of cultures, transcending language itself. The art could be harmonic or dissonant. It could accelerate or decelerate from one moment to the next. Hip-hop made the immediate moment the most valuable commodity in human experience. It offered an escape from industrial and digital routines. Nothing is more important in a world gone mad with violence, where everyone struggles to develop some sense of meaning.

Illmatic Consequences reverses this polarity by offering chapters that operate like the verses on Nas's classic debut album. Each voice brings an original analysis that contributes to a larger, interdisciplinary engagement with the horror of the conservative "white lash" that unfolded in 2020. Donald Trump's political alliance dedicated itself to a white nationalist vision of the world, in conjunction with the radical authoritarianism of Vladimir Putin's Russia and Li Keqiang's China. An open, equitable world, based on the principles advocated in Martin Luther King Jr.'s concept of the beloved community and the constitutional promises of Nelson Mandela's South Africa, was the enemy. Here, the next generation of scholars and artists come together to clap back against the forces of global fascism. There are three thematic sections: The Crisis, The Clapback, and The Consequences. The Crisis offers an assessment of critical race theory, its misrepresentation by its detractors, and the flaws in educational practice that allowed the attack to thrive. The Clapback provides a detailed analysis with multiple analytical tools from the humanities and social sciences to explain the deception involved in the attacks on critical race theory. The Consequences presents the terrorism inherent in white nationalism, while offering solutions through the lens of the Black Speculative Arts Movement and Afrofuturism.

Mos Def, Talib Kweli, and Hi Tek asked, "A Black Star, who, me?" in their classic album *Mos Def and Talib Kweli Are*. One of the key lyrics was "we be shinin and shinin, while we rhymin and rhyming." The lyrics and the whole album represent the spirit that Nas created with his album *Illmatic*. Love and appreciation for the range and depth of Black cultures is the keystone to this text, as well as Black Speculative Arts Movement and Afrofuturism. It is a fundamental love for Black people and, indeed, the entire human family. This core commitment requires the clapback against those who critique critical race theory. The struggle for human and civil rights is the highest calling within global society over the past four centuries. From this perspective, all people can embrace an Indigenous and African consciousness. It requires the repudiation of white nationalism in all of its forms. As readers consider the ideas in this text, they must continually ask themselves, "A Black Star, who, me?"—as they undertake the challenge that Nas' offered in his classic song "Represent."

> The corners is a hot spot, full of mad criminals / who don't care, guzzling beers, we all stare / at the out-of-towners, they better break north / before we get the four-pounders, and take their face off / the streets is filled with undercovers, homicide chasing brothers / the DA's on the roof, trying to watch us and knock us / and killer coppers, even

Introduction: Straight Up (Sh)It Is Real   xix

come through with helicopters / I drink a little vodka, spark a L and hold a Glock for / the fronters, wannabe ill . . . and spot runners / thinking it can't happen til I trap em and clap em / and leave em done, won't even run about Gods / I don't believe in none of that shit, your facts are backwards / Nas is a rebel of the street corner / pulling a tec out the dresser, police got me under pressure.

The crisis is now. The clapback is here. The consequences cannot be denied.
Who will you represent?

SECTION I
The Crisis

George Floyd was a man. Through his murder, he became a symbol. Breonna Taylor was a woman. Through her murder, she became an icon. At the heart of the modern world are these stories of injustice and death that define a "logos of violence"—a law that defines the parameters of civil society. The deaths of Floyd and Taylor are only the most recent symbols of injustice that explain the racial order around the world. Critical race theory provided civil rights attorneys with the tools to challenge this system of exploitation in court. Its opponents invented an endless stream of rhetoric to prevent this analysis.

Lee Ross, Christel Temple, LaTanya White, Andre Smith, Ronda Racha Penrice, Benjamin Levy, Dwayne Matthews, and Walter Greason explain the nature of the current threat. From the specific defenses of critical race theory through the exploration of rhizomatic education and legal storytelling, these chapters assess the limits of white nationalism as a legal and cultural construct. These perspectives invoke Nas's *Illmatic* as a template for opening a democratic and inclusive society in the next decade.

CHAPTER 1
Resistance to Critical Race Theory: Much to Do About Nothing?

Lee E. Ross

The past isn't dead: It is not even past.

—William Faulkner

THE GENESIS OF CRITICAL RACE THEORY

The genesis of critical race theory can be thought of as a paradigm that goes back to the Frankfurt School of Critical Theory, where theorists argued that before we can understand modern society, we have to first understand the nature of the power relationships among members and groups (Cole, 2019). Decades later, legal scholar Kimberlé Williams Crenshaw coined the term "critical race theory." However, the late Derrick Bell, whose scholarship is the subject of this essay, is often regarded as the spiritual godfather of critical race theory (hereinafter CRT). His work explored (among other things) what it would mean to understand racism as a permanent feature of American life and whether it was easier to pass civil rights legislation in the United States because those laws ultimately served the interests of white people. Since its inception, there have been various spinoff "frameworks" of CRT. Conceived as a part of critical legal studies, its branches have evolved to focus on the particular experiences of Indigenous, Latinx, Asian American, and Black people and communities.

Other pioneers in the field of CRT include Patricia Williams, Cheryl Harris, Richard Delgado, Mari Matsuda, Alan Freeman, and Kimberlé Williams Crenshaw. Collectively, these individuals recognized that overt practices of racism often resulted in more subtle and covert forms of racism, rendering it far more difficult to discern—much less to address. Consequently, formal rules that demanded color-blind treatment proved effective to curb only the most flagrant forms of racism. One of Bell's most significant theoretical contributions was to argue that the landmark 1954 civil rights case *Brown v. Board of Education* was a result of the self-interest of elite white people rather than a desire to desegregate schools and improve education for Black children. In short, Black people achieve civil rights victories only when white and Black interests converge, hence the term "interest convergence." In addition, Bell critiqued the field of law itself, highlighting exclusionary practices at elite schools, such as Harvard Law School, where he was on the faculty. He even resigned his position to protest Harvard's failure to hire women of color as faculty (Bedenheimer, 2021; see also Crenshaw et al., 1995; Ross, 2017). Before leaving Harvard, however, he pioneered a new field of CRT and legal scholarship when he was asked to write an article for the prestigious *Harvard Law Review*. His article, "The Civil Rights Chronicles" (1985), which focused on civil rights, race, gender, and equality, became the basis of several books written by Bell subsequently. These include *Faces at the Bottom of the Well: The Permanence of Race*, *And We Are Not Saved: The Elusive Quest for Racial Justice*, and *Silent Covenants: Brown v. Board of Education and the Unfulfilled Hopes for Racial Reform*.

CRITICISMS OF AND RESISTANCE TO CRT

Various CRT scholars, including Crenshaw, Delgado, and Stefancic, detail the earliest opposition to CRT in the 1990s, principally from neoconservative opponents of affirmative action. Critics viewed CRT scholars as leftist radicals and claimed that some aspects of CRT such as legal storytelling—which focuses on stories by people of color and is used to challenge dominant narratives—did not make CRT a rigorous method of analysis (Delgado & Stefancic, 2012; see also Valdes et al., 2002). These critics also objected to the notion that people of color were more knowledgeable about their own experiences and, thus, better equipped to represent them than white scholars and writers. They were also suspicious of the movement's tendency to question the existence of an objective truth. Their suspicions increased as CRT scholars challenged the notions of truth, objectivity, and meritocracy by exposing the often invisible workings of white supremacy. In the case of affirmative action, for instance, proponents of CRT cite the ways in which whites have always benefited from such practices within higher education. Bell noted that the people who benefit from racism have little incentive to eradicate it (Bedenheimer, 2021). These practices included legacy admissions, the GI Bill, and achievements on standardized testing that were influenced by a person's economic status rather than an authentic measure of one's intelligence. After all, intelligence is what intelligence measures. According to Crenshaw (2006), "the primary beneficiaries of affirmative action have been Euro-American women."

While these critics sought to delegitimize and discredit CRT, they never sought to ban its teachings or advocate its abolition. However, more recently, CRT has become the target of censorship and legal prohibition in many parts of our country, making national and international headlines. Like roaches that congregate in the darkness, suddenly the use of the term is prevalent everywhere. According to the watchdog Media Matters, as of July 14, 2021, Fox News had mentioned "critical race theory" about 1,900 times in a brief period of only 3.5 months. When Donald Trump was president of the United States, Fox News inspired him to issue an executive order censuring "critical race theory" in federal diversity seminars. Since then, eight states have passed legislation against it: Idaho, Oklahoma, Tennessee, Texas, Iowa, New Hampshire, Arizona, and South Carolina (Elnaiem, 2021). Culture wars over CRT have turned school boards into battlegrounds, and in higher education, the term has been ensnared in tenure battles. Dozens of U.S. senators have branded it "activist indoctrination."

CLARIFYING CRT

There appears to be mass confusion about the meaning of CRT. What many people refer to as CRT is best understood as a set of different frameworks (or basic tenets) used to understand the intersectional nature of power, race, privilege, and oppression. These basic legal tenets include (a) the construction of race and the normality of racism, (b) interest convergence, (c) differential racialization, (d) intersectionality, and (5) first-person narratives (or voices of color). While these multisyllabic terms permeate academic discussions, many laypersons—including our families—have a very limited idea of what these terms mean or imply. But critical race theorists say they are mainly concerned with understanding the racial disparities that have persisted in institutions and systems. Given Bell's contributions, I review three of the major tenets of CRT.

Three Tenets of CRT

Beginning with law, the first tenet (*racism as normal*) states that racism is a structured part of everyday life in the United States, as opposed to an aberration or a function of the attitude of a few racist individuals (e.g.,

Neo-Nazis). The second tenet (*interest convergence*) argues that the interests of people of color will only be advanced to the extent that they also advance white interests (Cabrera, 2018). The third tenet is "storytelling" (or *first-person narrative*), which implores marginalized people of color to express themselves and stand in their reality as viewed through an experiential lens. So what is it about CRT that has some people so alarmed? As we review these legal tenets, we can quickly eliminate the concept of *interest convergence* as it is perhaps the least threatening. This is one of those "I scratch your back, you scratch mine" notions. Perhaps the latest manifestation of this tenet is the national celebration of Juneteenth, which became a federal holiday in 2021. In terms of timing, it came on the heels of a social protest in response to the police brutality on Black men and women. Here, the nation sought peace and calm among the masses in exchange for national reconciliation and an acknowledgment that Black lives mattered. Others are quick to point out, however, that African Americans have not been fighting for a holiday. Rather, they have been pushing for reparations, police reform, criminal justice reform, small-business investments, education reform, and other such issues (Abdul-Jamin, 2021).

Far more threatening are tenets regarding the "normality of racism," where manifestations of white privilege are too obvious to ignore yet are quickly denied by its most likely beneficiaries. Another threatening feature of CRT is the use of the *first-person narrative* (or storytelling) by those victimized by racial injustice and other myriad forms of discrimination. This is similar to the educational tenet: a challenge to the dominant ideology, which focuses on how social science claims of objectivity, meritocracy, and neutrality represent the interests of power and serve to re-create systems of oppression.

WHAT'S ALL THE FUSS ABOUT?

So why has a theory formed in the 1980s become a simmering political hot button 40 years later? Ostensibly, the reasons vary, but most of them appear deeply ensconced in the fabric of political conservatism, undoubtedly triggered by recent social protests. Moreover, the murders of unarmed black women and men, including George Floyd; the burgeoning Black Lives Matter movement; and even the 1619 Project, which recounts America's history of systemic racism, are plausible explanations for the CRT backlash. Or is it our refusal to mythologize the founding of America? Whether we call it an *epiphany* or being "woked," more and more people of color are becoming aware of and actively attentive to important facts and issues (especially issues of racial and social justice). They are no longer asleep at the wheel of injustice. For some, the controversy demonstrates not only how CRT has been politicized but also a lack of understanding of the theory itself (Oputu, 2021). Rep. Antonio Parkinson, a Democrat from Memphis and chair of the General Assembly's Black Caucus, asserts, "Anything that tells the truth about our history, for whatever reason, their fragility comes into play and it is exposed" (McGee, 2022).The Christian Bible (Luke 12:3) suggests that what is done in darkness will eventually come to light. Therefore, whatever we are trying to conceal will surface as surely as the sun will rise tomorrow. Overall, the tenets and frameworks of CRT are threatening to some as it illuminates the present and sheds light on our nation's dark past.

Indeed, since January 2022, the conservative fraternity has raised a hue and cry, sounding the alarm against CRT. Consequently, legislatures across the country have moved to restrict how race and other sensitive topics are taught in public classrooms. Here are five examples:

1. Some advocate banning the teaching of CRT in schools under the pretense of restoring "excellence" in schools and avoiding "divisive concepts."
2. According to NBC News, a Florida school district recently canceled a college professor's civil rights lecture for teachers saying they had concerns over CRT, although his seminar had nothing to do with it.
3. In Alabama, many parents claimed that teaching Black history is a form of CRT.
4. South Dakota governor Kristi Noem signed legislation that would prohibit public universities in the state from using training material that could cause racially based "discomfort" (Beals, 2022).
5. During the confirmation hearings for Supreme Court justice candidate Ketanji Brown Jackson, a Tennessee senator revisited CRT, saying that Jackson ought to give parents the right to prevent CRT from being taught in public school classrooms (Tinsley, 2022).

As expected, the road to understanding CRT meanders down the path of least resistance. Here, people conveniently ignore the use and meaning of these terms, occasionally in pursuit of expedient motives, convoyed by politically driven narratives of misinformation. As a result, many use the term "critical race theory" with little to no understanding of its basic tenets and framework. Imagine the following scenario in the hallway of a public middle school in Ashburn, Virginia. The first bell is about to ring, and Johnny and Samantha run excitedly down the hall to their American history teacher, Mrs. Hamilton. The following exchanges occur:

Johnny: Good morning, Mrs. Hamilton, we have a quick question.

Mrs. Hamilton: Sure, Johnny, what is on your mind?

Johnny: We are hearing a lot of talk about critical race theory—and I heard the governor is opposed to allowing it into our school's curriculum.

Mrs. Hamilton: Ok—and . . .

Johnny: Well, we were wondering if you could just tell us in simple terms—what is critical race theory, what is all the fuss about, and why we can't discuss it in our class.

Mrs. Hamilton: I can't answer that.

Johnny: Why not?

Mrs. Hamilton: Johnny, the reason we will never discuss critical race theory in class is simply because I and your other teachers have no idea what the hell it is.

Disappointed and confused, Johnny is overheard telling his friend Samantha, "This is the fourth teacher we have asked, and no one seems to know what the hell critical race theory is."

Samantha: Well, if no one knows, why is the school so worried about it being taught and discussed?

Johnny: Well, I am not sure, but on social media, some say that critical race theory makes white people, like us, feel uncomfortable and guilty about America's past—especially its history in race relations. The discussions about racism are divisive and all about shaming us and accusing us and making us feel guilty about things we had nothing to do with.

Samantha: I don't feel guilty. Besides, if it is based on history, what is there to feel guilty about?

Johnny: I am not sure.

Samantha: Well, either way, it is what it is. Yes? Haven't we all heard about historical racism and the need for diversity training?

Johnny: Yes, I guess when we get to college, talking about critical race theory will be safe for our little ears.

Samantha: Yes, this kind of reminds me of how we eventually learned about Santa Claus. At first, we were too young—until our friends spilled the beans.

Johnny: Do you have any Black friends?

Samantha: No, not yet.

Based on this narrative, it is difficult to convey and understand the true meaning of CRT unless we have a clear understanding of what it is, what it entails, and its ramifications. Rather than be distracted by all the "white noise" and public fears bred by disinformation, we rely on the pioneering works of Bell to advance our understanding and appreciation of laws and practices that promote the obscured nature of systemic racism and structural inequality in the United States. In doing so, we quickly realize that, like history, "CRT is what it is": a critical examination of the American legal, education, and medical systems, where much of the opposition to CRT is baseless and much to do about nothing. In the words of Dr. Bernice King, CRT is not the problem. Rather, "racism is the problem, poverty or extreme materialism is the problem, and militarism, war is the problem" (Rauls, 2022).

REFERENCES

Abdul-Jamin, M. (2021, June 19). *Juneteenth, the evolution of American slavery and important lessons for Black Muslims*. https://americanmuslimtoday.com/details/2a8ad640-bedc-482d-bb57-a84c81ccc8a3

Beals, M. (2022, March 21). *Noem signs bill that rejects "divisive" race trainings at South Dakota universities*. https://thehill.com/homenews/state-watch/599122-noem-signs-bill-that-rejects-divisive-race-trainings-at-south-dakota

Bedenheimer, R. (2021, June 11). *What is critical race theory? Definition, principles, and applications*. https://www.thoughtco.com/critical-race-theory-4685094

Bell, D. (1985). The civil rights chronicles (Foreword). *Harvard Law Review*, 99(1), 4.

Brown v. Board of Education of Topeka, 347 U.S. 483 (1954).

Cabrera, N. L. (2018). Where is the racial theory in critical race theory? A constructive criticism of the Crits. *The Review of Higher Education*, 42(1), 209–233. https://doi.org/10.1353/rhe.2018.0038

Cole, L. C. (2019, October 15). *The Frankfort School of Critical Theory*. Thoughtco.com. https://www.thoughtco.com/frankfurt-school-3026079#

Crenshaw, K., Gotanda, N., Peller, P., & Thomas, K. (Eds.). (1995). *Critical race theory: The key writings that formed the movement*. New Press.

Crenshaw, K. W. (2006). Framing affirmative action. *Michigan Law Review First Impressions*, 105, 123. https://repository.law.umich.edu/cgi/viewcontent.cgi?article=1093&context=mlr_fi

Delgado, R., & Stefancic, S. (Eds.). (2012). *Critical race theory: An introduction* (2nd ed.). New York University Press.

Elnaiem, M. (2021, September 2). What is critical race theory? *The Daily*. https://daily.jstor.org/what-is-critical-race-theory

McGee, N. A. (2022, January 26). *Black Tennessee legislators feel ignored and unheard on issues of racism*. https://www.theroot.com/black-tennessee-legislators-feel-ignored-and-unheard-on-1848428333

Oputu, E. (2021, August 5). *Untangling the controversy around critical race theory*. https://news.temple.edu/news/2021-08-05/untangling-controversy-around-critical-race-theory

Rauls, M. (2022, January 12). *Reverend Bernice King urges to redirect attention towards racism and not focus on "false narratives" about CRT*. https://www.theroot.com/reverend-bernice-king-urges-to-redirect-attention-towar-1848344686

Ross, L. E. (2017). Critical race theory. In A. Brisman, E. Carrabine, & N. South (Eds.), *Criminological theory and concepts* (pp. 258–262). Routledge.

Tinsley, B. (2022, March 23). Race deconstructed: The bad-faith scrutiny reserved for Black SCOTUS nominees. *CNN Politics*. https://www.cnn.com/2022/03/23/politics/gop-criticism-ketanji-brown-jackson/index.html

Valdes, F., Culp, J. M., & Harris, A. P. (Eds.). (2002). *Crossroads, directions, and a new critical race theory*. Temple University Press.

CHAPTER 2

The Critical Race Theory Legacy of A. Leon Higginbotham's Vision of the Colonial Period

Christel N. Temple

A. Leon Higginbotham's *In the Matter of Color: Race and the American Legal Process: The Colonial Period* (1978) is not necessarily the first source scholars tend to mention in contemporary discussions of critical race theory. In the foreword to *Critical Race Theory: The Key Writings That Formed the Movement*, Cornel West (1996) credits Higginbotham's work with being one of a small number of "prophetic voices in the legal wilderness" (p. xi) from which critical race theory eventually evolved. However, Higginbotham's monograph is an exceptional history whose value lies in its chronological, colony-by-colony point of view. Higginbotham presents a straightforward survey of how European colonial era colonizers structured and altered the legal and even religious standards of their home countries in the North American regions where they planted their countries' flags. He surveys six key colonies, Virginia, Massachusetts, New York, South Carolina, Georgia, and Pennsylvania, in his case study. They relied on a highly racialized and discriminatory logic as they took advantage of their geographical distance from their European civic societies, the limited (or delayed) oversight by the mother country, and the confusion between the norms of European society and matters of race and religion to make local decisions about laws for governing African people in the colonies. Higginbotham's colony-by-colony revelations of how European colonizers used the settler colonial law to restrict the opportunities and life experiences of enslaved Africans, Indigenous Americans, and even white indentured servants are essential to an understanding of critical race theory.

Critical race theory is "an important discourse that developed in the midst of the ongoing dialog between civil rights and Black power advocates and activists, especially as it relates to law and political struggle" (Karenga 2006, p. 173). The contribution that Higginbotham made to critical race theory in the late 1970s is an indication of his intellectual grit; *In the Matter of Color* predates the work of Derek Bell (1989, 1992) and Crenshaw et al. (1995). Higginbotham's preface to *In the Matter of Color* reveals a legacy of intense thinking about race, racist social norms, policy, and the law and how they affected him in his personal experiences. Working backward from Higginbotham's personal reflections, even before his exemplary career as a judge, he revealed an understanding of the racialized legal practices that affected him at an early age. The personal anecdote that Higginbotham chose to introduce his volume was a practical choice. In 1944, he was a 16-year-old college student at Purdue University, forced into housing in a below-freezing, segregated, and overcrowded, barracks-style dorm of 12 Black students. When he made an appointment with the university president to advocate for equality in living quarters, the president told him, "The law does not require us to let colored students in the dorm, and you either accept things the way they are or leave the University immediately" (p. viii). This is a strikingly unsympathetic response from the highest university official, especially since a 16-year-old (a minor, technically) and the other 11 students had been placed in a cold, unheated attic by the university unit tasked with assigning housing to its students.

After the president's cold rejection of what to Higginbotham was a reasonable request, Higginbotham reflected on the irony that just that morning he had attended a lecture on the "genius of the founding fathers" (p. viii), who wrote the Declaration of Independence. The timing of this racial indignity also paralleled the nation's negative treatment of Black soldiers returning from and still actively participating in the Second World War. Higginbotham's sense of self and community, and activist resolve are powerful:

> Almost like a mystical experience, a thousand thoughts raced through my mind as I walked across campus. I knew I had been touched in a way I had never been touched before, and that one day I would have to return to the most disturbing element of this incident—how a legal system that proclaims "equal justice for all" could simultaneously deny even a semblance of dignity to a 16-year-old boy who had committed no wrong. Shortly thereafter, I left Purdue University and transferred to Antioch College. Ultimately, I chose the law as my vocation, and in 1952 I graduated from Yale Law School. (pp. viii–ix)

Chapter 2: A. Leon Higginbotham's Vision of the Colonial Period

Higginbotham convincingly acquaints readers with how routine indignities are related to a broader, more systemic alignment of racial discrimination in the United States. His thesis for *In the Matter of Color* is based on a commitment to "acquaint myself with the part the legal process played, to learn the lessons of racial history, to ascertain to what extent the law itself had created the mores of racial repression" (p. ix). He shares with readers how he shifted his analytical framework from a process of studying current racial episodes to a more methodical, historical undertaking where he goes back to the nation's colonial origins to pinpoint "the interrelationship between the law and color in America" (p. ix). As a methodology, Higginbotham encourages critical race theory practitioners to return to the historical archives of the United States to gain a chronological sense of the early steps taken by colonial era colonizers to create a nation that benefited Europeans only. Derek Bell's literary persona, Geneva Crenshaw, from *And We Are Not Saved* (1989), whose chronicles recount experiences with the white men who ran the Constitutional Convention, proceeds along a similar vein as Higginbotham in his attention to the role of experiences of the nation's origin in creating legal inequality.

In his survey of the types of early-colonial legal oppression present in Virginia, Massachusetts, New York, South Carolina, Georgia, and Pennsylvania, Higginbotham reserves the most vitriol for the state of Virginia as "the leader" of aggressive prejudice toward enslaved Africans. It is the starting point of the book's interest in the first 200 years, documenting "how the entire legal apparatus was used by those with the power to do so to establish a solid legal tradition for the absolute enslavement of blacks" (p. 14).

Higginbotham describes the Virginia colony as "a leader in the gradual debasement of blacks through its ultimate institutionalization of slavery" because "it pioneered a legal process that assured blacks a uniquely degraded status—one in which the cruelties of slavery and pervasive racial injustice was guaranteed by its laws" (p. 19). Chronologically, he noted the ambivalence of the Massachusetts colony's initial approach to enslavement and inequality. In 1700, the colonists had a "moral pretention" against enslavement but acknowledged that it was "an act that was legal and justifiable under the auspices of the legal process" (p. 61). Even the New York colony, with its early acceptance of half-freedom for Blacks, eventually incorporated enslavement codes that represented the fears of the colonists, and prohibitions to restrict Black freedom that by 1702 emerged as repressive laws that were later aimed at preventing Blacks from having economic equality. In fact, Black New Yorkers by the end of the eighteenth century found that they had freedom but without equality. Whites had "a perception that blacks were inferior human beings and thus not entitled to equality and fairness under the law" (p. 150).

Higginbotham necessarily includes the South Carolina colony in his assessment because even though Africans were the majority population, white colonists sought to imitate the West Indies model of absolute repression of Blacks. The colonists sought to keep slavery as a profitable institution and maintain slaves "in total subjection" (p. 168). South Carolina's legacy is such that the legislature mobilized to maintain the brutal and inhuman condition of enslavement in order to perpetuate white privilege and control over the colony in the centuries that followed. Even though the Georgia colony had an unusual trajectory that first rejected enslavement, Higginbotham notes that its unique first antislavery law of 1735 "was not passed for humanitarian reasons; nor did it move Georgia courts to a more sympathetic view of their responsibilities toward black Georgians" (p. 219). Instead, it "contained racist provisions, and subsequent judicial decisions based on these provisions were unnecessarily harsh and attest to the absence of any widely held Georgian regard for black welfare" (p. 217). Finally, Higginbotham highlights the Pennsylvania colony's legal system as being repressive yet less brutal than most others, but it still included provisions for the "the subtle and legal debasement of free blacks" (p. 308). Its role became more profound eventually as an agent of change when the colony passed a gradual enslavement act that was an improvement over the other colonies' distorted efforts.

The legacy of Higginbotham's contribution to critical race theory is that he viewed colonial history primarily

> through the special focus of a legal lens, to examine the *pathology* (italics added) of the law, its creation, its sanctioning, intolerance, and its occasional eradication of the racist practices that caused one group of human beings to receive such special, harsh, and disparate treatment. (p. 14)

"Pathology" is a remarkable legacy term for Higginbotham's study. Pathology is the science of the causes and effects of disease and illness, and in this case, the illness is behavioral. Higginbotham's legacy is his approach to viewing systemic racism from its national origins to the present—a method for charting disparity. It is thus appropriate to link Higginbotham's contribution to critical race theory with a traditional African studies view of pathology. Black psychiatrist France Cress Welsing offered the most comprehensive definition of racism, one that empowers thinkers to be acutely aware in deciphering the connections between the United States' racial past, present, and future. Welsing (1991) clarifies that racism (or white supremacy) is

> the local and global power system and dynamic, structured and maintained by persons who classify themselves as white, whether consciously or subconsciously determined, which consists of patterns of perception, logic, symbol formation, thought, speech, action, and emotional response, as conducted simultaneously in all areas of people activity (economics,

education, entertainment, labor, law, politics, religion, sex and war), for the ultimate purpose of white genetic survival and to prevent white genetic annihilation on planet Earth—a planet upon which the vast and overwhelming majority of people are classified as nonwhite (black, brown, red, and yellow), by white-skinned people, and all of the nonwhite people are genetically dominant (in terms of skin coloration) compared to the genetic recessive white skinned people. (p. ii)

This is the same pathology to which Higginbotham referred. The legacy is that we have the responsibility to take a long view of history that equates seventeenth century prejudice and inequality with the twentieth century racism that Higginbotham experienced and the twenty-first century systemic racism that critical race theorizations continue to deconstruct.

REFERENCES

Bell, D. (1989). *And we are not saved: The effusive quest for racial justice.* Harper.
Bell, D. (1992). *Faces at the bottom of the well: The permanence of racism.* Basic Books.
Crenshaw, G., Gotanda, N., Peller, G., & Thomas, K. (Eds.). (1995). *Critical race theory: The key writings that form the movement.* New Press.
Higginbotham, A. (1978). *In the matter of color: Race and the American legal process: The colonial period.* Oxford University Press.
Karenga, M. (2006). Revisiting *Brown*, reaffirming Black: Reflections on race, law, and struggle. In M. K. Asante and M. Karenga (Eds.), *Handbook of Black studies* (pp. 165–184). Sage.
Welsing, F. C. (1991). *The Isis papers: The keys to the colors.* Third World Press.
West, C. (1996). Foreword. In K. Crenshaw, N. Gotanda, G. Peller, & K. Thomas (Eds.), *Critical race theory: The key writings that formed the movement* (p. xi). New Press.

CHAPTER 3
Wicked Problems and Illmaticism: A Systems View
LaTanya White

> *I just told it crazy real, and it just talks about how to live in the circumstances and goes beyond, dreaming at the same time. Never just stay in the situation that you're in.*
>
> —Nas, as told to Clash Music (Brydon, 2014)

Before *Illmatic*, there was "Live at the Barbeque"—the world's first taste of Nas's signature recipe for lyrical genius. He established his position as a hip-hop legend by combining poetic complexity and multisyllabic internal rhyming (Classic Album Sundays, n.d.) with the emotional grit and resilience needed to navigate and survive Black life in America. In his guest verse on Main Source's 1991 track, Nasty Nas, his moniker at the time, recounted the "the racial, criminal, and economic problems of the world through his detailed storytelling" (Lust, n.d.).

In and of itself, the word "illmatic" was defined by Nas as "supreme ill. It's as ill as ill gets . . . the science of everything ill" (Markman, 2009). Through my worldview as a social scientist and inclusive scholar-practitioner, I dissect the science of every ill thing through the lens of solving wicked problems (Rittel & Webber, 1973). Wicked problems are those that are virtually impossible to solve because of their complexity and interconnectedness. Nearly all public policy issues—especially the crime, education, health, housing, and wealth issues lyrically unpacked in *Illmatic*—are wicked problems.

As Rittel and Webber (1973) informed us, "One of the most intractable problems is that of... finding wherein the complex causal networks the trouble really lies" (p. 159). On the surface, rap music—and especially *Illmatic*—uses language, marketing, and naming to undermine the power and authority of the established systems and institutions of mainstream society (Baszile, 2009). In every bar, Nas's lyrics retell the story of linguistic imperialism through a narrative of freedom and resistance, and a counternarrative, in a way, having "learned to make it incorporate... ancestral legacy and memory and recreate all [he] encounter[s], making it undeniable Black culture" (Rosier, 2020). At its core, *Illmatic*—like every wicked problem—is couched in the dichotomy of power versus privilege, margins versus access, and anything that challenges the dynamic that enables the ruling class to continue ruling.

While hip-hop emerged as a strategy that represented, reproduced, and resisted politics (Baszile, 2009), critical race theory (CRT) achieved the same objectives by shining much-needed light on America's languishing systems and policies, which are cloaked as justice. CRT arose as a tool through which legal scholars would shape the most inclusive approach to education, enlightenment, and elucidation regarding racial injustice in America. This approach challenges the discourse of America's power dynamic and hence has been met with virulent pushback from the right—naming CRT as "historically-dubious buzzwords and propaganda" (McConnell, 2021).

The theory, described as "the relationships among multiple dimensions and modalities of social relationship and subject formations" (McCall, 2005, p. 1771), can be wielded as a policy advocacy tool that addresses the intersecting inequalities of class, gender, race, religion, sexual orientation, and other identity forms (Crenshaw, 1989). CRT and intersectionality provide a lens through which people of color can be seen and heard. However, these theories have not yet penetrated America's entrepreneurship ecosystems and the pathways to wealth that those ecosystems produce.

THE WICKED PROBLEM OF AMERICA'S RACIAL WEALTH GAP

As America's wealth becomes concentrated in fewer and fewer hands, data reveal that one third of the 400 wealthiest Americans inherited their wealth through the entrepreneurial endeavors of earlier generations in their families (Collins & Hoxie, 2018). As it relates to Black business ownership and wealth accumulation, much of this story is underpinned by Stuart's (1940) economic detour theory. Referring to the oppression and racial discrimination faced by Black business owners, Stuart observed that they were forced to start businesses just to ensure that they had access to various products and services. This type of "race business" (Stuart, 1940, p. xvii) resulted in what is referred to as an economic detour. Legalized segregation, brought about by the 1896 U.S. Supreme court ruling in *Plessy v. Ferguson*, prevented Black and African Americans from having access to professional services in the open market, thus forcing them to build and create their own businesses, including insurance companies, funeral parlors, barbershops, and beauty salons. Being locked out of the labor market typically resulted in lower-income Black households (Brown, 2021); thus, the consumers who supported these businesses often had less purchasing power. Consequently, Black-owned businesses could generate significantly less revenue than their white counterparts. Butler (2005) referred to this divide as economic segregation, which still exists at the time of this writing.

THE DICHOTOMY OF AMERICAN HISTORY

While Senator Mitch McConnell's (R-Kentucky) letter to Secretary of Education Miguel Cardona makes the argument that young Americans should have a rigorous exposure to civic education and American history (McConnell, 2021), the position that he and more than 30 other Republican senators take against CRT quintessentially captures the dichotomy of American history. McConnell (2021) purports that "actual, trained, credentialed historians with diverse political views have debunked the [1619] project's many factual and historical errors, such as the bizarre and inaccurate notion that preserving slavery was a primary driver of the American Revolution." Yet everything new is old again: The earliest documented whitewashing of slavery in America goes back to the 1920s, with historians describing slavery as a premodern institution with no ties to profit seeking or American capitalism (Baptist, 2014).

In the introduction to their work on slavery's contribution to American capitalism, Baptist (2014) told the story of a character "accumulating evidence of two very different stories of the American past—halves that did not fit together neatly" (p. xv). In much the same vein, Gary Peller, a white male law professor and critical race theorist, shared the realization that came to him about the creation of knowledge as a poor southern kid attending Harvard Law School. In a panel discussion on Kimberle Crenshaw's *Intersectionality Matters!* podcast (2021), Peller shared that he grew up very conscious of inequality owing to his upbringing in Atlanta, the seat of the 1960s' civil rights movement.

Naturally, these phenomenological encounters shaped his experience as a student. Peller further shared that his aim in attending Harvard Law School was to use what he presumed to be the neutral arguments of the aw to fight for justice. However, he learned a hard lesson about constructivism that challenged his view of knowledge. Peller learned that knowledge was not as he had assumed—collected, distributive, and equally accessible. Through this lived experience as a student at Harvard Law School, he learned that the ruling class created knowledge that "told itself that it wasn't the ruling class, convinced itself that something else was going on" (Crenshaw, 2021).

In entrepreneurship spaces, also largely dominated by the white male paradigm, accelerator programs, business incubators, and investors tell themselves that their diversity, equity, and inclusion efforts are effective, yet Black and diverse founders are not applying to their programs. The application of CRT in this space is imperative as it addresses how America's wealth was created, distributed, and denied among the races. In the case where such structures do not recognize systemic racism and discrimination, this further marginalizes those who have been historically oppressed. In entrepreneurship ecosystems, Black founders are marginalized because they have not raised a seed round of funding from friends and family. These are typically the same friends and family who are still being underpaid compared with their white counterparts (Brown, 2021). Black founders today are further disadvantaged by not operating in the tech and STEM fields of entrepreneurship. Systemic racism plays a substantive role in the economic prowess of minority women, and separately so for minority men (Harvey Wingfield, 2008).

Systemic gendered racism accounts for the economic outcomes of both genders differently. As Harvey Wingfield (2008) argued, this is based on the dominant white racist frames for African Americans, Asian Americans, and Latin Americans, operating in what Harvey Wingfield referred to as a racial enclave economy. Emphasizing "the role of systemic gendered racism as a preeminent factor shaping the experiences of minority entrepreneurs" (Harvey Wingfield, 2008, p. 20), Harvey Wingfield suggested possible racial enclave economies for African American women and men, Asian American women and men, and Latin American women and men in the United States. They include hair salons and barbering or music for the African American group, nail salons and convenience stores for Asian American groups, and hair/beauty services and food services for Latin Americans. These industries are labor intensive and difficult to scale, and rarely leverage technology. Thus, the lean-startup, venture-funded, tech-enabled narrative in entrepreneurship ecosystems is a monolith that may not apply to Black founders.

Discourse establishes and shapes how something is presented, and the prevailing approaches that shape research include the assumptions that go unquestioned along with those that are excluded (Ahl, 2006). In comparing the current one-dimensional data collected using a white male lens with a "data model supporting CRT and intersectional theories" (Sterner,

2019, p. 7), the researcher's position was to evaluate whether the existing model needed to be replaced or modified, and indeed it does, as White (2022) noted:

> Most small business development programs and entrepreneurship accelerators focus almost solely on only the quantifiable aspects of [entrepreneurship]. . . . Dynastic Wealth™, a comprehensive entrepreneurial approach to wealth building, is the result of both quantitative and qualitative forms of wealth (Alberts, 2018; Hughes et al., 2018). It accounts for the lived experience and ancestral narrative of Black entrepreneurs in a way that no other entrepreneurship curriculum has done to date. (p. 123).

Researchers estimate that for the average Black and Latin American family, it will take 242 years to match the average wealth of a white American family in 2016 (Nieves & Asante-Muhammad, 2018). Notwithstanding the detriment to the broader American experience, if as a culture Black people do not deeply engage with their past and strategically plan to build Dynastic Wealth™ (White, 2022), Black America will stay on the road to zero wealth (Asante-Muhammad et al., 2017). "The redistribution of wealth in America is going to largely depend on the redistribution of access to information about several constructs" (White, 2022, p. 123); simultaneously, the white majority must continue to be informed and made aware of the deep roots of their implicit bias—the very thing that CRT aims to accomplish. Without CRT, the consequences will be illmatic indeed.

REFERENCES

Ahl, H. (2006). Why research on women entrepreneurs needs new directions. *Entrepreneurship Theory and Practice*, 30(5), 595–621. https://doi.org/10.1111/j.1540-6520.2006.00138.x

Asante-Muhammad, D., Collins, C., Hoxie, J., & Nieves, E. (2017, September). *The road to zero wealth: How the racial wealth divide is hollowing out America's middle class*. Institute for Policy Studies & Prosperity Now. https://ips-dc.org/wp-content/uploads/2017/09/The-Road-to-Zero-Wealth_FINAL.pdf

Baptist, E. E. (2014). *The half has never been told: Slavery and the making of American capitalism*. Basic Books.

Baszile, D. T. (2009). Deal with it we must: Education, social justice, and the curriculum of hip hop culture. *Equity & Excellence in Education*, 42(1), 6–19. https://doi.org/10.1080/10665680802594576

Brown, D. A. (2021). *The whiteness of wealth: How the tax system impoverishes Black Americans—and how we can fix it*. Crown.

Butler, J. S. (2005). *Entrepreneurship and self-help among Black Americans: A reconsideration of race and economics* (Rev. ed.). SUNY Press.

Brydon, G. (2014, September 4). Interview: Nas on the mass hysteria of "*Illmatic.*" Clash Music. https://www.clashmusic.com/features/interview-nas-on-the-mass-hysteria-of-illmatic

Classic Album Sundays. (n.d.). *The story of Nas "Illmatic."* https://classicalbumsundays.com/the-story-of-nas-illmatic/

Collins, C., & Hoxie, J. (2018, October). *Billionaire bonanza: Inherited wealth dynasties of the United States.* Institute for Policy Studies. https://ips-dc.org/wp-content/uploads/2018/11/Billionaire-Bonanza-2018-Report-October-2018-1.pdf

Crenshaw, K. (1989). Demarginalizing the intersection of race and sex: A Black feminist critique of antidiscrimination doctrine, feminist theory and antiracist politics. *University of Chicago Legal Forum, 1989*(1), Article 8. http://chicagounbound.uchicago.edu/uclf/vol1989/iss1/8

Crenshaw, K. (2021, September 2). The insurgent origins of critical race theory (No. 39) [Audio podcast episode]. In *Intersectionality matters!* African American Policy Forum. https://soundcloud.com/intersectionality-matters/39-looking-back-to-move-forward-the-insurgent-origins-of-critical-race-theory

Harvey Wingfield, A. M. (2008). *Doing business with beauty: Black women, hair salons, and the racial enclave economy.* Rowman & Littlefield.

Lust, B. (n.d.). *About Nas: Part intellectual. Part metaphysician. Part wordsmith. All Nas.* Hiphop Archive & Research Institute. http://hiphoparchive.org/artists/nas

Markman, R. (2009, March 6). FEATURE: Nas, the genesis. *XXL Magazine.* https://www.xxlmag.com/feature-nas-the-genesis/

McCall, L. (2005). The complexity of intersectionality. *Signs, 30*(3), 1771–1800. https://doi.org/10.1086/426800

McConnell, M. (2021, April 29). *Final DOE Civics Education signed 04.29.21.* Newsroom. https://www.republicanleader.senate.gov/imo/media/doc/FINAL%20DOE%20Civics%20Education%20Signed%204.29.21.pdf

Nieves, E., & Asante-Muhammad, D. (2018, March). *Running in place: Why the racial wealth divide keeps Black and Latino families from achieving economic security.* Prosperity Now. https://prosperitynow.org/resources/running-in-place

Rittel, H., & Webber, M. (1973). Dilemmas in a general theory of planning. *Policy Sciences, 4*(2), 155–169. https://doi.org/10.1007/BF01405730

Rosier, D. (2020). *Linguistic imperialism: An analysis of the political rhetoric of domination against and through the African American lens* (Publication No. 28315288) [Doctoral dissertation, Howard University]. ProQuest Dissertations and Theses Global. https://www.proquest.com/openview/129cf6377df913514130e1d51fed3906/1?pq-origsite=gscholar&cbl=18750&diss=y

Sterner, S. L. (2019). *An analysis of community college achievement outcomes using critical race theory and intersectionality* (Publication No. 13811132) [Doctoral dissertation, Fielding Graduate University]. ProQuest Dissertations & Theses Global.

Stuart, M. S. (1940). *An economic detour: A history of insurance in the lives of American Negroes.* Wendell Malliet.

White, L. (2022). *Dynastic and generative intent for first-generation Black wealth creators in a modern racial enclave economy* [Doctoral dissertation, Antioch University]. Antioch University Repository and Archive. https://aura.antioch.edu/etds/758

CHAPTER 4

The Ubiquity and Formlessness of Hip Hop and Critical Race Theory: Why Bans Against Critical Race Theory May Be Unconstitutional, as Against the Non-Delegation Doctrine

Andre L. Smith

HIP-HOP AND CRITICAL RACE THEORY, FROM BIRTH TO UBIQUITY

In the 2020s, hip-hop and critical race theory (CRT) are both everywhere and nowhere at the same damn time. Extensions of previously established resistance culture, first considered inferior then maturing from outcast and outsider status to distinct and respected cultural discourses, the parallel expansion and popularity of both hip-hop culture and CRT render them currently ubiquitous in terms of their presence throughout the worlds of music and academia, respectively, and yet considerably amorphous and formless as neither has remained true to the principles of its founders. Hip-hop has devolved from a radical rejection of societal norms—emanating primarily from the underground, from Derrick Bell's (1992) *Faces at the Bottom of the Well*—to merely any style of music by anybody with any purpose so long as it has rapping in it, and CRT has transformed from the pursuit of legal pretext in the interpretation of statutes and legal principles to now being popularly understood as any writing dealing with racism.

Considered by many to be important aspects of Black culture, both critical race theory and hip-hop can claim African origins, where hip-hop continues the predominance of the drum in Black music stretching back for millennia prior to European colonialism, while CRT represents a broader commitment to equal protection of the law that distinguishes "African" or "Black" jurisprudence since the reign of Ma'at from its Eurocentric counterpart—as reflected in ancient Egyptian texts such as *The Teachings of Ptah Hotep* or the *Tale of the Eloquent Peasant*; as reflected in Greek texts attributing the first abolition of the death penalty to Nubians, who controlled the Nile Valley as the 25th Dynasty; as reflected in the ubiquitous concept of matriarchy and matrilineality throughout the African continent prior to outside invasions; as reflected by the recognition of group rights in Mali's thirteenth century declaration, the *Karoukan Fouga*; and as reflected by the sixteenth century Ethiopian philosopher Zara Yacob, who included women in his antislavery theory, which claimed, prior to Immanuel Kant, that all men are created equal.

Both hip-hop and CRT can claim African American antecedents. The spoken word and styles of beatboxing or scatting precede hip-hop records; at the same time, Black professors produced scholarship exposing the connection between law and racial subordination prior to Bell's installation as the first tenured Black law professor at Harvard University. For example, see George Ruble Woolfolk's "Taxes and Slavery in the Ante-Bellum South," published in 1960, describing how state and local taxes on every conceivable aspect of the slave industry—from insurance to brokerage, to leasing—funded over half of many state budgets in the nineteenth century South, with significant portions earmarked toward antipoverty programs reserved exclusively for poor whites.

But then, Bell, considered the first critical race theorist, published his seminal course book *Race, Racism and American Law* in 1973, which happens to be the same year when DJ Kool Herc is credited with inventing hip-hop music—August 11, 1973, is widely accepted as the birth date of hip-hop. Yet neither Kool Herc nor Bell invented the monikers "hip-hop" or "CRT." The incomparable Kimberlé Crenshaw is credited with inventing the term "critical race theory." If Derrick Bell is the DJ Kool Herc of legal scholarship, then Kimberle Crenshaw is perhaps akin to Sylvia Robinson, the founder of the first major rap label, Sugar Hill Records, which produced the first commercial rap records, one of which was "Rappers' Delight" with emcee Wonder Mike uttering the words "a hip, hop."

CRT and hip-hop emerged as radical alternatives to the scholarship and music that Black people were expected to produce at the time; both were considered "raw" in the sense that they peeled back power-serving narratives about justice and racial progress to reveal unyielding subordination, marginalization, and dissatisfaction with milquetoast or syrupy responses to racial tyranny. Black leaders and artists of the time certainly spoke on civil rights issues, but they adhered to norms and limits with which hip-hop and CRT refused to comply. Rather than working within the system to better the system, early hip-hop and CRT called the system out as bullshit, as unworthy of its accolades, as impoverished morally as the founders of hip-hop were financially—both offering poignant and entertaining narratives to illustrate the point. But although both hip-hop and CRT see themselves as detached and distinguishable from the more universal disillusionment with the societal status quo, CRT derives in part from what is called critical legal studies, similar to the way hip-hop follows chronologically the white anti-establishment and beatnik types of the late 1960s, who challenged not just the content of popular music but also the excessive formalisms of music theory.

While described as Black even in this essay, the origins of hip-hop and CRT were more inclusive than is popularly imagined, considering first how a very strong Latino presence in both contexts has been either ignored or erased. With the heavy Puerto Rican presence in the Bronx, and in New York City generally, at the time hip-hop was invented, breakdance and graffiti crews featured innumerable Latino and Latina hip-hop dancers and artists. When hip-hop established itself on the West Coast, the Chicano influences on the genre there resembled the Latino participation on the East Coast. In the parallel universe of CRT, Hispanic figures such as Richard Delgado loomed large within the field. Ultimately, "LatCrit," short for Latino/a critical theory, became the official, incorporated spin-off from CRT at the same time when reggaeton asserted itself as family to, yet distinct from, hip-hop. Just as there were white and Jewish early critical race scholars, early hip-hop embraced the Beastie Boys, Blondie, Malcolm McLaren, Kraftwerk, and the Art of Noise. One of the first nationally popular rap groups outside the New York City area was Luke Skyywalker and the Too Live Crew, featuring the Afro-Asian American rapper, Fresh Kid Ice, who referred to himself sometimes as "Chinaman."

In the 1980s, CRT and hip-hop both defined themselves in ways that were important and nonarbitrary, yet contingent and nonexclusionary. Hardly different from the infamous emcee battles between BDP and the Juice Crew or LL Cool J and Kool Moe Dee, critical legal scholars debated among each other what it meant to be a critical race theorist. CRT scholars gathered for the first time at a conference at the University of Wisconsin in 1989. Some CRT scholars insisted that writing in a narrative form—storytelling that was inconsistent with the traditional style for law review articles—was an essential element of the genre, the absence of which rendered a work within the realm of race and law scholarship that had always existed. Similarly, hip-hop intelligentsia such as KRS-One promoted emceeing, deejaying, breakdancing, and graffiti as the essential elements of hip-hop, the absence of which arguably rendered a work within the genre of "rapping," which had always existed in one form or another. For instance, Lakeside's "Fantastic Voyage" includes a rapping verse but is never listed as an early hip-hop song. Neither is Teena Marie's "Square Biz."

Besides narration or storytelling, CRT's other foundational tenets might include Bell's interest convergence theory, his theory that racism is permanent; Cheryl Harris's whiteness as property; and a critique of liberal or colorblind discourse on race. None of these forms or tenets have proven particularly rigid, however. In the 2020s, academic and musical works are routinely described as CRT or hip-hop without satisfying any of the foundational elements. It is for this reason that hip-hop and CRT in the 2020s are both everywhere and nowhere, ubiquitous yet formless.

CRT and hip-hop expanded considerably during the late 1980s and early 1990s. After incubating in important yet niche environments, elite law schools for CRT and New York City's surrounding mid-Atlantic corridor for hip-hop, they both expanded nationally. Crenshaw arrived at UCLA Law School around the same time as N.W.A. made Los Angeles the center of gangster rap, a style of hip-hop that would eventually swallow the whole, not unlike how Crenshaw's "intersectionality" became the most important construct produced by CRT. The infinite permutations therefrom led ultimately to ubiquity on one hand and formlessness on the other. Thematically, the Kimberlé Crenshaw of hip-hop would be Queen Latifah and her seminal 1989 record "Ladies First," which reflected the emergence of a Black women's perspective that had been marginalized until then, notwithstanding the presence and influence of critical scholars and female emcees who had been there from the beginning, from Roxanne Shante and Linda Greene to MC Lyte and Mari Matsuda.

CRT and hip-hop each faced significant challenges from those attempting to obliterate their ideas entirely, only to overcome them and spread even more widely than before. In the early 1990s, both hip-hop and CRT produced extraordinarily popular works that crossed over to the mainstream, as in the case of MC Hammer's "Can't Touch This," and from the shelves of legal scholars to common Black households, as with Patricia Williams's (1991) *The Alchemy of Race and Rights*. Bell's (1992) *Faces at the Bottom of the Well* could then be found on syllabi for undergraduate African American studies classes. In fact, the Hudlin Brothers produced a cinematic version of Bell's "Space Traders," in which Americans had to vote on whether to accept an offer from a visiting alien race to cure all diseases in exchange for all Earth's Black residents.

After enjoying widespread popularity, both experienced significant backlash from mainstream media and academics. In the early 1990s, hip-hop was condemned by powerful and well-funded groups for disregarding and violating social norms, from church leaders like Reverend Jerry

Chapter 4: The Ubiquity and Formlessness of Hip Hop and Critical Race Theory

Falwell, political insiders like Tipper Gore, to some Black civil rights activists like C. Delores Tucker. Disparate ideological boxes threaded together in the belief that the artists and their young audiences were equally unqualified to deliver or listen to the messages in the music intelligently. Analogously, Richard Posner and other conservative legal scholars took aim at CRT, specifically targeting Williams's (1991) *The Alchemy of Race and Rights* and its reliance on personal narratives to tell the story of systemic racial subordination in modern-day America. Just as those who are hostile to CRT criticized the absence of case-crunching analysis, which was thought until then to be essential for legal scholarship, hip-hop's critics pointed to the lack of traditional musical elements like melodies to claim that hip-hop was not music at all, something even less than bad music.

Nevertheless, hip-hop and CRT flourished in the face of its detractors. Young emcees and scholars signed up with record labels and universities all across the nation, as well as a few international writers in both fields, Deborah Waire Post and Kardinal Offishal, both representing Toronto, for example. CRT expanded outside of law schools to other disciplines within the university, to the point where today one can find scholarship relating the insights of early CRT legal scholars in disparate fields such as education, literature, urban planning, psychology, sociology, anthropology, and even architecture and archeology. Likewise, artists merged elements of hip-hop with other musical categories to create go-go music, hip house, reggaeton, dancehall reggae, and so on. Once Kid Rock incorporated rapping into music raced as "white," like rock and heavy metal music, hip-hop was firmly established and entrenched within American culture. By the mid- to late 1990s, the same could be said for CRT, as several books were produced celebrating its most poignant insights, most notably *Critical Race Theory: The Key Writings That Formed the Movement*, edited in 1995 by Crenshaw and colleagues. Representing "Big Tent" CRT, examining group subordination far beyond the Black/white paradigm, Richard Delgado and Jean Stefancic's (2013) *Critical Race Theory: The Cutting Edge* was also first published in 1995.

By 2000, hip-hop had risen from the South Bronx to a global phenomenon. One could find hip-hop communities and culture in Japan, Africa, Europe, and South America. Promoters established annual world deejay and breakdance competitions and championships. Similarly, the discussion of racial and group subordination, particularly when supported by color of law, had also expanded past the U.S. borders to the United Nations and universities across the globe. But the impressive diffusion of hip-hop and CRT may have come at a cost to each, the loss of not just its form but also its original purpose of representing the outsider's perspectives, the faces at the bottom of the well. While both seem stronger and perhaps more vibrant than ever from the public view, a pessimist can argue that both have succumbed to systemic white supremacy represented by Eurocentric universities (herrenvolk socialism) and corporate entertainment interests (racial capitalism), that the lion's share of discourse dubbed critical race theory or hip-hop nowadays reaffirms the status quo rather than challenges or provides alternatives to it.

In 2006, Nasir "Nas" Jones, considered one of the greatest hip-hop artists of all time, asked, "Is hip-hop dead?" Many from inside the culture now criticize the corporate rap music industry for making a caricature of hip-hop, a tool for negatively stereotyping Black people; it is no longer what Chuck D called the "CNN" of the ghetto. Whereas the originators seized upon whatever little was available to them to create material and normative styles independent of the dominant culture around them, the corporate takeover of hip-hop by the rap music industry is reflected by the overwhelming percentage of discourse holding the material trappings of elite white society as the preeminent purpose of life itself.

The case that CRT may be captured by elite interests within a Eurocentric educational system to the detriment of the majority of Black people, who remain impoverished in the United States, is somewhat harder to make, especially by one who considers himself within the construct and has great affection for its members, as I do. If CRT in its early years is defined in large part by Bell's insistence that traditional legal approaches to civil rights amounted to a ruse upon the public—courtroom machinations over race that seem positive are and forever means for maintaining an illusion of racial inclusion—then current CRT scholarship, the bulk of which still calls on the law and legal actors to "do something," will reinforce current racial hierarchy instead of challenging it directly.

In "The Afrolantica Awakening," Bell conceives of a mythical island halfway between America and Africa on which only Black people can breathe. While Bell's purpose for writing it was to explore how white people have asked Black people to leave America if they don't like it at the same time that they penalize those, like Marcus Garvey, who actually endeavor to do so, it is confounding why critical race theorists have not seized on the concept of Bell's "Afrolantica" to try and construct whole new systems of governance that aspire to promote justice better than the kind we experience in the United States.

CRT as an academic genre and hip-hop music as an art form have analogous chronologies. Both CRT and hip-hop originated and found themselves at the same time and for the same reasons in the 1970s and 1980s as a backlash to the capitulating expressions that dominated discourse before them. Both were incorrectly described as exclusively Black; the founders of each were far more diverse than the current narrative presents, the erasure of their Latino presence being most obvious. Both established a form in the 1980s, narrative writing with respect to CRT and the famous first four elements of hip-hop—emceeing, deejaying, graffiti, and breakdancing. In the 1990s, both left their original locations in law schools and the East Coast for national recognition across disciplines, followed by international acclaim in the 2000s and then ubiquity in the 2010s, to the point where in the 2020s both genres are almost completely formless in practice, rendering them therefore everywhere and nowhere at the same damn time. One can argue that the backlash against CRT is stronger now than any organized political movement against hip-hop because hip-hop is more easily controlled through commerce. From an afro-pessimistic perspective, both intend to be counterculture, but neither succeeds.

LEGAL CONSEQUENCES OF CRT AND HIP-HOP'S FORMLESSNESS

The wildly popular Broadway play *Hamilton* relies heavily on rapping and other urban aesthetics related to hip-hop; but is the play *Hamilton* to be considered hip-hop? Because the play critiques racial dynamics, is it representative of CRT such that it may be banned by one of the local school boards with regulations against CRT?

Formlessness can have legal consequences in the context of newly enacted statutes and promulgated regulations intending to ban "critical race theory" in public school systems around the country, because those laws may be set aside or struck down by judges invoking what is called "The Nondelegation Doctrine," a juridical construct that finds laws unconstitutional when they authorize the deprivation of liberty or property rights without an "intelligible principle" to cabin the discretion of executive branch decision makers, like public school boards burning books and firing teachers and administrators who purport to teach CRT, without any salient or comprehensible definition of what is and what is not CRT.

Whodini once rapped, "You can look the word up again and again, but the dictionary doesn't know the meaning of 'friends'." A state legislature cannot constitutionally enact a law that authorizes the government to penalize "unfriendliness" because to do so would give law enforcement officials unfettered discretion to pick and choose whom to sanction; since no appeals officer could say the state actor is within or without the intention of the legislature, rendering each low-level officer a lawmaker unto him or herself, the potential for abuse is obvious. A law requiring everyone to "love one another" would probably fail for the same reasons. Even if we assume that lawmakers have the best intentions, the formlessness of a law requiring "love" provides ample cover to unscrupulous legal actors who would enforce the law whimsically, against political rivals, or toward improper purposes like racial subordination.

Consider a hypothetical law banning "hip-hop" in schools. Because hip-hop no longer has any form or concrete definition, such a law or regulation would authorize school officials to punish teachers who play some songs with beats and rhythm and not others based on the official's personal whim because there is no reliable standard for defining the outer perimeters of hip-hop that an appellate review can use to derail the original decision. Imagine a ban on "hip-hop" after which a Black teacher is fired for playing songs from Gil Scot Heron while the marching band from the same school receives praise for a rendition of a Kid Rock song. The formlessness of hip-hop would allow the school's administrators to defend the maintenance of racial subordination by claiming that the songs of Gil Scot Heron, who is the godfather of rap to many, fall within the definition of hip-hop, then turn around and claim that Kid Rock's music is close to but outside of hip-hop. A judge considering the Nondelegation Doctrine should recognize that the converse is also true, that the district could just as easily claim that Gil Scot Heron is not hip-hop but Kid Rock is, and hold therefore that a statutory ban on hip-hop is statutorily impermissible for lack of intelligible principles, for its inability to support intelligent and principled decision making, and for denigrating the rule of law.

This type of unfettered discretion is anathema to equal protection of law, further decaying the already tenuous threading of America as a would-be tapestry of cooperating cultures. It is also violative of the rule of law and separation of powers as a constitutional principle. To wit, lawyers for those aggrieved should invoke the Nondelegation Doctrine to prevent school boards from banning rap music by Black people or books on race written by Black people under the guise of banning CRT or hip-hop.

Such a situation is far from being hypothetical. The first Black principal in the history of Colleyville High School in Texas, James Whitfield, was recently placed on administrative leave by the schools superintendent after being accused of teaching CRT by several audience members at a school board meeting, who called for his firing despite rules prohibiting direct attacks on personnel at such proceedings. In 2019, the same school board supported racist parental complaints against the educator by asking Dr. Whitfield to remove from his social media a picture showing him and his wife, who is white, embracing to celebrate their wedding anniversary. After a parent asked, "Is this the Dr. Whitfield we want as an example for our students?", the school board asked him to remove the photo.

As for the current controversy over teaching methods, the ousted principal stated, "These people flipped what we were doing in the wake of George Floyd's murder and turned the tide on the push for diversity, equity, inclusion, and anti-racism by placing them under the umbrella of this false narrative of critical race theory." Dr. Whitfield asserted,

Chapter 4: The Ubiquity and Formlessness of Hip Hop and Critical Race Theory   33

There's no credence to the CRT claims. . . . This group that has spoken out against me has a problem with inclusivity, with embracing diversity and with providing equitable experiences for all students. . . . I am not the CRT boogeyman. I am the first African American to assume the role of principal at my current school, and I am keenly aware how much fear this strikes in the hearts of a small minority who would much rather things go back to the way they used to be.

A ban on CRT (or hip-hop) raises First Amendment speech concerns, claims relating to Fifth Amendment equal protection of the law, and other legal doctrines. It is best to assert them all instead of relying on one. But as Professor Bijal Shah writes, lawyers should not neglect basic administrative law principles designed to keep government officials in check. The Nondelegation Doctrine, as one example, is a potential weapon against CRT bans specifically because the doctrine is designed to combat executive tyranny generally.

In service of a well-functioning democracy, one in which the legislature is superior to the executive and judicial branches, the judiciary oversees executive-level bureaucrats to ensure that their actions are always within the scope of authority given to them by the lawmakers, so that the power of the state cannot be arbitrarily or capriciously used against citizens, such as those disfavored in a particular community. Toward these goals, the Supreme Court of the United States developed the Nondelegation Doctrine, which prohibits legislatures from giving the executive a blank check to do whatever it wants to whomever it wants. The basic idea is that Congress cannot delegate its lawmaking authority to others. Congress cannot pass a law that states, "The President is hereby and hereafter authorized to create the laws of the United States," under the principle that the Constitution was designed to reject the monarchical system that formerly governed its authors.

By contrast, the Kebra Nagast, the holy book of the Ethiopian Coptic Church, says that Queen Makeda (aka the Queen of Sheba) abdicated her traditional matriarchal authority as Queen Mother of the nation to declare that only kings follow her son Menelik, whom she conceived with King Solomon of Israel.

The Nondelegation Doctrine was developed along with the growth of the administrative state to ensure a system of checks and balances where judges must be able to discern the parameters of enacted legislation and make sure determinations made pursuant to them are properly within the intent and purposes of the lawmakers. To guide judicial review of executive agencies, all legislation must include "an intelligible principle," which means it must have words and phrases susceptible to thoughtful and consistent judicial interpretation—which in the case of outlawing either hip-hop or CRT is perhaps doubtful given that the popular conception of CRT is anything that has race in it, just as the popular conception of hip-hop is now anything that includes rapping.

Now, to be realistic, the Nondelegation Doctrine does not have strong teeth within federal Supreme Court jurisprudence, having been used to strike down a law from Congress only on rare occasions. In fact, federal courts rarely set aside regulations and administrative decisions based on their being arbitrary and capricious, which is an easier standard to meet than claiming that the statute covering them has no intelligible principles at all. Legislatures are free to reword the legislation in more specific terms than simply "banning critical race theory." There are also several legal theories a petitioner may rely on for redress, including asking a court to set aside an action because the decision was unsupported by the facts, which should happen in the case of the Texas high school principal. But to remove the law banning CRT off the books as unconstitutional, the aggrieved should invoke the Nondelegation Doctrine and attack the logic of the language in the statute itself.

In "Deploying the Internal Separation of Powers Against Racial Tyranny," Shah (2021) contends that the interests of legal formalists and those of racially subordinate minorities converge when executive officials overreach their authority or act in ways contrary to the rule of law. Her essay suggests that

> unjust racial dynamics perpetuated by the government indicate the existence and persistence of race-based tyranny as a descriptive matter. In doing so, it takes a small step toward developing a critical theory of the separation of powers and builds on recent scholarship by Professor Richard Revesz and others that have considered the distributional consequences of regulation.

Professor Shah takes aim at former president Donald Trump's "travel ban" against predominantly Muslim countries as an exercise in racial tyranny. Several critical scholars complain that the "War on Terror" was and remains a war primarily on Muslims. Scholars such as Kenneth Nunn demonstrated how the "War on Drugs" was and remains a war primarily on young Black and Brown people. In the early 1990s, the war on hip-hop focused on Black artists, while the same critics ignored more violent and prurient and misogynistic entertainment industries such as the movie industry. Similarly, the current war against CRT is a pretext for maintaining white racial solidarity in the face of the changing demographics in the United States, where white people will no longer constitute the majority and will therefore have to reestablish, redirect, and reinvigorate political institutions toward tightening a loose racial caste, if white people regardless of class are to remain on the highest social rung and retain the economic benefits thereof, now and for generations hereafter.

Hence, this essay explains why administrative law principles may be brought to bear against recent state and local statutes and mandates against 'critical race theory, how a juridical construct known as the Nondelegation Doctrine can be deployed against laws that set the government off on wild-goose chases, like bans on critical race theory, because when completely rudderless authority is given to bureaucrats, it will inevitably be exercised arbitrarily and tyrannically. In a democracy based on the rule of law, one that preaches the supremacy of a legislature as the people's representative, it is impermissible for the executive branches to pursue secret or unstated motivations—in this case, ill-intentioned and thinly disguised missions to conserve racial hierarchy. Government bureaucrats are tasked with administering that and only that which is authorized openly by duly enacted legislation. To overreach that authority imbues those branches with tyrannical powers, powers that can be wielded at racial minorities, like Black people, and then subsequently on nonracial minorities, like the wealthy, once the precedents are set.

Far from lamenting the formlessness of hip-hop or CRT, their ambiguous or amorphous natures may actually have negative legal consequences for those attempting to maintain racial subordination by pretending to ban CRT in the name of reducing racial divisiveness, when the real goal is to promote white supremacy by eliminating discourse challenging the current racial order while retaining that which defends it, by terminating the voices of people of color who challenge the current racial order while retaining the voices of those who defend it.

A legislature that writes a vague and ambiguous law regarding so-called CRT has improperly given school boards the authority to surreptitiously wield their power in ways that would not pass constitutional muster if expressed in plain words, to ban books and fire persons of legitimate educational quality whose only transgression is weakening white racial solidarity. Dr. Whitfield, the Black high school principal in Texas who was fired for violating a ban on CRT, claims that his dismissal was for having an interracial relationship as well as promoting diversity, equity, and inclusion. Beyond racial subordination, his dismissal is also an example of executive tyranny, which separation of powers doctrines are designed to prevent.

Yet, even if soundly presented, adding the Nondelegation Doctrine to a legal quiver does not guarantee or even necessarily increase the odds of successfully attacking bans on CRT. While CRT has several definitions or important tenets, none of which can claim universal acceptance or application, critical race scholars identify and amplify the inconsistencies between this country's legal system and its grand declarations of commitment to justice and equity in the Constitution and elsewhere, but without the expectation that the same system that created racial subordination will turn around and earnestly attempt to end it. Racism in the United States is permanent, says Bell and innumerable adherents.

Against the most extreme versions of afro-pessimism, however, we note that a system of white supremacy, no different from any other system or construct across known space and time, cannot be undefeatable or indefatigable, and that hope for those in resistance lies in the fact that white supremacist systems must morph and change and adapt to defend themselves at all, because history demonstrates that they cannot do so perfectly and perpetually. Recalling how the godfather of hip-hop, Gil Scott Heron, rapped in the 1970s that Arabs used to be considered the Third World but had put a down payment on the First World, it would be amazing to hear today his take on the rise of China in global geopolitics and commerce. I suggest that if one takes a long, global view, afro-pessimism should yield to afro-pragmatism, where Black people resist white supremacy the best we can considering the circumstances, which should mean taking unflinchingly honest assessments of costs and benefits, relying more on likelihoods and probabilities than on hopefulness and possibilities yet understanding that we need not know exactly how the tides will turn but can be sure that they always do eventually even if centuries or millennia must pass in between.

REFERENCES

Bell, D. (1973). *Race, racism and American law*. Little, Brown.
Bell, D. (1992). The Afrolantica awakening. In *Faces at the bottom of the well: The permanence of racism* (pp. 39–58). Basic Books.
Bell, D. (1992). *Faces at the bottom of the well: The permanence of racism*. Basic Books.
Crenshaw, K., Gotanda, N., Peller, G., & Thomas, K. (Eds.). (1995). *Critical race theory: The key writings that formed the movement*. New Press.
Shah, B. (2021). Deploying the internal separation of powers against racial tyranny. *Northwestern University Law Review Online, 116*. https://ssrn.com/abstract=3954548
Stefancic, J. (2013). *Critical race theory: The cutting edge* (R. Delgado, Ed.). (Original work published 1995)
Williams, P. J. (1991). *The alchemy of race and rights*. Harvard University Press.
Woolfolk, G. R. (1960). Taxes and slavery in the Ante-Bellum South. *Journal of Southern History, 26*(2), 180–200. https://doi.org/10.2307/2955182

FURTHER READING

Appert, C. (2019). *In hip hop time. Music, memory, and social change in urban Senegal*. Oxford University Press.
Bridgewater, P., cummings, d. p., & Tibbs, D. (2015). *Hip hop and the law*. Carolina Academic Press.

Chang, J. (2005). *Can't stop, won't stop: A history of the hip-hop generation.* St. Martin's Press.
Clark, M. K. (2018). *Hip hop in Africa: Prophets of the city and dustyfoot philosophers.* Ohio University Press.
Clay, A. (2012). *The hip hop generation fights back: Youth, activism, and post-civil rights politics.* New York University Press.
Condry, I. (2006). *Rap and the paths of cultural globalization.* Duke University Press.
Fernandez, S. (2011). *Close to the edge: In search of the global hip hop generation.* Verso.
Fricke, J., & Ahearn, C. (2002). *Yes, yes y'all: The Experience Music Project oral history of hip-hop.* Perseus Press.
George, N. (2005). *Hip hop America.* Penguin.
Gray, J. (2016). *Hip hop studies: An international bibliography and resource guide.* African Diaspora Press.
Hess, M. (2010). *Hip hop in America: A regional guide.* Greenwood Press.
Hill, M. L. (2009). *Beats, rhymes, and classroom life: Hip hop pedagogy and the politics of identity.* Teachers College Press.
Kitwana, B. (1995). *The rap on gangsta rap: Who run it? Gangsta rap and visions of Black violence.* Third World Press.
Kitwana, B. (2006). *Why white kids love hip-hop: Wangstas, wiggers, wannabes, and the new reality of race in America.* Basic Civitas.
KRS-One. (2005). *Ruminations.* Welcome Rain.
KRS-One. (2009). *The gospel of hip hop: First instrument.* PowerHouse Books.
Mitchell, T. (2001). *Global noise: Rap and hip-hop outside the USA.* Wesleyan University Press.
Morgan, J. (2000e). *When chickenheads come home to roost: A hip-hop feminist breaks it down.* Simon & Schuster.
Neal, M. A., & Forman, M. (2004). *That's the joint!: The hip-hop studies reader.* Routledge.
Parmar, P. (2009). *Knowledge reigns supreme: The critical pedagogy of hip-hop artist KRS-One.* BRILL.
Parmar, P. (2015). *Rebel music: Resistance through hip hop and punk.* Information Age.
Perry, I. (2004). *Prophets of the hood: Politics and poetics in hip hop.* Duke University Press.
Rose, T. (1994). *Black noise: Rap music and Black culture in contemporary America.* University Press of New England.
Rose, T. (2008). *The hip hop wars: What we talk about when we talk about hip hop—and why it matters.* Basic Civitas.
Terkourafi, M. (2010). *The languages of global hip hop.* Continuum.

CHAPTER 5

Hip-Hop Represented Long Before Critical Race Theory Became a Conservative Rallying Point

Ronda Racha Penrice

Critical race theory (CRT), as defined by Republicans and other conservatives who consistently oppose or block it from school curriculums, is essentially a refutation of American history as a glorious celebration of white men and white men only. How else can we explain anyone charging that the Frances Ruffin and Stephen Marchesi's 2000 book *Martin Luther King Jr. and the March on Washington* is "anti-American, anti-white, and anti-Mexican," as the anti-CRT group Moms for Liberty did in Tennessee in November 2021? They could do so because in May of that year, the state made legal provisions against topics they deemed as CRT being taught in schools. One of Moms for Liberty's objections to *Martin Luther King Jr. and the March on Washington* included its display of images showing segregated water fountains as well as white firefighters blasting Black children with water. Not only did these things happen, more than sufficient real-time documentation exists to prove it.

Long before the present-day culture war erupted, putting CRT—which began over 40 years ago with the core idea that race is systemic and embedded in the legal system and then broadened to include the very fabric of the country, including its many institutions and wide-ranging public policies—at the center, hip-hop had challenged those force-fed "facts" about Black Americans in American history. In Boogie Down Productions' 1989 hit "You Must Learn," KRS-One gives a shout out for

Black history makers such as inventors Granville Woods, Lewis Latimer, and Garrett Morgan, as well as Dr. Charles Drew, abolitionist Harriet Tubman, and entrepreneur Madam C. J. Walker. That same song also put a focus on African history, particularly the accomplishments of Egyptians, as well as the concept of white supremacy, specifically naming influential race theorist Johann Friedrich Blumenbach.

While hip-hop is frequently written off as frivolous, the truth is that it has been an important tool for education and empowerment. The absence of Black history and culture from American school curriculums is no secret. That reality is the backbone of "You Must Learn," which includes the lyrics "What do you mean when you say I'm rebellious/ Cause I don't accept everything that you're telling us" and "I sit in your unknown class while you're failing us/I failed your class cause I ain't with your reasoning/You're tryin' make me you by seasoning." Because early rappers were almost overwhelmingly educated in public schools, they were very familiar with the erasure of the Black experience in the curriculum. And for the vast majority of them, the economic and social inequities in American society were not and are not merely academic talking points but, rather, a lived reality.

Public Enemy certainly upped the ante in what is now challenged CRT territory with their 1988 sophomore album *It Takes a Nation of Millions to Hold Us Back*. In a time when African and other non-Western nations, or, more bluntly, "nonwhite" nations, were officially deemed "Third World countries," Public Enemy proclaimed them "First World" and even symbolically protected them through the S1W (Security of the 1st World). Like BDP, Public Enemy also challenged white supremacy and anti-Black racism, which are the main points of contention for CRT critics. "Left or right, Black or White/Attack lies in the books that we're readin'/It's knowledge of yourself that you're needin'/I'm like Vesey or Prosser, we have a reason why" are lyrics from "Prophets of Rage," one of the critically acclaimed songs from the album. In this song, Public Enemy's front man Chuck D alludes to the alternate history in many mainstream American books that exclude Black Americans and likens himself to abolitionists Denmark Vesey and Gabriel Prosser, Black men, one free and the other enslaved, who were behind notable slave rebellion efforts.

Conscious rap, as it is more popularly known, as a genre, was more influential during that era than has been acknowledged. Although groups like X-Clan, Poor Righteous Teachers, and Brand Nubian did not have the mainstream record sales success of more mainstream hip-hop groups like Public Enemy, their discographies represent a social undercurrent of the times. Major changes were adrift in Black communities across the nation, and hip-hop, in many ways, reported on those changes. Grandmaster Flash and the Furious Five's "The Message" (1982) is widely credited with paving the way for conscious rap. Achieving commercial success by putting the spotlight on timely social issues, and especially focusing on the systemic oppression in the cities, "The Message" proved that rap could give marginalized Black people a much-needed voice. That positive impact emboldened other artists to raise their voices in a purposeful and intentional manner for rap to function in the capacity of what Chuck D famously described as "Black people's CNN."

Through that lens, hip-hop became an important corrective that filled in a lot of gaps, introducing scores of listeners to a narrative centered on Black empowerment and self-determination. It was in this landscape that Nas's debut album, *Illmatic*, arrived in 1994, though it would take Nas a number of years to share this narrative with greater clarity and transparency, as exemplified by his controversial *Untitled* album, released in 2008. On the album's cover, Nas references the well-known photo of an enslaved Black man whose back bears the horrific scars of a whip in the form of an "N," meant to indicate the signature racial slur that was originally supposed to be the album's title. Outrage derailed that plan, however. What was not derailed is the album's many references to history. In fact, this symbolism is not just an essential element of the album but a reflection of the Queens native's personal belief system.

While speaking with *The Financial Times* in 2021, the largely self-taught Nas, who never finished high school, echoed the sentiment many Black Americans feel about the importance of Black history and its ongoing marginalization in the American educational system. "To be black has been a long journey, yet there's a certain lineage that gets ignored, covered up and disrespected constantly. You can't just start Black history in schoolbooks with slavery; that's just wrong in every single way!"

With *Untitled*, Nas covers much ground. For example, in the single "You Can't Stop Us Now," he rhymes, "Minstrel shows, from gold to shackles and back to gold/We act like we home, matter of fact, we are home/Bad attitudes, octoroon skin tones/Slave food turned to soul food, collards to neck bones"—which drops various topics that can be further explored. Minstrel shows are a prime example. Beginning in the early 1800s, minstrel shows, in which white performers initially performed in blackface to intentionally ridicule and devalue Black Americans, became very popular. Over the course of time, however, Black performers became fixtures in the format, themselves performing in blackface. By the early twentieth century, minstrel shows were regular fixtures but often featured Black performers sharing the latest and greatest of their creations. As with "slave food turned to soul food," Black performers put a positive spin on the minstrel format created to demean them. That spirit of resilience is what permeates Black history and a lot of hip-hop.

In "N.i.g.g.e.r. (The Slave and the Master)" from the same album, Nas refers to the erasure of Black people from mainstream American history in the chorus: "Man this history don't acknowledge us/We was scholars long before colleges." And because debates about Black history have consistently been a point of contention in the mainstream landscape, the lyric " . . . any time we mention our condition, our history or existence/ They calling it reverse racism" sadly remains timely. Rappers, particularly in the 1980s and 1990s, were very clear about Black American history being a necessity for Black people to form a healthy identity and used hip-hop to promote that history with full knowledge that a lot of the "education" in their rhymes was an important tool in that self-discovery. And though Nas has achieved international success and acclaim, he, like many others, has not abandoned that mission primarily because the need has not disappeared.

The fallacy behind recent efforts to reinforce teaching and philosophies rooted in white supremacy by those challenging CRT is the assumption that the conversation is new when, in actuality, there is just more mainstream coverage of it now. Black people have been resisting the demonization and devaluing of our humanity for centuries, and hip-hop has been no exception. And that resistance doesn't just look like a fist in the air either. It is even found in songs like Chubb Rock's 1991 party jam "Treat 'Em Right," where he references the racially motivated 1989 murder of Yusef Hawkins—whom an estimated 10 to 30 white youth attacked, along with his younger brother and two other friends, in Bensonhurst, a predominantly white area of Brooklyn in New York City, before killing him—with the lyric "In your hearts and minds never forget Yusef Hawkins."

LL Cool J is not known as a conscious rapper, but he has also used his music to affirm Black humanity and Black joy as well as to call out social injustice. "Illegal Search," released in 1990, is the song that immediately comes to mind. In it, LL brings attention to racial profiling or, more succinctly, "driving while Black." This was at a time when the practice was not in mainstream conversation. So LL's acknowledgment of it as a victim as well as an observer is important. "On the turnpike, and everything's right/In the background is flashin lights/Get out the car in the middle of the night/It's freezin cold, and you're doin it for spite/Slam me on the hood, yo, that ain't right," he rhymes. While it did not generate the media frenzy of N.W.A.'s more aggressive 1988 release "Fuck Tha Police," which angered the FBI, it also bore witness to the pervasiveness of law enforcement's practice of racially profiling young Black men.

Jay-Z's "99 Problems" from *The Black Album*, released in 2003, also reaffirms that routine practice.

> I ain't stepping out of shit, all my papers legit
> 'Well do you mind if I look around the car a little bit?'
> Well my glove compartment is locked, so is the trunk in the back
> And I know my rights so you goin' need a warrant for that,

Chapter 5: Hip-Hop Represented Long Before CRT   43

he retorts, presumably hipping some of his Black listeners to the fact that they are not required to exit their vehicle without a warrant. Of course, knowing your rights does not exempt Black people from being harmed by the police. Philando Castile knew his rights and cooperated fully with police officer Jeronimo Yanez, who shot and killed him in Falcon Heights, a suburb of St. Paul, in 2016 as Castile's girlfriend Diamond Reynolds livestreamed the encounter. Her four-year-old daughter, Dae'Anna, witnessed Yanez killing Castile. And this is despite Castile informing Yanez that he had a firearm that he was licensed to carry. Yet Yanez, who pleaded "not guilty," was acquitted of killing Castile. Rappers who have referenced Castile, along with others like Sandra Bland, Tamir Rice, and Alton Sterling, in their songs include T.I., and The Game and Big Sean with "Warzone" (2016), "Let Me Know" (featuring Jeremih, 2016), and "No Favors" (2017).

Reflecting the Black communities from which Black rappers overwhelmingly emerge has been a critical element of hip-hop. This is what has kept many aspects of the social justice struggle visible. For instance, Tupac Shakur regularly referenced Latasha Harlins in his music, who was just 15 when Korean store owner Soon Ja Du shot and killed her over a $1.79 bottle of orange juice. One of those references came a year after his own death in 1996 in the song "Hellrazor," where he rhymed, "Dear Lord if you hear me tell me why/Little girl like Latasha had to die."

Rappers have long shed light on the myriad issues and challenges Black communities face. The politically charged rap duo Dead Prez alluded to the school-to-prison pipeline as well as how the tentacles of slavery still grip us in their 2000 song "They Schools" with these lyrics: "The same people who control the school system control/The prison system and the school system/Every since slavery . . . ." The Chicago-bred rapper Lupe Fiasco, who was raised Muslim, has been a prominent voice in even challenging mainstream Black American perspectives and practices in dealing with racism. Lupe has never hesitated to share his discontent with this country, especially its history of Jim Crow laws and racial subjugation, and that is evident in his 2012 song "Strange Fruition" from the very beginning. "Now I can't pledge allegiance to your flag/Cause I can't find no reconciliation with your past/When there was nothing equal for my people in your math/You forced us in the ghetto and then you took our dads," he opens, immediately drawing attention to the country's wrongs against him and Black people and the lasting impact of housing segregation and the dissolution of the nuclear Black family through the removal of Black fathers. Common tied the civil rights movement of the 1950s and 1960s to the 2014 Ferguson protests in the theme song for Ava DuVernay's 2014 film *Selma*, which is about the iconic campaign led by Dr. Martin Luther King Jr.

Black male rappers dominate hip-hop and as such dominate conversations in the CRT terrain. In keeping with a patriarchal society, visibility in this space has been granted to men. But women have also made contributions. It just may look different. For example, in 1989, Queen Latifah's "Ladies First" came with a groundbreaking message, especially with the video starting with images of Harriet Tubman, Sojourner Truth, and other historic Black women, which is continued throughout. Not only does she share the stage with the British-born rapper Monie Love, whom she introduces, the video also features other Black women rappers, including Ms. Melodie, who was a member of the BDP camp. The video also inserted Black women into the narrative of Black nation building, even showing Queen Latifah in front of a map of Africa as she moved her chess pieces, at a time when Black women were even less acknowledged in both Black American and mainstream American history.

Taking a cue from *The Mis-Education of the Negro* by Carter G. Woodson (1933/2007), the historian behind Negro History Week, which evolved into Black History Month, Lauryn Hill named her debut album *The Miseducation of Lauryn Hill*. Rapper Rapsody has been even more explicit about incorporating Black self-determination and empowerment, which threatens anti-CRT critics. In her 2019 release "Nina," which paid homage to the great Nina Simone, who also hailed from her native North Carolina, Rapsody rhymes,

> A new dawn, another deed, I try to do some good
>
> I felt more damned than Mississippi was
>
> They deny Nina in Philadelphia
>
> And still we persevere like all the 400 years of our own blood, Africa
>
> Old panthers lookin' back like who gon' come up after us.

With these words, Rapsody references slavery and systemic oppression along with the civil rights movement and the Black Panther Party's fight for self-defense and self-determination.

The deaths of Trayvon Martin in Florida and Mike Brown in Ferguson are frequently credited with ushering in the Black Lives Matter era. Adding fuel to that fire have been the deaths of many others, including Eric Garner in Staten Island, Alton Sterling in Louisiana, Freddie Gray in Baltimore, Sandra Bland in Texas, and Tamir Rice in Cleveland—far too many more. Hip hop, as aforementioned, through songs referencing a Minnesota policeman killing Philando Castile in 2016, responded quite passionately with an astounding uniformity and unity. Joyner Lucas's 2017 release "I'm Not Racist," an innovative stand against white supremacy, references the movement quickly. "With all due respect/I don't have pity for you n***as, that's the way I feel/Screamin' Black Lives Matter/All the black guys rather be deadbeats than pay your bills" is how the song begins.

George Floyd's brutal murder at the hands of a Minneapolis policeman, Derek Chauvin, caught on camera in 2020, as well as the deaths of Breonna Taylor, who was killed by Louisville Police as she slept, and Ahmaud Arbery, who was killed by three men, including an ex-policeman, in Georgia, ignited the hip-hop community even more. Songs that appeared in 2020 in the wake of those tragedies include Lil Baby's "The Bigger Picture," Jeezy's "Oh Lord," Tobe Nwigwe's 45-second "I Need You to (Breonna Taylor)," and Master P's "Say Her Name."

Hip-hop, even with its varied styles and approaches, has been one of the most consistent challengers of the erasure of Black American history and culture. That is the work recognized in the establishment of the Nasir Jones Hip-Hop Fellowship by the Hip-Hop Archives and the W. E. B. Du Bois Institute at Harvard in 2013. It is what is reflected in books like *Pulse of the People: Political Rap Music and Black Politics* by the 2018 Nasir Jones Hip-Hop Fellowship recipient Lakeyta Bonnette-Bailey. Criticisms of hip-hop being misogynistic, nihilistic, materialistic, violent, and all other ills frequently dominate mainstream conversation. Little regard is paid to the music genre's responsiveness to issues like education, history, police brutality, and social injustice, which means a lot to its many Black consumers and supporters. When it comes to clapbacks to those who misrepresent CRT as it challenges institutional racism and systemic oppression, especially in the educational system, the truth is that hip-hop has been on the job.

REFERENCES

Bonnette, L. M. (2015). *Pulse of the people: Political rap music and Black politics*. University of Pennsylvania Press.

Ruffin, F. E. (Author), & Marchesi, S. (Illustrator). (2000). *Martin Luther King Jr. and the march on Washington*. Penguin Young Readers.

Woodson, C. J. (2007). *The mis-education of the Negro*. Lightning Source. (Original work published 1933)

CHAPTER 6

Rhizomatic

Benjamin Perry Levy

INTRODUCTION

The project of understanding pasts is a difficult one, with countless ways of approaching it. Growing up, I remember my maternal grandmother constantly reminding me to not "forget where I came from," to not "forget who I am," and to not "forget who my people are." Resonating deeply with me, these words have shaped how I engage with pasts, with my grandmother always reminding me of them in pivotal moments in my life until her death. This ingrained within me the realization that it is particularly important to remember oneself in a deep sense, to recall pasts in moments when you are engaging with futures. While this anecdote is intensely personal, the learning I was able to gain from it has much broader implications for how we all must interact with remembering. This remembering becomes particularly important for those who hold socially dominated identities, for whom memory and *complete* recitations of pasts are often rare as they have been stripped by those who stand within dominant positions.

Macalester College prides itself on being a school that emphasizes engagement with its neighboring communities, so when I heard of an orientation activity during my first week at this institution that would take us out into the community, I was incredibly excited. On the day of the trip, I was told I would be visiting "rondo," which at the time meant almost nothing to me. Led by the college's Civic Engagement Center, we drove over to an outlet on a road near the I-94 highway. Prior to leaving the bus, we were offered a brief framing: We were in what "was" once the "Rondo neighborhood," St. Paul's predominantly Black neighborhood that was destroyed by the construction of I-94.[1] Macalester employees offered no further information. As we left the bus later on and visited the Hallie Q. Brown cultural center, I was met with more thorough depictions of pasts, of pasts that held joy and energy, not just memories of a community's destruction and its depiction as something that *was*. How may these realities be foregrounded in a way that pushes back against the structures of white supremacy that aim to reduce them?

Just as important as remembering itself is how we string together our memories, how we prioritize information. It is with this that we must be doubly cautious as our relationships with technology grow deeper, as the realities we create outside the digital space and those created within grow closer and closer. There is potential to use technology as a catalyst for engaging more deeply with our memories, but there is also potential for technology to entrench harm. It is with this that I argue that the combined use of new media, particularly the internet, and rhizomatic educational structures can allow for the creation, and perpetuation, of memories of resistance that can be engaged to highlight the life, brilliance, and complexity of Black communities in St. Paul, Minnesota, and, taking a broader lens, peoples whose pasts have been violently destroyed by white supremacist structures of power.

To do this, I shall first differentiate history and memory in order to discern the value and power of memory. With this understanding established, I will turn to the groundbreaking work of Safiya Umoja Noble (2018), *Algorithms of Oppression: How Search Engines Reinforce Racism*, to situate memory within the context of new media. I shall then break down the concept of rhizomatic education as a tool for creating and upholding memories of resistance, using the works of Zelia Gregoriou and Mwalimu J. Shujaa to frame and support my arguments throughout. Rreturning to media analyses, I will examine how this rhizomatic education plays out in *The Matrix* (Silver et al., 1999), to begin the process of drawing the theoretical into the realities in which we live. Synthesizing everything into an analysis of the Rondo neighborhood(s), I shall then offer ideas on what memories of resistance there may look like and how they may be structured using frameworks of rhizomatic education—drawing on guidance from Kim Gallon's (2016) definition of the "Black digital humanities" and André Brock's (2020) analysis of Black Twitter.

MEMORY, POWER, AND THEIR STRUCTURING(S)

History, as noted by David W. Blight (2019), is something that is "interpreted" and something that must be constantly revised. Conversely, memory, according to Blight, is something that is "owned," something that is passed between generations and "carries the more immediate authority of community membership and experience." With memory being something that is owned and intensely personal, yet also communal, one can understand that there is a unique power associated with it, a power specifically deriving from the truths that are connected to who people are. Understanding history is crucial to gathering a full context for the creation of memories, but history alone cannot provide strength enough to, for example, undertake work against structures of oppression and domination.

In her work "The Site of Memory," Toni Morrison (1999, p. 95) dissects the way in which reflections on those who came before her provide the greatest insight into *who* she is in the present, and how she is able to situate herself in the context of their lives, stating, "These people are my access to me; they are my entrance into my own interior life." Holding tremendous weight, Morrison's reflections on how ancestors offer insight into oneself, and quite plausibly into any engagements one may have with one's futures, provide a framework for understanding the function of memory. It is from this that one is able to further contextualize memory. Memory at its core, drawing on the knowledges of one's ancestors, dictates how we operate in the present and frames how we move through our lives, which is supported by Morrison as she notes that she must "trust [her] own recollections" as well as "the recollections as others": "Thus memory weighs heavily in what I write, in how I begin and what I find to be significant" (p. 91). As Morrison addresses the importance of memory in her work, in accordance with and in support of Blight's (2019) analysis, she begins to touch on the notion of collective memory. While memories of individuals may be passed down through generations within a family, collective memory ties together large communities through shared perceptions of the world. As used in this context, collective memory refers to the way in which groups of people with a shared identity, particularly identity that has been politicized in such a way that it is attached to social power and structures of dominance and of being dominated, remember themselves through the amalgamation of individual memory. Collective memory influences how identity is constructed and viewed through the minds of those who share it.[2]

With memory being created through physical artifacts and texts, one must also consider the role the media plays in the creation of memory, particularly collective memories. As digital technologies have become a core part of our lives, defining the way in which we engage with information, the world, and each other, they have undoubtedly shaped the way we remember. This is corroborated by a 2013 article in Scientific American penned by Daniel M. Wegner and Adrian F. Ward (2013), wherein they discuss the way in which the internet has effectively become a "hard drive for our memories" (p. 58), allowing us to simply Google information rather than remembering it, blurring the lines between memories that exist outside the influence of the internet and ones that do not. Going on to further justify this, Wegner and Ward suggest that these new technologies will allow people to "transcend some of the limits on memory and thought imposed by the shortcomings of human cognition" (p. 61). Although this may be a superficially exciting possibility, the replacement of our ability to remember by these technologies and the blurring of the lines between what we remember and what is "remembered" through the internet present a complex situation: How must we contend with information therein that is harmful to the socially dominated bodies of people? This is not to say that the use of these new digital technologies is in and of itself "bad"; rather, we must recognize the work that must be done to ensure that these technologies are not made into a tool of oppression for socially dominant peoples, ad infinitum.

To focus an analysis of the formation of collective memories from new media and offer insight into the question above, I will concentrate on memories created within marginalized communities, particularly Black communities, through representations and depictions in new media. Noble (2018) explores, in her work Algorithms of Oppression: How Search Engines Reinforce Racism, the ways in which search engines, in general, reinforce racism through the use of algorithms that prioritize profit over all else while selectively bringing up harmful depictions of Black women, in particular. The dangerous impact of this is intensified as she asserts that the information aggregated at the top of search pages is "assumed to be fact (by virtue of its legitimation at the top of the information pile)" because of the profitability of "racism and sexism . . . under our system of racialized capitalism" (Noble, 2018, pp. 31–32). Limited depictions of Black women in particular,[3] create deceptive realities, realities that offer an image of dominated peoples only as they exist to benefit those who dominate, those who harm them. The danger of their deception, however, takes effect when they are conflated with fact, by virtue of their prioritization within search results, erasing the impact of more complete realities that hold the depth of hundreds of years of resistance to domination, of more complete realities that would be conducive to breaking down all facets of white supremacist power structures and creating a future for Black communities. To this end, these deceptive realities create, in accordance with the ideas presented by Noble, Wegner, and Ward, memories that serve to uphold structures of white supremacy that destroy futures for Black communities, especially Black women and those who exist beyond gender binaries.

While this paints a bleak picture of the relationship between new media and memory for dominated peoples, and indeed it is so, it is important to turn an eye to the ways in which it can be fought against. If deceptive realities lend themselves to the creation of memories that entrench patterns of domination, more complete realities lend themselves to the creation of memories that break this pattern: *memories of resistance*. Just as deceptive realities—in the context of new media—and the power thereof, in the form of the memories they create, are contingent on the structuring of information in line with systems of (racialized) capitalism, more complete realities and memories of resistance must be constructed in a manner that is wholly antithetical to these systems. Manuel Lima, an authority on visual cultures and data visualization, offers a potential solution to this concern—rhizomatic networks. Should one understand memories that uphold domination to be created by search engines (and other new media that structure information in linear scrolling lists) that structure information in "upside-down tree[s]" of knowledge, insofar as they hierarchize information to reinforce broader social hierarchies (Lima & Stephenson, 2012), then memories of resistance can be created by rhizomes that decentralize, decolonize, and layer knowledge(s) through the formation of networks with numerous nodes. This possibility is strengthened further as Lima notes that "networkism doesn't happen in only two dimensions," thus opening discussion for how rhizomatic networks can be applied across time—or rather through layering of knowledges across time—to generate complete memories that will challenge racialized violence (Lima, 2015).

RHIZOMES AND *THE MATRIX*: EXPLORING AFROFUTURES

Afrofuturism may be characterized as a program for recovering the histories of counter-futures created in a century hostile to Afrodiasporic projection and as a space within which the critical work of manufacturing tools capable of intervention within the current political dispensation may be undertaken.

—Eshun (2003, as cited in Anderson, 2016, p. 228)

Afrofuturist Groundings

As described by Kodwo Eshun (2003), a Ghanian British author and filmmaker, Afrofuturism is a movement of art, literature, theory, and more that centers Black people (and is produced by Black people), people of the African diaspora, and layers the past and present—harm, joy, and everything in between—to critically imagine futures through the use of technologies. Rhizomes and memories of resistance provide a powerful framework through which one can unpack Afrofuturist thought. Within rhizomatic educational frames, as provided by Shujaa and Gregoriou, one intentionally layers pasts into the present to construct more complete realities in order to establish the conditions necessary for memories of resistance. The Oracle in *The Matrix* takes this approach and demonstrates the way in which something, or someone, that exists within conditions of oppression can bring about the destruction of the system through the engagement of rhizomatic education in technological contexts.

In "Further Considerations on Afrofuturism," Kodwo Eshun (2003) examines in greater depth the importance of science fiction in Afrofuturist thought, noting that "science fiction was never concerned with the future, but rather engineering feedback between its preferred future and becoming present" (p. 290). Blurring the lines between what is assumed to be fiction and nonfiction, he implores one to realize that the former is at its core a "significant distortion of the present" (p. 290). Afrofuturism, therefore, cannot be a project of the future, and neither can futures be relegated to a time other than the present.

Rhizomatic Education

On the whole, rhizomatic networks and structurings of information present one with quite a nebulous concept to grasp, a concept that may seem to be detached from any realities that may be constructed with immediacy. While constructing entirely new technologies to embrace rhizomatic structures falls into this realm, for the time being, there is possibility in bringing approaches that rely on rhizomatic structures into existing technologies to modify them in order to facilitate the development of memories of resistance. Taking this approach, I turn to the concept of rhizomatic education, developed out of the work of Gilles Deleuze and Félix Guattari. At its core, rhizomatic education, as discussed by Zelia Gregoriou (2008, as cited in Humphreys, 2013), emphasizes the rejection of codification in order to centralize community, emphasizes the rejection of preconstructed materials that are not responsive to and dependent on the community in which they are built. Understanding the relationship between communities of learning and the learning that is done is a crucial aspect of rhizomatic education—as the former cannot be formed without the latter—and highlights the lack of beginning or end, a process that, in line with Lima's visual engagement of rhizomes, allows for the folding of time to engage with multiple dimensions. This infinite co-constitution demands that the past be engaged with the present, in all spaces in which futures may be imagined.

Grounding rhizomatic education in theories of education that are directly pertinent to dominated social bodies,[4] I turn to the work of Mwalimu J. Shujaa (2003), namely his article "The Widening Gap Between Schooling and Education in the Post 9/11 Era." Deftly differentiating schooling and education, Shujaa argues that schooling is a *tool* for the purveyance of

Chapter 6: Rhizomatic   53

"conformist thinking" to "perpetuate and maintain society's existing power relations" in order to uphold "participation in socially valued and controlled patterns of action" (p. 181), whereas education serves as a *conduit* for the "intergenerational transmission of cultural identity through knowledge of the values, beliefs, traditions, customs, rituals, and sensibilities" (p. 182). Immediately, one is able to draw parallels between schooling, trees of knowledge, and memories that uphold structures of domination, as all seek to enforce hierarchies and sameness. However, there is a more exciting possibility in exploring the beautifully complex relationship between rhizomatic education and the creation of memories of resistance. As Morrison (1999) notes the relationship between ancestors and the creation of memory, of knowledge and power embodied, Shujaa (2003) reinforces this, arguing for the importance of maintaining the past, of maintaining the complete knowledges of ancestors in the present.

Providing an additional framework for considering this argument, Shujaa (2003) addresses the usefulness of education in closing the gap between students' knowledge bases and worldviews, operating within the context of re-Africanization. It is through this framework that Shujaa asserts the importance of engaging in this "cultural combat" to challenge systems that reinforce a lack of cultural knowing. To do this, he draws into relief the importance of working past resignation and uncritical acceptance of information to moving into a space of deconstructing everything that attempts to undermine the development of a connection between one's knowledge base and worldview, of reconstructing information in a manner that is consistent with a student's worldview, and of constructing new knowledge that is born out of this congruence. Shujaa's understanding of education, particularly education as a mechanism for Black liberation—although he does not explicitly state this—is inherently rhizomatic. With no defined start, stop, or inherent structure, education will come about naturally as time is folded in this cultural combat to fill out students' knowledge bases. Thus, seeing as how education that is fundamentally rooted in who students are is, at its very core, rhizomatic, one can see the potential for the creation of memories through complete representations, depictions of complete realities, of Black folk of the African diaspora that are intensely personal yet rooted in communal pasts and presents and reflective of whole truths—memories of resistance.

The Oracle: Engaging Rhizomatic Education and the Present Future[5]

Core to the efficacy of this examination of memory generation in the context of media is the movement of analysis between spaces of traditional "social reality," as provided by the work of Morrison and Shujaa, and digital spaces—as to blur the lines between the two is to emphasize their inextricable nature. It is with this that I shift again to the realm of media to analyze *The Matrix* and the role of the Oracle therein (Silver et al., 1999), grounding the theory discussed above. Within this movement, there are several things to unpack: (1) the representation and construction of the Oracle as a Black woman, (2) the role of the Oracle in engaging education to challenge what is perceived as factual or "real," and (3) the potential of the Oracle to create memories of resistance.

A core character in *The Matrix* franchise, the Oracle is a program, core to the function of the Matrix itself, that has the power of foresight (Silver et al., 1999). In the first *Matrix* film, the Oracle is portrayed by Gloria Foster, an older[6] Black woman. Although this may have been simply in line with concerted efforts made in the 1980s and 1990s to increase non-white representation in the media, and in all facets of U.S. life for that matter, the impact of a Black woman playing the role of a character so transformational in the franchise, regardless of the intent behind her assuming the role, is felt. However, the importance of her representation can only be understood in its entirety when one has a grasp of the function of the Oracle within the Matrix. First introduced after Morpheus instructs Neo to visit her, the Oracle makes clear her power of foresight by consistently asking Neo questions that force him to reckon with the formation of reality, even in a space as small as the kitchen they are in: "Would you still have broken the vase if I hadn't said anything? Do you think you are the one?" (Silver et al., 1999, 1:13:28-1:14:04). Through this one can understand the purpose of the Oracle—to force Neo and Morpheus to question the very nature of what they assume to be factual simply by its existence. However, it is crucial to note the way in which the Oracle engages with her work. At no point does she offer solutions to Neo, nor does she use her foresight to warn Neo of futures that have yet to be realized;[7] rather, she leads through questioning.

This incredible power of the Oracle is felt throughout the entire film, as—although she only appears on screen for roughly five minutes in the movie—she is the central figure in the human resistance to the Machines. Her use of questioning falls in line with the hybrid construction of rhizomatic education as a tool for liberation, as described above. She does not assume there to be a design for her questions or foresight that exists outside of her interactions with Neo, Morpheus, and the resistance on the whole, as is evident through her intensely personal questioning of Neo, making her approach rhizomatic.

As her interactions with Neo unfold, she draws attention to the Latin words above the entrance to her kitchen: *temet nosce*, meaning "Know thyself." The Oracle stresses that answers will not come easily from external sources but rather from knowing oneself. Through this, one can readily draw parallels with Morrison's (1999) work and the use of memory to form oneself and engaging it to make decisions—as the

Oracle implores Neo to do. These are, then, memories of resistance. Melba Joyce Boyd (2004) reminds us of the importance of this as she argues, in her analysis of *The Matrix*, that the film is itself, by virtue of the efforts of characters such as the Oracle, in partnership with Neo, Morpheus, and the human resistance, "a statement against the fixation of boundaries—a resistance to 'residual self-images' that restrict creative and liberating possibilities" (p. 131). Ostensibly, the "residual self-images" referred to by Boyd are equivalent to memories that uphold domination—the Matrix itself—which are created through the presentation of deceptive realities as fact. It is this that allows one to see the usefulness of memories of resistance. When structured in a rhizomatic format, allowing them to constitute it while being constituted by it, memories of resistance are able to create futures that break down present realities that reinforce "hierarchical binar[ies]" that exist only as "culturally constructed realities" (p. 131). If current pedagogical approaches visualize education as a spiral that begins with the teaching of a basic set of facts and continues by adding depth to students' understandings thereof, I propose a shattered, three-dimensional spiral as a visualization of rhizomatic education: one in which the student becomes the center and is able to engage across layers as they are guided by their interests and ways of knowing that are closest to them. This shattered spiral rejects the boundaries that are imposed by institutions of education and highlights the importance of education and learning in all spaces.

THE SITE OF MEMORIES OF RESISTANCE: THE RONDO NEIGHBORHOODS

Situating Memories

With plenty of theoretical grounding and offerings presented in the media, one must situate and understand the applicability of rhizomatic education as a catalyst for the generation of memories of resistance within social realities—for how else can one hope to breathe life into futures in the present? To do this, I shall turn my focus to the Rondo neighborhood in St. Paul, a central point of the Black community in the Twin Cities for much of the twentieth century—and because of this, a space that was intentionally destroyed; the memories and recollections that those who are a part of the community have of it; and how they can be built into memories of resistance.

Delving into the pasts and present futures of the Rondo neighborhood, it is key to develop a sense of the broad context of the area. While the name of the neighborhood is itself new,[8] the community is far from new:

Coming together throughout the first half of the twentieth century, the Rondo neighborhoods spanned north and south from Rondo Avenue to what are now University Avenue and the Summit-University neighborhood, respectively; they consisted of the Oatmeal Hill, more affluent middle class, and Cornmeal Valley, lower middle class, neighborhoods (Cavett et al., 2017). A thriving area of Black life, the Rondo neighborhood was home to more than 85% of St. Paul's Black residents by the early 1950s (McClure, n.d.). In spite of the life and energy in these communities, the construction of the I-94 highway along St. Anthony Avenue in 1956 destroyed this neighborhood, splitting it in half and taking with it much of the nonresidential life that aided in making it the hub that it was—with the estimated average economic incomes of those born in Rondo being under half of those born in the neighboring Macalester-Groveland neighborhood, the former estimated to make roughly $29,000 a year at 35 years of age and the latter, $64,000 a year at the same age (*The Opportunity Atlas*, 2021). Although it is important to recognize this, it cannot become one's primary focus. Predicted outcomes are just that, and to reduce people and their possibilities to predictions disengages the present future, the future that is drawn in through sustained memories of resistance. Creating context offers understanding, but it should not create understandings that paralyze or limit us.

It is only with the context established that one can begin to engage the memories of Rondo—as the former amalgam of neighborhoods shall be referred to from here forward for simplicity's sake—in an effort to imagine futures. Before this, however, I will draw on what I will term as the construction of memories that uphold the domination that restricts Rondo. A brief Google search for "Rondo neighborhood"[9] highlights results that focus on the destruction of Rondo by the construction of I-94, which is corroborated by the anecdote I shared in the introduction to this essay. While it is undoubtedly important to realize the consequences of the highway construction, it is essential to more broadly address the more complete histories, the more complete realities, of the community. By simplifying this narrative and omitting particular details, the neighborhood is formalized and historicized in the view of those who are not privy to the more complete reality that the Rondo area existed, and exists—creating memories that uphold domination, that uphold the destruction of the community.

To work against this, then, one must center more complete realities—realities that include the lives and stories of those who lived in the neighborhood, who fought against the (ongoing) destruction thereof—to build memories of resistance. The collection of oral histories of the elders of the community[10] compiled by Kate Cavett (Cavett et al., 2017) offers just this. Born in 1903, Mary Chambers Bradley Hamilton was nearly 101 years old at the time of her interview with Cavett (Cavett et al.,

2017). Having lived through the very formation of these Black communities, Bradley Hamilton recounted the story of her family moving to St. Paul and of both her mother's experiences attending segregated schools as a light-skinned Black woman and her own while also bringing attention to the joy that the music and dances at Union Hall brought them every Saturday night. While Bradley Hamilton was the eldest of those interviewed, others[11]—including Deborah Gilbreath Montgomery and Mary Kalleen Murray Boyd—highlighted their experiences growing up in Rondo in the late 1940s and 1950s. Through their stories, one can learn of the churches that served as focal points for sociopolitical organizing—with the local NAACP youth group having 650 children in it at one point (Cavett et al., 2017)—and of the innumerable educational opportunities present in schools, churches, and the community—such as the Three Fours Club, which started while Murray Boyd was in elementary school (Cavett et al., 2017). These are layered memories of pain and joy, and the resistance that lies in their dissonance, rooted in a large, rich community. These are only a few of the many experiences that must be brought to light, that must be arranged together, accessibly, for memories of resistance to be built.

Toward Resistance

With the focus of this essay, after all, being on the ways in which digital technologies aid in the construction of memories of resistance, it is necessary to turn back to them to imagine the role they may play in facilitating their creation in Rondo. Before this, however, it is crucial to define what memories of resistance are in the context of Rondo.

Memories of Resistance. These are the stories of the elders of the community. These are the stories of the hopes of the younger generations. The memories of resistance within Rondo are the memories—histories embodied and imbued with power—that draw in the full humanity of all who exist within it, all who ever have, and all who ever will. They actively work against creation of memories by deceptive realities that serve to dismiss Rondo as a neighborhood that was destroyed, and that do not address its future and past in the same breath.

With memories of resistance being ones that center the people of Rondo, what may it look like for rhizomatic educations—the mode of enacting, and ensuring the future generation of, memories of resistance—to be created in digital space?[12] Offering thoughts on this in "Making a Case for the Black Digital Humanities," Kim Gallon (2016, p. 47) defines the importance of the Black digital humanity to be in "its emphasis on humanity as an evolving category" and states that in "recognizing that humanity is a construct, . . . digital humanists [must] come to terms with the contingency of digital projects" (p. 47). With the Black digital humanities, one can imagine the construction of rhizomatic education in digital space to be, at its core, both a method of sustaining a push toward memory and the dismantling of oppressive structures through recognition of the inefficacy of fixed structures.

To address the shortcomings of Wikipedia as a widely used model for digital rhizomatic structures, I draw into consideration Black Twitter. As described by Brock (2020) in Distributed Blackness, it is "Twitter's mediation of Black cultural identity, expressed through digital practices and informed by cultural discourses about Black everyday life" (p. 37). This fusion of the digital and what has been understood as nondigital mirrors the arguments I made earlier in this essay and reemphasizes the importance of thoroughly considering digital space as a nexus for memory generation. Beyond this, however, the use of hashtags and other "technical" elements of Twitter—what Brock names as "cultural-digital" practices (chap. 3)—justify its description as rhizomatic, which is further reinforced by the way in which it shatters space to draw all Black people of the diaspora into community together. Drawing together the voices of numerous people within this space, Jason Parham's (2021) three-part "A People's History of Black Twitter" describes it as a "living archive" of Black life, as the most "unfiltered, dynamic . . . [and] honest" depiction thereof. With everything from protests (and communications related to them) to joy, Black Twitter presents a full depiction of the realities of Black people and facilitates the sustained creation of memories of resistance; memories that are inextricably intertwined with each other through the numerous cultural-digital practices engaged on Twitter. These are the Black digital humanities. To this end, what may it look like for memories of resistance, the complete realities, to be structured in a way that allows users of technologies to access them as they please, by topic, regardless of when they were published or at what time they occurred, removed from the temporal hierarchies imposed by Twitter's "timeline"? What may it look like for memories of those in Rondo to be brought into a digital space akin to this?

In exploring all of this, I want to emphasize the importance of multidimensionality within rhizomatic structuring. One could superimpose, perhaps, these rhizomes of realities, of memories, on layered maps: maps of present-day St. Paul and of St. Paul as it existed before the construction of I-94, with the old Rondo neighborhoods intact. Layering memories onto maps highlights the sites of memories of resistance and would allow community members to flatten time and view the past and present together, with memories of the elders written onto the map of the present and memories of the younger generations written onto the maps of the old neighborhoods. It allows the past to be rebuilt and sustained. This beautiful joining of memories across time and (shattered) space is at the heart of rhizomatic structures and allows those who interact to do so without the confines of hierarchized information—structurings of information that would, as noted in Appendix A, prioritize information that destroys any hope of resistance. In doing this, one fully leans into systems of rhizomatic education that center the experiences of those interacting with the material and allow them to take in information without certain pieces being prioritized in a manner that upholds racialized capitalism.

CONCLUSIONS

From differentiating memory and history and making sense of the embodied power of the former through a combined analysis of Blight (2019) and Morrison (1999), an analysis of rhizomatic education in the context of memories of resistance as a method of creating present futures, demonstrated by the Oracle in *The Matrix* (1999), to exploring how all of this may allow one to create digital representations of the Rondo neighborhood(s) in St. Paul that sustain resistance to white supremacist structures that consistently seek to undermine them, this essay offers an exploration of the possibility digital media offers in building memories of resistance that are able to catalyze a drive against structures that uphold the domination of whiteness.

Turning an eye toward present futures, it is crucial to examine how these ideas of rhizomatic education within digital space to build memories of resistance may be engaged outside the context of the Rondo neighborhood. Within this possibility, there are several things to consider. First is the question of universal applicability: Is it be possible to create a structuring that can be translated into almost any situation? The brief answer to this is that it is not possible. Rather, an honest engagement of rhizomatic educational design necessitates different constructions in every situation, varying to best suit the cases presented by those who will be engaging with the digital structures. Second is the question of where in digital space such sites will be constructed. It is difficult to create space that is able to fully generate memories of resistance and wholly present realities within platforms such as Twitter, given the way they continue to prioritize information in hierarchies rooted in racialized capitalism (i.e., timeline). One must then contend with the difficulty of creating platforms that are widely and easily accessible if the decision is made to abandon such (private) "public" spaces, with it becoming much harder to avoid the cloistering tendency of academia. There is no "simple" answer to this question. It requires a broader project to be undertaken, a project that works to create truly public digital spaces that can effectively house spaces of rhizomatic education while being widely known and easily accessible.

A full consideration of the importance of this work is essential. The project of remembering is a difficult one. Yet undertaking it to build memories of resistance that are sustainable in light of the ways in which the media influences how we remember demands that the work happens now. Futures cannot be relegated to the future; they must be engaged alongside pasts in the present. We must create the conditions and frameworks necessary for building sustainable memories of resistance. We must lean into the present future.

NOTES

1. Since then, this has become less surprising to me. Macalester proudly states its "commitment" to community engagement but routinely encourages students to blunder out into space, center themselves, and reproduce harms through white saviorist approaches—even when these are not consciously undertaken.
2. This is in line with the definition of collective memory offered by *Oxford Bibliographies Online*, which states that "*collective memory* encompasses both the shared frameworks that shape and filter ostensibly 'individual' or 'personal' memories *and* representations of the past sui generis, including official texts, commemorative ceremonies, and physical symbols such as monuments and memorials" [italics added] (Simko, 2019).
3. By "limited "depictions of Black women, I refer to both harmful depictions of Black women and depictions that exist primarily to generate profit, which are considered to be "better." For example, Noble's search for "Black girls" brought about a search page populated with pornographic results (Noble, 2018), while a Google search I performed in September 2021 placed emphasis on music videos, websites such as "Black Girls Code," and social media accounts such as "BLACK GIRLS ROCK!" Thus, one can see, in search results separated by a decade, how search engines prioritize profit in a manner that limits one from fully understanding the reality of Black women as they exist outside the confines of subjugation by (racialized) capitalism (Levy, 2021).
4. For the remainder of this essay, I shall focus on the experiences of Black people. Centering Black experience, I shall critically be able to engage with futures closest to myself and feed emotion and care(fulness)—which it is necessary to do—into my writing.

5. In the context of this work, I use the term "present future" to refer to the creation of the conditions necessary to generate desired futures (sustained memories of resistance) in the present. I elect to use this language to emphasize the importance of layering time to deepen our understanding of both the realities we live in and the ones we will live in.
6. At the time of the release of *The Matrix*, Foster was roughly 66 years old.
7. Note her refusal to provide further explanation for (relatively) trivial matters, such as when she notes, "No wonder she likes you," to which Neo replies, "Who?" (Silver et al., 1999, 1:13:42).
8. David Vassar Taylor, in the foreword to *Voices of Rondo*, notes that the name "Rondo" is a more contemporary term that arose out of an effort to recapture the community that was (by the accounts of dominant narratives) "destroyed" (Cavett et al., 2017, p. xii).
9. Note Appendix A.
10. Interviewing elders is particularly important as their deep-lived experiences and wisdom offer guidance from which younger generations can grow and create futures.
11. Although Cavett compiled the oral histories of 33 residents of Rondo (Cavett et al., 2017), I elected to focus on these three—Bradley Hamilton, Montgomery, and Murray Boyd—as (a) Bradley Hamilton was the eldest of those interviewed and therefore offers experiences of a different time period and (b) the latter two were noted in a series of pamphlets created by the present Rondo community that highlighted various aspects of community life. By virtue of their presence in these materials, one can infer them to be *important*—by the definition of those in the community itself—members of the community and therefore people whose lived experiences and insight are critical in constructing a robust position on the importance of building memories of resistance.
12. To preface this, I must note that this work should not, and cannot, happen without entering the space alongside and behind the Rondo community members. Although this theorizing may allow for the production of some potential configurations, they mean nothing unless they are co-created with those whose memories will be core to this endeavor. With that in mind, one can begin to engage rhizomatic education frameworks in the cultural combat of building and using memories of resistance.

REFERENCES

Anderson, R. (2016). AFROFUTURISM 2.0 & THE BLACK SPECULATIVE ARTS MOVEMENT: Notes on a manifesto. *Obsidian*, 42(1), 228–236. http://www.jstor.org/stable/44489514

Blight, D. W. (2019, October 25). Historians and "memory." *Commonplace*. http://commonplace.online/article/historians-and-memory/

Boyd, M. J. (2004). The African American presence and the resolution of race in the matrix trilogy. *Black Renaissance*, 5(3), 129–143.

Brock, A. L., Jr. (2020). *Distributed blackness: African American cybercultures* (Critical Cultural Communication, Vol. 9). New York University Press.

Cavett, K., Taylor, D. V., & Rondo Oral History Project. (2017). *Voices of Rondo: Oral histories of Saint Paul's historic Black community* (Fesler-Lampert Minnesota Heritage Book Series). University of Minnesota Press. https://doi.org/10.5749/j.ctt1pwt76v

Eshun, K. (2003). Further considerations on Afrofuturism. *CR: The New Centennial Review*, 3(2), 287–302. https://doi.org/10.1353/ncr.2003.0021

Gallon, K. (2016). Making a case for the Black digital humanities. In M. K. Gold & L. F. Klein (Eds.), *Debates in the digital humanities* (pp. 42–49). University of Minnesota Press. https://doi.org/10.5749/j.ctt1cn6thb.7

Gregoriou, Z. (2008). Commencing the rhizome: Towards a minor philosophy of education. In I. Semetsky (Ed.), *Nomadic education: Variations on a theme by Deleuze and Guattari* (pp. 91–109). Sense.

Humphreys, C. (2013). Rhizomatic writing and pedagogy: Deleuze & Guattari and Heidegger. *Journal of Educational Thought (JET)*, 46(3), 191–205. http://www.jstor.org/stable/24713039

Levy, B. (2021, September 23). *Away from trees: Representation, racialized power, and memory in new media*. [Unpublished manuscript].

Lima, M. (2015). *A visual history of human knowledge* [Video]. TED Conferences. https://www.ted.com/talks/manuel_lima_a_visual_history_of_human_knowledge/transcript?source=facebook#t-648728

Lima, M., & Stephenson, A. (2012). *RSA ANIMATE: The power of networks* [Video]. YouTube; Royal Society of Arts. https://www.youtube.com/watch?v=nJmGrNdJ5Gw

McClure, J. (n.d.). Rondo neighborhood. *Saint Paul Historical*. https://saintpaul-historical.com/items/show/160

Morrison, T. (1999). The site of memory. In W. K. Zinsser (Ed.), *Inventing the truth: The art and craft of memoir* (pp. 83–102). Houghton Mifflin.

Noble, S. U. (2018). *Algorithms of oppression: How search engines reinforce racism*. New York University Press.

Parham, J. (2021, July 29). A people's history of Black Twitter, part III. *Wired*. https://www.wired.com/story/black-twitter-oral-history-part-iii-getting-through/

Shujaa, M. J. (2003). The widening gap between education and schooling in the post 9/11 era. *Journal of Negro Education*, 72(2), 179–189. https://doi.org/10.2307/3211167

Silver, J. (Producer), Wachowski, L., & Wachowski, L. (Directors). (1999). *The matrix* [Film]. Warner Bros.
Simko, C. (2019, February 27). Collective memory. In *Oxford bibliographies online*. Oxford University Press. https://www.oxfordbibliographies.com/view/document/obo-9780199756384/obo-9780199756384-0215.xml
The Opportunity Atlas. (2021). Opportunity insights. https://opportunityatlas.org/
Wegner, D. M., & Ward, A. F. (2013, December 1). How Google is changing your brain. *Scientific American, 309*(6), 58–61. https://doi.org/10.1038/scientificamerican1213-58

INTERLUDE
Multitasking
R-Son the Voice of Reason

I may never pop the top of the bottle of
Or spend time dropping opulent monologues
any L I take is a lesson not a loss
but I slay puppet masters like killing Marty Kroftt
Freeing slaves at all cost, Harriet for hire
Black Vangelis riding Chariots of Fire
rappers swear they nice with their very rich attire
but anybody claiming that they're better is a liar

spit Vitamin verses for healthier bars
Negro League rap, Philadelphia Stars
you think I'm in this to get wealthy but naw
Tiger Woods good, hitting well below par
standing on the green, dropping my bombast
impacting like the Nagasaki bomb blast
maintaining your connection, not Comcast
The freman that stops the fre, Guy Montag
Just ask, I multitask, see I'm the
Spirit, the Shadow, modern day crimefighter

I'm Hendrix and Kendrick, rock and roll rhyme writer
laying in the cut, basking in the limelighter

An old-timer despite the fact
that I'm young at heart and my black don't crack
my people came from a lane full of torture and pain
but I'm making damn sure that we won't go back

No retreat, no surrender
mental acumen of a million Mensa members
standing at the center of the room sending censures at pretenders
for faking the funk, I condemn ya
with that Main Source mannerism
Hulk strength mixed with Bruce Banner wisdom
strategize and plan the mission
so it don't end with a brother man imprisoned
I'm the future the elders said they can envision
in between the acts of violence and vandalism
every verse got a little of their phantoms in 'em
calling us out for somnambulism
so if you're the sleepwalking dead
letting the days go by like talking heads
going wild in the streets like you of your meds
and justifying all the things that are often said
consider this the antithesis
push the boulder up the hill, I'm not Sisyphus
making moves but if I get stopped

I rock my own body cam to ensure witnesses
watch it, so you get the proper optics
tryin to raise my boys the same way that pops did
Makin sure they know they got options
& their masculinity's the opposite of toxic
the Vox is the cure for toxins and poxes
thinking man's thinking man, out of the boxness
the kind that led to slavery being abolished
here to make America live up to its promise
so I'm gonna do what I CAN
dynamic formulas and subtle plans
Send a message every hood can understand
John Lewis, Marvin Gaye, Good Trouble Man
dropping science while I pop shit
part James Baldwin, part James Todd Smith
even with, all of this
sometimes it's hard to make it pop with the populace
still I float about the rhythm

Interlude: Multitasking

unknown might like Dr. Spectrum's Power Prism
The algorithm flouts my altruism
ignore the knowledge if you want but you just can't doubt the wisdom

Source. https://music.youtube.com/watch?v=
KSg2u19QC1Y&feature=share

CHAPTER 7

Five Mics and Five Tenants: A Content Analysis of Illmatic to Understand Critical Race Theory

Dwayne Matthews

INTRODUCTION IS ILLMATIC

Before Drs. Michael Eric Dyson and Sohail Daulatzai's critical analysis of Nas's (1994) album *Illmatic* in their book *Born to Use Mics*, before the Library of Congress announced that *Illmatic* will be inducted into the National Recording Registry for "being a groundbreaking album that continues to be imitated by artists today," before the Nasir Jones Hip Hop fellowship at Harvard University, and well before any other ivory institution could give it their stamp of approval, *Illmatic* was already certified where it mattered the most—The Streets. Nas spoke for hustlers, thinkers, those behind the wall, and anyone else marginalized because of their social location. Nas had agency: He had the lyrical license to convey his thoughts in a manner that hip-hop had never seen before. There was only one publication at that time that meant something to any hip-hop enthusiast, and that was *The Source* magazine. *The Source* provided information about new rap artists, the latest sneakers and clothing, and world politics, and most important, it rated rap albums. The greatest rating any rap album could get was five mics, which solidified the album as a hip-hop classic, and that determined who was hip-hop's elite. *Illmatic* received five mics in *The Source*. Hip-hop writer and cofounder of *The Source* John Shecter (1994) stated the following about *Illmatic*: "Nas captures poetic images so intense they force you to take heed then once you're in his grasp he takes your mind deep into the essence of surviving, maintaining, and dealing with life in a vicious society."

Nas's ethnographic lyricism throughout *Illmatic* is about survival—surviving a society that was socially constructed to prevent him and others like him in urban settings of color from succeeding in life. Though Nas does not directly say it, he details the insurmountable obstacles caused by white supremacy and how they are embedded within every social institution. He talks about his distrust of law enforcement, the lack of economic opportunity, and a school system that had failed to hold his interest with half-truths.

Critical race theory (CRT) was crafted by legal scholars of color who were concerned about racial subjugation in society. These activists and legal scholars launched a movement to understand and challenge race, racism, and power. Critical race theorists, or CRITS, formed the movement for all marginalized communities of color and identified each community under its own umbrella—those who identify as Latinx (for whom they formed LatCrit), Asian Pacific Islanders, those who identify as LGBTQ+, and Muslims—but each with their own set of priorities (Delgado et al., 2017). Since then, a growing body of scholarship in education uses CRT as a framework to examine a variety of educational issues at both K–12 and postsecondary levels. Most CRITs believe that racism is the way society does business, which is the everyday experience of most people of color, through social determinants like environmental racism, economic instability, inadequate health facilities, and lack of access to quality education. In recent times, there has been a contention from state officials and parents that CRT pedagogy in K–12 classrooms will make white kids feel bad about being white, so an anti-Black narrative has been the response. A Eurocentric curriculum that is exclusionary of Black people's lived experiences (and any of their derivatives like diversity and inclusion, identity, social constructs, or Black Lives Matter) is not considered damaging to white people's existence. In fact, CRT does not admonish white people or attempt to erase history, but rather, it details racism within systems that benefit white people because of historical sociopolitical changes like welfare reform, and public lynchings done by white organizations like the Ku Klux Klan.

The real travesty is teaching Black kids and other kids of color that they have the same positionality as their white counterparts. We know that this is not true. From a historical materialist perspective dating back to slavery, Jim Crow, civil rights, and now Black Lives Matter, the qualitative narrative will consistently be adverse for Black people with regard to the quality of life that African Americans have had to endure within the American social structure and its institutions. The goal of CRT is to raise consciousness, to insist on action, and to understand racism in our society. Dominant social groups racialize different minority groups at different times to suit their own purposes. A common and repeated example involves the labor market. For example, white people will racialize Mexicans and say that they are lazy and are taking up space in America meant for people who want real jobs. However, that narrative shifts when they want to employ cheaper labor to do masonry, yard work, or other laborious jobs that they do not want themselves. Ruling-class and working-class whites have created and popularized negative images and stereotypes of various minority groups such as minstrels or created narratives about "superpredators," which is why CRITS stress the importance of Black people creating their own narratives, using storytelling as a way of persuasion to illustrate and critique the ways in which American culture typically sees race. Richard Delgado and Derrick Bell argue that people of color should speak from experiences framed by racism and the stories that people of color are born with. This different frame of reference imparts to them a voice that is different from the dominant culture of hegemonic whiteness. CRITs argue that for the majority to understand the minority, the story of the individual must be understood in terms of the individual's own experience. "Legal storytelling" is a method that can sometimes prove useful in bringing to light minority experience, especially within the law (Delgado et al., 2017). This kind of storytelling is what Nas does in *Illmatic* as he goes down the memory lane of his street life, which led him to self-medicating, shootouts with the police, and dropping out of school. In this essay, I discuss the experiences of urban Black people with the societal institutions of housing and education and the criminal justice policies that subjugate them, using CRT tenets and Nas's *Illmatic* album as my framework for a critical analysis of white supremacy in American structures and systems.

HOUSING IS ILLMATIC

The question of race, welfare, class, and poverty is one that many CRITs explore. Bell posed these questions. Is racism a means by which whites secure material advantages? Or is there a culture of poverty that causes racial minorities to be positioned low in the social strata? In terms of housing, it's both; currently, African Americans are disproportionately represented in urban public housing developments. These neighborhoods are generally characterized by high rates of poverty, violence, toxic environmental exposure, and disorganization. However, this wasn't always the case. Between 1934 and the time of the 1940 Census, the U.S. government built and leased 30,151 units of public housing across 46 cities in 22 different states (Allen & Riper, 2020). This was a direct response to the Great Depression, the economic downturn that left many Americans unemployed and on the brink of homelessness, under President Franklin Roosevelt's Public Works Administration. This initiative was created to stimulate the economy by providing contracts to the construction industry that went toward the employment of skilled and unskilled laborers. One of the housing projects that was built was Queensbridge Housing, located in Queens, New York.

Queensbridge is the largest housing project in North America; the 3,149-unit development was built in 1940. In 1941, the Queensbridge population consisted of 3,097 white and 52 African American families (Petrus & Rosner, 2019)—that is, until the G.I. Bill of 1944 made homeownership more affordable for white families to move to the suburbs. This particular access incited white flight to cul de sacs around the United States. African Americas who had served in the war should have also had the access to those houses but were discriminated against with redline practices that stigmatized poorer neighborhoods and labeled them as risks, so banks would not lend money or provide insurance to Black war veterans. As white residents left, so did resources, such as the closure of community-based businesses like grocery stores and health care facilities, which meant less access for Black community members. By 1947, the New York City Housing Authority began evicting tenants whose annual income exceeded $3,000, which made it harder for higher-income residents to live there but much easier for poorer people to enter public housing. By 1969, the demography of Queensbridge Housing had completely shifted; the population was now 63% black, 21% white, and 16% Puerto Rican, with 19% on welfare. Racist local and federal housing policies perpetuated the culture of poverty among African Americans in Queensbridge Housing. The once-resident white working class of Queensbridge no longer exists; it is now a breeding ground for crime, a place with substandard living conditions (Petrus & Rosner, 2019). Nas raps about his time growing up in Queensbridge Projects "My windows faces shootouts/drug overdoses/live amongst no roses, only the drama/for real a nickel plate is my fate, my medicine is the ganja."

If you've ever seen Nas in concert or on your TV screen, it's not uncommon to see him with a diamond-encrusted QB pendant, because he is from Queensbridge Projects. It's evident that he wants to represent his people—which explains why he raps with such fervor when addressing "The Bridge," a touchstone for his skill as a lyricist—through years of observation that served as an inspiration for his magnum opus, *Illmatic*. The album artwork shows an emotionless mugshot of an adolescent Nas with the Queensbridge Housing Projects as the backdrop, with very little color, only shades of brown with a red tint. The back of the album artwork is more telling. Nas divided the track listing into a table of contents—the first five tracks under the header "40th Side North" and the second half under "41st Side South," as if to provide the exact geographical location for his maturation, morality, and masculinity. Further details of the artwork include a cushion-less sofa inside a recreational area with the housing project in the background, with more color saturation of brown and red. The details of the artwork are important as it addresses a much larger phenomenon of racism, structural determinism—a mode of thought or a widely shared practice that determines a significant social outcome, usually without our conscious knowledge (Delgado et al., 2017). Similar to Nas's album artwork is an example taken from the CRT text (Delgado et al., 2017) that is used to provide an example of structural determinism, where children who are raised in smoggy Mexico are said to paint pictures of the sky with a brownish-yellow color, never blue.

> I'm the young city bandit, hold myself down single-handed
> For murder raps, I kick my thoughts alone, get remanded
> Born alone, die alone, no crew to keep my crown or throne
> I'm deep by sound alone, caved inside, a thousand miles from home
> I need a new nigga for this black cloud to follow
> 'Cause while it's over me it's too dark to see tomorrow
> Trying to maintain, I flip, fill the clip to the tip
> Picturing my peeps, now the income make my heartbeat skip
> And I'm amped up, they locked the champ up, even my brain's in handcuffs.
> (Nas, 1994)

The structural segregation of minorities and the social determinants of impoverished communities can lead to social factors that cause mental health issues such as depression and suicide ideation. According to the National Institutes of Health, African Americans who are diagnosed with depression are less likely to receive treatment than their white counterparts. Disadvantaged communities of color cope with problems differently. The social problems of Queensbridge include broken families, crime, staggered employment, high educational dropout rates, and even poor air quality from industrial smokestacks, causing asthma. However, nothing compares to Nas's narration of the damaging and yet lucrative effects crack cocaine had on his community: "I know this crackhead who said she's got to smoke nice rock/And if it's good, she'll bring you customers in measuring pots/But yo, you gotta slide on a vacation, inside information/Keeps large niggas erasi' and their wives basin'."

In the 1980s, crack cocaine hit Black low-income communities hard throughout the United States. This led to the distribution of the drug particularly by young Black men, coupled with Ronald Reagan's war on drugs and community violence against fellow Black men, which left many dead, in jail, or succumbing to the drug. The epidemic was another component of the poverty that tore Queensbridge's social fabric, intensifying feelings of fear and mistrust and increasing posttraumatic stress syndrome, which would cause people to self-medicate or take the extra precaution of protecting themselves (Petrus & Rosner, 2019). The epidemic of crack cocaine use in urban Black neighborhoods made it to mass media outlets, ultimately racializing crack and ghettos as Black social problems, adding to the stigmatizations that African Americans already had to endure, such as coons or welfare queens. The negative depictions and stereotypes of socially disadvantaged Black folks constantly circulated on media outlets, as it was during the height of the war on drugs, are hard to live down. These images of Black people addicted to drugs frightened middle white America, giving support to the belief of some of them that Black people are less civilized. The mistaken belief that sweeping social reform can be accomplished through speech and incremental victories within the system is what CRT refers to as an empathic fallacy (Delgado et al., 2017). Nancy Reagan's "Just Say No" campaign, which called on many Black entertainers of the time to influence drug users and distributors to stop this behavior, was not going to stop drug abuse. What was going to help people overcome the drug menace was more safety nets and treatment, not speeches.

EDUCATION IS ILLMATIC

First month of ninth grade, that was my last month. School aint shit, the teachers is full of shit, the whole system is bullshit, to me.... I wanted to finish school, I didn't want to drop out of school, I wanted to finish school and do something/ . . . I used to write all type of shit when I was young, I thought I was blessed. But that crushed that type of shit, they crushed that in my head. I dropped out of school, start to smoke weed, that's what it was all about. (Nas, 1994)

The landmark 1954 case of *Brown v. Board of Education* was celebrated as the end of the segregation of schools by race. This was reported as a major social win for Black folks and a moral victory for lawmakers. Bell questioned this victory, asking, "Why now?" He theorized that the groundbreaking decision to end segregation in schools because the United States needed favorable attention globally. The country had just ended the Korean War and World War 2 and was currently involved in a Cold War. The optics required that the United States should not be seen to be in a state of war with their Black citizens, who had also fought in those wars. CRT explains this analysis as interest convergence. Bell (1989) argued that whites advance the interests of people of color only when they converge with and advance white interests. White people fear that systemic changes will threaten them in personal ways (e.g., loss of status or control) and gains for people of color mean losses for whites. Although *Brown v. Board of Education* (1954) was a landmark case of desegregation by race, racism within the American system still hindered complete integration

(Delgado et al., 2017). Later, segregation by school districts was established. Communities with more money and resources were provided with better funding for schools and access to better after-school facilities. Housing projects like Queensbridge were intentionally drawn up so that Black neighborhoods had less access to quality education, resulting in perpetuation of the cycle of poverty. According to *Voices of Queensbridge: Stories From the Nation's Largest Public Housing Development* (Petrus & Rosner, 2019), it was common for families to live for multiple generations in Queensbridge—in some cases, right back to the 1940s. Furthermore, according to American Community Survey data, it is most common for Queensbridge residents to have less than a high school diploma (38%) and least common for them to hold a college degree (11%). In the surrounding Long Island City neighborhoods, it was most common for residents to hold a bachelor's degree or higher (51%) and least common to have a high school diploma or equivalent (13%). While the average income in the broader neighborhood is $80,908, the average earnings for Queensbridge residents with earnings greater than zero are less than half that amount at $33,096.4 (Petrus & Rosner, 2019).

> Sometimes I sit back with a Buddha sack/Minds in another world, thinkin
>
> How can we exist through the facts? Written in school textbooks, bibles, et cetera
>
> Fuck a school lecture, the lies get me vexed-er

The commonly held belief is that we live in a meritocratic society, where everyone has an equal chance of success. All a person has to be do is work hard and acquire the appropriate in-demand skill set. After doing so, that person will be rewarded with social mobility and ascend to their desired social location as though there are no barriers in place that hinder free enterprise or the quality of life. Social barriers were set in place against Black people to impede their growth across the board in education. A good example of this is trying to pass the ACT or SAT to get into school. White privilege allows white parents to pay for a fixed entry exam for their child who slacked for an entire four years during high school. In CRT, color-blind racism becomes systemic and institutionalized through four ideological frameworks that people use to interpret information concerning race relations and to explain racial differences in outcomes:

1. *Abstract liberalism*, which involves ideas associated with political liberalism, such as "equal opportunity"
2. *Naturalization*, which allows white people to find an explanation for racial phenomena by suggesting that they are natural occurrences

3. *Cultural racism*, which relies on arguments that are racial stereotypes, such as "Black folks do not put much emphasis on education" or "Blacks have too many babies, which is why they need welfare," as a way to explain the rankings of minorities in society
4. *Minimization of racism*, suggests that discrimination is no longer a central factor affecting the life chances of Blacks and other people of color (Silva, 2018)

INCARCERATION IS ILLMATIC

What up kid? I know shit is rough doin' your bid

When the cops came, you shoulda slid to my crib

But fuck it black, no time for looking back it's done

Plus congratulations, you know you got a son

I heard he looks like you, why don't your lady write you?

Told her she should visit, that's when she got hyper

Flippin', talk about he acts too rough

He didn't listen, he be riffin' while I'm tellin' him stuff

I was like yeah, shorty don't care, she a snake too

Fuckin' with the niggas from that fake crew that hate you. (Nas, 1994)

The idea that Black behavior is linked to criminality had become ingrained in the American fabric post–Civil War. This general conception would ultimately lead to the demise of any social progress in any institution for Black people, as it pertains to adequate housing, health, policy, and education. Rather than seeing Black people as an asset to the economic system if they were educated, they were viewed as "genetically inept" by eugenicists, so educating them would lead them to become better criminals. As a result, it was considered advisable to keep Black folks uneducated, subservient, and dependent (Muhammad, 2010). CRT critiques the processes of legal subjugation by policies of the criminal justice system, Supreme Court decisions, mandatory sentencing guidelines, and drug laws. The crack cocaine epidemic in the 1980s debilitated poor urban Black communities throughout the United States, which led to an increase in drug trafficking, drug use, homicides, and overpolicing. The 1986 Anti-Drug Abuse Act established mandatory minimum sentences for federal drug offenses. This particular act affected African Americans negatively and was one of the biggest contributors to the destruction of the nuclear Black family. The act set in place mandatory minimums for possession of cocaine. However, depending on its form, whether it was rocks (mostly in Black communities) or powder (mostly in white communities), the act stipulated different sentencing. Five grams of crack cocaine received a minimum sentence of five years in prison with no parole, and 500 grams of powder cocaine received the same sentence, even though the chemical compounds are the same. Additionally, in 1986, Queensbridge experienced more murders than any other public housing project in the city. In Queens, in general, the murder rate increased by 25% from 1987 to 1988. About 38% of the homicides were directly related to crack cocaine (Petrus & Rosner, 2019). The idleness of many lower-class Black males, resulting in part from chronic unemployment, is a major factor contributing to their being available to participate in street-related activities. Black male unemployment is on average twice higher than the unemployment rate among white males. In addition, Black males earn 62 cents for every dollar earned by white males. Black men socialized as breadwinners for the family have a harder time providing for their families due to the lack of decent wages, resulting in them looking for alternate ways of making money that may not be legal (Oliver, 2006), such as the distribution of crack. As a result, they find themselves under state supervision and in opposition with police officers.

> I got so many rhymes I don't think I'm too sane
>
> Life is parallel to Hell but I must maintain
>
> And be prosperous, though we live dangerous, cops could just
>
> Arrest me, blaming us, we're held like hostages. (Nas, 1994)

Throughout *Illmatic*, Nas raps about shootouts with police officers and the growing unrest between Queensbridge residents and local law enforcement. In 1989, the death of Richard Luke while in Housing Authority Police custody was a moment when tensions ran high as Luke died face up in a restraining blanket. The Housing Authority officers said his death was from a cocaine overdose and heart failure. Queensbridge residents did not believe the police narrative, which led to a two-day protest on the Queensboro bridge against police officers. After a state investigation, it was established that Luke choked to death on his own vomit while being restrained by the police (Petrus & Rosner, 2019). Stories like the death of Luke are far too common in urban African American communities. Racist policies, like stop and frisk, that allow police officers to racially profile individuals legally whom they deem reasonably suspicious have disproportionally affected both Black and Latinx communities simply because crimes such as distribution of drugs or drug use have been highly racialized. However, what preceded stop and frisk was President Bill Clinton's 1994 Crime Bill, "the largest crime bill in the history of the United States." The bill promised $10 billion to the states for prison construction between 1995 and 2000 but only for those states that passed truth-in-sentencing laws, which eliminated most "good time" provisions and required convicted offenders to serve a minimum of 85% of their prison sentence. The effect on state policy was almost immediate; the number of states with truth-in-sentencing statutes grew from 4 in 1992 to 27 in 1998. The bill also provided funds for the hiring of 100,000 additional police personnel. These provisions of the bill could affect Black incarceration either through the overall incarceration rate or through an effect on "racial disparity" (Souto, 2018). The congressional authors of the legislation implemented a three-strikes rule, mandating a lifetime in prison for those convicted of a serious violent crime who had two or more prior convictions, including for drug possession.

HEALING IS ILLMATIC

I sip the Dom P, watching Gandhi til I'm charged

then writing in my book of rhymes, all the words past the margin

To hold the mic I'm throbbin, mechanical movement

Understandable smooth shit that murderers move with the thiefs them,

play me at night, they wont act right

the fiend of hip hop has got me stuck like a crack pipe

the mind activation, react like im facin time like pappy mason, with pens im embracing (Nas, 1994)

According to Nielsen N-Score data, in 2018, hip-hop became the leading music genre, beating rock and roll, making it the genre most listened to, an increase from 4.1% in 2017 to 8.1% in 2018. According to Nielsen N-Score data—a proprietary metric that assesses a celebrity's potential for partnerships based on awareness, likeability, and other attributes including influence—hip-hop personalities were rated as number 1 compared with artists in any other genre. Nielsen's Audience Insights report that the largest demographic of fans of hip-hop/rap music were African American and Hispanic males 18–24 years of age (Kitwana, 2002; Nielsen, 2015). By comparison, the third highest cause of death among African American men in the same age-group is suicide according to the National Institute of Minority Health and Health Disparities. Use of rap and hip-hop by African American males as a mental health coping method would directly correspond with the genre's creation as an expression to engage with the community and share perspectives. Violence, death, and suicidal ideation have been long-standing themes in rap music, and more recent offerings in hip-hop include narratives about mental and emotional vulnerability.

Chapter 7: Five Mics and Five Tenants

Artists more readily evoke help seeking—a virtue seemingly unfamiliar to those who align more with the prevailing themes of escapism, self-control, and hypermasculinity. Hymns, gospel, blues—Black music has been the primary means of cultural expression for African Americans, especially during difficult social periods. Rap is no different; it articulates life in urban America for African Americans who are at the bottom of the capitalist society as they are disenfranchised and alienated, finding themselves facing conditions of accelerating deterioration; rap's urgent, edgy, and yet life-threatening resonances will become a more important and more contested social force in the world.

Clinical psychologist Don Elligan coined the term "rap therapy" in 2000 as an intervention method while working with Black youth. The emergence of rap therapy (Alvarez, 2011) as well as hip-hop psychology (Roychoudhury & Gardner, 2012) offers two conceptual and practical frameworks to both encourage and understand how and why artists vocalize depression and thoughts of suicide. The impact that rap music has on young Black men as a form of expression and catharsis should be acknowledged by more mental health professionals, who can use it as a therapeutic resource to engage with young Black men in a better way. Mental health professional T. Tomas Alvarez utilized rap therapy as an intervention when working with at-risk youth of color in Oakland, California, who were frequently exposed to community violence that potentially led to posttraumatic stress disorder. According to a report issued by the Urban Strategies Council, out of the 125 people murdered in Oakland in 2008, 9 out of every 10 were male, 8 out of every 10 were African American, 2 out of every 3 were under the age of 30, and 9 out of 10 were shot by a firearm. African Americans make up 37% of the Oakland population but accounted for 80% of the homicides. Alvarez noticed a pattern of Black males getting labeled as oppositional or defiant, and he wanted to use rap therapy as a community-driven model to provide culturally relevant strengths to the community. He was able to do this by understanding the stigma surrounding mental illness in African American communities and the barriers to mental health treatment. So Alvarez pioneered a performance-based rap therapy program called Beats, Rhymes, and Life to engage young men of color in therapy, and this program has operated in schools where young people learn to use it to talk about their struggles and to solve problems. The BRL rap therapy program now operates in Oakland and in the South Bronx, in New York City, where empirical studies have been conducted on it (Alvarez, 2012).

> Sentence begins indented, with formality
> My duration's infinite, money wise or physiology

> Poetry, that's a part of me, retardedly bop
> I drop the ancient manifested hip-hop, straight off the block

Hip-hop and rap are most popular among and dominated by African American men. The genre, which has birthed a multibillion-dollar industry, originated as a result of living in harsh and oppressive social and environmental conditions. Research has shown that rap music can be cathartic and expressive, and give self-worth through a written or spoken coded language that allows an escape from harsh social conditions; it has been proven to lessen morbidity and reduce mortality rates among African American men by means of the modulization of rap therapy. However, rap lyrics are now being used by criminal justice agents as admissions of guilt or as proof of motivation for crimes committed within communities. In the article "When Music Takes a Stand" (Lutes et al., 2019), the researchers note the existence of a pattern where an increase in the number of rap songs is matched by an increase in the number of criminal court cases where rap lyrics were used as evidence by prosecutors. To examine how rap lyrics were used as evidence, the researchers did a content analysis of 160 federal and state court cases that used rap lyrics as evidence. Rap lyrics have been widely used in court cases to find defendants guilty or to tarnish their character in front of jurors. In many instances, it is not clear whether the rap lyrics posed a legitimate threat, plainly stated, to cause harm to another person. If rap music became more popular as a therapeutic tool among practitioners and within the academy, it would have more validity and will be viewed as a viable option to be used as a coping mechanism by those who are inspired by the art form, instead of getting criminalized (Lutes et al., 2019). If the art form of rap is going to be put on trial by those who do not understand it, this will continue to perpetuate feelings of insignificance, resulting in a new generation of African American men with poor mental health.

CRITs also acknowledge the contribution of scholar Paul Butler in introducing the idea of hip-hop theory in *Let's Get Free*, which holds that the purpose of hip-hop music and culture is the reconstruction of the criminal justice system so that it is more humane and responsive to the Black community. This is the first step in imagining a hip-hop nation. Hip-hop as a theory and music genre exposes the American justice system, just as Nas had done with *Illmatic*. Hip-hop as a culture champions the human rights of all people. It is as concerned with fairness for drug sellers, as it is for law-abiding middle-class people who are stopped by the police for "driving while Black." There is no respectability for politics that hinders fairness of justice in a hip-hop nation. However, for hip-hop to command moral authority, as stated by Paul Butler, it needs to give up its endemic sexism and homophobia. So it is imperative that it addresses all forms of subordination within the hip-hop nation. If a hip-hop nation is to be successful, it would need to develop an intersectional lens of race, class, and gender, just as CRT has (Butler, 2009).

Illmatic may be the most important album in hip-hop history, and it deserves to be celebrated and acknowledged within pop culture, revered among hip-hop heads, and studied within the academy. When Illmatic was released, it refined storytelling among MCs. There is a reason why *Illmatic* has been at the helm for the past 20 years: It is because it was created out of desperation by a 19-year-old Black man from a decaying housing project in Queens characterized by urban blight and neglect, whether by city officials or community members. CRITs understand the importance of narratives by individuals of color who have these lived experiences, which can be used to influence the majority narrative, and Nas has done that. Both CRT and *Illmatic* reflect the historical impact of white supremacy on, in this particular case, Queensbridge Housing Projects. Each reveals the ideological, political, and economic tools used by America to accomplish unrivaled hegemony. CRT and *Illmatic* can both be used as tools to understand the transgression of life in urban Black communities. Within each, the dialectical relationship between the material conditions of the oppressed and the oppressor is an enduring source of conflict. Without proper resources for social structures like housing, education, and incarceration, the oppressed have struggled to find their agency in effecting their own liberation. What is certain, however, is that the historical arc trends toward freedom and self-determination as the manifest aspiration of Black people in urban communities throughout the United States. In the context of racism, privilege, and white supremacy as expressed through the global capitalist economic order, Black people will continue to resist these oppressive systems to secure their own political and economic security as citizens of the world and members of the human race.

REFERENCES

Allen, R., & Riper, D. V. (2020). The new deal, the deserving poor, and the first public housing residents in New York City. *Social Science History*, 44(1), 91–115. https://doi.org/10.1017/ssh.2019.41

Alvarez, T. T. (2011). Beats, rhymes, and life: Rap therapy in an urban setting. In S. H. Yancy (Ed.), *Therapeutic uses of rap and hip hop* (chap. 7). Routledge.

Bell, D. (1989). *And we are not saved*. Basic Books.

Brown v. Board of Education of Topeka, 347 U.S. 483 (1954).

Butler, P. (2009). *Let's get free*. New Press.

Delgado, R., Stefancic, J., & Harris, A. (2017). *Critical race theory: An introduction*. New York University Press.

Dyson, M. E., & Daulatzai, S. (2009). *Born to use mics: Reading Nas's Illmatic*. Civitas Books.

Kitwana, B. (2002). *The hip-hop generation: Young Blacks and the crisis in African American culture*. Basic Books. https://www.fulcrum.org/concern/monographs/x059c806w

Lutes, E., Purdon, J. A., & Fradella, H. (2019). When music takes the stand: A content analysis of how courts use and misuse rap lyrics in criminal cases. *American Journal of Criminal Law, 6*. https://papers.ssrn.com/sol3/papers.cfm?abstract_id=3369175

Muhammad, K. G. (2010). *The condemnation of blackness*. Harvard University Press. https://doi.org/10.2307/j.ctvjsf4fx

Nas. (1994). *Illmatic* [Album]. Columbia.

Nielsen. (2015, July). *Hip-hop nation: How the genre is turning it up in 2015*. https://www.nielsen.com/us/en/insights/article/2015/hip-hop-nation-how-the-genre-is-turning-up-in-2015/

Oliver, W. (2006). "The Streets": An alternative Black male socialization institution. *Journal of Black Studies, 36*(6), 920–921. https://doi.org/10.1177/0021934704273445

Petrus, S., & Rosner, M. (Eds.). (2019). *Voices of Queensbridge: Stories from the nation's largest public housing development*. LaGuardia and Wagner Archives, LaGuardia Community College/CUNY.

Roychoudhury, D., & Gardner, L. (2012). Taking back our minds: Hip-hop psychology's (HHP) call for a renaissance, action, and liberatory use of psychology in education. In B. J, Porfilio & M. J. Viola (Eds.), *Hip-hop(e): The cultural practice and critical pedagogy of international hip-hop* (pp. 234–248). Peter Lang.

Shecter, J. (1994, April). The second coming. *The Source*, p. 45.

Silva, E. B. (2018). *Racism without racists*. Rowman Littlefield.

Souto, W. E.-C. (2018). Racial disparity in U.S. imprisonment across states and over time. *Journal of Quantitative Criminology, 35*(2), 365–392. https://doi.org/10.1007/s10940-018-9389-6

CHAPTER 8

Represent: Education, Still Groovy but Smoother

Walter D. Greason

In 1831, Nat Turner staged a revolt that shocked the Anglophone world. Countering hegemonic logics about the docility and happiness of enslaved Africans, Turner's rebellion inspired thousands of people around the world to support new calls for the abolition of slavery. However, new scholarship has demonstrated that the patterns of African resistance stretch further back and much deeper than was previously documented. Most notably, scholars have begun to connect the understanding of the Haitian Revolution to the increasing frequency of resistance among enslaved Africans in the early nineteenth century. With groundbreaking publications winning international awards every year, a reassessment of these traditions of African liberation in the western hemisphere is now due.

Only recently has the United States chosen to love Black people. It has loved the Confederacy deeper and longer and with greater loyalty. Stone Mountain spits in the face of our supposed destiny: How deeply must a nation hate a people to carve their destroyers into the landscape *in perpetuity*? After a year that included the shootings of Breonna Taylor, Ahmaud Arbery, George Floyd, and Jacob Blake, we still lack a national consensus to end racism and the violence it has hurled on Black Americans. The year 2020 was a year of revelation for some, but it has been a year of minimal progress for others. We must continue the work of dismantling white supremacy. By age 12, I fully understood the layers of violence that maintained racial injustice in America. During a swimming class, a student tried to drown me because I was Black. On another occasion, a group caught me alone in a classroom and beat me to the floor because I was Black. The interpersonal violence reinforced the structural segregation that I had experienced every minute of every day for decades.

As a young educator, I longed to teach a course on racial violence. Drexel University gave me the opportunity to create a syllabus on racial hatred in 2002. Teaching that syllabus opened my eyes to the challenge ahead of us. It was an evening course, meeting for almost three hours once a week. The class fulfilled a core requirement; two dozen students enrolled. I remember thinking that I would have to offer extraordinary reassurances to the Asian and white students in the class because it was very unlikely that they had read the material previously. There were only two African American students in the class. My first lecture focused on the early nineteenth century, examining white violence against Blacks in Pennsylvania and Ohio. Cincinnati's 1829 riots were a consequence of laws prohibiting Black migration to Ohio, which existed almost from its statehood in 1803. Philadelphia's Flying Horse riot in 1834 destroyed a Black neighborhood, displacing dozens of families. The determination to maintain racial segregation through terrorism became a pattern that continues today. In 1851, white terrorists (who called themselves "slave catchers") tried to invade the town of Christiana, Pennsylvania. With the support of U.S. marshals, they attacked the farm of William Parker, a free African American. The terrorist leader was killed in the assault, but the abolitionists who repelled the invaders faced charges of treason.

My students, working from the syllabus I called "Collective Racial Violence in the United States" were not prepared for a history that had been kept from them. Nor were they emotionally ready for a sustained confrontation with this evidence. The material turned their heads in countless ways. They learned about festival lynching—advertised assemblies to murder criminal suspects before their trials—and the use of planes, cannons, and firebombs to destroy neighborhoods and businesses, any evidence of Black excellence. It was easy for them to see that this history shaped a century of racial terrorism that still influences law enforcement practices today. This knowledge shattered their assumptions about white supremacy. After three weeks, they would leave class to weep or to vomit. After six weeks, they began to sob uncontrollably in the classroom. Their horror was so jarring that I decided a week after the course ended to break the content into multiple courses over several semesters, which in many cases only delayed but not stopped the emotional scarring. After years of social activism that often confronted threats and violent action, my choice to teach a course about that tradition required a degree of caring (for myself and my students) that I lacked initially. Seeing my students glimpse the burden that Black people carry constantly forced me to find a different path. Unlike my other courses, there was no pleasure in teaching about this carnage.

Over the next 15 years, I taught suburbanization, the evolution of American media, enslavement at the Cape of Good Hope, and the economic evolution of global markets. All of the courses involved aspects of our violent history but did not put them at the center. Then, in 2017, I published the racial violence syllabus online. Countless Americans now know about the entire communities that were nearly reduced to memories—in Eatonville, Florida; Independence Heights, Texas; and Pergolaville, New Jersey. Our national park system has a chance to preserve these places as it does plantations across the South.

In the past two decades, scholars like Walter Johnson and Sven Beckert have demonstrated the power of social history in understanding the developing American economy in the nineteenth century. Calvin Schermerhorn opened important new doors to this knowledge by examining the language of business that originated in the plantation system. Daina Ramey Berry and Christine Sears have added depth and insight to the initial breakthroughs in creating a social history of capitalism.

All of this work fits into the framework provided by the 2016 historical reader, *The American Economy*. At its root, it combines the quantitative analysis of Sir Partha DasGupta with the historical sociology of world systems pioneer Immanuel Wallerstein. Advancing the work of an earlier generation led by Oliver Cromwell Cox, W. E. B. DuBois, and Eric Williams, the product of this analysis is a sharp, balanced account of the historical evolution of industrialization in the trans-Atlantic context. Most important, it demonstrates the ways in which agricultural wealth evolved into systems of cities and industrial infrastructure. Ultimately, these systems produced the core assumptions that shaped globalization over the past sixty years.

On January 6, 2021, the world saw the threat to freedom and democracy posed by a slice of white America. Most people do not understand the movement's depth and endurance—or its history. While the nation has never had a stronger, common commitment to equity for all people, these darker, authoritarian forces are determined to use every resource they can to ensure that injustice prevails. Most scholars who study the second half of the twentieth century in the United States would recognize the term "massive resistance." The call from Senator Harry F. Byrd (D-Va.) in 1956 sparked 50 years of ongoing defiance of racial inclusion. The past 30 years of white nationalism in federal politics helped seed the rise of mass incarceration between 1994 and 2012 and the crippling of the Voting Rights Act in 2013. The historic election of President Barack Obama in 2008 only intensified this movement. This resistance movement helped Republicans win 12 governor's offices and 958 legislative seats between 2010 and 2016. Now those state legislatures are moving almost in lockstep to restrict access to the ballot for people of color.

The United States is a decade or two away from becoming majority non-white. The Republican Party has been quietly trying for years to delay that moment; now it isn't even trying to hide its efforts. Senate Minority Leader Mitch McConnell (R-Ky.) proudly celebrated his leadership in this effort when he declared his determination to limit Obama to one term in early 2009. He considers the denial of a Supreme Court nomination in 2016 one of his greatest political achievements; he knows the court is key to furthering the delay. He followed that effort by working overtime to confirm the appointment of more than 270 federal judges between 2017 and 2021, while Donald Trump was president.

The events of January 6 were predictable and foretold. The Unite the Right rally in August 2017, less than a year after Trump's election, brought the movement into the open again and revealed its core assumptions about citizenship and belonging in the United States. In my home state of New Jersey, these assumptions play out across many parts of daily life. Some social clubs and youth athletic teams build their identities around racial exclusion. A local school board member in Middlesex County attacked state attorney general Gurbir Grewal with an anti-Sikh slur in 2018. A white referee forced a 16-year-old high school wrestler to cut his dreadlocks before a match near Atlantic City. Last year, the state government itself issued a report that assessed the risk of violent white supremacist extremism as "high." We don't need to see men marching with tiki torches to know that the forces of white supremacy are alive and at work. As my colleague, polling expert Patrick Murray noted, hatred runs deep in New Jersey.

Constant reminders that Muslims, Asians, Latin Americans, and Black Americans are threats to national traditions filled the headlines and airwaves every moment for five years. The total exhaustion with this reckless, unchecked rhetoric drove the celebrations of a new administration in early November. Yet the determination of the zealots to undermine the election, to sabotage the certification process, and to distort election law continues unabated. The forces of authoritarianism aren't going to lay down their weapons voluntarily. The only way to stop the movement is to prosecute the individuals who participate in events and to condemn the ideology that encourages them.

In the wake of the increasing violence against Asian Americans, Latino migrants, American Indians, and African Americans, now is the time to break the traditions of white nationalism in the nation's civic institutions. From the military and law enforcement to finance and philanthropy, the United States must rid itself of white supremacists. The Biden administration has an opportunity to deliver justice in a nation still bound by segregation. Today, consumers are bound by the troubling assumptions of the market (rooted in historic patterns of enslavement). The systemic reinvention of society and the marketplace is the basic requirement of freedom in the twenty-first century.

INTERLUDE

Systemic Racism: A Theory of Oppression (2006)

by Joe Feagin

"Systemic racism includes the well-institutionalized, society-wide array of white anti-others practices, unjustly gained white societal power embedded in a racial hierarchy, huge resource inequalities along racial lines, and a dominant white racial frame rationalizing unjustly gained white privilege and power."

To achieve societal change, racism education beyond simple conscious raising is needed. More people need to learn about the dominant white racial frame, and ways to de-frame their views, reframe them, and dissent in everyday settings. The Southern Poverty Law Center reported that teachings about the civil rights movement in classrooms typically center around two key figures, Martin Luther King Jr. and Rosa Parks; only a handful of states require educators to devote significant attention to the movement, and more than 30 states require minimal or no instruction at all.

Beyond schoolrooms, local and national leaders need to establish organizations that aggressively identify individual and systemic racism and teach ways to challenge those practices and attitudes in everyday life. Based in Minnesota, the Antiracism Study Dialogue Circles Metamorphosis is one such group that has experienced success in developing antiracism curriculum models and expanding group facilitator training. The group is growing organizational outreach to take its programs beyond Minnesota.

As Frederick Douglass said in 1857: "If there is no struggle, there is no progress. Those who profess to favor freedom, and yet depreciate agitation, are men who want crops without plowing up the ground. They want rain without thunder and lightning. . . . Power concedes nothing without a demand. It never did and it never will" (https://today.tamu.edu/2017/10/18/texas-am-professor-discusses-systemic-racism-white-racial-frame/).

SECTION II
The Clapback

Thousands of social scientists subscribed to a series of assumptions called "the culture of poverty" to explain the deficit models of Black, Latinx, and Indigenous cultures in Western societies. Most notable among these voices was Patrick Moynihan, an elected official and public scholar, who crafted public policy to maintain a welfare state against the prevailing forces of white supremacy. For decades, these ideas reinforced systems of racial segregation and expanded the racial wealth gap, which prevented any chance of progress toward justice and equity.

Bijoun Eric Jordan, Maurice Broaddus, Ryan J. Petteway, Harry Allen, Michael Dando, Stacy Robinson, Matthew Teutsch, Michael A. Gonzales, and Kat Moore diagnose the ways in which white identity mobilized institutional power through state, federal, and corporate policies to destroy organizations that promoted Black liberation. These chapters lay bare the horror of racist terrorism in many of its forms, revealing the range of public powers that used critical race theory as a symbol to preserve white authority. The clapback described in these chapters presents the ways in which hip-hop and Afrofuturism transform art, language, and science in service to human dignity and global peace for all people.

CHAPTER 9

Static: The Illmatic Consequences of the Critical Race Theory Boogeyman

Bijoun Eric Jordan

Time is Illmatic, keep static like wool fabric
Pack the four-matic to crack your whole cabbage.

—Jones and Cruz (1994, "Life's a Bitch")

On the third track of *Illmatic*, with the words quoted above, Nas describes history and time, asserting that reconciliation is evasive and far from inevitable. Today, right now, our lives are woven into a figurative fabric that holds social conflicts as static, amassed since 1492, since 1619, since 1775, since 1861, and so on. History charges time with ammunition, and time discharges unpredictably, with lethal consequences. We are not able to forecast the next tragedy sparked by this cloth. Yet each and every time it comes, it fits into familiar and painful patterns. Even though the strife you and I have inherited has its origin in the past, neutralizing our collective static cling requires us to confront the influence of our country's history. There have always been factions who insisted that our path forward required us to stop "dwelling" on the past, even though a number of current trends make it glaringly apparent to those willing to consider them that "what is past is prologue." We must continually contend with that legacy; without grappling with it, we only bind ourselves. Race is the one issue we are somehow supposed to address by not talking about it. But we *must* talk about it, and movements clashing over how to fight for a better future and deal with race as it is constructed in the United States battle most vocally today over critical race theory (CRT). Meanwhile efforts to ban the framework from society and education threaten to arrest our progress, thus holding us in stasis.

Allow me to introduce myself early on. I have 17 years of experience as a public high school English teacher in Brownsville, Brooklyn. I ensure that my students learn the historical context of what we encounter in literature, and so we explore history, society, power, and privilege on a daily basis. I am directly responsible for bringing forth educated, self-aware citizens who use their knowledge of from where and from whom they came to guide them to where they are going. I have skin in the game. But the events and new prohibitions introduced last year demonstrate that this is not, in fact, a game. Truth itself is at risk, and false social narratives are permitting atrocities and anguish on massive scales—a case in point: the January 6 insurrection, enabled by the Republican "Big Lie" about the true victor in the 2020 presidential election.

Truth is the bedrock of a stable society able to rely on an informed citizenry, and a pesky and destructive part of the backlash against critical race theory is that backlash's dishonesty, which we can see most easily through how loosely the term has been defined and applied. CRT's detractors have benefited from its obscurity and seized on the chance to interpret it as they see fit, and their (mis)interpretations have set the terms of discussion. In her book *All About Love*, bell hooks (1999) illuminates the way in which "definitions are vital starting points for the imagination. What we cannot imagine cannot come into being. A good definition marks our starting point and lets us know where we want to end up" (p. 14). And so the terms with which we engage, and everything about the way in which we employ them, shape what is possible. The issue of preciseness is not a matter of snobbish semantics when half of the United States have issued or are considering new legislation affecting the education of tens of millions of students, when school boards are bombarded with protest and even incidents of violence, and in an era when a misguided and reckless tweet can reach and mobilize millions in minutes. The mob violence and numerous casualties in January's seditious coup attempt had profound implications—among them, just how completely the truth and the potential for peace or insurrection are linked. Another metaphorical discharge of the static in the fabric of time.

One of the main threads of argument in this essay is that the misinterpretation of critical race theory as a concept is stoking societal paranoia about interrogating history, truth, and what it means to be American. This misinterpretation is a tool by itself, one that is being leveraged as a distractor to muddy the waters and ratchet up skepticism to sabotage those pursuing different types of social justice. Approaching issues of race, gender, and class in our culture and education system fairly—or more accurately, at least—could begin to bridge or even lessen the cavernous political divisions that feed increasing conflict. Of course, a certain level of conflict is part of the human condition, but national civic discord fueled by disinformation and distortion will cause our society itself to deteriorate. It is crucial that we slow down this deterioration and lay the groundwork for a process of restoration. Let's address what critical race theory is, how the term is being misused as a tool of deception and control, and where we go from here.

Let's consult a proper source to outline a framework originating in legal scholarship. The American Bar Association defines critical race theory as "a practice of interrogating the role of race and racism in society," with its roots in legal scholarship and with the purpose of critiquing "how the social construction of race and institutionalized racism perpetuate a racial caste system that relegates people of color to the bottom tiers" (George, 2021). It must be noted that intersectionality (a concept coined by law professor Kimberlé Crenshaw, who also gave CRT its honorific) acknowledges that racial identity intersects with other identities, including sexuality, gender identity, and others" (George, 2021), such that our racial selfhood interacts with other aspects of who we are.

Another observation of CRT is that "the legacy of slavery, segregation, and the imposition of second-class citizenship on Black Americans and other people of color continue to permeate the social fabric of this nation" (George, 2021; listen to the crackle of that static cling). Other principles include the understanding that "race is not biologically real but is socially constructed and socially significant" (George, 2021) and racism is embedded within society's systems and institutions, which replicate inequality. This means that attempts to confine racism's effects to "a few bad apples" are dismissive of the true nature of racial oppression. Racism is not defined in its more typical sense as "the consequence of discrete irrational bad acts perpetrated by individuals" but rather as usually "the unintended (but often foreseeable) consequence of choices" (George, 2021). Yes, race is constructed on a large, social scale, but its *consequences* cannot be imagined away or ignored into obsolescence. The flawed conception of racism as a matter of individual acts of cruelty on an interpersonal level essentially implies that if you *act nice, the problem of racism is solved*. But as Nas said, it is *time* that is illmatic and perpetuates cycles of "static," of hostility and strife. We can either discern that reality and develop insight into the patterns in the fabric or get our "cabbage" cracked and fall victim to the repercussions of a sporadic release of that figurative static.

I'm out for presidents to represent me. (Say what?)
I'm out for presidents to represent me. (Say what?)
I'm out for dead presidents to represent me. (Jones, 1994b, "The World Is Yours")

Over the previous year, I've heard little discussion of former president Donald Trump's September 2020 Executive Order 13950, outlining what is permissible in federal workplace diversity trainings. But that mandate was one of the first dominoes to topple in what has evolved into a full-on attack against antiracist teaching in public education. Like most of the anti-CRT legislation that has come to be since then, the Executive Order on Combating Race and Sex Stereotyping (2020) does not name CRT explicitly (in fact, the term has only become notorious in 2021), although its provisions overlap with exaggerated or misinterpreted CRT concepts. The order bans practices such as "instructors and materials teaching that men and members of certain races, as well as our most venerable institutions, are inherently sexist and racist" and defines nine concepts deemed divisive (Executive Order on Combatting Race and Sex Stereotyping, 2020). Imagine instructors in thousands of courses who might find themselves in a precarious position—for example, while discussing a discomforting truth such as how the Three-Fifths Compromise enshrined chattel slavery in our Constitution alongside lofty claims about universal equality—accused of asserting that American institutions are inherently racist and finding their courses outlawed.

The man whose presidential campaign was characterized by his description of Mexican immigrants as rapists and murderers, one of whose first acts as president was to preemptively ban immigration from seven Muslim-majority countries (would purges follow?), and under whose watch race-based hate crimes and open accosting escalated and were basically broadcast through social media, now assumed the rhetorical posture of colorblindness and claimed to be an agent of equity. At a moment when the Black Lives Matter (BLM) movement had gained so much ground, the obvious effect of Order 13950 was to suppress any direct discussion of racial discord, any attempt to raise the specter of white supremacy—in a nation founded on it—while the coronavirus pandemic endangered lives and embittered the national mood.

There is a common understanding that the killing of George Floyd on May 25, 2020, was the initiating spark that forced us, Americans, to look again at the role of racism in our society, which led to a new backlash (Schwartz, 2021), although some point to the seismic journalistic impact of Nikole Hannah-Jones's 1619 Project, published on August 14, 2019, due to its overarching goal of "refram[ing] American history by considering what it would mean to regard 1619 as our nation's birth year" (CNN Business,

2021). Rep. Brian Seitz of Missouri called the project a "Trojan horse" that smuggled ideas now broadly labeled as CRT—a term that appears nowhere in the project—into public school classrooms (Schwartz, 2021).

But if the activist reporting of the 1619 Project and widespread educator efforts to help students understand racist brutality prompted the conservative backlash we are now seeing, there is still the question of who initiated or led that reprisal. Benjamin Wallace-Wells of *The New Yorker* identifies a single engineer. In his 2021 article "How a Conservative Activist Invented the Conflict Over Critical Race Theory," Wallace-Wells first rewinds 2021's toppled dominoes to July 2020 and the increased transparency and screen-shot accountability of the new pandemic Zoom era. (Meeting virtually means more documents are shared by email, and as a result a document could be leaked more easily; portions of meetings are much easier to record secretly and share undetected.) In that context, a Seattle worker "documented an anti-bias training session and sent the evidence to a journalist named Christopher F. Rufo, who read it and recognized a political opportunity" (Wallace-Wells, 2021). Rufo sought out materials from the seminars and came across a number of antiracism principles and practices in them, such as learning new "ways of seeing that are hidden from us in white supremacy." In a piece for the right-leaning Manhattan Institute, Rufo (2020) stated that under the pretense of antiracism, "Seattle's Office of Civil Rights is now explicitly endorsing principles of segregationism, group-based guilt, and race essentialism—ugly concepts that should have been left behind a century ago." Rufo received more leaks from workers completing their own antiracism training. Wallace-Wells (2021) describes what followed:

> Reading through these documents and others, Rufo noticed that they tended to cite a small set of popular anti-racism books, by authors such as Ibram X. Kendi and Robin DiAngelo. Rufo read the footnotes in those books and found that they pointed to academic scholarship from the nineteen-nineties, by a group of legal scholars who referred to their work as critical race theory, in particular Kimberlé Crenshaw and Derrick Bell. These scholars argued that white supremacy of the past lived on in the laws and societal rules of the present. As Crenshaw recently explained, critical race theory found that "the so-called American dilemma was not simply a matter of prejudice but a matter of structured disadvantages that stretched across American society."

Rufo felt that the effect of the city's "segregated" trainings was to "induct white employees into the cult of critical race theory." He next engaged in intellectually lazy thread pulling. According to Wallace-Wells (2021), "Rufo thought that he could detect the seed of their ideas in radical, often explicitly Marxist, critical-theory texts from the generation of 1968," but Crenshaw, one of genuine CRT's most important luminaries, dismisses this as selective "red baiting" that ignored obvious controverting examples such as Martin Luther King Jr., whose alleged communist ties right-wingers seem content to ignore (perhaps so that they can continue sanitizing and reducing his teachings to quote him and perform antiracism every January). Wallace-Wells consulted Rufo directly, who described his campaign without hiding its contrived and strategic nature. He concocted a plan to use the public's reaction to CRT *to put wind in right-wing sails* given that "conservatives engaged in the culture war had been fighting against the same progressive racial ideology since late in the Obama years, without ever being able to describe it effectively" (Wallace-Wells, 2021). They needed "new language" for social issues, and while terms like "political correctness" and "cancel culture" had flaws that limited their tactical usefulness, the phrase "critical race theory" was "the perfect villain," in Rufo's own words. He said that each word of the phrase carries negative connotations for many Americans, and most important to its utility, "it's the label the critical race theorists chose themselves." Although even CRT's most vocal opponents still struggle to articulate its nature and characteristics, its proponents would remain perpetually on the defensive, having to own, define, and defend their ideology instead of addressing issues and policy.

On September 2 of that year, Rufo appeared on the Tucker Carlson show to introduce his new menacing phantom, which he claimed "pervaded every aspect of the federal government," even though Trump had helmed it at the time (Wallace-Wells, 2021). He dubbed CRT an existential threat to the country and called on the Trump administration to "immediately issue an executive order to abolish critical-race-theory training from the federal government." On September 3, Trump's chief of staff, Mark Meadows, contacted Rufo; the ensuing executive order arrived on the 22nd of that month. With Christopher Rufo in the role of mastermind, and experiencing a meteoric rise, it was not long before the conservative movement seized on the "new language" Rufo had extracted and selected to galvanize the static in their political fabric. They now had what they must have imagined was a secret codex for the kinds of rhetoric, training, and education they vehemently opposed but had been unable to define or defuse, and they succeeded in fabricating a hair-raising boogeyman by convincing susceptible audiences that an ideological invasion was taking "their" country from them.

History has provided playbooks for the creation and animation of such hobgoblins. Anti-CRT rhetoric relies heavily on mythology and even utilizes many of the same tools as fascism yet pretends to use those instruments to gallantly expand liberty. In his 2018 book *How Fascism Works*, professor Jason Stanley outlines 10 facets of fascism, many of which map quite neatly onto the campaign against so-called CRT. One principle is what Stanley calls the mythic past—the idea that there is a "we" descending "from a glorious, patriarchal past" and a "they" that exist to "threaten that legacy." We see this over and over again as anti-CRT critics contend that our children are being taught to hate America. On unreality, Stanley says, "Facts are debased, and without a common understanding of reality, reasoned debate becomes impossible." Especially useful here are the mechanisms of propaganda: "The language of democratic ideals takes on corrupted, opposite meanings. Corrupt politicians run anti-corruption campaigns; freedom of speech claims are used to suppress speech" (pp. 24–35). Remember Rufo's strategic characterization of workplace trainings on race as "segregationism, group-based guilt, and race essentialism"? His tactic of projecting and deflecting while arguing that antiracism work is racist is backward enough to cause a rhetorical whiplash. About suppression of speech, Stanley asserts, "Every legislative act discussed here, every piece of stricken educational content, every school board skirmish, is occurring with the stated goal of preventing children from reading or hearing about 'dangerous' perspectives" (p. 33).

Think back to Trump's executive order "combatting stereotyping." There's a familiar stench of egregious pretense and hypocrisy present; posturing as a guardian of justice and equity (in order to hamstring actual initiatives that mitigate racial tensions through education) does little to hide their true concern about white participants being made uncomfortable by having to acknowledge our country's original sin, its unfading stain. The attempts by many conservatives to pose as spokespeople for equity while fighting to suppress measures that would advance racial progress, and accusing their proponents of being the "real racists" because they directly address race, are embarrassingly ahistorical, logically delusional, and only intelligible if one completely ignores the relevant history and context. Up is not down.

> Visualizing the realism of life in actuality
>
> Fuck who's the baddest; a person's status depends on salary. (AZ, "Life's a Bitch")

Through deception, manufactured panic, and even fascistic propaganda, conservatives have unleashed a new social specter—and along with it the consequences in the fabric of time, which are truly illmatic. For instance, the new debate over CRT is not merely a matter of public opinion; it is rapidly reshaping the educational landscape. Lists of banned texts are proliferating; school board activists propose book burnings to "purify" our society; political futures are being launched, with the most prominent example in 2021 being Glenn Youngkin getting elected to the governorship of Virginia, where education was suddenly among voters' top concerns, polling well above the ongoing pandemic. Just over a year ago, before the conjuring of the CRT boogeyman, it would have been abnormal for any political race, let alone a gubernatorial contest, to be so influenced by classroom practices.

In 2021, there were numerous accounts of states and districts limiting the reach of curriculum with regard to race. The Brookings Institution reported in November that the states of Arizona, Idaho, Iowa, New Hampshire, North Dakota, Oklahoma, South Carolina, Tennessee, and Texas had passed anti-CRT legislation, although Arizona's was overturned that month by the state's Supreme Court (Ray & Gibbons, 2021). Such legislation does not usually mention CRT explicitly (Idaho and North Dakota's laws do, though); instead, it bans "the discussion, training, and/or orientation that the U.S. is inherently racist as well as any discussions about conscious and unconscious bias, privilege, discrimination, and oppression" (Ray & Gibbons, 2021). Notably, their laws ban certain discourse on gender as well. (Maybe they've just really got intersectionality nailed down?) Additionally, in around 20 states that have proposed or are planning such bans, state school boards, like those in Georgia, Kentucky, North Carolina, and Virginia, can enforce suppression without laws being passed. Many local boards have gone prohibitionist as well, and we are witnessing a tidal wave of activism against antiracist teaching.

Idaho's bill is one of those that names CRT directly, stating that its tenets "exacerbate and inflame divisions on the basis of sex, race, ethnicity, religion, color, national origin, or other criteria" and threaten the "unity of the nation and the well-being of the state of Idaho and its citizens" (An Act Relating to Dignity and Nondiscrimination in Public Education, 2021). *So Idaho lawmakers would have us believe that a system of legal scholarship that addresses the consequences of the idea of race is putting our nation and its states and citizens in peril.* The same law, signed and enacted on April 28, contains a "dignity and nondiscrimination in public education" clause, which states that the statute's intent is for all educational institutions to "respect the dignity of others, acknowledge the right of others to express differing opinions, and foster and defend intellectual honesty, freedom of inquiry and instruction, and freedom of speech and association." Deploying a warped reinterpretation of CRT as antithetical to freedom of inquiry, to dignity and respect, and even to honesty in the same clauses that serve to eliminate exploration and scrutiny of our nation's history of racism is truly ironic. How do you allege restriction of freedom of inquiry and outlaw a vast avenue of inquiry in the same act? Dignity and respect for whom, when a righteous reckoning with white supremacy's reach is outlawed? How is sweeping uncomfortable truths into a dustpan and disposing of them intellectual honesty? Something very, very wrong has been enacted here and woven into the fabric of society.

Let's consider Texas's HB 3979 legislation, which stipulates that teachers participating in the trainings must not be made to feel "discomfort, guilt, anguish, or any other form of psychological distress on account of the individual's race or sex" (An Act Relating to Dignity and Nondiscrimination in Public Education, 2021). We have to pause for a while on this issue of people's feelings about race—of how it is used to short-circuit discussions that offer to probe racism's roots, in order to extricate and untangle them. It is hard to imagine engaging in real discussions about the stakes of race without provoking discomfort, which is a normal human response—a compassionate one, really. This is where we can apply what bell hooks called "radical openness," which allows people to have deep disagreements about some parts of their beliefs but remain in conversation regardless; furthermore, disagreement and conflict in discussions of issues like race are to be expected and not a sign that something is wrong. No one is campaigning for Holocaust curricula to be banned and justifying the ban because that history engenders feelings of shame or sorrow. A key difference, of course, is that slavery, Jim Crow, and the "new Jim Crow" are America's own shame. Additionally, when laws like HB 3979 legislate against emotional reactions such as guilt, a reckless level of latitude is given to plaintiffs to claim that they have been victimized simply because they have been made to face those shameful parts of American history.

Let's look at more of the Texas law's language. When teaching a topic made questionable by the law, teachers must "strive to explore the topic from diverse and contending perspectives without giving deference to any one perspective," which is a bizarre requirement in the context of racial injustice (An Act Relating to Dignity and Nondiscrimination in Public Education, 2021). Taken at face value, this provision could require me to "balance" materials affirming that the primary cause of the Civil War was slavery with authors arguing that the slave states *didn't* secede to defend human bondage, *without* deferring to the view backed up by the Confederate states' own articles of secession. The law as it was updated on September 1 now includes prohibitions against teaching "that the advent of slavery in the territory that is now the United States constituted the true founding of the United States" (practically a direct charge against Hannah-Jones's 1619 Project; CNN Business, 2021) or "that, with respect to their relationship to American values, slavery and racism are anything other than deviations from, betrayals of, or failures to live up to the authentic founding principles of the United States, which include liberty and equality." Incredibly, the law requires teachers in the state to teach that slavery and racism are aberrations and not manifestations of the country's character. If you dare to teach that 1619 is more foundational than 1776 or that in the framing of what came to be the United States, the framers who buried the calls for abolition *did it on purpose,* you run the risk of being denounced for "indoctrination." If you take the position that the treatment of nonwhites during the bulk of American history, 361 years, from the first colony at Jamestown and the extermination campaign that followed, to the end of the civil rights era in 1968, is indicative of the predominant character of the United States, then you are "teaching our children to hate America." They made one more addition: Including the 1619 Project in a district's required curriculum is now prohibited as well. Lessons like my current junior English unit pairing Octavia Butler's *Kindred* (1979/2003) with the 1619 Project are now banned in a number of states. It would be easy to be at rest knowing I am here in New York State, where it is "safe"—except that the proposed New York assembly bill A8253 contains the very same 1619 Project ban. We are on a new social landscape, with a political hijacking of teaching practices never seen before.

Scene: It is the state of Washington and a site of protest. Demonstrators clamoring outside an assembly bang on the windows. Mixed with the booming sound of their blows are several hurled obscenities. Before long, the meeting is forced to adjourn. One man in the mob threatens two meeting attendees with a weaponized flag pole, causing them to flee for safety. Hurled objects and more obscenities trail them. One official attempting to drive away finds his car swarmed. The scene is of a school board meeting.

In recent months, education coverage has been rife with images and sound bites of school board meetings that have become crucibles as well as courts of public opinion on CRT and one of the spaces in which public opinion and political urging are manifesting in policy. Although these might seem to be grassroots battlegrounds with understandably impassioned opponents, journalist and lawyer Judd Legum characterizes our country's local school boards as being "under attack." In an October article, he describes recent hostilities and even acts of repressive violence, including the scene above—incidents of aggravated battery, disorderly conduct, unmasked protestors forcing their way into school board meetings, hostile confrontations, and death threats—in every region of the country (Legum et al., 2021). Legum clarifies that the protests are over both CRT supposedly being "in schools" and COVID protocols, but while the COVID-19 issue might seem to be an unrelated one, the response to both masking mandates and the boogeyman of CRT in schools maintains the same energy as in events like the January 6 insurrection, in the belief that an oppressive and "anti-American" society is infecting our institutions, that the insurrectionists are the "real patriots," standing up for freedom and justice, and that democratic processes have failed them, when they have simply been outvoted, and so to advance their aims at all costs, processes are pointless and violent means are a proper substitute. It is frightening to see our democracy under attack and even more hair-raising to see the anti-CRT movement effectively reframe concerns about identity, stymie the movement for social justice, and achieve policy victories in mere weeks and months, rivalling the results of true grassroots movements that took years to achieve breakthroughs. Legum, founder of the independent newsletter *Popular Information*, has been tracking the intrusion of dark money organizations into educational institutions and describes how groups such as the Virginia-based Parents Defending Education (PDE) use their deep pockets and resources to subvert what they view as "woke indoctrination" of our country's young people. Legum states that while such groups pretend to have risen organically, they are in fact networked with figures like the Koch brothers and are "suspiciously well-organized." PDE, for example, incorporated only in January 2021, but as observed by former political science professor Maurice Cunningham, "The next thing you know, this group of moms is hiring a law firm that has represented Donald Trump, has a sophisticated PR approach, has extensive . . . instructions on how to go about the things they're encouraging people to do" (Legum et al., 2021). PDE's president Nicole Neily has worked with multiple organizations headed by individuals such as "a former head of a Koch-backed trust and two conservative attorneys from Koch-funded programs," as reported in *The Nation* (Moattar, 2018). With their vast resources, these groups are mobilizing and goading legions of parents into a kind of educational reform army we have never seen before—one that is rapidly reversing progress toward openness and inclusion in education, through a platform of distorted reality.

Think back to hooks's words about the generative power of a "good definition." What would be the effect of its inverse, terms utilized recklessly, or in bad faith, to organize and build bedrocks for mass movements? To study anti-CRT coverage is to peel back layers of manipulations, convenient omissions, and outright falsehoods. We see a textbook straw man fallacy at work—in this case, opponents creating and then attacking a warped version of CRT or the antiracist, "woke" ideology in front of an overly credulous audience, many of whom have been groomed for this moment since the campaign against "political correctness" in the Reagan era.

As I write this essay ("Sentence begins indented," Nas mystically invokes), Florida governor Ron DeSantis is unveiling the Stop the Wrongs to Our Kids and Employees Act, or Stop WOKE for short, which will "put into statute the Department of Education's prohibition on CRT in K–12 schools" (Bella, 2021; Staff, 2021). Not only does it register a backlash against the CRT straw man, its name is also meant as a cultural clapback with the term "woke," which originated as a Black marker of political and social consciousness but now is used derisively by right wingers to allege a senseless self-righteousness. By late 2021, in bans like this one, CRT was being explicitly named and no longer tacitly targeted.

It has entered kitchen table conversations, even though it continues to have no prominence in K–12 curricula. DeSantis declared, "No taxpayer dollars should be used to teach our kids to hate our country or to hate each other." Refusing to ignore or hide the inconvenient truths of our country's past and present is now tantamount to teaching hate; again, a lawmaker all but says he believes our children should receive mythology and not complete or balanced facts, adding for a little razzle dazzle, "You think about what MLK stood for. He said he didn't want people judged on the color of their skin but on the content of their character." Once again, we see the propagandistic technique of posing as a protector of fairness and equality in order to sabotage actual antiracist concepts and practices.

The *Washington Post* points out that Florida's prohibition came despite a lack of evidence that CRT is being taught in K–12; it is truly an imagined offense, yet the act will likely have disastrous and real consequences. One of Stop WOKE's most troublesome provisions is that it will

> give parents the "private right of action" to sue if they think their kids are being taught critical race theory as well as let parents collect attorneys' fees if they win the lawsuit. This proposal, which promises to be "the strongest legislation of its kind in the nation," would also apply to the workplace. (Bella, 2021)

In a civil context in which CRT's meaning has broadened to apply to practically any ideology that grapples with race's role in history and society, we may soon see a flood of frivolous or misguided lawsuits filed by parents against teachers who they perceive are using unlawful curriculum or methods (which shouldn't be banned or unlawful in the first place), or by coworkers who see themselves as being subjected to racial indoctrination. It is hard to imagine that this will have anything less than a chilling effect, where teachers by the thousands who are considering delving into a troubling truth about race in our society will simply consider it better to omit that part of the story. In essence, policies like Stop WOKE threaten to revert us to the levels of incompleteness, erasure, and exclusion of history and the American story that we've had for most of public education's existence following the Civil War.

Not only do anti-CRT laws like the ones discussed here seek to codify colorblindness, their legislative maneuvers will conceal and actively revise the role of race in our history. To quote sociologist Victor Ray (2021), "Making laws outlawing critical race theory confirms the point that racism is embedded in the law." We also must remember that all laws are open to misinterpretation as well as errors and overreach in application; anti-CRT laws provide the wrong kind of fertile ground, provoking more activists and parents enraged by disinformation skirmishes in school boards to level accusations, attacks, and a multitude of legal actions against teachers working in good faith. Perhaps most frightening of all, right-wing demagogues and dark money have achieved this despite the fact that actual CRT is absent from K–12 curricula and always has been.

Let's say that *timing* is illmatic. It is no coincidence that the current controversy is rocking school boards and the chambers of legislation precisely after the righteous outrage and collective action coordinated largely by BLM peaked in mid-2020. To look at just a few measures, the organization's 2020 impact report listed June 2 as the day its website had the heaviest traffic, up 5,000% from its most active day the preceding March (BLM, 2021). It reported a 3,370% increase in its international impact as the movement began to globalize; 6,000 volunteers engaged 5.4 million voters in the swing states as BLM shifted its approach and directly took part in the political process, establishing a political action committee, among other courses of action, with 44 BLM-backed candidates seeing success that year. *The New York Times* identified June 6 as the day when the protests peaked and published an infographic map illustrating a nation aflame with the outcry. On that day, there were approximately 550 demonstrations—which followed over a month of sustained protest at a rate of 140 actions a day—and a number of analyses showed that 15 to 26 million Americans protested in this short time period (Buchanan et al., 2020). Unlike previous BLM-centric protests, 95% of the U.S. counties in which actions took place were majority white, and almost 75% of the counties were more than 75% white, showing that a new kind of allyship was emerging and helping to prove that the goal is dissolving racial divisions, not deepening them (Buchanan et al., 2020). The "race war" that conservatives warned righteous indignation could incite did not materialize. And the movement was producing some concrete gains: The *Times* mentions a number of cities and states banning police chokeholds, Mississippi lawmakers' decided to retire their state's flag as a remnant of the Confederacy, New York policymakers repealed a law that kept police disciplinary records secret, and leaders in Minneapolis, where George Floyd was murdered, pledged to dismantle its police department, although that proposal failed in 2021 to gain the votes required.

A national conversation that previously focused on pitting the semantics of BLM against All Lives Matter, and later on the implications of calls to "defund" the police, now saw diverse but unified masses of citizens mobilizing for policy changes. Public opinion had shifted as well; the *Times* notes that in the two weeks preceding a June 10 report, voters' support of BLM had leaped as much as it had in the two preceding years—and that support had started in the net negative (Cohn & Quealy,

2020). Opinion on contentious or political matters rarely changes much, if at all, and yet here we were. As for the die-hard All Lives Matter crowd, it is hard to imagine that they simply sat by and watched these changes without concern for the direction "their" country was taking. Such a massive shift in the public's view of race matters had to be combatted. An antidote was needed. The most reliable golden oldie in white supremacy's playbook is stoking white fears and racial animus in order to check social progress. Cut to late September 2021, when Hannah-Jones appeared on CNN's Reliable Sources to commemorate banned books week and spoke of the perils of the current moment. In sum, she said that she sees an attempt "to control the collective memory of this country" by "purg[ing] uncomfortable truths" (CNN Business, 2021). On November 15, she spoke with her Howard University colleague Ta-Nehisi Coates at the Brooklyn Academy of Music during an event commemorating the expanded edition of the 1619 Project. I was lucky enough to be present. The fanfare and celebratory tone of the event lay in contrast with the starkness of the realities they discussed. At one point, she quoted Peter H. Will, stating, "Nations hold their shape by managing [their] history" and added that "the history that we're taught is not about the country that we actually live in. It's a fictional country; it doesn't exist." What we are in the midst of in the current anti-CRT moment is another leg of a centuries-long thrashing out of *what the American story will be*—in the process, manufacturing an elaborate lie meant to serve power itself, perhaps to create a kind of inexhaustible amnesty. Hannah-Jones concluded,

> So you can do all these terrible things if you say, "But we are a great country founded on great ideas, but sometimes we don't live up to them." The narrative of 1776 doesn't explain the insurrection on the Capitol on January 6th. It doesn't explain George Floyd. It doesn't explain why we're the most carceral nation in the world. It doesn't explain why we have the worst wealth inequality of all of the democratized Western nations that we like to compare ourselves to. That narrative is explained by 1619. (CNN Business, 2021)

Think back to laws like those requiring educators to teach that racism is an anomaly when it was incorporated by design and as such has always needed to be reckoned with. The heart of the CRT debate is that it puts us at a familiar crossroads: We can choose today and tomorrow to pick up the work our ancestors began of making this country what it promised to be, or we can declare the renovations complete and ignore the leaks, the crumbly spots, the foundation. As I said earlier, a peculiar feature of how America deals with race is that we are supposed to resolve racial tensions by not talking about them; it's obvious that this approach serves only the guilty party, not the injured. It is far too convenient and suspicious for the fox and his descendants to wish to call it even and ignore the loss of the hens, even with the feathers stuck to their jaws, their bellies still full, and those of the farmers' descendants empty. Nothing less than the American story is at stake, and a nation of people who were told a different story—an incomplete one crafted to promote resolution without restitution—will never wake up to any need for redressal.

> Inhale deep like the words of my breath
> I never sleep, 'cause sleep is the cousin of death. (Nas, "New York State of Mind")

The anti-CRT rhetoric was immediately suspect to me. I had last heard the term around 2002 in a college course, and suddenly I was hearing it from the mouths of conservatives and pundits almost ecstatic in their revulsion. Hearing of CRT from these individuals, even just the term, felt eerie and unsettling. They said teachers were being pressured to use CRT in their classes, but I hadn't heard CRT even being mentioned in any teacher training in 17 years. I came to know since college that CRT was born in the 1970s; was the framework enjoying a renaissance, or was the right-wing media simply misusing the term? The latter was far more likely.

The more I followed the story, the more I noticed a particular tell. In the flood of coverage I've seen, there hasn't been one complaint of a district, school, or teacher teaching events in our nation's history inaccurately. Pundits and protestors could barely pretend it was really about the truth. Parents claimed their children were being harmed by facts, when we knew the harm of the lies being told. Talking heads trotted out the tired line that we are not motivated by a love of rightness and justice but rather by hatred of our country. If you think that teaching facts about race, history, and society—the kind that were suppressed, forgotten, or ignored for generations—is antiwhite or anti-American, then what does that say about what it means to be a white American?

Those who seek a righting of wrongs and a balancing of scales, a final discharge of time's static, are the real engineers of progress and development of our social landscape. There is no appropriations bill that could repair this kind of infrastructure, only reckoning and reconciliation. The author bell hooks argued that a love of justice is missing and said,

> It is impossible to have a love of justice if your society has erased the ledger of unpaid and even unacknowledged debts that oppression and exploitation have accrued—in order to obscure the accumulation by theft that came along with it. (Horton, 2021)

We must be cognizant of any and all efforts to present erasure as harmony, and wary of those who would lure us into imagining that we can forget our way toward a just society. We would simply allow a new set of atrocities to inherit the places of the old ones, and bring forth even more durable systems of injustice. But about our necessary accounting, hooks also wondered, "How do we hold people accountable for wrongdoing and yet at the same time remain in touch with their humanity enough to believe in their capacity to be transformed?" (Horton, 2021). For those who value CRT's reckoning, it is easy to imagine that our role is to become soldiers or mercenaries, but more to the heart of the matter, we can be standard bearers of the revolutionary understanding that we must confront pain in order to transform society and ensure everyone's freedom. When hooks spoke with *Jet Magazine* in 2013, she expanded on what a love of righteousness will provide us: "We can't combat white supremacy unless we can teach people to love justice. You have to love justice more than your allegiance to your race, sexuality and gender. It is about justice" (Horton, 2021).

It shouldn't be hard to select a place to stand. Which groups are arguing for the inclusion of a history that for generations has been suppressed? Which groups advocate a suppression they claim is benign? This is Politics and the English Language 2.0. Joseph McCarthy is dancing in his grave; George Orwell is rolling in his. But while our view of the path may be clear, what we contend with is unavoidable. As Crenshaw herself put it back in 1988, "Reform itself creates its own backlash, which reconstitutes the problem in the first place" (Wallace-Wells, 2021). What's more, the enemy we seek to destroy—not people but immoral principles, not infantries but institutions—is constituted in words, in intangibles. We stand for justice; therefore, our protest is powered by optimism. And still, recoil will meet us at every forward step. In this way and others, time is illmatic.

REFERENCES

An Act Relating to Dignity and Nondiscrimination in Public Education, ID Code § 33-138 (2021). https://legislature.idaho.gov/wp-content/uploads/session-info/2021/legislation/H0377.pdf

Bella, T. (2021, December 15). *DeSantis invokes MLK as he proposes stop woke act against critical race theory.* https://www.washingtonpost.com/politics/2021/12/15/desantis-stop-woke-act-mlk-crt/

Black Lives Matter. (2021, February). *2020 Impact report.* https://blacklivesmatter.com/wp-content/uploads/2021/02/blm-2020-impact-report.pd f

Buchanan, L., Bui, Q., & Patel, J. (2020, July 3). Black Lives Matter may be the largest movement in U.S. history. *New York Times.* https://www.nytimes.com/interactive/2020/07/03/us/george-floyd-protests-crowd-size.html

Butler, O. E. (2003). *Kindred.* Beacon Press. (Original work published 1979)

CNN Business. (2021, September 26). *Nikole Hannah-Jones on "Banned Books Week"* [Video]. https://www.cnn.com/videos/business/2021/09/26/nikole-hannah-jones-on-the-meaning-of-banned-book-week.cnn

Cohn, N., & Quealy, K. (2020, June 10). How public opinion has moved on Black Lives Matter. *New York Times.* https://www.nytimes.com/interactive/2020/06/10/upshot/black-lives-matter-attitudes.html

Executive Order on Combatting Race and Sex Stereotyping. (2020, September 22). https://trumpwhitehouse.archives.gov/presidential-actions/executive-order-combating-race-sex-stereotyping/

George, J. (2021, January 11). *A lesson on critical race theory*. American Bar Association. https://www.americanbar.org/groups/crsj/publications/human_rights_magazine_home/civil-rights-reimagining-policing/a-lesson-on-critical-race-theory/

Hannah-Jones, N., & The New York Times Magazine. (2021, November 16). *The 1619 project: A new origin story*. One World.

hooks, b. (2000). *All about love: New visions*. William Morrow.

Horton, A. (2021, December 15). A life in quotes: bell hooks. *The Guardian*. https://www.theguardian.com/books/2021/dec/15/bell-hooks-best-quotes-feminism-race

Jones, N. (1994a). Memory lane [Recorded by Nas]. On *Illmatic* [MP3 file]. Columbia.

Jones, N. (1994b). The world is yours [Recorded by Nas]. On *Illmatic* [MP3 file]. Columbia.

Jones, N., & Cruz, A. (1994). Life's a bitch [Recorded by Nas]. On *Illmatic* [MP3 file]. Columbia.

Legum, J., Zekeria, T., & Crosby, R. (2021, October 14). *The right-wing operatives orchestrating the attack on America's school boards*. https://popular.info/p/the-right-wing-operatives-orchestrating

Moattar, D. (2018, July 9). The dark money behind campus speech wars. *The Nation*. https://www.thenation.com/article/archive/dark-money-behind-campus-speech-wars/

Ray, R., & Gibbons, A. (2021, November 22). *Why are states banning critical race theory?* Brookings Institution. https://www.brookings.edu/blog/fixgov/2021/07/02/why-are-states-banning-critical-race-theory/

Ray, V. [@victorerikray]. (2021, June 12). *I've said a version of this before. But making laws outlawing critical race theory confirms the point that racism is* [Tweet]. Twitter. https://twitter.com/victorerikray/status/1403437961367240711?s=20

Rufo, C. (2020, July 29). *Separate but equal*. https://christopherrufo.com/separate-but-equal/

Schwartz, S. (2021, July 19). Who's really driving critical race theory legislation? An investigation. *Education Week*. https://www.edweek.org/policy-politics/whos-really-driving-critical-race-theory-legislation-an-investigation/2021/07

Staff. (2021, December 15). *Governor DeSantis announces legislative proposal to stop W.O.K.E. activism and critical race theory in schools and corporations*. https://flgov.com/2021/12/15/governor-desantis-announces-legislative-proposal-to-stop-w-o-k-e-activism-and-critical-race-theory-in-schools-and-corporations/

Stanley, J. (2018). *How fascism works: The politics of us and them*. Random House.

Wallace-Wells, B. (2021, June 18). How a conservative activist invented the conflict over critical race theory. *The New Yorker*. https://www.newyorker.com/news/annals-of-inquiry/how-a-conservative-activist-invented-the-conflict-over-critical-race-theory?fbclid=IwAR3_TX2i3W4qlwGrRzPwyuNQ42_XR0JaJfWlfbd4Lnml3O9XWhpjkKFebq

CHAPTER 10

Decolonizing Public Minds and Public Places

An Interview With Maurice Broaddus

Danian Darrell Jerry

Danian Darrell Jerry: Before we start, I have a brief introduction that I want to read. You, Maurice Broaddus, writer, educator, community activist, are the Kheprw Institute's resident Afrofuturist. You have published dozens of novels—including *The Usual Suspect, Pimp My Airship*, and *King Maker: The Knights of Breton Court*—and hundreds of short stories. Your digital novella *Sorcerers* is being adapted into a television series for AMC, and your latest novel, *Sweep of Stars*, is available on Harper Collins. You are the founder of the self-named science fiction convention, MoCon, that has been going strong for over a decade. You do so much for the city of Indianapolis, and your work has impacted countless lives, both in Indiana and beyond.

Your work as an educator in Indiana provides a great doorway into a conversation on "critical race theory," which leads me to my first question. As a teacher in Indianapolis, Indiana, you have always been on the front lines of public education. How has the recent debate on critical race theory affected your teaching and your interactions with students, especially in areas like social studies and literature?

Maurice Broaddus: My job switched this year, so I'm mostly the school librarian. That being said, let me give you a bit of background on my school. So I teach at a private Christian school, and they follow what's called the classical educational model. I work at this school because they distinguish themselves as a Christ-following school, not a Christian school. Which is also how I would describe my faith. Someone says are you Christian? I'm like, I prefer Christ follower, because "Christian" now brings up so many connotations I want to avoid. The other thing is our school aspires to be on the front edge of racial reconciliation. So our school tries to maintain a percentage of 40, 40, 20. That's 40 percent Black, 40 percent white, 20 percent other. I'm trying to paint this picture. You have this school, which uses the classical education model steeped in Europe's greatest hits while trying to maintain a leading edge in racial reconciliation.

It's like we're basically trying to fight white supremacy by propping up white supremacy. This is where we are. Frankly, if there is no critical thought given to what we're doing, this is where we will find ourselves by default, which means we have to be active and intentional in how we go about crafting our curriculums, crafting our lesson plans, even curating the library. I just had a conversation with the administration about redoing the library for events because it was the original home of the Paul Dunbar Library, the first Black library in Indianapolis. The first library that served the Black community in our city, so they're looking to restore that library with me being the face of the face program. We would restore the space. Then I would make it a community facing peace, so I would basically host a writer and artist residency program from the school. I'm like, yes, I will gladly do this with the following condition. I want to use the books that we stock in the library to change the conversation about what a classical education model looks like.

Does it have to be Europe's greatest hits? The answer to that is no, and I can trace it all the way back to the words that we use and how we define the kind of books we want to engage. We want living books. Books that are relevant. Books that allow us to talk about difficult subjects. Books that allow us to engage and wrestle with profound ideas. By that definition, they do not all have to be written by dead white guys. What would it look like for us to decolonize our library space and use that sort of decolonizing to have a conversation on what a classical education model looks like. Better yet, what can it look like? That's the conversation I'm interested in having, while dodging terms like "critical race theory," because that'll take me down a path which . . .

There was a huge, huge "critical race theory" protest gearing up on the north side of town. Right. I know some of the people who are organizing it, and I'm like, y'all couldn't pick critical race theory out of a lineup. You don't even know what you're protesting.

Danian Darrell Jerry: What has it been like curating the books in the library? Have certain books ever been removed because of their content or the messages they send towards, I guess, marginalized groups or what have you?

Chapter 10: Decolonizing Public Minds and Public Places 111

Maurice Broaddus: I do this on three fronts. I am close friends with the humanities teacher, and I'm close friends with the art teacher, so we regularly have these conversations about what it looks like to decolonize these spaces. With the art teacher, it's been a lot easier because he has full control over the curriculum, so he's just been sliding in stuff. He'd been phasing out some artists and replacing them with marginalized artists and artwork from the same periods, but they get overlooked because art is a curated experience. This is my mantra. I'm driving home like, art is a curated experience. History is a curated experience. Critical race theory allows us to wrestle with the fact that what we are taught is curated, so how do we address the curation? Critical race theory is all about addressing the whole idea of what's been curated and how. The humanities teacher, she's been struggling. Because the curriculum has been shifting in ways that she does not like. In some ways, it's good because the curriculum has been saying, hey, we want to spend more time in the pre-Greek era. They want to expand, so they're touching on African culture and Asian culture as a part of world history. In that regard, it's great. Unfortunately, they're taking out, so the shift has been in order to have room for that, we need to take room from somewhere else.

They've been taking from their study of the Harlem Renaissance, for example. The humanities teacher is like, no, we need these. For history to be relevant to where our students are today, we need to draw that line. Because we can't go back to history is slavery, Civil War, civil rights. That can't be the entirety of the story that gets told. The humanities teacher says, no, we need things like the Harlem Renaissance. We see this on multiple fronts. They appease you in this area but take it out of that area. It's like it's a clever battle. It's a clever move. We see you, but now we've been talking about what it looks like to push back and how we push back. What do we want to accomplish? Those are the conversations we're trying to have now. We're decolonizing the art spaces, the common lines, the library spaces, but history is still curated above our pay grade, frankly.

I just thought about this while I was talking to you. It's easier for us to make shifts in art and shifts in the library because those aren't considered core classes. We can even do that with the music program. We could decolonize that space because it's not considered a core program. Humanities, history, that sort of thing. Those are considered core classes, which means they have much greater scrutiny.

Danian Darrell Jerry: When you say "scrutiny," you're referring to shareholders and parents, and even those dynamics change depending on the situation. For example, you work at a private school. You're not employed by the state, like a public school educator, but the shareholders at your school do have vested interests in the state machine.

Maurice Broaddus: Absolutely. And that can be our financial support, our parent base. All those relationships [have] vested interests in the status quo.

Danian Darrell Jerry: That makes education a balancing act, with the students suspended in the middle. You're trying to maintain integrity as an educator, raise them up in spaces that are decolonized, implement programs and lessons that benefit them, while getting this pushback. In the end, the students are the ones who either gain or suffer.

Maurice Broaddus: I still substitute teach some of the classes. Which is at your own risk because I teach how I teach in these situations, and I inevitably hear pushback because the parents always know when Mr. Broaddus has taught a class.

We will always have discussions that are frank and honest. Quietly, the humanities teachers know this. So I have a couple of teachers who get strategically absent. They're like, hey, I'm going to be absent. Can Maurice sub for me? Not any sub, I need Maurice. Then I look at the curriculum for what he has to teach, and I'm like, okay.

I see you. You want me to have *that* civil rights conversation? Which gives the teacher cover because I'm the substitute. If I go off the script, that's just me. If I'm teaching civil rights, for example, I don't use the textbook per se. I mean, I use a textbook, but I bring my own set of pictures. If we're going to talk about the civil rights movement, I don't do black-and-white photographs. I use color pictures to remind them this wasn't that long ago. It's that subtle programming. Oh, it's a black-and-white photo. That was a long time ago. Let me remind you, this was not a long time ago. If I'm subbing and teaching about slavery, I remind the students that my name is Mr. Broaddus, spelled with two Ds. Why is it two Ds? If I trace my family tree, I only have to go back three generations before I have to sift through the receipts of my family.

There was a spelling error in one of the receipts, which is why we went from one "Broadus" to "Broaddus"—due to a slavery transaction. That was just a few generations ago. The curation of history likes to paint it like this was a long time ago, faraway problems that people shouldn't have to deal with today. I'm like, no, this is in my living memory. When parents want to talk to me about "critical race theory," I remind them I'm not talking about your idea of critical race. I'm talking about living, breathing history and the fact that history has been curated to your advantage, not mine.

Danian Darrell Jerry: That's living, breathing history, and you use examples from your own life to add that personal edge so the students can make sense of the information.

Maurice Broaddus: Absolutely. Frankly, parents can argue "critical race theory," but they can't argue my story.

My youngest son, my students, all want to talk about Martin Luther King. That's great. My son's name is Malcolm Xavier, and that's because my wife wouldn't let me get away with just saying X, because my son is Malcolm X. I come from a different philosophical background. What is

Chapter 10: Decolonizing Public Minds and Public Places 113

that, Mister Broaddus? I'm glad you asked. Let me tell you . . . I can bring a whole different lens because students aren't taught Malcolm X in school. We hear about the civil rights movement, and it's basically Rosa Parks, Martin Luther King, and they're kind of done at that point. Yes. That is not what brought me to the movement. I came in through Malcolm X. Let's expand what we're talking about.

And it's all done through the lens of my family, my story. My father was a Black Panther. My son was named after Malcolm X. Again, parents can argue "critical race theory," but I'm just talking about my story at this point. When I was hired, the administration said, Maurice, you're a unicorn because Black male teachers are unicorns. We're trying to gather as many unicorns as we can as a way to subvert the system. They're having the "critical race theory" conversations without having the "critical race theory" conversations. They're never going to use those terms because those words are too politically charged, but they can create and support a system that is doing the work without saying a thing.

Danian Darrell Jerry: That's what it's all about, assuming agency, doing what we can to effect measurable change. Let's switch gears and focus on your community activism and the work you do with the Kheprw Institute. I remember when I attended McConn and saw what you all were doing in Indianapolis. You bought houses. You had students working in the houses, sustaining themselves and the living space, independently, you know. The whole scene was amazing.

Maurice Broaddus: That was before we had the gardens going, so now we grow our own food on top of it.

Danian Darrell Jerry: You've carved out time to be a teacher, a prolific author, and a key supporter of a well-respected community empowerment group, the Kheprw Institute. Between neighborhood gardens, community-based startups, reclaiming properties, reversing gentrification and supporting the next generation of entrepreneurs, the Kheprw Institute has left an indelible mark on the landscape of Indianapolis. What conditions created the need for the Kheprw Institute? And how do these issues impact its work?

Maurice Broaddus: Kheprw has been around for at least 18 years now. I've been there for the last 6 years. Things have just taken off, even in the short time I've been there. Kheprw came about because the founder's son was someone who was failed by the school system. His cousins and his friends were failed by the school system. They were all in bad spaces, gradewise. The Kheprw Institute started by being a support for these young Black men. It was an after-school tutoring program, and they said, hey, we're going to provide you entrepreneurial experiences to drive home the lessons and give you some money to pocket. That's how the institute started. Now it's grown into an octopus. Our tendrils are in everything, but they have to be because of the different areas where the system has failed us. It's not like folks are sitting around saying, you know what we'd love to do. We'd love to grow some gardens. No, we live in a food desert, one of the largest food deserts in the entire state.

In the 14th largest city in the country, we live in a food desert. The system has failed us. There are no grocery stores nearby. We have to walk or catch buses in order to get food. The system has failed us. Going and begging them, after they've failed us makes no sense. How do we rely on our own agency? How do we rely on the gifts and talents of our neighbors to support one another? How do we create community wealth, starting with the folks around us in our relational base, our relational pool? How do we start and build from here? That's the ethos in which we work. We look at the tendrils. Planting the gardens in order to feed ourselves, starting after-school programs, STEAM programs. Having Afrofuture Fridays, for example, as a way to have book discussions, ways to talk about history and art, to have models of sustainability, models of resistance and resilience. When we talk about the Afrofuture, we go all the way back to Martin Delaney and W. E. B. Dubois in terms of science fiction work. Afrofuturism allows us to reimagine ourselves.

How does that apply to where we are? That's what Afrofuture Fridays is about. Education, food, buying up houses, restoring those houses, that's a twofer. That's establishing Black businesses in terms of the house rehab work, and rehabbing properties to provide housing for some of our young people. This year we also launched Alchemy, which is our community wealth-building program. It has two sides, Alchemy and Cafe Creative, which is Alchemy that features our artists in the city. Our artists as entrepreneurs. To do what? To build our own infrastructure, support ourselves as artists in the city, so that we aren't relying on institutions which have neglected, if not forgotten, us this entire time. We do our KIF, Kheprw Integrated Fund, so we can do microloans in the community to support these businesses, to dole out grants to artists. All that's been going on around 18 years, and this is where we find ourselves.

That being said. These days all those institutions which had failed us beforehand, well now, they're like, Black lives do matter. Now some of the institutions are playing catch up. They know they have neglected us for decades, but now they want to come alongside us. Kheprw will take the money on our terms. But it's only to bolster the stuff that we were already doing without them. Now we're discussing how to work alongside these institutions. Including some of the art institutions in the city who have apparently discovered Black artists in the last three years. Oh wait, there are Black artists in the city. Go figure. We've all been discovered right now. Indianapolis artists are some of the hardest-working people because everyone wants us—for now. Black artists are hot right

Chapter 10: Decolonizing Public Minds and Public Places 115

now. Our lives matter right now. The opportunities are coming for us. In the meantime, we continue to either create institutions and support our own institutions, so that when we are forgotten again, which history has told us and taught us—if it's not being curated against us—that eventually there will be pushback and these opportunities will close. In the meantime, we create our own institutions, so we can support ourselves when these institutions forget about us again.

Danian Darrell Jerry: I saw an interesting term on the Kheprw website, "democratizing data." Hmm. Can we talk about democratizing data? From my understanding, the idea involves making data accessible to individuals and small companies. Allowing the smaller entities to go around the larger third-party data providers that may not have the community's best interests at heart.

Maurice Broaddus: I can talk about it in big-picture terms because despite being an Afrofuturist, I am not a tech guy, but one Afrofuture Friday, my co-host from the Kheprw Institute, Russell Palmer, sat in with another young brother, Modibbo for Day, who's a futurist out of Ohio. Basically, it was an Afrofuturist interviewing two Black futurists. With democratizing our data, the basic gist or the big picture begs the question. Who is controlling our stories? Because our stories are going to be written. If you look at politicians, they write the stories of our community and use all sorts of statistics to define our community. Numbers don't lie, but people do. So who is controlling those stories? That's what democratizing data is about. It's about bringing data down to the community level so the community can access this data and tell our stories from our perspective. Numbers don't lie. It's a matter of what numbers are you looking at? You defined our community using these numbers, but wait a second. These numbers over here tell an entirely different story.

Let's tell that story. Rather than waiting on the media to define us or politicians to define us or the police to define our city, we'll put the data in our hands. We can tell our own story.

Danian Darrell Jerry: Has the program been successful?

Maurice Broaddus: You mean, is it one of the most successful arms of Kheprw at the moment?

Danian Darrell Jerry: Yes.

Maurice Broaddus: The program is definitely expanding. We'll just say that.

Danian Darrell Jerry: That's what Afrofuturism is all about, thinking outside the box, using our imaginations to imagine better futures that we can build in real life.

Maurice Broaddus: In that program, you see a lot of things that Kheprw is about in that one moment. Its headed up by Russell Palmer. That dude is like 23, 24 maybe. He teaches two main classrooms, a group of elders for a start, and a group of high schoolers. In this one area, you see intergenerational learning and intergenerational conversations, which is beautiful. Watching these elders grapple with data and technology and then pick it up so well. You see this beauty of community in action. Talk about joy. There's several levels of joy. There's the joy of young people sharing with older people, older people learning and sharing their wisdom with the younger people a couple of generations down. You have the joy of just learning because this isn't part of a school program. This isn't a formal education thing. This is a bunch of people who want to learn, coming together, which is a totally different vibe. There's joy in imagining the stories for our community and imagining the different applications of data to tell our own stories.

Danian Darrell Jerry: I love Kheprw Institute's multigenerational aspect. You have young people, elders and every generation in between cooperating on an extraordinary level.

Maurice Broaddus: I just met with one of the elders earlier today. We were thinking ahead about our Kwanzaa celebration. I've been informed by said elder that I am not an elder in this space. I'm in fact on the verge of being a baby elder. That's as much as I can claim. I don't even get full baby elder status. I'm a baby elder in training.

When it's all said and done, community is about relationships—relationships that are rooted in history. That's what our elders represent. They represent the stories, our living history, our living wisdom. Whether they realize it or not, they are the griots of our community. Learning happens just by coming and sitting at their feet and going, hey, just tell me a story. I'm there every week to scoop up these stories, to learn from my elders and then spin those stories and imagine them into the future. That's my job.

Danian Darrell Jerry: You do that job well. This is a good place to segue into a conversation about writing. According to my research, you're best known in Indianapolis and beyond for your award-winning science fiction and fantasy books. Over the years, you have served both as an editor, highlighting new voices, and a writer of well-respected, beloved science fiction. In 2021, you served as the Ray Bradbury lecturer and visiting writer at the Center for Ray Bradbury Studies. Alongside Kheprw and Imhotep Adisa, you founded Afrofuturism Friday. Your goal was to demonstrate to Hoosiers viable solutions for networking relationships between technology and the humanities in order to create viable and sustainable futures—while acknowledging the interactions of various social constructs like race and gender.

How does this work as an Afrofuturist examining the past, the present, imagining the future, countering the mythologies imagined by opponents of antiracist initiatives, restorative justice, and accurate historical reporting that have been conflated under the guise of "critical race theory"?

Chapter 10: Decolonizing Public Minds and Public Places 117

Maurice Broaddus: You're trying to get me into trouble. I'm going to talk about two books of mine, *Pimp My Airship* and *Sweep of Stars*. *Pimp my Airship* takes place in this alternate history version of America. In this version, America lost the Revolutionary War and remained a colony of England. It's an alternate history. It's a steampunk novel, and at its heart, it's interrogating this one idea I was thinking through at the time. I'm just a writer. How do I use my gift to impact my community? That's literally all I was thinking about at the time, and that's what plays out in *Pimp My Airship*, right? You have a spoken-word poet named Sleepy. He's joined by a couple of his compatriots, and they become inadvertent revolutionaries. Changing the system. Keep in mind, the reviews always say *Pimp My Airship* is a fun romp of a novel. However, during my fun rompingness, if that's a thing, what am I examining? I'm examining overpolicing in our neighborhoods, mass incarceration, redlining. This is my way of just examining not just where Black people are but why we are here. We didn't find ourselves in these neighborhoods by accident. There were systematic things put in place, one to put us into these neighborhoods, two to keep us in these neighborhoods.

We were put in our place, and people try to keep us in our place. And there are historical institutions, historical processes, historical systems which did this. Through this lens, I examine the history of the Klan, especially the Klan in Indiana, because in the 1920s, one in three members, one in three citizens of Indiana, one in three Hoosiers were card-carrying members of the Klan. And once you factor in Black people were part of that three. Right? Like that's an awful lot of folks that weren't us card-carrying members of the Klan. And to the point where our governor was a grand dragon, a grand wizard, I mean. Our governor. When people talk about systems, these systems are created by laws. Laws are put in place by lawmakers. If you have a governor that's a member of the Klan. The laws being passed and introduced will not work in our favor. So there's a system there, there's a history there, and it's one that I wanted to examine. Sure, I throw in airships and giant robots. That'll happen. But at its root. Those are all genre affectations.

I am examining one, how do I use art to change the system? What is it then in the system that we need to change? Here is the system. Here are all the tendrils of this system. There's this history that put these tendrils into place. As modern-day artists, we have to fight against all of it. We have to pick our spots and break down that system using our gifts. Gifts are twofold. One, they are our words, our art. They cast a vision, and they move hearts. That is the role of art.

Then organize. Bring people together through story, through celebration. Bring them together through art. We come together, and we organize. That creates another leverage point. It's about our agency.

How do we own our agency and move forward, not just as individuals? Individuals only get so far, but as a group, a collective of informed citizens and neighbors. So that was *Pimp My Airship*. I'm examining, critiquing the past, setting the present in order to create a better future. *Pimp My Airship*, that's my work as an Afrofuturist.

Danian Darrell Jerry: One of the characters in *Pimp My Airship* is a literal sleeping giant, so the novel wrestles with themes and ideas about artists learning their talents and transforming into a better instrument in the process.

Maurice Broaddus: One of Kheprw's things is the credo *empowerment through self-mastery*. You master your craft, master what you do. That mastery empowers you and enables you to empower the community.

Danian Darrell Jerry: The chapters in *Pimp My Airship* have titles taken from some of the greatest rap records of all time. Can you talk about hip-hop's influence over your novel's composition?

Maurice Broaddus: There was this weird thing I fell into. Whenever I started working in the steampunk genre, it was always tied to music. The world in *Pimp My Airship* was created by me listening to Parliament Funkadelic as my entry point into steampunk. Which is why the airships are called bop guns and things like that, why they have to go after the star child. These are all Parliament Funkadelic elements that have worked their way in. A lot of my work is influenced by a love of culture, and I grew up as a hip-hop head. I mentioned that my son was named after Malcolm X. I came to my knowledge and study of Malcolm X through hip-hop. Through Public Enemy, Leaders of the New School, Boogie Down Productions. It was through X-Clan that I learned about Malcolm X. I learned a lot about history, frankly.

When I'm coming to hip-hop, I am. It's 1987. I've graduated high school. I've gone through America's basic educational system. I'm like, who are these figures Public Enemy is talking about? I don't know any of this history.

After high school, because I love the music I'm listening to, I'm researching historical figures. That's how I came to Malcolm X. That's why I have yet another copy of his autobiography within reach. I go through it so often when I'm mentoring people. I end up giving away my copy, so I have to keep buying more copies. I came to Malcolm X through music. Music has had a profound effect on me, so plenty of those chapters are named after Public Enemy songs. That's what brought me into the culture, period.

Danian Darrell Jerry: I learned about Malcolm X from "Proud to Black" by Run DMC. At first, I thought Malcolm X was a DJ, like Terminator X. Before that, I had never heard of him, and the fact that I had never heard of him made me believe what he said. That's what made it stick. I felt angry. I felt cheated. Something wasn't right, and I knew it was deliberate. I didn't know how, but I sensed that the absence of Malcolm X from my textbooks and my classes was deliberate.

Maurice Broaddus: It absolutely was deliberate and systematic. That was in *Pimp My Airship*, but then there's *Sweep of Stars*. Again, it's doing my work as an Afrofuturist. It's critiquing the present, but now I'm projecting a hundred or so years into the future. I kept telling the folks at Kheprw this. *Sweep of Stars* is like, what if Kheprw was its own galactic empire? What if we win? That's literally the question I posed to them when I was beginning the world building for *Sweep of Stars*. It's like, what if we won? What if we could build and design our own world? What would it mean to dream about the possibilities? What are we working towards?

That became a fun mental exercise. What could a different educational model look like? What could a different economic model look like? We started doing all these what-if games, one, to help me world-build. Two, we kept imagining the future we wanted to create and taking the time to dream about those kinds of futures. I'm the Afrofuturist resident, but we're all Afrofuturists in that space.

When I talk about being an Afrofuturist, it's like, what is our work? Our work is to dream alongside community and to create spaces and opportunities for us to just dream and let our imagination just go. Which is a huge work that in and of itself sets us apart from other organizations in the city. I can't tell you how many organizers I bumped into who basically said, we are so locked into surviving today, we don't have time to dream.

There's more to life than survival. If we're just surviving, we're not getting anywhere. *Sweep of Stars* is my imagination exercise about what the future could look like. What could community look like if we could build any sort of society we wanted? It looks a lot like my neighbors in space. It looks a lot like my sister and her friends as the guardian military of this community. It looks a lot like elders leading the way in an intergenerational manner of living together, being together. It looks like a community that has found healing and joy.

CHAPTER 11

ANTIBODIES//Shots: Engaging Public Health Critical Race Praxis to Counter Epistemic Violence in the Discourse of Dual Pandemics

Ryan J. Petteway

KEEPING STATIC, NEVER SLEEPING

Or, That One Time the U.S. Office of Minority Health Told Black Men to "Wear Blue" on Juneteenth in 2020 During the Pandemics of COVID-19 and Racialized Police Violence

so analyze me, surprise me, but can't magnetize me
scannin' while you're plannin' ways to sabotage me

—Jones (1994, p. 10)

COVID-19 has laid bare a true pathology at the root of population health inequities: unapologetic, litigiously defended structural racism. Discourse and evidence to this effect span various national contexts, from the United States (Bailey et al., 2020; Bailey & Moon, 2020; Egede & Walker, 2020; Krieger, 2020; Yearby & Mohapatra, 2020), to Brazil (Araújo & Caldwell, 2020; Oliveira et al., 2020), to the United Kingdom (Razai et al., 2021; Syal, 2020), to Canada (Tuyisenge & Goldenberg, 2021). In the United States, we have seen the consequences of structural racism not only in exposure, infection, and mortality inequities (Garcia et al., 2020; Gawthrop, 2022; Khazanchi et al., 2020; Laster Pirtle, 2020; McClure et al., 2020; Millett et al., 2020) but also in government-backed racist rhetoric on the "Chinese virus" (Gover et al., 2020)). More broadly, we've witnessed its insidiousness via the pervasive individualist, racialized, and pathologizing narratives of "people at risk" and "vulnerable communities"— narratives that emphasize personal responsibility and decontextualize the root causes of "preexisting" conditions (Petteway, 2020). And with multiple vaccines now available, we've observed the effects of structural racism on COVID-19 vaccination rates (Acosta et al., 2021).

And as if one pandemic were not enough, we've continued to experience the pandemic of racialized police violence against Black, Brown, and Indigenous communities around the globe. While this violence is not unique to the United States, the country has served as a focal point in a growing international movement for Black lives, especially since the murder of George Floyd in May 2020 (Bhaumik, 2020; Collins, 2020; Kirby, 2020; Mohdin & Campbell, 2020; Nakhavoly, 2021; Phillips, 2020; Staff, 2020). In December 2020, it was estimated that COVID-19 had killed at least 1 in 1,000 Black Americans—a chilling statistic matched only by the grim reality that 1 in 1,000 Black men in America can expect to be killed by the police over their lifetime (Edwards et al., 2019). As of the time of writing, COVID-19 now killed 1 in 555 Black Americans (Gawthrop, 2022), and the police have continued to murder and brutalize Black Americans (Rosenberg & Evans, 2021; Stelloh, 2021). Moreover, COVID-19 social distancing and masking mandates have been used to further subject Black and Brown communities to racialized policing practices (Kajeepeta et al., 2022).

Public health has been front and center during these crises. In the United States, the confluence of COVID-19 and racialized police violence has prompted long-overdue calls from numerous professional, academic, and governmental organizations to declare structural racism a public health crisis (AMA, 2020; American Public Health Association, 2020a, 2020b; Pew, 2020). Alas, this is America. And even in the face of all of this . . . well, let's just put it like this.

Scene

It's June 2020. Black Americans are dying from two pandemics. Structural racism is running rampant in the streets. The police are taking Black lives like COVID. It's Pride Month. Black trans lives are taken just the same.

Enter stage left

The U.S. Office of Minority Health (OMH) sends out various email and Twitter communications to encourage communities of color to celebrate

Chapter 11: Antibodies/Shots   123

"Wear Blue Day" on June 19 because it's Men's Health Month. Blue. On Juneteenth. In 2020. During an international uprising and movement in support of the value of Black life. No emails or tweets mentioning structural racism or racial health inequities. No emails, tweets, or statements in solidarity with the movement for Black lives. Just . . . wear Blue. On Juneteenth.

Scene

A curious observer does a casual investigation (i.e., on the internet) into the leadership and "core values" of OMH to determine how in the entire f#@! something like this made it through comms approval. The observer finds the following information (see Figure 11.1), reaches for his cellphone, opens a music-streaming app, presses play on Nas's "It Ain't Hard to Tell," and pours some Heineken brew for his deceased crew on memory lane.

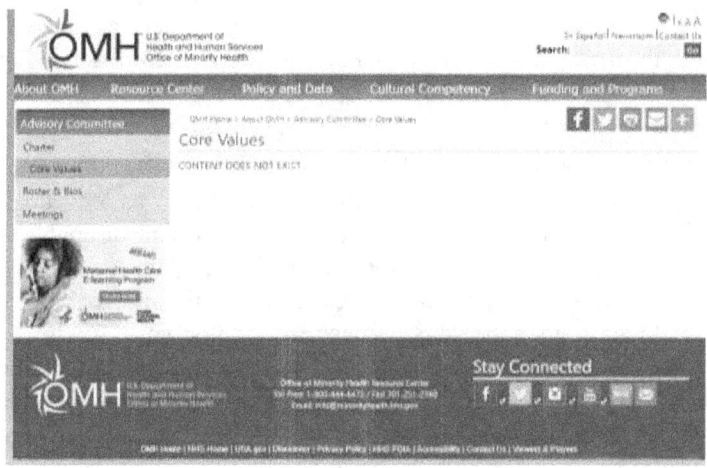

Figure 11.1 Screenshot of the Office of Minority Health's "Core Values" page

NEVER PUT ME IN YOUR BOX IF YOUR SH*T EATS TAPES

On the Epistemic Violence of a Structurally Racist Public Health System

Silenced. We fear those who speak about us,
who do not speak to us and with us.
We know what it is like to be silenced.

—hooks (2015, p. 152)

As grotesque as it was, here I suggest that the OMH's public communication is just one illustrative example of what Black feminist philosopher Kristie Dotson (2011) refers to as an "instance of silencing," and part of a larger "practice of silencing" and epistemic violence as routinized in public health. At risk of oversimplification, Dotson describes how epistemic violence manifests within various communication exchanges wherein one party is speaking from a marginalized social position—such that this speaking from the margins presents as a form of potentially "unsafe" and "risky" testimony. Here, the notions of *testimonial quieting, testimonial smothering*, and *testimonial incompetence* become critically important. First, as described by Dotson, *testimonial quieting* occurs "when an audience fails to engage a speaker as a knower" (p. 242), thereby creating a scenario in which the speaker is effectively silenced. In the OMH instance discussed above, I read the OMH as essentially quieting the testimony of Black Americans as related to racialized police violence—that is, failing to engage with or even acknowledge what Black men, for example, were experiencing and embodying. And the juxtaposition of that quieting—as either a dismissal or a refusal to "hear"—against a message in support of "wearing blue," on Juneteenth in the midst of international protests against racialized police violence, places the act of epistemic (and symbolic) violence in clear relief.

Second, Dotson (2011) describes *testimonial smothering* as occurring when a speaker "perceives one's immediate audience as unwilling or unable to gain the appropriate uptake of proffered testimony" (p. 244). In essence, a would-be speaker reads the room and decides (read: through coercion) that speaking/sharing one's ideas/knowledge/truths is not worth the foreseeable epistemic, psychic, and/or physical risks. In effect, such testimonial smothering has the potential to not only further enable existing dominant narratives that misrepresent the lived and factual contexts of the speaker's history/reality but also to coerce a self-silencing of potential counternarratives. In this way, testimonial smothering presents as a coerced truncation and withholding of (counter)stories that could potentially offer resistance and facilitate meaningful action. In the OMH instance, given that there appear to have been multiple Black Americans in leadership positions at the time, I (charitably, perhaps) read their acquiescence as a form of coerced silence—a smothering of what I can only hope would have been their better selves if not subjected to the pressures of their employing institution. Perhaps they did not feel that to resist—to counter—the intended communications was a professionally and psychically safe thing to do, and thereby smothered testimony that, perhaps, may have denied the "wear blue" message and replaced it with a message in solidarity with the movement for Black lives.

Third, as described by Dotson (2011), *testimonial incompetence* is "the failure of an audience to demonstrate to the speaker that she/he will find proffered testimony accurately intelligible" (p. 245). In other words, the audience consists of folks who "don't get it" and are not at all prepared—either epistemically or affectively—to do the work of listening, hearing, and holding space. In the OMH instance, I read the failure of anyone in the entire organization to catch the troublesome nature of their communications regarding "wearing blue" as a sign of an institution rife with testimonial incompetence. That is, in addition to those who may have smothered their testimony of resistance, there are many others who—by training and design—are conditioned to not even see how it could be problematic—wholly unfit to represent the health interests of Black Americans.

As Dotson (2011) articulates, an *instance of silencing* (e.g., the OMH tweets) can be read as a *practice of silencing*—a mode of epistemic violence—when it is part of a repetitive and "reliable" pattern of discursive practices that suppress, truncate, dismiss, or otherwise devalue the knowledges, lived experiences, and testimonies of those at the margins. It is my position here that the dynamics discussed in the OMH example routinely play out within the public health field at large. Why, for example, would a scholar of color, a public health student of color, or a community co-researcher/research participant trust us (public health) with their testimony (their story, their knowledge, their truths from the margins) if, in my view, the bulk of our research and practice enterprise signals death by epistemic violence? In this manner, testimonial quieting, smothering, and incompetence—particularly as codified via/embedded within status quo research and practice processes, including public communication—present as a practice of silencing that threatens continued epistemic violence against those of us who dare speak of what we know from the margins.

This violence has been legible, for example, in generic, catch-all, colorblind frames attempting to project a common sense of mutuality and solidarity during COVID-19 (e.g., "We're all in this together" and "Let's flatten *the* curve"—emphasis on "the," as if everyone is affected the same and on a singular "curve"). We've also witnessed this violence in narratives that pathologize Black Americans as being "at greater risk" (Petteway, 2020) versus being repeatedly and actively *risked* by the architecture of structural racism (Bailey et al., 2020; Bailey et al., 2021; Gee & Ford, 2011). And we've seen it in narratives that portray Black Americans as being "vaccine hesitant" versus Black Americans having plentiful historic and present reasons to have a healthy and necessary level of distrust and suspicion in the context of public health and medical systems/practices (Corbie-Smith, 2021; Gamble, 1997, 2010; Washington, 2008). Moreover, narratives of Black vaccine hesitancy obscure concerns regarding inequitable vaccine access (i.e., vaccine apartheid) and the fact that available data have actually shown that it is white Evangelical Christians and Republican men who are the quintessential "vaccine hesitant" populations (NPR/PBS, 2021), not Black Americans.

As I've discussed elsewhere (Petteway, 2022), by engaging in and/or encouraging various practices of testimonial quieting and testimonial smothering, public health has inculcated a culture of testimonial incompetence, to the extent that, I suggest, even organizations like the OMH have been constructed, conditioned, and/or co-opted into public communication and "branding" practices that decenter (or outright ignore) core critical race theory and public health critical race praxis (PHCRP) principles like centering the margins, the primacy of racialization, structural determinism, critical approaches, voice, and intersectionality (Delgado et al., 2017; Ford & Airhihenbuwa, 2010). And the OMH itself has a history of such practices (Petteway, 2020). The net effect, I submit, is to systematically truncate potentially productive discourse and action on structural racism as relevant to racial health inequities—to silence narratives that more critically and expressly challenge the power structures that function to preserve racial inequality and continually cast Black lives as simultaneously "essential" and expendable. Hence, the imperative of public health to more thoroughly engage PHCRP to better identify, contest, and counter practices of silencing that subject Black Americans to yet another form of violence. Otherwise, it would appear that perhaps even in the context of public health, Derrick Bell was right: COVID-19 claiming the lives of 1/555 Black Americans is only of national public health concern/interest because COVID-19 is also claiming millions of white lives. But the 1/1,000 Black Americans killed by the police? Silence. Public health keeps trying to sell us some broken amps and hoping that we won't notice.

"OUTRO": "MY POETRY'S DEEP, I NEVER FELL"

ANTIBODIES//Shots

Through poetry, I engage PHCRP to interrogate matters of misrepresentation and institutional silence surrounding COVID-19 and racialized police violence. Specifically, I engage/enact PHCRP principles of disciplinary self-critique and voice to expose and counter the epistemic violence that public health has repeatedly subjected Black Americans to in times of crisis—rendering legible the manner in which the present discourse of "returning to normal" is, in fact, a return to the invisibilization of the endemicity of structural racism. Crafted as a counternarrative and in the counterstorytelling tradition of critical race theory (Delgado, 1989; Solórzano & Yosso, 2002), ANTIBODIES// Shots weaves together a sampling of 28 tracks as a listening trail for readers to (re)encounter 40+ years of lyrical protest and resistance, rearticulating the COVID-19 discourse of viral "antibodies" and "shots" as embodied/manifest within racialized police violence—that is, the *other* anti-(Black)bodies and shots that claim 1/1,000 of us.

ANTIBODIES//Shots

Or, A Critical Race Theory Analysis of Infection Endemicity Using Purposive Sampling

Straight up, shit is real

. . . and any day
could be your last when you're essential;
working-class hands
keep the beat, instrumental;
more than instruments
our intellect is influential;
are we still in this together
come November and the rent's due?

Lookin' for a Change,
found a quarter in the cushion;
kickin' it with Curtis,
told me Keep on Pushin';
Brown Babies need food,
I'ma keep on cookin';
they keep on shootin',
I'ma keep on lookin' . . .

And they shootin'

No bandanas
on the face of the Shook,
Ones in a pocket,
wallet Commonly mistook;
Nina said Please
but our pleas are overlooked;
hotels shutting down,
DCs overbooked.

Cruisin' in a six . . .
to buy food for the fam;
pulled down by the river,
so we kneel next to Sam;
brown liquor on the pave,
ICE Cube in the hands
of a lady named America,
Working on her tan.

It's Alright if we Hussle
and keep working the mop;
counterclockwise,
true sign of a Boss;
so much Sauce
gets dripped in a stop
made from the same fruit
that the poplars drop.

Now on the count of three . . .
look out for the one time;
the Math don't lie,
it's not happening one time;
it's a cold, Cold World,
but it's hot in the Sunshine;
got N-95 problems
who they got on the frontlines?

Flash!
Keep your hands on the dash;
keep your mouth shut,
and don't move too fast;
don't reach for your phone,
don't remove your mask;
they said they got calls
you took 1200 cash.

And they shootin' . . .

REFERENCES

Acosta, A. M., Garg, S., Pham, H., Whitaker, M., Anglin, O., O'Halloran, A., Milucky, J., Patel, K., Taylor, C., Wortham, J., Chai, S. J., Kirley, P. D., Alden, N. B., Kawasaki, B., Meek, J., Yousey-Hindes, K., Anderson, E. J., Openo, K. P., Weigel, A., . . . Havers, F. P. (2021). Racial and ethnic disparities in rates of COVID-19–associated hospitalization, intensive care unit admission, and in-hospital death in the United States from March 2020 to February 2021. *JAMA Network Open*, 4(10), e2130479. https://doi.org/10.1001/jamanetworkopen.2021.30479

American Medical Association. (2020, June 23). *AMA Board of Trustees pledges action against racism and police brutality*. https://www.ama-assn.org/about/board-trustees/ama-board-trustees-pledges-action-against-racism-and-police-brutality

American Public Health Association. (2020a). *Racism is a public health crisis*. https://www.apha.org/topics-and-issues/health-equity/racism-and-health/racism-declarations

American Public Health Association. (2020b, May 29). *Racism is an ongoing public health crisis that needs our attention now.* https://apha.org/news-and-media/news-releases/apha-news-releases/2020/racism-is-a-public-health-crisis

Araújo, E. M. de, & Caldwell, K. L. (2020, June 10). COVID-19 is deadlier for Black Brazilians, a legacy of structural racism that dates back to slavery. *The Conversation.* http://theconversation.com/covid-19-is-deadlier-for-black-brazilians-a-legacy-of-structural-racism-that-dates-back-to-slavery-139430

Bailey, Z., Barber, S., Robinson, W., Slaughter-Acey, J., Ford, C., & Sealy-Jefferson, S. (2020). *Racism in the time of COVID-19.* Interdisciplinary Association for Population Health Science. https://iaphs.org/racism-in-the-time-of-covid-19/

Bailey, Z. D., Feldman, J. M., & Bassett, M. T. (2021). How structural racism works: Racist policies as a root cause of U.S. racial health inequities. *New England Journal of Medicine, 384,* 768–773. https://doi.org/10.1056/NEJMms2025396

Bailey, Z. D., & Moon, J. R. (2020). Racism and the political economy of COVID-19: Will we continue to resurrect the past? *Journal of Health Politics, Policy and Law, 45*(6), 937–950. https://doi.org/10.1215/03616878-8641481

Bhaumik, S. (2020, June 23). Black Lives Matter comes to Colombia. *The Bogotá Post.* https://thebogotapost.com/black-lives-matter-comes-to-colombia/46928/

Collins, L. (2020, June 18). Assa Traoré and the fight for Black lives in France. *The New Yorker.* https://www.newyorker.com/news/letter-from-europe/assa-traore-and-the-fight-for-black-lives-in-france

Corbie-Smith, G. (2021). Vaccine hesitancy is a scapegoat for structural racism. *JAMA Health Forum, 2*(3), e210434. https://doi.org/10.1001/jamahealthforum.2021.0434

Delgado, R. (1989). Storytelling for oppositionists and others: A plea for narrative. *Michigan Law Review, 87*(8), 2411–2441. https://doi.org/10.2307/1289308

Delgado, R., Stefancic, J., & Harris, A. (2017). *Critical race theory* (3rd ed.). New York University Press.

Dotson, K. (2011). Tracking epistemic violence, tracking practices of silencing. *Hypatia, 26*(2), 236–257. https://doi.org/10.1111/j.1527-2001.2011.01177.x

Edwards, F., Lee, H., & Esposito, M. (2019). Risk of being killed by police use of force in the United States by age, race–ethnicity, and sex. *Proceedings of the National Academy of Sciences, 116*(34), 16793–16798. https://doi.org/10.1073/pnas.1821204116

Egede, L. E., & Walker, R. J. (2020). Structural racism, social risk factors, and COVID-19: A dangerous convergence for Black Americans. *New England Journal of Medicine, 383*(12), e77. https://doi.org/10.1056/NEJMp2023616

Ford, C. L., & Airhihenbuwa, C. O. (2010). The public health critical race methodology: Praxis for antiracism research. *Social Science & Medicine, 71*(8), 1390–1398. https://doi.org/10.1016/j.socscimed.2010.07.030

Gamble, V. N. (1997). Under the shadow of Tuskegee: African Americans and health care. *American Journal of Public Health, 87*(11), 1773–1778. https://doi.org/10.2105%2Fajph.87.11.1773

Gamble, V. N. (2010). "There wasn't a lot of comforts in those days": African Americans, public health, and the 1918 influenza epidemic. *Public Health Reports, 125*(Suppl. 3), 114–122.

Garcia, M. A., Homan, P. A., García, C., & Brown, T. H. (2021). The color of COVID-19: Structural racism and the disproportionate impact of the pandemic on older Black and Latinx adults. *Journal of Gerontology: Series B, 76*(3), e75–e80. https://doi.org/10.1093/geronb/gbaa114

Gawthrop, E. (2022, November 22). *The color of coronavirus: COVID-19 deaths by race and ethnicity in the U.S.* American Public Media. https://www.apmresearchlab.org/covid/deaths-by-race

Gee, G. C., & Ford, C. L. (2011). Structural racism and health inequities. *Du Bois Review: Social Science Research on Race, 8*(1), 115–132. https://doi.org/10.1017/S1742058X11000130

Gover, A. R., Harper, S. B., & Langton, L. (2020). Anti-Asian hate crime during the COVID-19 pandemic: Exploring the reproduction of inequality. *American Journal of Criminal Justice, 45*(4), 647–667. https://doi.org/10.1007/s12103-020-09545-1

Kajeepeta, S., Bruzelius, E., Ho, J. Z., & Prins, S. J. (2022). Policing the pandemic: Estimating spatial and racialized inequities in New York City police enforcement of COVID-19 mandates. *Critical Public Health, 32*(1), 56–67. https://doi.org/10.1080/09581596.2021.1987387

Khazanchi, R., Evans, C. T., & Marcelin, J. R. (2020). Racism, not race, drives inequity across the COVID-19 continuum. *JAMA Network Open, 3*(9), e2019933. https://doi.org/10.1001/jamanetworkopen.2020.19933

Kirby, J. (2020, June 12). *"Black Lives Matter" has become a global rallying cry.* Vox. https://www.vox.com/2020/6/12/21285244/black-lives-matter-global-protests-george-floyd-uk-belgium

Krieger, N. (2020). Enough: COVID-19, structural racism, police brutality, plutocracy, climate change—and time for health justice, democratic governance, and an equitable, sustainable future. *American Journal of Public Health, 110*(11), 1620–1623. https://doi.org/10.2105/AJPH.2020.305886

Laster Pirtle, W. N. (2020). Racial capitalism: A fundamental cause of novel coronavirus (COVID-19) pandemic inequities in the United States. *Health Education & Behavior, 47*(4), 504–508. https://doi.org/10.1177/1090198120922942

McClure, E. S., Vasudevan, P., Bailey, Z., Patel, S., & Robinson, W. R. (2020). Racial capitalism within public health: How occupational settings drive COVID-19 disparities. *American Journal of Epidemiology, 189*(11), 1244–1253. https://doi.org/10.1093/aje/kwaa126

Millett, G. A., Jones, A. T., Benkeser, D., Baral, S., Mercer, L., Beyrer, C., Honermann, B., Lankiewicz, E., Mena, L., Crowley, J. S., Sherwood, J., & Sullivan, P. S. (2020). Assessing differential impacts of COVID-19 on Black communities. *Annals of Epidemiology, 47*, 37–44. https://doi.org/10.1016/j.annepidem.2020.05.003

Mohdin, A., & Campbell, L. (2020, November 13). "So many people care!" The young Britons whose lives were changed by Black Lives Matter. *The Guardian.* http://www.theguardian.com/world/2020/nov/13/how-black-lives-matter-has-inspired-a-generation-of-new-uk-activists

Nakhavoly, M. (2021, February 4). *The history of Black Lives Matter Toronto and its momentous fight for change. CityNews.* https://toronto.citynews.ca/2021/02/04/the-history-of-black-lives-matter-toronto/

Ndugga, N., Hill, L., Artiga, S., & Haldar, S. (2022, July 14). *Latest data on COVID-19 vaccinations by race/ethnicity.* KFF. https://www.kff.org/coronavirus-covid-19/issue-brief/latest-data-on-covid-19-vaccinations-by-race-ethnicity/

NPR/PBS. (2021, March 8). *Nature of the sample: NPR/PBS News Hour/Marist Poll of 1,227 national adults.* http://maristpoll.marist.edu/wp-content/uploads/2021/03/NPR_PBS-NewsHour_Marist-Poll_USA-NOS-and-Tables_202103091124.pdf#page=3

Oliveira, R. G. de, Cunha, A. P. da, Gadelha, A. G. dos S., Carpio, C. G., Oliveira, R. B. de, Corrêa, R. M., Oliveira, R. G. de, Cunha, A. P. da, Gadelha, A. G. dos S., Carpio, C. G., Oliveira, R. B. de, & Corrêa, R. M. (2020). Racial inequalities and death on the horizon: COVID-19 and structural racism [in Portuguese]. *Cadernos de Saúde Pública, 36*(9). https://doi.org/10.1590/0102-311x00150120

Petteway, R. J. (2020). LATENT//missing: On missing values, narrative power, and data politics in discourse of COVID-19. *Health Education & Behavior, 47*(5), 671–676. https://doi.org/10.1177/1090198120950194

Petteway, R. J. (2022). On epidemiology as racial-capitalist (re)colonization and epistemic violence. *Critical Public Health, 33*(8), 1–8. https://doi.org/10.1080/09581596.2022.2107486

Pew. (2020, June 15). *Racism is a public health crisis, say cities and counties.* Pew Charitable Trusts. https://pew.org/2AsZVRC

Phillips, T. (2020, December 7). Killing of two girls stokes outrage over Brazil's horrific toll of Black lives. *The Guardian.* http://www.theguardian.com/world/2020/dec/07/brazil-girls-killing-black-lives-matter

Razai, M. S., Kankam, H. K. N., Majeed, A., Esmail, A., & Williams, D. R. (2021). Mitigating ethnic disparities in COVID-19 and beyond. *BMJ, 372,* m4921. https://doi.org/10.1136/bmj.m4921

Rosenberg, G., & Evans, N. (2021, February 5). *Bond set at $3 million for fired Columbus police officer who killed Andre Hill.* NPR. https://www.npr.org/2021/02/05/964466831/bond-set-at-3-million-for-fired-columbus-police-officer-who-killed-andre-hill

Solórzano, D. G., & Yosso, T. J. (2002). Critical race methodology: Counter-storytelling as an analytical framework for education research. *Qualitative Inquiry, 8*(1), 23–44. https://doi.org/10.1177/107780040200800103

Staff, R. (2020, June 6). *Protests worldwide embrace Black Lives Matter movement.* Reuters. https://www.reuters.com/article/us-minneapolis-police-protests-global-idUSKBN23D0BO

Stelloh, T. (2021, February 1). *3 Officers suspended after 9-year-old girl pepper sprayed in Rochester.* NBC News. https://www.nbcnews.com/news/us-news/police-pepper-spray-9-year-old-girl-rochester-n-y-n1256313

Syal, R. (2020, October 27). Structural racism led to worse COVID impact on BAME groups—report. *The Guardian.* http://www.theguardian.com/world/2020/oct/27/structural-racism-led-to-worse-covid-impact-on-bame-groups-report

Tuyisenge, G., & Goldenberg, S. M. (2021). COVID-19, structural racism, and migrant health in Canada. *The Lancet, 397*(10275), 650–652. https://doi.org/10.1016/S0140-6736(21)00215-4

Washington, H. A. (2008). *Medical apartheid: the dark history of medical experimentation on Black Americans from colonial times to the present* (Illustrated ed.). Anchor.

Yearby, R., & Mohapatra, S. (2020). Law, structural racism, and the COVID-19 pandemic. *Journal of Law and the Biosciences, 7*(1). https://doi.org/10.1093/jlb/lsaa036

INTERLUDE
The Sinking White Middle Class: A Political History of Debt, Misery, and the Drift to the Right

David R. Roediger

What *Sinking* argues is that historically and in the present the majority of the middle class—clerks, salespeople, nurses, government workers, teachers, and even unionized workers in heavy industry—have experienced exploitation on the job to be sure but also a set of other miseries beyond those of wages. These anxieties center on debt—credit was long associated with middle-class status—and management of personalities by the employer, a practice much more and earlier associated with white-collar work than blue. Overwork in terms of hours of labor has also often been a problem associated with the middle class, insofar as unpaid overtime featured in some salaried positions. Debt itself drives overwork, and vice versa. Managed closely in terms of productivity and personality, the middle class "needs" more to make ends meet both financially and psychologically.

Because middle-class problems are material ones but reach far beyond those on which, say, unions bargain, we ought to be able to speak to workers thinking of themselves as middle class with fair hope that social movements can be built around their miseries on and off the job.

Source. https://www.versobooks.com/blogs/4948-an-interview-with-david-roediger.

CHAPTER 12

Don't Believe the Right: A Message From the Media Assassin

An Interview With Harry Allen

Danian Darrell Jerry

Danian Darrell Jerry: To start, I want to thank you for giving us this interview. I'm a long-time fan. The first time I heard the name Harry Allen, I was listening to Public Enemy, "Don't Believe the Hype." I remember Chuck D shouting out your name. He referred to you as the Media Assassin. I love how he said your name in a way that gave it context with the song.

Harry Allen: That's very kind. I appreciate your kind comments.

Danian Darrell Jerry: Outside of being a member of one of hip-hop's greatest groups of all time, you've written for *Village Voice*, *Time Magazine*, *The Source*, The BBC, CNN, MTV, and others. You produced a film series that featured decades of photographs of Public Enemy. Rockstar Games hired you to work on *Grand Theft Auto*. You've gathered awards and honors from the Smithsonian and the Nasir Jones Fellowship at Harvard. It is a pleasure to meet you, Mr. Allen.

Harry Allen: Thank you for the information that you read concerning my bio.

Danian Darrell Jerry: Jumping right in, I always wanted to ask. Why did you name yourself the Media Assassin?

Harry Allen: I became a Media Assassin because I decided to become one. I needed, as a writer, a certain kind of way, a certain kind of presence for my work, a certain kind of power. I chose to exemplify a certain kind of assassin, and that seemed to be the metaphor that best described how I wanted to approach the act of writing. And it was also based on the conviction that certainly when I started, and certainly now, media, for the most part, does not serve the interests of Black people either at all or well.

Yes, sir. It's too white, doesn't take (tell the story). It's written from a white perspective, almost overwhelmingly. Yes, sir. It doesn't take into account the goals of Black people. It doesn't seek to convey those goals in a way that does not please or satisfy white central politics. To specify, I mean, it's both too white in terms of the people who write and especially the people who edit.

When I started writing in the late 80s, it was even more visible, I mean unapologetically so. I decided I didn't want to be happy to be a part of that. I didn't want to declare myself, you know, thrilled to be here or present that position or posture. I was someone who had entered the space in order to take out its power center. How did I do? I failed miserably. It's still a dominant and powerful and white political enterprise.

I guess what's required is a better front from people who are going to be journalists and from readers who consume media.

Danian Darrell Jerry: We need a stronger stance from journalists and consumers? What does that look like?

Harry Allen: Doing so with an end in mind, in other words asking, why am I a journalist? Why am I here? What is it I'm trying to accomplish? The same thing with consumers with an end in mind. How am I consuming media? Why am I consuming the media, I'm consuming right now? For what reason? What purpose? The last thing anyone should be is a mindless consumer of media, because media requires you to turn on your mind.

Going back to journalism, I think there's a lot of careerism, stuff that journalists do because it's the job and they intend to keep the job. They get addicted to the safety of the job. I think that stuff inevitably undermines Black interests because Black interests have nothing to do with the job.

It's an information source. So where are you? Why are you taking in this information? What are you going to do with it? We all need to be more purposeful in terms of our actions and our thoughts, even thinking about our thoughts. Not to mention our words. We have to consume media, and I don't just mean the news. I mean *The Bachelor*. I mean, you know, whatever.

Danian Darrell Jerry: Thoughtful consumption of media takes me back to "Don't Believe the Hype." When I think of Chuck D's lyrics in that song, I'm reminded of Noam Chomsky's *Manufacturing Consent* and the connections between lawmakers, corporate owners, and media producers.

Harry Allen: It might correspond with those ideas, but from my understanding, "Don't Believe the Hype" was something that Chuck's parents used to say around the dinner table. As parents, good parents, they would sit with their children and talk about what happened that day or what's going on in the neighborhood.

Chuck's late dad and his living, wonderful, beautiful mother would often say, "Don't believe the hype" to inspire cynicism in their children about what they might see or hear. His parents were politically conscious and active people. Chuck talked about the fact that the part of his education that led him to form Public Enemy was a program taught by erstwhile Black Panthers out in Long Island. This was during a time when we had people whose work had been Black Consciousness, teaching young people.

The program was run by people who had been members of or still were members of the Black Panther Party. So even the decision to send their child to a summer program run by such people shows that Chuck's parents had a certain way of seeing the world. This was a view and a way of seeing they passed on to Chuck D through these first tutors. I'm sure that significant parts of our views in Public Enemy correspond with Noam Chomsky's ideas. I've seen a lot of the things that he said. He's incredibly, awesomely astute. I've never read the book *Manufacturing Consent*, though it certainly is on a long list of things that I must and should read. I'm sure that a lot of what he says, we'd agree with, but Noam Chomsky wasn't, to my knowledge, the inspiration for "Don't Believe the Hype."

Danian Darrell Jerry: Responsible consumption is a good place to segue into a conversation about news media manufacturing of a "critical race theory" monster. When I watch CNN, Fox, NBC, whatever, I see political campaigns, legislation, parents protesting, school boards banning books—all complaining about critical race theory. As a consumer of media, I find myself bombarded by these images and reports on "critical race theory." To start, I would like to ask, how does the news media shape public perception of "critical race theory"?

Harry Allen: The first thing one has to ask before they address the question is something that you've addressed, but I haven't, and that is *What is critical race theory?* My understanding is based on statements by Kimberlé Crenshaw. One of the co-founders or early students of Derrick Bell. He named a character in one of his books after Kimberlé Crenshaw. I think in his book *Faces at the Bottom of the Well*. From my understanding, critical race theory is the scholarly study of how racism affects law. Yes. The end.

Danian Darrell Jerry: How does the news media work to define "critical race theory" to the general public?

Harry Allen: It affects it by being confusing, unclear. One of the things that the media has done well. For the most part, the news media does not fact check the use of the term "critical race theory." The term is typically used by activists on the right, screaming out of control, parents screaming or holding up signs. The media does not interject by saying critical race theory is the scholarly study of how racism affects law, which it seems given the reality of racism, the reality of law and the reality of scholarship would be a reasonable pursuit and certainly not a subject over which to pull one's hair or melt into a puddle of tears.

However, when one understands that "critical race theory" in the common mind, especially the common white mind, typically means talking about racism and talking about who to blame for racism. Whom to hold responsible for racism, that's what it means in my impression when most white people generally use the term, and when many Black people use the term and speak about it as something they are against. Then it becomes the basis of hysteria. It's a stereotype the news media hasn't done much to reverse or dissuade.

I think I'm just aware of it less because I'm watching a lot less TV these days. I find the projects on developing far more engaging than almost any television show. I did finish watching *Hannah*. All right. Now I'm watching *The Expanse*, a TV show I absolutely adore, I came across the very first edition of the *Charlie Rose* show.

Even though he's been disgraced, his shows are often there and they're often pretty good. And I had never seen the very first one. I turned it on, and I was surprised to see that the very first guest on the *Charlie Rose* show was a professor from City University of New York named Leonard Jeffries. The show was broadcast in the early 90s, late 80s. I don't remember. He had come under criticism for making statements about Jewish people in the context of a debate about a subject called the curriculum of inclusion.

I had forgotten. The curriculum of inclusion was an effort by the New York State Board of Regents to formalize the inclusion of historical information about non-white peoples in New York City schools. There would be more Black history, more Asian history, more Latino history, et cetera, in the school curriculums. Notoriously, this provoked the responses that we now see from parents over "critical race theory." Then it hit me. "Critical race theory" is just another form of the curriculum of inclusion, but the curriculum of inclusion is just another form of the Kerner Commission Report.

That document discussed racism in American society in the 1960s. Lyndon B. Johnson commissioned a group to study the causes of riots in America in the 1960s. They came back with two words—white racism, and they began to talk about how to remediate it. They wouldn't release the report, and Johnson would not sign off on it. But the Kerner Commission report was just another version of Reconstruction for the historical fact of it. I would add the fact that most Americans, even most Black Americans, who study the history of the United States, do not know that there was a period immediately after slavery during which black people prospered and rose to great heights politically.

This period lasted around a decade or a little more. It's never taught in schools. It's invisible. It's not even part of how we discuss the history of the world. And this period of prosperity was suppressed by a white response, primarily through violence and the Ku Klux Klan. But Reconstruction was just another version of Special Field Order Number Fifteen. General William Tecumseh Sherman and others had put forward the order as a remedy for the effects of slavery. Hundreds of thousands of acres of coastal property in southeast New York would be taken away from white slave owners and given to their former slaves to inhabit and develop.

The idea was that each free slave would get 40 acres. Now, they say 40 acres and a mule. The mule gets added later. But 40 acres was an idea that Sherman put forward. There was motion and some development behind it until Abraham Lincoln was assassinated and Andrew Johnson became president. Johnson immediately squashed all that Lincoln did—the entire proposal. "Critical race theory" is just the manifestation of the next otherwise-to-be-named phenomenon that will crop up in a decade or two that will represent white hostility and resentment to adjusting the effects of racism.

Whenever non-white people attempt to address the effects of racism and start to turn the gears of the mechanics behind it, white people howl. And they howl because on some basic, fundamental level they don't usually address, they understand that this thing is rigged in their favor, like that Chris Rock joke: *There's not a white person in the room who would trade places with me, and I'm rich.*

"Critical race theory" is a camera. A shivering, shimmering hologram, a refraction through time of previous phenomena. I say "critical race theory" not in terms of its actual content but in terms of this phantasm that's been sprung upon people that provokes hours of entertainment, screaming and howling as non-white people continue to suffer. Yes, there's debilitation under white supremacy.

Danian Darrell Jerry: Whenever the news media mentions critical race theory, I never hear them mention Kimberlé Crenshaw or Derrick Bell or Kendall Thomas.

Harry Allen: You may every now and then, but you don't see enough of it. You don't see it systematically. You don't see a fact check in real time. In this regard, the media has let this one go and built it because it's a great story. It bleeds and thus leads. At every instance, every time the term "critical race theory" is used, they should say what it is and say these people are outraged because they don't want racism to come home.

The media's role is to tell the truth, right? I don't mean all of it, like *The Bachelor* is a part of media, but its job is not to tell the truth. I'm talking about news and journalism primarily, when I say media assassin. I'm talking about the news: the papers, the shows, the programs. Their job is to filter that nonsense. The people fighting "critical race theory" are being irrational. If they had been handled that way, you'd see a lot less of this. There should be more about the historical basis, which I've tried to allude to in my comments, and more about why this is happening now.

It's happening in an axial kind of perpendicular way. It's happening for the same reason that more white men are killing themselves than ever. Has this rise in suicide among white men been seen before in history? There are fears about America becoming overwhelmingly non-white, which is going to happen in our lifetimes or certainly in the lifetimes of our children. Those kinds of things have more to do with the outrage over "critical race theory" than the actual legal discipline.

Danian Darrell Jerry: Who gains when the news media let's it go and fails to fact check?

Harry Allen: The news media is not separate from the history of racism in America. It's not isolated or sitting by itself on some distant planet observing us. It's part of the current, so addressing racism honestly, would itself endanger the news media because it is part of the process. The news media is part and parcel of the entire confluence around race and history in the United States. Radiating from there are all the advertisers, all the people who buy from those advertisers. They aren't unrelated to this story.

There is a white supremacy power system. There is no one with power who is not like or related in some way to the story of how race gets told. No one related to the power system is going to say, yeah go ahead. Tell them everything.

Danian Darrell Jerry: The benefits can also inspire an individual, or an individual's participation within the power system.

Harry Allen: White supremacy is an extremely efficient political system. It spins off benefits rapidly, easily, and accurately. It's very easy if you're white to get something out of it, so everyone who is white has to tighten up the sphincter a bit when the subject goes to race because the spotlight might hit one of them at any minute.

Danian Darrell Jerry: That's why Kimberlé Crenshaw applies "critical race theory" like a verb. The laws that govern us are created by individuals who profit from oppression. For that reason alone, the institutions and the laws that affect our daily lens warrant analysis through the lens of race.

Harry Allen: That's why it's called a scholarly study of how racism affects law.

Chapter 12: Don't Believe the Right 141

Danian Darrell Jerry: How does the news media act in order to control the narrative, the information we consume?

Harry Allen: News media controls the narrative through its presence, through repetition, through contextual framing, and illustrating. I always ask people looking at a news broadcast to observe every shot change. What does the shot have to do with the story being told? If they say, burglars broke into the store, is the shot showing that burglars broke into the store? If not, why is it there, right?

The news media is always teaching, conveying, telling us things in often subtle, even invisible ways. In college, I majored in communications at Adelphi, and that meant hands-on media production: radio, television, film—how to load cameras, shoot video, et cetera. I remember reading or hearing that once you learn how a cut is made, you never look at the world the same. Most people have no idea how a cut is made or that a cut even took place. It's the visual language we understand, but we don't think about. Media is a sophisticated tool made for people who are not sophisticated about media. When you're not sophisticated about the tool that someone is using to affect you, you're going to be affected beyond your control.

But media doesn't talk enough about media. The story you'll never see on CNN is how the news media supports racism, or reinforces white supremacy. You will never see an explosive nine-part story about that.

Danian Darrell Jerry: So the whole framework is presented in a way that uses perception to manipulate the consumer.

Harry Allen: Whiteness is framed in a way that feels normal and natural. We're not encouraged to see it as aberrant. We're encouraged to see whiteness as the way things should be.

Danian Darrell Jerry: Now, as a student of hip-hop culture, I want to ask, *How has the news media defined and shaped public perception of hip-hop?*

Harry Allen: To a great extent, hip-hop parallels the treatment of "critical race theory." This is not surprising, because both have to do with relationships to race. Hip-hop is currently in a place where there are people with children who grew up on it, who grew up with it. As you mentioned in my bio, it's been nearly two decades since I was at *Rockstar Games*, and I remember the alarm over video games at that time for any number of things that still go on but do not provoke alarm any longer.

Race is always alarming. That's the difference. If you're a Black person at a party or you're at dinner with a lot of white friends talking about any subject. At a moment in the conversation, you say, *What does racism have to do with that?* The conversation will stop at least long enough for people to deflect because race is always a new conversation. Every white generation will think in one way or another that they've solved the dilemma. They will bear children who are not going to converse about racism, even as it persists.

Hip-hop once provoked similar outrage. There was a period of time I remember very well. The word "rap" in the news media was always followed by the word "violence." *Rap violence* meant there was a concert and someone started shooting. It seemed like there was never any reporting about rap music unless there was shooting involved. What you heard was the association of hip-hop with violence, hip-hop labeled as the favorite music of people who were violent or deprived, despondents looking for camaraderie through gang affiliations. But that's shifted, especially as hip-hop has become more mainstream, which means more white people involved. The discussion of racism doesn't get that kind of reprieve. It's new every day.

I've long said, *Ask someone to write all the adjectives to describe hip-hop*—loud, aggressive, edgy, noisy. *Then ask them to describe Black males*—loud, aggressive, edgy, noisy. You would see an identical lump, an identical bell curve of adjectives.

Danian Darrell Jerry: The misrepresentation of Black people, the depiction defined by the music they create. All of which are demonized in order to perpetuate subjugation. Then the same people and their voices are demonized for existing in the state of subjugation.

Harry Allen: Correct, I see them as kind of part and parcel. I don't see it as odd that the creations, even the abstract creations of mistreated people, would also be mistreated—or mistreated until they were deemed safe.

But deemed unsafe at first, like unsafe at first. Like. And then over time, checked. Ok, this is safe.

Danian Darrell Jerry: Yet I've never seen a news report that says Sony or Universal or any other record corporation that sells music. Violence in hip-hop is funded by and through corporate America. Being a rapper on a major record label is equivalent to having a job. In order to work for the corporation, the rappers have to do and say certain things and display particular kinds of behavior. I've never seen an exposé that focuses on the connections between corporate America and the street-level violence disseminated in rap music or hip-hop culture.

Harry Allen: Or I would say you'd be hard pressed to see an analysis of either A, the musicological brilliance of hip-hop, or B, how that brilliance is constricted and constrained by white supremacy.

How white supremacy works to keep that brilliance subject to itself, like these are not appropriate subjects for news pieces. Subjects about how white supremacy works as a system are not appropriate for news pieces.

Chapter 12: Don't Believe the Right

That's too close to where the lemons get squeezed. I wouldn't even put it in terms of corporations. I would say corporations are just another way of talking about racism—a synonym for racism.

Danian Darrell Jerry: Yes. Especially like in today's times, corporate America has become a bastion of racism. When you think about allocation and access to resources. I've never thought about it like that, but I have felt these sentiments on an unconscious level.

Harry Allen: I hear that a lot. People, I felt it, but I hadn't put it like that. For example, you hear a lot about institutional racism. Which is another term I do not use. Because an institution just means tools, right? A corporation, a 501C3, a stapler, windows and desks, doors, a fax machine, maybe a computer, file. An institution to me is white people and their tools. Tools can't be racist, right? So the talk about institutional racism puts an unnecessary layer of complication on a critical kind of analysis.

I think that's what you're leaning towards when you say corporations, because corporations are institutions, right? Usually, people say "institutional racism" when they mean to show how non-profit organizations, NGOs, other kinds of corporate assemblages, even for-profit organizations, judicial systems, and municipalities can be racist. A building cannot be racist. A letter of incorporation cannot be racist. A doorknob cannot be racist, even though you have all those things in an institution. People can be racist. So what we're really talking about is racist people and their tools. But that's the same stuff anyway, right? If the Ku Klux Klan is not institutional racism, then why would anything else be?

Danian Darrell Jerry: We talked about the news media. We talked about racism. Now, I'm thinking about the law, the way public policy is constructed. How does the news media affect the way laws and public policy are created?

Harry Allen: News media serves as a megaphone. No one likes unpopular laws, especially the people who make them. They want laws to be popular because they want to keep making them. News media helps make certain laws popular and certain laws unpopular. The media can frame a subject. Using all its tools, it can show people how to think about this thing. It can even tell people if we should be thinking about this thing. There are lots of laws, lots of policies that are made that the news media doesn't talk about—the overwhelming majority of them, in fact.

Later, you find your city council had a session where they voted to throw aluminum and sulfates in the lake. No one knew about it because it was done in a secret session at night. Now corporations can go to our beautiful lake and drop chloride, and it's legal, and the media said nothing. The media might have stayed silent because someone actively said, "I don't want this covered." They could have been focused on other things. They could say that we can't cover every single thing. Either by pointing at something they think should be heralded and praised or something they don't think should be heralded and praised, the news media can influence the consensus around an issue. For example, name the two young people who were killed around the time of George Floyd, the young man who was shot when he was jogging.

Danian Darrell Jerry: Ahmaud Arbery . . .

Harry Allen: And the young lady who was in her home.

Danian Darrell Jerry: Breonna Taylor . . .

Harry Allen: When Ahmaud Arbery and Breonna Taylor were killed, if you read the early reports, the issue was lack of coverage. There was no relevant coverage of these killings. I remember the dominant cry from those fighting on Ahmaud and Breonna's behalf. *We need to make people aware of these issues.* When the news media turned its spotlight on, these killings began to get noticed. One could say they did it soon, or not enough, or if they should have kept the spotlight on. That's up for discussion, but without news media, these stories were going a certain way. Then with lots of people talking about the crimes and focusing on them, other things began to happen.

Media as it pertains to policy, to law can illuminate. It can discuss the people signing these laws and ask them questions. Consumers of news media can get a sense of their lawmakers. Are they sober minded? Do they have my goodwill at heart? Where can you go? Who can you write? Whose home can you march on in protest? Media brings us useful information, because ideally, at least in concept, it tells us what's true, and truth is vital for any correct action. Truth is the beginning of doing. Is this true? That's the first question anyone should ask. If somebody calls you a name, the first thing you should ask is, Is this true? Yes, the news media can make that task simple or not. And the chief issue that the news media ignores is the issue of the media. It essentially, relentlessly ignores the issue of itself.

Danian Darrell Jerry: How can we as consumers hold the news media responsible for the images it depicts and for the messages that it sends—like, what can I do? How can I increase control over the information presented to me by the news media?

Harry Allen: First thing is deciding to do so. You asked me how I became a media assassin, and I said I decided to name myself. No one gave me this name. I came up with it. I wanted to work, talk, and act in a certain manner. The same way that people can decide against being fed indiscriminately. You can learn about the people who write and produce stories. You can learn how news media works. You can study it in a college classroom or read books like Manufacturing Consent and others that explain how news media works. You can write letters contradicting or complaining—in a way that's not noisome or sibilant but that's calm, effective and fact based—about things that you read and find displeasing. You can protest. There's a term used a lot these days called "cancel culture." People used to call it boycotting. If you don't like the way news media handles the stories in your community, just wait till the commercials come on, and write down the names of the companies that run the advertisements. Contact those companies, and tell them you are dissatisfied with their actions.

All news media has advertisers. That's just the way commercial media is set up in this part of the world and in most. Start talking to them. Say, we're not going to buy your products as long as your company continues to sponsor this news program. There are ways you can become the news media yourself. We live in a world where it's a lot easier to both write and tweet. So much of the media these days is built on carrying camera phones and holding them vertically instead of turning them horizontally, which is how TVs are shaped, and shooting video. One of the most important stories of the twenty-first century, the murder of George Floyd, was captured by a young woman who used her cell phone camera to record his strangulation. She refused to turn it off or move it and her relentlessness to hold that camera, her tenacity changed the narrative. Without that video, it would have been a different kind of story. We might have never heard of George Floyd.

We can critique media. We can understand media, and we can be media. We can watch media that serves our interests and tune out media that doesn't because it works by ratings, by how many people are watching. Streaming and those kinds of technologies enable us to count very closely when news programs are being watched and when they're not being watched. Before it was just a guess. Now, I can tell when you turned on MSNBC and when you turned it off. It's very accurate, very easy to see the effectiveness of the news media. We can respond accordingly. Be media. Critique media. Watch media you support, and protest media you don't like. You can do one or two things that fit your temperament. This is all based on thinking about what you're seeing and reading and not consuming just because it's on TV or in the paper.

Danian Darrell Jerry: Thank you, Mr. Allen. That's a good place to leave our audience, with a call to action.

Harry Allen: Support news media that serves our interests, especially little media. There are lots of little shows and blogs. There are people who tweet, who are committed to getting information out like. Yeah. It might be micro but that's a form of media.

People on Tik Tok are trying to get concrete information out in a multitude of areas. This is not just people dancing all the time or telling jokes. These people are trying to get information out. There's one, there's one sister who just covers racism. I don't remember her name, but she covers racist things that she's read about or seen. There's another very funny Tik Toker that has a wild way of covering animal life and nature, but he has an incredible way of writing that I love. That's media. It's micro, but it's media all the same, and it's increasingly being covered by the mainstream.

Danian Darrell Jerry: So the same tools that have allowed hip-hop artists to establish their independence and autonomy can be used to counter the news media.

Harry Allen: Black people are really good at finding those funny little crevices, those spaces that aren't being filled. We can thrive in those smaller places because we're often kept out of the seats of power. We know how to look around and hack. We find new names and identify ourselves with Twitter handles to put out information with lots of critique and a little bit of snark. The same way that hip-hop used tools the wrong way in order to make the music we wanted, we found another way to get at this thing. That kind of hacking is consistent across hip-hop and various kinds of mediation that we see in today's world.

CHAPTER 13

The Lion Man Project: Creating Critical Comics as Counterstorying

Michael B. Dando, John Jennings, and David Brame

INTRODUCTION

Speculative storytelling has always been directly connected to hip-hop and comics—whether it was Ice Cube envisioning "a good day," MF DOOM taking up the iconic mask, or Milestone envisioning a universe of Black superheroes, creating visions of what might, could, and should have been a way of life. As KRS One rightly observed, it is "something you live." In addition to being unassailably cool, or *illmatic* as NAS puts it, these forms of storying are necessarily educative. These cultural exchanges have the capacity to encode, decode, and recode ways of thinking, knowing, and being. Young people have opportunities daily to hear, tell, and create stories. Perhaps, in no other place is this more possible than in the classroom. Learning communities, either passively or actively, are generating, legitimizing, and stigmatizing particular stories and supporting some ways of life as viable "funds of knowledge" while invalidating or otherwise erasing other ways, particularly those of BIPOC (Black, Indigenous, and people of color) communities. But what if there was a space where students could re-story? What if there was an agentic space for them to create forms of self-expression that spoke back to the grand narratives presented to them daily? What would such a space look like? And what might it take to realize it?

This essay chronicles the development and implementation of an 8-week after-school design space that invited students to imagine, create, draft, and produce speculative Afrofuturist artifacts and graphic narratives and share them with their wider community. Ultimately, this article examines how comics can be enacted as a promoter of critical multimodal literacy development, self-actualization, and democratic engagement.

To situate this article, I rely on the following questions. To what extent can speculative fiction through comics serve as a space for critical multimodal literacy development and democratic engagement? How can participants use speculative fiction and design through comics as a counter-storytelling method? That is, how can comic narratives conceived, generated, and produced by young people who occupy particular historic, sociocultural, and political spaces serve as an illmatic clapback to dominant and oppressive ways of thinking, knowing, and being?

When we ask students to write about themselves or their communities, we are asking them to be vulnerable. We are asking them to examine the world in which they live, break down their protective walls, and expose themselves to the feelings that result from the broken barriers. Therefore, when we ask students to write, we are asking them to be courageous enough to share their truths with us, despite the intense level of openness required to do so. Yet even though it requires students to be vulnerable, "writing enables them to name problems they face, to show adults assets where we might see deficits, and to reframe who they are" (Burke & Greene, 2015, p. 393). That is, by being vulnerable while writing, students can speak back to confining narratives, and they can prompt educators to reimagine the ways they view students and the communities in which they live.

The ability to change requires the capacity to imagine. As Robin Kelley (2002) noted, "Freedom must begin in the mind." Likewise, hooks (2000) argued that "to be truly visionary we have to root our imagination in our concrete reality while simultaneously imagining possibilities beyond that reality" (p. 110). What this means is that to realize meaningful change, people must engage in imaginative processes that are grounded in, but not confined by, current social, political, and tangible realities. Speculative fiction and comic books invite and indeed encourage this form of imagination as they ask audiences to consider themselves in their current reality while also dreaming of realities yet to be. This radical imagining of possibilities and this dreaming forward lie at the very heart of speculative fiction and the medium of comics. New lives and civilizations as well as new ideas and possibilities are born every day and very often within the classroom, a space that hooks called "the most radical space of possibility" (p. 12).

Chapter 13: The Lion Man Project 149

Educators have the opportunity to effect social change by collaborating with students to build different futures—Octavia Butler's proverbial "new suns." And the comics in the classroom invite us to consider them, but some critical questions must be taken up before doing so. It's here that critical race theory (CRT) offers a robust analytic framework for doing so. What are today's young people dreaming about? What obstacles do they face? Perhaps more important, what are they fighting for? Comics and graphic novels can take up these questions in meaningful ways that embrace the un-possible, and can offer a clapback to limited, oppressive conceptions of literacy, thinking, knowing, and being by explicitly centering stories of and by people who are not frequently centered in a medium dominated by cis-gendered, straight, white, male writers, artists, and characters.

Using comics in the classroom is hardly a new strategy. As far back as the 1930s and Classics Illustrated, teachers were trying to use comics to teach the so-called classics, like *Frankenstein*, *Macbeth*, and *The Three Musketeers*. To this day, school libraries are awash with comics from every content area, from how volcanoes work to phonemes trying desperately to capture student attention and disseminate information. High-interest texts have been used as reading interventions for students in language arts classrooms to get students interested in reading or literature, but this has led to a grave tactical and pedagogic error: These interventions forgot to consider their audience. They neglected the very real wants, needs, desires, and concerns of the very people they were trying to teach, in favor of a perhaps well-intentioned but woefully misguided effort to repackage and repurpose dominant understandings of knowledge construction and literacy, which as the research has demonstrated are steeped in white supremacy.

As Kress and the rest of the New London Group argue (Cazden et al., 1996), *how* we communicate has changed and our response as educators must be to change our thinking about texts and literacies in our pedagogies rather than to see other modes as hindrances, gimmicks, or intermediate steps to the command of the printed page. Therefore, how people are (re)presented and by whom becomes an issue of the utmost importance. Knowledge and understandings of self and society are mediated through these semiotic moments, and this is especially true for popular cultural forms.

I center these questions not to generalize but to examine the possibilities of speculative fiction for young people, particularly those in BIPOC communities, which are too often marginalized or neglected in formal educational spaces. I begin this analysis by examining multimodal storytelling as a form of counter-storytelling through narrative and artifact construction. I follow this story with a researcher-constructed narrative of participants' words and artifacts, connecting her speculative story to their personal stories. In closing, I analyze each narrative through the lens of critical multimodal storytelling, highlighting how students use speculative narrative acts as a counterstory.

COMICS, COUNTERNARRATIVE, AND CRT

CRT recognizes the legitimacy of experiential and embodied knowledge and maintains that the voices and stories of people of color are vital to comprehending, analyzing, and educating about racial injustice (Anderson, 2015; Chambliss & Greason, 2016; Delgado & Stefancic, 2001; Ladson-Billings & Tate, 1995; Martinez, 2013; Solórzano & Yosso, 2002a, 2002b). The desire to examine the lived experiences of historically marginalized communities led CRT scholars to focus on and develop the practice of counter-storytelling (Miller et al., 2020), a method that allows people of color to describe their reality. CRT holds that because of their different histories and experiences with oppression, Black, American Indian, Asian, and Latino/a writers and thinkers may be able to communicate to their white counterparts about matters that the whites are unlikely to know (Delgado & Stefancic, 2001).

While "counternarrative" and "counterstory" have often been used interchangeably (Rodela & Rodriguez-Mojica, 2020), it is important to make a distinction between a counterstory (told by someone) and the broader idea of a counternarrative (told about something) here. As a white researcher, I can use my researcher positionality to support a broader counternarrative methodology of the communities I work with, namely by telling their stories in contrast to the racialized, dominant stories told about them—but educators of color must lead that work in telling those stories. It is their counterstories that must drive it. Those individual counterstories include all that we think of as storytelling "allegories, chronicles, parables, dialogues, other fictional forms" (Delgado, 1989, p. 2438). Those stories are purposefully told in contrast to majoritarian narratives, and in the field of education, they have been used by a variety of scholars across a variety of educational settings.

These stories challenge the discourse of students of color being "at risk" or in need of remediation, positioning them instead as informed learners and agentic in the face of institutional and cultural racism. CRT work in education also uses these stories to counter majoritarian narratives which have been used in specific ways against particular racial groups. A counternarrative specifically disrupts majoritarian narratives that perpetuate myths of meritocracy for white people and victim blaming and deficit arguments for people of color. "Majoritarian stories function as master narratives and re-inscribe the myths of meritocracy and colorblindness, purport neutrality and commonsense, and invoke stereotypes that vitiate people of color as dim, criminal, and depraved and exalt whites as intelligent, lawful, and moral" (Aleman, 2017, p. 75).

Naming one's truth is essential as it can elucidate the constructed nature of social reality, catalyze social change by challenging oppressors' mindsets, and create space for people of color to heal (Ladson-Billings & Tate, 1995). In this way, counterstories uplift the narratives of minoritized people while also challenging dominant narratives, providing windows into new realities that allow readers to envision possibilities for a world beyond the one in which they currently live (Delgado, 1989). There are at least three counter-storytelling formats:

1. Autobiographical narratives, which describe an individual's experiences
2. Biographical stories, which relate another person's experiences
3. Composite narratives, which combine various data to create characters and situations that describe how racialized others experience oppression (Solórzano & Yosso, 2002b; Yosso, 2005)

Ladson-Billings and Tate (1995) also outline the numerous formats of counter-storytelling, contending that critical race scholars use "parables, chronicles, stories, counterstories, poetry, fiction, and revisionist histories to illustrate the false necessity and irony of much of current civil rights doctrine" (p. 57). Thus, counterstories are not solely limited to realistic narratives. Acknowledging the various counter-storytelling formats, some CRT scholars have used allegory, an extended metaphor "in which the entire narrative introduces and elaborates upon a metaphorical source domain to evoke larger than life themes" (Gibbs, 2011, p. 49). Allegory enables writers to create metaphorical renderings of real situations and engage readers in a thought experiment that asks them to transfer their ideas about stories to events in the real world. Bell (1987) argued that allegory offers a way to explore real situations and remove the distortion of jargon. Delgado (1995) offered that allegorical storytelling can challenge reality, construct a counter-reality, and dismantle dominant narratives. In addition, Martinez (2013) argued that allegory is "a trope by which to render invisible forms of racism (structural or colorblind), visible" (p. 2). Essentially, allegory is a storying method that allows the author to transform the realistic world into a fantastic tale, and CRT scholars have used this method to create counterstories that can make visible the stories of marginalized people and communities.

The rhetorical practice of call-and-response is a dialogic exercise between a speaker and a listener that is deeply rooted in the Black church, in which "all of the speaker's statements ('calls') are punctuated by expressions ('responses') from the listener" (Smitherman, 1977, p. 104). The focus on both situates call-and-response as a shared event that requires the participation of the community and an agreement that everyone will perform. Boone (2003) and Richards-Greaves (2016) noted that call-and-response is often associated with the Black church, where a preacher will ask for a specific response from the audience. Boone argues that the literacy practice of call-and-response can occur anywhere in the Black community if there is a speaker and an audience. It can occur in a conversation among friends and family, in an academic presentation, in a secondary classroom, or in the pages of a comic book or graphic novel, not only to produce knowledge but also to construct truth and provide "counterknowledge" (Dillard, 2000).

WHY AFROFUTURISM?

As Kelley (2002) notes,

> Progressive social movements do not simply produce statistics and narratives of oppression; rather, the best ones do what great poetry always does: transport us to another place, compel us to relive horrors and, more importantly, enable us to imagine a new society.

This is in keeping with the very questions Mark Dery (1994) posed when coining the term "Afrofuturism" in "Black to the Future." Indeed comics, particularly the Milestone imprint, were an integral part of that article, demonstrating the social and political import of the medium and the movement.

Afrofuturism involves evaluating the past, the present, and the future through literature, music, technology, and the arts; it allows us to envision a world with just conditions for Black people—a world that does not violently oppress Black communities—and invites us to imagine and dream of a better future. Afrofuturism is a complete re-envisioning of the past using combinations of elements of magic realism, Afrocentricity, fantasy, speculative fiction, historical fiction, science fiction, and non-Western beliefs to speculate about the future. It is more than just conceptualizing the world using the power of fiction and fantasy but is rooted in challenging the existence of our present world. It requires the imagining and telling of stories from a particular perspective that eschews the white gaze in favor of a particular counterfuture.

Afrofuturism invites subaltern communities to realize a new universe of possibilities—a world in which we can use our creativity and ideas to create a more balanced and equitable future with the ability to think and innovate more freely. Afrofuturism is a way of telling stories that creates a greater and better world than the one that exists. The high-tech, utopian world in *Black Panther* shows us the possibilities that exist in a society where Black men and women protect their history and embrace their advancement. As Nelson (2002) notes, "They excavate and create original narratives of identity, technology, and the future and offer critiques of the promises of prevailing theories of technoculture" (p. 9).

From *Black Panther* to George Clinton, to a period room in the Met, Afrofuturism writ large on the public square invites communities to invest in their futures, create opportunities for youth engagement, and make active efforts to create a lasting, meaningful presence in fields such as arts and STEM. Contemporary challenges perhaps make it difficult to retain that futuristic vision where everything and anything is possible, but this focus is an essential aspect of equity, liberation, and the destruction of oppressive and violent power structures. These stories and worldviews invite us to the future, and to plan a way to get there. Embracing Afrofuturism is one step forward on this journey. Indeed, as Butler points out, "I was attracted to science fiction because it was so wide open. I was able to do anything and there were no walls to hem you in and there was no human condition that you were stopped from examining."

WHY COMICS?

As Butler again points out, "There is nothing new under the sun, but there are new suns." If people are to create other ways of being, they must create new stories, which requires imagining that which does not yet exist. This itself is a radical and generative act because in the dreaming, there also lies creation. And human beings read the world through the stories they tell. These stories are often told in myriad formats. Still, there is scant research on how Black girls engage in alternate methods of storytelling. One striking example is Dyson's (1995) study of how Tina, a Black girl in the third grade, used superhero-centered fiction, specifically the *X-Men*, to alter the constructed world and the constructed self.

Comics provide a speculative avenue to explorations of self, identity, culture, and belonging in a way that no other medium can offer. Not only do comic books invite audiences with a wide range of reading proficiencies, but they also require multimodal engagement, visual rhetorical literacy engagement, and an innate constructivist framework wherein the learner pieces together information in a variety of cognitive domains to create a cohesive, coherent, and cogent experience.

THE LION MAN TEAM

Michael Dando is an educational researcher who focuses on critical multimodal literacy development through popular culture, specifically hip-hop and comics. A former high school language arts teacher, he has examined how students develop abilities to question and critique social, political, and cultural structures and mobilize their talents to engage in community upliftment and democratic engagement. Jennings and Brame are an artistic collaboration known as The Blackatz. I had worked with John on a previous project (Holbert et al., 2020) and was aware of his love for and scholarship with speculative fiction and comics as a medium. John had worked with David on a previous project for Abrams's Megascope imprint titled *Black Rain*, and he immediately recommended him for this project.

All of us hold terminal degrees in education or art and have taught at the collegiate and/or secondary level. This gave us perspectives, insight, and training regarding visual rhetoric, design, aesthetics, and critical approaches to education. John and David identify as African American and male and have been among the 3% of Black males in higher education (National Center for Education Statistics, 2018). These two artist-scholars brought their considerable talents to bear on the production of, critically oriented social justice comics. Their work, such as the critically acclaimed adaptation of Nnedi Okorafor's *After the Rain*, clearly proves that they love comics and Black folks at the same time.

But most of all, we love comics and know well the formative power the medium holds for communities and individuals in navigating identity and encoding, decoding, and contesting messages of race, gender, ability, class, and more. Cosmologies, epistemologies, and ontologies all lie within and among the margins of the comic page. Ways of thinking, knowing, and being are bound up in the ink and newsprint, which possess the ability to influence global culture and even reach across time and space. In many ways, democracy may depend on a good comic.

While our individual cultures and backgrounds of origin varied, our commonality lay in the centrality of the BIPOC youth experience to the project. This required that we make explicit choices throughout the project to position participants as the authority on their own experiences. In other words, while we were well versed in comics, we were what participants called "oldheads," a hip-hop phrase meaning a member of a respected, kindred but outdated generation. We had to make room for the new while embracing that which came before—that is, we had to *Sankofacise* the space. To that end, during the series, we invited local BIPOC comics artists and creatives into the space and facilitated a co-constructed generative conversation around representations of BIPOC communities in popular media. We particularly wanted to showcase how these artists and storytellers challenge these often negative representations in their work.

ENVISIONING SPECULATIVE ANCHOR TEXTS

In our creative team's discussions about comics and stories we wish existed, Jennings brought up Lion Man, a character from 1947, produced by *All-Negro Comics* (ANC). Published in 1947, *ANC* was a single-issue, small-press anthology comic that was the first known comics magazine written and drawn solely by African American writers and artists. Publisher Orrin C. Evans, noted in the issue's opening pages,

> Every brush stroke and pen line in the drawings are by Negro artists. And each drawing is an original: that is, none has been published ANYWHERE before. This publication is another milestone in the splendid history of Negro journalism.

The 8-page Lion Man story featured an American-born, college-educated, and yet un-named Lion Man, a young scientist sent by the United Nations to watch over the fearsome Magic Mountain of the African Gold Coast. Within its crater lies the world's largest deposit of uranium, enough to make an atom bomb that could destroy the world. Lion Man's mission is to report on the doings of any treacherous nation that might attempt to steal any of the lethal element for nefarious purposes. Sadly, the first issue of *ANC* was also its last. Nonetheless, Lion Man stands as the first Black superhero.

Drawing inspiration from the 1947 iteration of Lion Man, we created a Speculative Anchor Text (SAT) as a common reading experience. The creative team brought back Lion Man (Figure 1), and this time it would be a full story. This incarnation of Lion Man, written and colored by Jennings and penciled and inked by Brame, was influenced by the 1990s' *DC Vertigo* and focused on a hero who defended children from nightmare demons. The story itself is intentionally tied to dreams, identity, and agency across space, time, and culture.

Figure 13.1 Interior pages of "Lion Man #1" (2021) by Jennings, Dando, and Brame.

We created the SAT to invite students to draw from a shared aesthetic and narrative experience while still bringing their own backgrounds, thoughts, and ideas to bear on interpretations, close readings, and other literacy practices as well as to provide a shared resource with which to develop and articulate critical positions regarding representation, (counter)storytelling, and self-actualization. It was with this in mind that we set out on bringing new-old stories—what Brooks et al. (2016) call "sankofarration" (p. 2), that is, stories that look back and forward simultaneously—into formal educative spaces to serve as a clapback to oppressive forms of teaching and learning.

There has been a long history of comics and graphic novels being used in classrooms as an intervention toward myriad curricular aims from stoichiometry to phonics, to reading comprehension. More recently, race and representation have been meaningfully and beautifully explored in works such as Wanzo (2020) and Black women in sequence by Whaley (2015), but these are not as related to education. There have also been books that have taken up teaching the art of reading, analyzing, and producing comics, such as the foundational *Understanding Comics* (McCloud, 1994), as well as several books and resources for classroom practice. There has also been recent emergent research on engaging students in more critical ways through comics but little on how understandings of race are mediated by young people through comics or how opportunities to construct graphic narratives of and on their own might provide avenues for self-expression, cultural identity construction, and political resistance. Despite the apparent popularity of using comics in the classroom, we have become increasingly dissatisfied with what appears to be a static conception of what it means to "teach comics."

THE LION MAN PROJECT: ADVENTURES IN SPECULATIVE (COUNTER)STORYING

The perfect opportunity to grow, change, and expand understandings of storying through comics, race, and education came when we began work on The Lion Man Project with a grant provided through the Center for Excellence in Teaching and Learning's Miller Scholar Award at St. Cloud State University, Minnesota. The grant was designed to enhance student learning, and we recognized that there was a fundamental disconnect between how comics were predominantly being used in the classroom (for remediation) and their sociocultural and political potential. Given our own interests and the seeming ubiquity of superheroes in the public square, we homed in on issues of critical multimodal literacy development and BIPOC youth identity formation through comics creation. What are(n't) comics talking about? Whose communities are(n't) represented, and how? What do they identify as their community and individual assets,

Chapter 13: The Lion Man Project   157

their social challenges, and their capacity to communicate their dreams and desires for the future?

To that end, we collaborated with four local, middle school art classes for the first iteration of this project. The classes met each day for 45 minutes and were taught by Jack, another veteran teacher with a masters in fine arts, who also shared a love of comics, art, and education. Approximately 90 students agreed to participate. The students collectively read a custom-

Figure 13.2 "Lion Man #1" (2021) by Jennings, Dando, and Brame. This served as the speculative anchor text for the experience.

made comic (Figure 2), analyzed it collectively, and engaged in the creation of their own speculative comic artifacts (Figure 3). The participants reported that prior to this workshop their experience with comics or graphic arts in school had been primarily as a lesser form of reading or as a stepping stone toward some other concept or content. Many indicated that they hadn't thought of comics as literature before. Furthermore, they indicated that most of the time their interests, backgrounds, or cultures were not regularly incorporated into their classes except for an example for a particular content area. To forge a more relevant and meaningful experience for the students, we constructed a workshop-style experience, drawing from tenets of culturally relevant pedagogy (Ladson-Billings, 2002), attending to academic excellence, foregrounding cultural competencies, and developing reflective practices and critical consciousness throughout.

Figure 13.3 Participant artifacts (left to right: Mina, Amira, Sierrra, and Dani).

Although the students depended on us to be the so-called experts in the room, we also depended on them to construct new ways of thinking about and understanding how these comics and aesthetics might be critically deployed to engage in conversations about critical concepts and constructs such as truth, justice, belonging, and others. We also depended on them to collaborate to realize new pedagogic strategies. For example, when we asked students about initial designs, they eagerly responded and engaged us in diverse social issues almost immediately.

Effective constructivist spaces are inherently inspirational. To imagine and subsequently create a space that would inspire the imagination of possible futures that center people of color, we filled the space with the images and work of Black storytellers and artists, African textiles, and ancient African symbology. Likewise, we placed African sculptures, BIPOC comics–oriented toys and posters, stacks of comics written about Black superheroes (e.g., *Black Panther*, *Icon & Rocket*, and *Naomi*), as well as other resources created by Black artists throughout the room. Guest artists also brought in additional materials each week, sharing news clippings, new comics, and images they found inspirational to their own work.

During these sessions, we took photographs of design iterations and making activity, journals, and in-process as well as final artifacts. A group interview was held at the beginning and end of the project. The initial group interview invited participants to discuss where they lived as well as their experiences as young women of color living in a dense urban city. In the group interview at the end of the final session, the participants shared their completed artifact and described their definition of Afrofuturism as well as their vision for the future. We also interviewed participants individually twice during the project. In each of these interviews, we invited participants to share their works in progress, talk a bit about how they came to their ideas, and consider how their project helped them think about the probable and the possible.

While the description of the Lion Man Project offers a brief overview of the project's design, the project itself evolved throughout its enactment as participants and the project team collaboratively constructed a Critical Constructionist Design Experience. This co-construction was supported both by the explicit design choices made by the project team as well as by participants' willingness to mobilize their own experiences and values in the construction of a personally meaningful artifact. By intentionally designing the space and activities according to core constructionist principles (particularly student-centered, discovery-oriented, problem-based learning) and inviting participants to create within an Afrofuturist aesthetic, the participants were encouraged to imagine speculative stories, characters, and artifacts that connected to both their family histories as well as their present experiences as young BIPOC women. To explore the critical implications of this project, we will focus on a small cohort of four young BIPOC students (two African Americans, one Somali, one South Asian). As Geneva Smitherman (1977) noted, the creator of Black arts literature envisions himself or herself as a necromancer, a skillful manipulator of the art of shonuff black magic, whose job it is to "heal" Black folks through the evocative power of art and transform their suffering into constructive political action.

That is, Black authors often assume the role of conjuror, using literary and linguistic magic to challenge oppressors and mitigate the everyday violence enacted on Black communities by those who continuously work to fortify our oppression. To invoke an image of justice, some authors transform the real into the fantastic, grounding their stories in the imaginary because justice has not historically been, nor is it currently, defined as a social reality. In this way, some Black authors entwine their truths with make-believe, combining testimony and counterstory in the hope that readers will bear witness and join the fight for justice.

The students in this series served as conjurers, weaving personal experiences into fantastic narratives and imagery to disturb, disrupt, and ultimately to inspire people to act. Not only did they ideate, iterate, and imagine what their characters looked like, they also created backstories and an imagined world in which they lived. That took the form of other planets and Minneapolis. Wherever these stories were set, one thing was clear—the students made very particular and deliberate social, cultural, political, and creative choices. When we talked with the young women about their ideas, they said,

> "I realized that I never really see female superheroes, so I decided to make her." (Sierra)
>
> "We need a role model in the world, so I made a female because there isn't [sic] that many in the spotlight of a comic." (Amira)
>
> "There isn't much Muslim representation in comics, so I made a hijab hero. I looked up superhero outfits, and drew inspiration from there, and designed the clothes for both modesty and superhero." (Mina)

In her reflections, creation, and concluding interview, Mina explicitly detailed the U.S. legacy and her own experience of surveillance by a police state. These young women intimately connected their characters with the history of disproportionate structural and systemic violence visited on Black people and communities. By connecting these characters to the real world, they embed the realistic into the fictional.

Ultimately, Mina uses her art to comprehend and consider injustice and then contemplate avenues for radical change, all staples of the counter-storytelling framework. But it is more than just a matter of focusing on the social world. Here, Mina centers herself. Specifically, she says she put herself in the narrative to understand the character better. They both wear hijab. Just like the main character, Mina cares for others and wants the world to be a place of peace. Just like her character, she desires justice for all and wants to build with others toward collectively realized, structural changes. Mina embedded her personal and social worlds into her comic creation and, through her artifact, establishes and realizes a counterreality that makes the injustices she has experienced visible (lack of representation); she illuminates her cultures of origin, validates her repertoires of practice, and (re)affirms her individual humanity. She simultaneously invites her audience to experience what it is to see her dream and to hear her voice. In this way, her art operates as a sort of visual, diegetic counterstory, enabling her to mobilize creative, fictive means to vocalize her very real perspectives and position those experiences as a critical commentary toward resistive ends (Grifin et al., 2014).

Furthermore, Lathan (2014) argued that testimony is rooted in the Black cultural tradition "of embracing critical intellectualism as an empowering activity: thinking, reasoning, and expressing that begins by embracing oppressive ideologies while sharing about literacy customs that consciously choose an empowering response" (p. 34). The world building alongside the character demonstrates that Mina critically engages her real world, analyzing and critiquing the various injustices she has experienced and witnessed. Counterstories can occur in any genre, as Black women and girls have used numerous means to name their truths. Mina engages in affirmation and Black joy by storying herself into a speculative space of activism and social change. She engages with her community by creating a space for people to bear witness and using art for collective justice. She engages in truth telling by using a fictionalized format to highlight events and situations that occur in the real world. Her creation is both her testimony and a counterstory.

IMPLICATIONS

We encountered several emergent themes when analyzing the data from our participants.

1. Students expressing their understandings of race by making intertextual references to and from comics
2. Students critiquing authors for racial exclusion (absence and underrepresentation) in comics
3. Students responding to the content of comics to initiate conversations about socio-racial phenomena, particularly along socioeconomic lines

4. Students making connections to their own racial identities in responding to comics

These themes were all expressed through the characters, profiles, and stories the participants created. When asked what might need to change in the world/country/future, these storytellers referenced a particular desire for ecological conservation, noting particularly a need for a decrease in pollution and a need for renewable energy sources. They also indicated that there was a need for peace, safety, and reconciliation as well as a need for more public input into decisions affecting their communities. Sienna noted that we need to begin "asking the public for opinions on decisions instead of making decisions without input." Amira echoed that sentiment, saying that what was really needed to effect change was "people's perspectives on power."

These themes are explicitly reflected in their creations as we see them draw themselves into the story with personal reflections on race, gender, and other markers of self (e.g., the hijab). Furthermore, their creations had a connection with energy, nature, or a particular sociocultural issue. Multiple characters were adopted and were still discovering their powers and identities.

While these connections are perhaps barely metaphorical, they also speak directly to counternarrative. Rather than being disaffected, disinterested, distracted, and delinquent, these young women of color demonstrated that they are clear-eyed, passionate, energetic, and informed experts on their own lives. Rather than being unintelligible, vacuous, and deficient, as they have been portrayed so often, these young people were capable, critical, creative storytellers intent on conveying their perspectives. Ladson-Billings and Tate (1995) outline the numerous formats of counter-storytelling, contending that critical race scholars use "parables, chronicles, stories, counterstories, poetry, fiction, and revisionist histories to illustrate the false necessity and irony of much of current civil rights doctrine" (p. 57). Thus, counterstories are not solely limited to realistic narratives. This is because the truth of the tale is in its telling.

CONCLUSION

What state departments, school districts, and school departments and teachers call "teaching comics" is too often a distortion or corruption of central critical tenets offered by CRT and notions of storytelling and counternarrative. The idea of bringing comics into education seems, at least at the day-to-day level, to be reduced to adding some picture books about BIPOC communities, comics about stoichiometry, or comics about the War of 1812 to the curriculum, which somehow, along with the inclusion of "diverse" or "high-interest" texts, makes it culturally relevant.

While study of multimodal literacies has clearly demonstrated effective strategies to reduce inequality and critically engage students, too often it has been reduced to an "activity" that groups implement for so-called low-level or disengaged students in their educative spaces.

But as Imarisha (2015) reminds us, all organizing "is science fiction" (p. 3). And nowhere is this clearer than in the pages of comic books and doubly so when rendered by communities who are systematically excluded and organizationally marginalized from these imaginative and generative spaces. Smitherman (1977) notes that "every black neighborhood in every city in the United States comes equipped with its own storytellers" (p. 148). Mina is one such storyteller, a young Black girl who mobilized her imagination to condense broad, theoretical observations about life, love, and humanity into a specific, speculative artifact. Through her character and story, Mina shares both her understandings of, and her experiences in, the world and provides audiences the opportunity to be present, look back, and dream forward. In other words, she was realizing new ways to read the word and the world and inviting her community to do the same.

Her personal mosaic, shown through her narrative, is an example of the many ways BIPOC communities, and women and girls in particular, chronicle their lives to remix, resist, and refuse traditional and oppressive boundaries. These creations, these worlds, along with the others generated in this space, offer a way to construct critical counterrealities, to "clap back" in ways that challenge oppressive narratives that seek to confine BIPOC youth to a limited vision of who they can be, what they can do, and what they can offer the world. Communities tell stories as a way to survive, as they afford opportunities to co-construct a vision of reality and preserve lives—both physical and communal—amid institutional and often physical erasure. People tell stories to envision possibilities beyond those they currently hold, to imagine more just, equitable futures. Through their stories, Mina and the other participants in the Lion Man Project shared their understandings and experiences of the world and provided readers an opportunity to listen and respond.

REFERENCES

Alemán, S. M. (2017). A critical race counterstory: Chicana/o subjectivities vs. journalism objectivity. *Taboo: The Journal of Culture and Education, 16*(1). https://doi.org/10.31390/taboo.16.1.08

Anderson, R. (2015). Critical Afrofuturism: A case study in visual rhetoric, sequential art, and post-apocalyptic Black identity. In F. Gateward & J. Jennings (Eds.), *The blacker the ink* (pp. 179–192). Rutgers University Press. https://doi.org/10.2307/j.ctt1hd186b.12

Bell, D. (1989). *And we are not saved*. Basic Books.
Boone, P. R. (2003). When the "amen corner" comes to class: An examination of the pedagogical and cultural impact of call–response communication in the Black college classroom. *Communication Education*, 52(3–4), 212–229. https://doi.org/10.1080/0363452032000156208
Brooks, K. D., McGee, A., & Schoellman, S. (2016). Speculative sankofarration: Haunting Black women in contemporary horror fiction. *Obsidian*, 42(1/2), 237–248.
Burke, K. J., & Greene, S. (2015). Participatory action research, youth voices, and civic engagement. *Language Arts*, 92, 389–402. https://www.researchgate.net/publication/281627393_Participatory_Action_Research_Youth_Voices_and_Civic_Engagement
Cazden, C., Cope, B., Fairclough, N., Gee, J., Kalantzis, M., Kress, G., . . . & Nakata, M. (1996). A pedagogy of multiliteracies: Designing social futures. *Harvard Educational Review*, 66(1), 60–92. https://doi.org/10.17763/haer.66.1.17370n67v22j160u
Chambliss, J., & Greason, W. D. (Eds.). (2016). Comics, race, and society [Blog series]. *Black Perspectives*. African American Intellectual History Society. https://www.aaihs.org/call-for-submissions-new-blog-series-on-comics-race-and-society/
Delgado, R. (1989). Storytelling for oppositionists and others: A plea for narrative. *Michigan Law Review*, 87(8), 2411–2441. https://doi.org/10.2307/1289308
Delgado, R. (1995). *The Rodrigo chronicles: Conversations about America and race*. New York University Press.
Delgado, R., & Stefancic, J. (2001). *Critical race theory: An introduction*. New York University Press.
Dery, M. (1994). Black to the future: Interviews with Samuel R. Delany, Greg Tate, and Tricia Rose. In *Flame wars* (pp. 179–222). Duke University Press. https://doi.org/10.1215/9780822396765-010
Gibbs, R. W. (2011). *Metaphor wars: Conceptual metaphors in human life*. Cambridge University Press.
Grifin, R. A., Ward, L. C., & Phillips, A. R. (2014). Still flies in buttermilk: Black male faculty, critical race theory, and composite counterstorytelling. *International Journal of Qualitative Studies in Education*, 27(10), 1354–1375. https://doi.org/10.1080/09518398.2013.840403
Holbert, N., Dando, M., & Correa, I. (2020). Afrofuturism as critical constructionist design: Building futures from the past and present. *Learning, Media and Technology*, 45(1), 1–17. https://doi.org/10.1080/17439884.2020.1754237
hooks, b. (2000). *Feminism is for everybody: Passionate politics*. Pluto Press.
Imarisha, W. (2015). Intro. In W. Imarisha & A. M. Brown (Eds.), *Octavia's brood: Science fiction stories from social justice movements* (pp. 3–5). A. K. Press.
Kelley, R. D. (2002). *Freedom dreams: The Black radical imagination*. Beacon Press.
Ladson-Billings, G. (2002). But that's just good teaching! The case for culturally relevant pedagogy. In S. J. Denbo & L. M. Beaulieu (Eds.), *Improving schools for African American students: A reader for educational leaders* (pp. 95–102). Charles C. Thomas.

Ladson-Billings, G., & Tate, W. F., IV. (1995). Toward a critical race theory of education. *Teachers College Record*, 97(1), 47–68. https://doi.org/10.1177/016146819509700104

Lathan, R. E. (2014). Testimony as a sponsor of literacy: Bernice Robinson and South Carolina Sea Island Citizenship Program's literacy activism. In J. Dufy, J. Christoph, E. Goldblatt, N. Graf, R. Nowacek, & B. Trabold (Eds.), *Literacy, economy, and power: Writing research ten years after literacy in American lives* (pp. 30–44). Southern Illinois University Press.

Martinez, A. (2013). Critical race theory counterstory as allegory: A rhetorical trope to raise awareness about Arizona's ban on ethnic studies. *Across the Disciplines*, 10(3). http://wac.colostate.edu/atd/race/martinez.cfm

McCloud, S. (1994). *Understanding comics: The invisible art*. William Morrow Paperbacks.

Miller, R., Liu, K., & Ball, A. F. (2020). Critical counter-narrative as transformative methodology for educational equity. *Review of Research in Education*, 44(1), 269–300. https://doi.org/10.3102/0091732X20908501

National Center for Education Statistics. (2018). *Race/ethnicity of college faculty*. https://nces.ed.gov/fastfacts/display.asp?id=61

Nelson, A. (2002). Introduction: Future texts. *Social Text*, 20(2), 1–15. https://doi.org/10.1215/01642472-20-2_71-1

Richards-Greaves, G. R. (2016). "Say hallelujah, homebody" and "I will call upon the Lord": An examination of call-and-response in the Black church. *Western Journal of Black Studies*, 40(3), 192–204.

Smitherman, G. (1977). *Talking and testifyin: The language of Black America*. Wayne State University Press.

Solórzano, D. G., & Yosso, T. J. (2002a). A critical race counterstory of race, racism, and affirmative action. *Equity & Excellence in Education*, 35(2), 155–168. https://doi.org/10.1080/713845284

Solórzano, D. G., & Yosso, T. J. (2002b). Critical race methodology: Counter-storytelling as an analytical framework for education research. *Qualitative Inquiry*, 8(1), 23–44. https://doi.org/10.1177/107780040200800103

Wanzo, R. (2020). *The content of our caricature: African American comic art and political belonging* (Vol. 25). New York University Press. https://doi.org/10.18574/nyu/9781479813636.001.0001

Whaley, D. E. (2015). *Black women in sequence: Re-inking comics, graphic novels, and anime*. University of Washington Press.

Yosso, T. J. (2005). Whose culture has capital? A critical race theory discussion of community cultural wealth. *Race Ethnicity and Education*, 8(1), 69–91, https://doi.org/10.1080/1361332052000341006

INTERLUDE
A House Divided and New Abolition

Zebulon Vance Miletsky

We find ourselves at a profound crossroads as a nation today. Many are speaking actively of a new civil war, and the violence that accompanied the conflicts in Charlottesville and other places speaks to this reality. It is how America responds to this new American dilemma that will decide our fate as a nation. As President Abraham Lincoln reminds us, "A house divided upon itself cannot stand." About the impending crisis, Lincoln warns, "I do not expect the house to fall—but I do expect it will cease to be divided. It will become all one thing or all the other."

Historically, African Americans have saved this country from war and chaos—during the Civil War and Reconstruction and then again in the 1950s and 1960s, when they helped America remember its ideals by spurring the country, as Martin Luther King Jr. said, to "live up to the true nature of its creed." What are some of the historical barriers to achieving full racial justice in America? How have we functioned in America as a "house divided"? When we characterize the country as having racist origins, for example, it is important to point out that historically not "all" of America has subscribed to white supremacist origins. Although British North America, and what eventually became the United States, certainly started that way, in the end some (maybe just about half) of white Americans were able to see beyond slavery and evolve into something that has tried to live up to the ideals and creed of American democracy and equality. We are essentially still, in the words of Lincoln, "a house divided." To help explain where we are in the country, we must examine the history that led us to this moment. This article makes the argument that it's important not to get into the mentality that the whole country has problems with race—when it's historically been more like half. That same half (in a different time) is why we had a civil war in this country—and that same half is why we had mass incarceration and policing after slavery—leading us to our present moment where "new abolitionists" have appeared to help us rethink everything from policing, suburban racism, and lack of equity to how cities work, how to reverse the adverse effects of redlining, and so many other issues. Much of this is critical to our survival as a country and a democracy in the twenty-first century.

In the 1990s and early 2000s, whiteness studies pioneer and critical race theorist, the late Noel Ignatiev—named a "dangerous mind" by *Rolling Stone* magazine—author of *How the Irish Became White*, American historian, and Marxist, founded the Society for New Abolitionists. He was best known for his work on race and social class, for his call to abolish or "renounce whiteness." Seeing the construction of whiteness as the essential problem in American life, Ignatiev's work built on the work by a number of scholars that began to emerge in the 1980s—including David Roediger, Theodor Allen, Karen Brodkin, Cedric Robinson, Nell Irvin Painter, Matthew Frye Jacobson, and David Theo Goldberg—who explored the idea of whiteness as an ideological, psychological, social, and political construct and a set of governing mechanisms rather than a biological or even determinatively cultural one. As part of these efforts, Ignatiev led a crusade to "abolish the white race" in order to draw attention to the destructive power of the uncritical belief in whiteness as an identity. A journal was established in 1993 called *Race Traitor*, which set out "to run the film backwards, to explore how people who had been brought up as white might become unwhite." It's masthead read, "Treason to whiteness is loyalty to humanity." John Brown, martyr to the abolitionist cause was portrayed as a hero and a model. The first words in its first issue urged readers to "abolish the white race—by any means necessary."

In today's climate of abolition—abolish ICE, abolish the police, not to mention drawing on the tradition of the abolitionists of the nineteenth century—and with the rise in open and unapologetic expressions of white supremacy, it is perhaps a good time to retake up the questions raised by The Society for New Abolitionists and see where "abolitionist futures" meet the much longer tradition of abolition, and offer a model of praxis for whiteness studies and antiracist education. So I propose "2022: A House Divided: The Emergence of the New Abolitionists," which would also look at some of the people doing the most important work in this regard.

CHAPTER 14

Illmatic Images: A Visual Essay

Stacey Robinson

The following collection of images are inspired by an amalgam of my cultural and artistic influences. To be clear, this work is critical, it's not only racial, but radical, and it's theoretical.

Comics book aesthetics, Black religious beliefs systems, science fiction to name a few are some of the leanings connecting these images to a theoretical working of Black liberation through Black creativity.

Black creativity, via its many manifestations is our gift to the world. Often our gifts are co-opted, commandeered, stolen, negated, rewritten, recontextualized, reimagined, etc., leaving us not only locked out historically but most often times left proving our cultural significance and contributions to global cultures collectively.

Hip-Hop is built on an algorithmic system of cultures. Systems like the 5 Percent Nation of Gods and Earths's Supreme Mathematics, and Supreme Alphabet have been foundational in Hip-Hop culture since its beginning. The 7 and the star with its crescent moon is an icon representing the 5 Percenters. In the piece titled "We Were Beginners" the celestial icon shines on one of Hip-Hop's most dynamic duo's as the sun itself.

Additional figures in the series include AZ, Pete Rock, Olu Dara (Nas's father). Dara is seen ascending into Nas, who ascends to his dependents. Dara's eye is focused forward while his sight is connected backward in time. Through his inevitable transition he will be resurrected through the birth of his heir.

The cover art and interior piece "Half-Man, Half-Amazin'" reference Nas's *Stillmatic* album cover as a sampled mashup between Nas, and the Amazing Spider-Man through the quoted lyric.

"One Love" illustrates Nas blowing the herb smoke through his nose in remembrance of "Shorty" a young brotha far too young and far too entrenched in an inescapable trap of drugs, violence, revenge, and oppression. Both understand and are powerless, embracing the horror that Shorty won't escape.

In "Memory Lane" Nas is a comet, invading the Earth as an Afrocentric Asian.

My goal with this visual essay is to provide enough context to intrigue the audience, many of whom will be a nostalgic fanbase, without taking away an interactive, and interpretive experience from the audience, whether they are familiar fans of Nas or newcomers to art and Hip-Hop culture.

Chapter 14: Illmatic Images

Figure 14.1 We Were Beginners
Source. S. A. Robinson (2022).

Figure 14.2 The Genesis
Source. S. A. Robinson (2022).

Chapter 14: Illmatic Images

Figure 14.3 One Time for Your Mind
Source. S. A. Robinson (2022).

Figure 14.4 One Love
Source. S. A. Robinson (2022).

Figure 14.5 Memory Lane
Source. S. A. Robinson (2022).

Figure 14.6 New York State of Mind
Source. S. A. Robinson (2022).

Chapter 14: Illmatic Images

Figure 14.7 Triple Cypher
Source. S. A. Robinson (2022).

Figure 14.8 My Resurrection
Source. S. A. Robinson (2022).

Figure 14.9 Half-Man, Half-Amazin
Source. S. A. Robinson (2022).

CHAPTER 15

Christian Nationalism and the Comic: Incognegro

Matthew Teutsch

Mat Johnson and Warren Pleece's *Incognegro: A Graphic Mystery*, focuses on constructions of race and the ways in which whites use these constructions to maintain power or achieve power. This graphic novel does not extensively engage in an examination of Christian nationalism, looking at the intersections between white supremacy and the church, but there are moments that cause readers to think about these intersections. This essay focuses on the ways that *Incognegro* highlights the social construction of race and how those social constructions manifest themselves in Christian nationalism to maintain control and power.

These moments in *Incognegro* play into the larger discussions surrounding white evangelicals' and Christian nationalists' attacks on critical race theory and intersectionality. Recently, the presidents of the Southern Baptist seminaries recommitted themselves to the Baptist faith and message, and by extension, as Jemar Tisby (2020) notes, "whiteness." Tisby argues that Christian nationalism is "the greatest threat to Christianity in the United States."

Christian nationalism is an interwoven network wrapping Christianity tightly in the robes of patriotism, embracing the nation just as much as, if not more so than, the Christian faith. Andrew Whitehead and Samuel Perry define Christian nationalism as "an ideology that idealizes a fusion of American civic life with a particular type of Christian identity and culture" (pp. ix–x). Tisby (2020) expands on this and points out that Christian nationalism fits right in line with white supremacy and the maintaining of whiteness. He writes,

It is Christian Nationalists who support draconian laws aimed at excluding immigrants from the US. It is Christian Nationalists who say Confederate monuments are about southern pride and not white supremacy. It is Christian Nationalists (even more than white evangelicals) who believe that the Republican party is the only Christian option for voting. It is Christian Nationalists who think Critical Race Theory and Intersectionality are the greatest threats to the gospel while doing nothing of substance about the racists and white supremacists in their midst.

All of this shows up in the three panels from *Incognegro* that I want to look at in this essay. The first panel occurs early in the text when Zane and Carl walk into town. While the two discuss why they are there, Pleece's illustration is what caught my attention. Pleece shows the men walking down what appears to be Main Street. We see utility polls with lines on the right side of the panel and cars lining the street on each side. On the left-hand side, we see a church, the steeple rising right alongside Carl's figure.

In this moment, we see the prevalence of the church within the community. No words tell us the significance, but the framing tells us that the church serves an important role within the town. It stands on Main Street. It's steeple towers above the other buildings and can be seen from any spot when someone walks around the town square. Some of Lillian Smith's relatives are buried in the cemetery behind Clayton Baptist Church in Clayton, Georgia, and the church sits on an elevated hill. Recently, as I walked through the cemetery looking for the graves, I looked down past the Baptist church and immediately spotted another steeple. At that moment, I began to think about how these structures serve to point the townspeople to the church, towering above the other buildings. The churches serve as centers for the community, pulling together influence and wealth. In her debut novel, *Strange Fruit* (1944/1992), Smith highlights this through the description of Rev. Dunwoodie and his revival services in the southern town of Maxwell, Georgia. Dunwoodie makes a list of all the influential men in Maxwell who he hopes will attend the revival services and get saved, because these men "must, in the nature of things, be counted upon for the major financial support of the church" (p. 249). One of these men is L. D. Stephenson, a member of the state legislature, who may one day become governor and have influence over the state. All of this is an undercurrent in the panel as Carl and Zane walk down the street beneath the towering steeple.

The next two panels appear near the end of the text. While the white townspeople of Tupelo lynch Carl in the town square, the sheriff looks through the bars of the jail cell and tells Alonzo, "There it is. America. Right out our window. Church-attending, moral-living, average men and women in all their glory" (p. 107). The sheriff's words drive home the enmeshing of Christianity and American nationalism, the ways the two

Chapter 15: Christian Nationalism and the Comic 183

have become so entwined that uncoiling the mess will take deep, hard work. Along with the sheriff's words, the panel positions the reader inside the jail cell, looking outward from Alonzo's perspective; in doing this, it puts the sheriff behind the bars. This perspective highlights the psychological effects that these entanglements have on the sheriff's white psyche also. Lillian Smith, in *The White Christian and His Conscience* (1945/2011), talks about the psychological compartmentalization that enables the intimate intermingling between Christianity and nationalism. She also points out the ways in which this meshing together harms everyone. She writes,

> Not only is it true that we Jim Crow Jesus Christ each time we Jim Crow any human being . . . but we Jim Crow our own children, segregating them from those human experiences that make a personality creative, rich and good—that make it grow. (p. 43)

Smith knew the effects of racism and nationalism on the psychological development of children and their impact on the oppressor. Even in *Incognegro*, we see this, especially when the white mother gives her white son rotten fruit to throw at Carl as the white citizens drag him through the town to lynch him in the square. In the first panel, the boy screams, preparing to throw a good piece of fruit, and the mother grabs his arm, saying, "No, honey, don't throw that" (p. 103). The next panel shows the woman smiling as she hands the boy a rotten piece of fruit and says, "We can still eat that one. Throw this one, it's rot" (p. 103). The final panel shows the fruit hitting Carl's head and spattering on the ground. The mother, in this moment and in what we do not see, teaches her son hate, stifling his ability to grow, mature, and connect with others.

The mother and son probably go to the church. They are two of the "Church-attending, moral-living, average men and women" that the sheriff mentions. Yet they stand in the street, violently spewing hate and throwing things at Carl. They do this, the sheriff tells Alonzo, because "they need something to hate. Something to blame for why things ain't perfect in the world. Something to explain their fear" (p. 107). This is the same thing that Christian nationalism does. It provides people with constructions to fear, which helps them feel better about their own exploitation by those above them. It does not allow them to see the ways in which those in power stoke the fears, working to maintain control, wealth, and power.

Early in *Incognegro*, as Zane looks at himself in the mirror, straightening his hair and preparing to pass for white, he transforms himself into *Incognegro*. After this scene, we see Zane going to Grand Central Station to catch a train to Tupelo, Mississippi. The page contains four panels, and over the course of the panels, Zane goes from the streets of Harlem to a subway train in Grand Central Station. As he moves through these spaces, he provides a narration:

> That's one thing that most of us know that most white folks don't, that race doesn't really exist. Culture? Ethnicity? Sure. Class too. But race is just a bunch of rules meant to keep us on the bottom. Race is a strategy. The rest is just people acting, playing roles. That what white folks never get. They don't think they have accents. They don't think they eat ethnic foods. Their music is classical. They think they're just normal. That they are the universal, and that everyone else is an odd deviation from form. That's what makes them so easy to infiltrate. (p. 19)

In his narration, Zane's comments lay bare the ways in which whiteness works to hold on to power. The ways it works to construct systems that oppress others. Zane mentions the "rules," deploying language similar to what Ernest Gaines uses in his novels when discussing the "rules" that structure life and societal interactions in South Louisiana.

Along with this, Zane points out what Smith (1942–1943) did in "Buying a New World With Confederate Bills" when she wrote,

> It is just possible that the white man is no longer the center of the universe. It is just possible that even German nazis, British imperialists, and white southerners will have to accept a fact that has been old news to the rest of the world for a long, long time. (p. 11)

Zane, like Smith and countless others, points out that whites do not think of themselves as "white," as distinct. Instead, we envision ourselves as "the universal," the "norm." Yet that is not the case. This belief comes from, as Smith (1942–1943) points out,

> the home, the church, the school, in books, in a hundred studied phrases, through a thousand jokes and innuendoes, by means of ten thousand unverbalized approvals and disapprovals, [where] the superiority of the white race was solidified into a sacred code ... to which our lives were molded. (p. 28)

The social construction of race becomes manifest in the institutions that educate and support the community, creating justification for systemic structures to exploit and oppress others. The church serves as the center of this praxis, as preachers and leaders stand in pulpits claiming credibility while espousing white supremacy, which highlights the fact that "racism is a feature, not a bug, of American evangelicalism" and Christian nationalism (Butler, 2021, p. 1).

Before we can move forward as whites, we must recognize our position. We must recognize that we have created adjectives. We have created images. We have created hierarchies. All of these, and more, work to benefit us, no matter if we are wealthy or poor. We have benefited because we have positioned ourselves as normality and others as some deviation from the norm. This construction hinders our work toward equity and equality because it posits that if someone does not adhere to these "norms" then that person is unworthy or inferior. This is why I always go back to Frank Yerby's condemnation of adjectives when he told James Hill (1995), "I reject adjectives. Adjectives, which are the enemy of nouns, don't mean anything" (p. 216).

All of this leads me to the illustrations that lie underneath Zane's narration. He talks about how easy it is for him to infiltrate white spaces due to white narcissism and our view that we are the center of the world. Working through the social constructions of race, we see Zane in the first panel walking along a street in Harlem. He is one of many African Americans strolling on the concrete. We see detail here. Each person has a level of detail that mirrors Zane's. In the second panel, we see Zane in a subway car. An Orthodox Jewish man stands behind a pole in the middle of the panel, half obscured from our view. On the right-hand side of the panel, Zane can be seen seated with Blacks and whites. Less detail appears on the passengers' faces than in the previous panel.

The third panel shows Zane walking up the steps from the subway station to the street. It is here that he talks about whites having accents, eating ethnic food, and viewing ourselves as "the universal." Here, the detail continues to fade from the image. We still see Zane's mouth and eyes, and the mouths and eyes of others; however, they are not like the faces in the first panel. The ones in the first panel have multiple lines, showing expressions, wrinkles, shadows, and more. In the third panel, we only see lines and dots depicting parts of the faces, not the details we encounter in the first panel.

An outward view of Grand Central Station appears in the fourth panel, and we see countless people walking around on the street and into the station. Here, Zane states, "That's what makes them so easy to infiltrate." In this panel, individuals' details are nonexistent. Instead, they appear as merely lines, devoid of expressions, faces, and more. The removal of these details serves two purposes. One, it proves Zane's point of how easy it is for him to infiltrate white spaces. Along with this, it showcases Zane's comment that whiteness views itself as the norm. No variety exists. No deviation exists.

The people become a mass of humanity, blurring into one another as they walk the streets. This aspect drives home the entirety of Zane's narration and calls upon readers to acknowledge their whiteness and that we are not the universal norm; rather, we are part of the universal humanity, a part that has accents, ethnic food, music, and other things that other members of humanity have. These do not make us superior. They make us human, along with everyone else who inhabits this whirling sphere as it hurtles through space.

To counter Christian nationalism, we must, as Smith (1942–1943) puts it, be like the men and women who fought back against "the hypocrisies of and empty, cowardly words of the segregated Christian churches and their parasitic preachers" (p. 14). We must "be more loyal to Jesus than to White Supremacy" (p. 14). We must, as the women who met at Junaluska put it in their slogan, be "determined never for a moment to refuse hearing a truth because it is new or to be afraid to dig under a belief because it is old and dearly loved." We must illuminate the entwining of Christianity and American patriotism, and we must be willing to learn and not be afraid of discovering that what we know and what we do serve to maintain white supremacy. It's not easy, but it must be done because if we don't, the "Church-attending, moral-living, average men and women" will remain in the town square perpetuating white supremacy under the guise of religion, enacting violence against others through their words and actions.

REFERENCES

Butler, A. (2021). *White Evangelical racism: The politics of morality in America*. University of North Carolina Press.

Hill, J. L. (1995). An interview with Frank Garvin Yerby. *Resources for American Literary Study, 21*, 206–239.

Johnson, M., & Pleece, P. (2008). *Incognegro: A graphic mystery*. Vertigo.

Smith, G. K. L. (2016). *The land south of the clouds*. University of Louisiana at Lafayette.

Smith, L. (1942–1943). Buying a new world with old Confederate bills. *South Today, 7*(2), 7–30.

Smith, L. (1992). *Strange fruit*. Harcourt. (Original work published 1944).

Smith, L. (2011). *The white Christian and his conscience*. Literary Licensing. (Original work published 1945)

Tisby, J. (2019). *The color of compromise: The truth about the American church's complicity in racism*. Zondervan.

Tisby, J. (2020, December 1). Southern Baptist seminary presidents reaffirm their commitment to whiteness. *The Witness*. https://thewitnessbcc.com/southern-baptist-seminary-presidents-reaffirm-their-commitment-to-whiteness/

Whitehead, A., & Perry, S. (2020). *Taking America back for God: Christian nationalism in the United States*. Oxford University Press. https://doi.org/10.1093/oso/9780190057886.001.0001

CHAPTER 16
Black Noise Whitewash
Michael A. Gonzales

It was the fall of 1978: the era of Jimmy Carter in the White House, Jerri curls on Black folks' heads, Frank Frazetta imitators airbrushing vans, *Welcome Back Kotter* on television, and disco blasting from passing cars. I was the new kid at Northwestern High School in Baltimore, and a red-headed kid with braces named Larry Ressin was the first person who was nice to me. We'd met during our first period of journalism class. Taught by the sweet but scattered Miss Stall; she was a round butterball of a woman who was also a Trekkie.

As a 15-year-old Black kid with a shapely Afro, blue jeans, and sneakers, I was constantly running. I didn't live in the school zone, and no matter what time I left my row house with the white marble stairs on the other side of town, I was always late. Larry sat across from me. One morning when I rushed out of the house, I'd forgotten my pens, and Larry lent me a blue Bic.

"You can keep it," he said.

"Thanks, man." Larry and I shared a few classes, including chemistry and biology. We shared a love for comic books and rock 'n' roll. He was a talented artist who also played lacrosse, a sport I'd never heard of before moving to Baltimore. Within a month of us meeting, we were making plans to become an artist–writer team on our own comic book project once we graduated three years later.

Opened in 1965, Northwestern was an impressive-sized school with a swimming pool, a football field, tennis courts, and archery taught in gym class. It was huge compared with the buildings where I attended classes in Harlem. With its many staircases and corridors, I got lost a lot my first week, wandering the locker-lined hallways that smelled of perfume, sweat, and chlorine vapors from the pool.

Located in the predominantly white neighborhood of "upper Park Heights" but serving as the zone school for the majority Jewish community and the Black neighborhoods of "lower Park Heights," it was integrated in ways that were unknown in the other parts of the city. That racial mix went for the teaching staff as well. Black and white together, everyone got along fine, and I never heard of any racial incidents.

Having spent most of my years in a Catholic school where it was mandatory to wear a jacket and tie, I was delighted to be in a place where jeans and sneakers were acceptable. That first year, I must've looked like a bum, but I was so happy to be free of a uniform that I took it to the extreme. Most of the Black kids at Northwestern were more fashion conscious than I, who usually dressed as though I were going to a rock concert.

Growing up, I had a diverse musical palette that included jamming Isaac Hayes and Curtis Mayfield soul records as well as those made by makeup-wearing rockers like Queen, David Bowie, and Kiss. Being a rock 'n' roll fan in Harlem sometimes got me teased by friends and my younger brother Carlos. To them, all rock was "white boy music" or simply "noise," but I didn't care.

As I got older, my musical taste got heavier. I began to go the Zep way in 1976, swaying to the screaming vocals, thunderous guitars, and booming drums that tore through the radio speakers the first time I heard "Stairway to Heaven." Some smart-assed DJ had played them on WNEW-FM moments after the station stereo simulcast the disaster film *Earthquake*, which aired on NBC television.

Standing in the living room of the New York apartment where I was raised, "Stairway" pulled me into its aural vortex. After relocating to Baltimore, I began listening to the local station 98 Rock exclusively and soon considered Led Zeppelin to be the best band in the world.

98 Rock played more Zeppelin records than I'd ever heard before, often spinning complete album sides on Saturday nights. Through that exposure, I started buying their albums, digging deeper into their catalog. The first one I bought was their untitled fourth disc, which most people referred to as *ZoSo* or *Led Zeppelin IV*; it celebrated its 50th anniversary in November 2021. The album, which contained "Stairway to Heaven," opened with "Black Dog," a track with lead singer Robert Plant wailing in, as I'd later define it, an ivory, faux-blues voice, "Hey hey mama said the way you move, gonna make you sweat, gonna make you groove," followed by drummer John Bonham playing with a violent energy that was brutal and beautiful, anchored by John Paul Jones on the bass. The electric guitar player was Jimmy Page, who was also the producer, the ax-man whose sound was worshipped and copied.

Chapter 16: Black Noise Whitewash

The album closed with their brilliant cover of the Memphis Minnie and Kansas Joe McCoy blues song When the Levee Breaks," a track about the Great Mississippi Flood of 1927. Of course, at the time, I had no idea that this was a blues cover since I barely knew what "the blues" were or how much that genre was the foundation of rock 'n' roll. Elvis might've proclaimed himself "the king," but the real royalty was a few "colored" folks from the other side of the tracks.

One day, my new friend Larry invited me to his house two blocks from Northwestern to hang out and listen to his older brother's records. Larry's mom, Katie, was a sweet woman from West Virginia, a housewife and an occasional substitute teacher at our school. Mrs. Ressin had three boys, including Larry's twin brother, Terry, and older brother, Robert. From our first meeting, she always treated me like another son.

The basement was junky with boxes of stuff, but there was an old record player that sounded great. Larry and I stuffed ourselves on snacks and soda while spinning records. While jamming to Zep, we played air-guitar to "Dazed and Confused," "Kashmir," and the overexposed single that had made many of us fans in the first place, "Stairway to Heaven."

Sometimes we stopped at High's convenience store and picked up the rock magazines *Crawdaddy* and *Circus*, flipping through them as we head-nodded to the music. They often published photos of Zep on tour, especially when they were in Los Angeles, causing havoc at hotels with their wild parties, groupies, and television sets thrown from windows. Renting the entire floor of the Continental Hyatt House (aka Riot House), those "boys" were complete devils in the city of angels with their drugs and debauchery.

In the summer of 1979, I went to New York City to visit my grandma in Harlem. I had read in a recent Rolling Stone that a new Led Zeppelin album was released. Although I'm not sure how the thought came to me, I decided that I was going to write an essay about the group for our school paper. Taking a chance, I called Atlantic Records and explained that I was a high school journalist and needed pictures of the group.

Much to my surprise, someone from publicity told me to come to the Rockefeller Center offices the following day and there would be a package for me in the lobby. When I arrived, there was a large envelope waiting for me.

Excited, I walked down the block and sat in front of a water-spouting fountain on 6th Avenue and tore open the envelope, which was packed with photographs, bios, and a copy of the recently released disc *In Through the Out Door*. This was years before I thought about being a music journalist, so I didn't realize that packages like these were usual. I thought I was special.

A few weeks later, back in Baltimore and school, I took the album to Larry's basement. I'd listened to it already but was looking forward to sharing the experience. The music was softer than on the previous records and featured a lot of bassist John Paul Jones, who wrote more than usual and introduced the Yamaha GX-1 synthesizer into the group's musical mix. Though I didn't know it at the time, Zep was going through a really bleak period that included the sudden death of Robert Plant's five-year-old son two years earlier as well as Jimmy Page's heroin problem and John Bonham's out-of-control drinking.

Apparently, *In Through the Out Door* was a record made under duress, with Plant and Jones doing most of the heavy lifting in production/songwriting during the day. Page and Bonham came to the studio at night to lay down their parts. It was different, but since Zep hadn't released any new material in three years, I was just glad to have a new record.

I had seen critic Charles M. Young from *Rolling Stone*, a magazine that hated on the band for years, going straight for the jugular. Heaping most of his distain on Plant's singing and songwriting, he wrote,

> Of the seven songs on *In through the Out Door*, only one has orchestral guitar rumble, and Plant's singing has fallen to the occasion in the other six. With this paucity of good music to work with, Plant fails to create phrasing good enough to disguise the lyrics, which are horrible.

Accusing Plant of having an "appetite for inanity," Young hated the howling lust of "I'm Going to Crawl" and completely ignored the ballsy ballad "All of My Love," which was my favorite song. The writer blamed Plant for whatever he thought was wrong with the album. "Fuck that guy," I thought, tossing the paper across the room. In my rebuttal, I wrote, "No matter what the rock press says or how the so-called critics feel about their music, they were still explosive."

Still, 11 years had passed since the band released their first album, and much of the music world had changed. The so-called dinosaur bands were considered relics by critics more attuned to punk or the emerging new wave. My forthcoming school paper essay "The Song Is Still the Same" was written in response to a negative review.

Miss Stall, in addition to being the journalism teacher, was the newspaper advisor of *The Northwestern Compass*. There was a small staff, but Larry and I typed up the copy, pasted up the type, and laid out the pages. During the process, Miss Stall had a heart attack. Fortunately, she lived, and we finished putting the paper together in her hospital room.

We were excited when it returned from the printer that November. In the masthead, I billed myself as "Rock Columnist." My passionate essay on

Chapter 16: Black Noise Whitewash

Led Zeppelin defended them from dreaded critics who thought they were overwrought and ridiculous. Reviewers had been writing negatively about the band from the beginning of their careers right up to their last studio album, and I thought it was my mission to defend them.

> The group has the ability to sell millions of albums, millions of concert tickets and themselves, year in and year out, no matter what the rock press says about them or how the so-called "critics" feel about their music. The music is what Plant, along with Page, is concerned with.

It was the first piece of pop journalism I ever penned, and I was so proud. More than 40 years later, I can't stop cringing thinking of it.

Shortly after the newspaper was published, my honors English teacher, Mrs. Sommer, kept me after class, along with my friend J. T. Zimmerman, to give us some work we'd missed when we were both absent the day before. J.T. was another friend, though he wasn't as good a buddy as Larry, and he was a bit of a bad influence.

The first time I ever cut class was at J.T.'s urging, and while hanging out with him at the city's sole punk rock club, the Marble Bar, one night, he encouraged me to take a Quaalude. "How will it make me feel?" I asked, before popping it in my mouth. J.T. smiled. "Like you just drank a six pack," he replied. The rest of the night was a blur.

Mrs. Sommer was a very smart liberal-minded white teacher who many of the boys, myself included, thought attractive. Between our schoolwork readings of Beowulf and *The Chocolate War*, she also schooled us on issues of race and class in America. After giving me and J.T. the assignments, she said, "Michael, I read your story on Led Zeppelin, and I enjoyed it, but you could've gone a bit deeper."

"Deeper?"

"Yes, like how much they and other rock groups were influenced by blues musicians or how Black people invented rock and roll." Although I read rock magazines on a regular basis, this was a new truth for me. Meanwhile, J.T. instantly refused to believe our teacher's words. "Black people did not invent rock 'n' roll," he said, his words dripping with snark, as though that achievement was too much for the race.

Mrs. Sommer laughed. "It's true, J.T. Have you ever heard of Little Richard, Ike Turner, or Chuck Berry? Those men were the music's pioneers. Mick Jagger, Led Zeppelin, and Eric Clapton were inspired by them as well as by blues musicians Muddy Waters, John Lee Hooker, and many others. It all comes from the blues."

Turning 99 shades of red, J.T. was speechless for a few minutes as he tried to wrap his brain around the notion that Black people had anything to do with creating the music he loved so much. Finally, he spat, "Black people didn't have anything to do with creating rock 'n' roll" and stormed out of the classroom.

Prior to his outburst, I never would've thought of J.T. as racist, but his disgust and anger changed my mind. His intense negative reaction to the Black foundation of what he (and so many others) perceived to be white greatness revealed more about him than I had known. Afterward, though I can't recall the details, our friendship dissolved.

Since Google hadn't been invented yet nor were there any *History of Rock* books in our school library, the argument, at least for J.T., was over. He was content with his ignorance while I realized that not only did I respect Mrs. Sommers but I also had a lot of reading and research to do.

So many of us Black folks don't know our own histories, and I was one of them. Still, there were so many others on both sides of the color line who didn't know or recognize the truth about "Whole Lotta Love" being swiped from "You Need Love," written by Willie Dixon and performed by Muddy Waters. Blind Lemon Johnson's track "Jesus Make Up My Dying Bed" would later be transformed into the 11-minute anthem "In My Time of Dying," and Howlin' Wolf's piano drive "How Many More Years" became "How Many More Times."

Having grown as a child of the "Elvis is king" propaganda machine and lots of other misinformation concerning rock history, I didn't know any better. Like many others, I thought of Jimi Hendrix as the lone Black rock star, and though the Thin Lizzy lead singer/songwriter Phil Lynott was obviously "of color," it was never mentioned. I felt a sense of cultural shame that I hadn't been schooled on the subject before.

Of course, one wouldn't expect to learn these things in school, where Black history usually consists of slavery, George Washington Carver, and Martin Luther King Jr. But still, I would've thought that someone in my family, especially my music-loving/audiophile Uncle Carl, might have enlightened me. It is for this very reason that, in 1985, Living Colour's lead guitarist Vernon Reid along with cultural writer Greg Tate founded the Black Rock Coalition, an organization designed to, among other things, educate people on the roots of these rhythms.

The members of Black Rock Coalition included musicians, writers, and visual artists as well as more business-minded folks who were unafraid to do their thing. "Black people started this music, and I take umbrage that I have to explain that," Reid said in a later interview.

The more I learned about Led Zeppelin's blues roots, the more it annoyed me that they had brazenly appropriated the music and claimed it as their own. While the group's members had no problem paying lip service to the blues men and women who inspired them, when it came to songwriting credits and royalties, it was a completely different story. As author Erik Davis documented in his 2005 book, 33 1/3, on *Led Zeppelin IV*, singer/lyricist Plant "honestly seemed to believe that these songs in turn emerged from some collective well of folk memory that welcomed all comers." It was this sort of "piracy" that would be "ultimately costly" as they later faced lawsuits from Willie Dixon and others.

While it could be argued that Led Zeppelin's cultural thievery brought recognition to otherwise obscure men, I'm sure they would've preferred to get a few dollars instead. I couldn't help but equate their actions to white men sailing to the New World and snatching land and resources from the natives, but instead of bullets, Zeppelin used lawyers. In the end, did it matter? The white guys would be the bigger stars, while the Black originators would remain footnotes?

A part of me tried to understand why the southerners in my life, namely my Richmond, Virginia–born grandma, who also had a hand in raising me, never told me about the musical ancestors who paved the way for so many. Was the blues as a musical form something that Black southerners like my grandma pushed to the back of their minds, the soundtrack to Jim Crow, lynchings, and their own fears? Was getting rid of the blues a way of forgetting all the bad things that music reminded them of, the dark days from long ago?

Despite their creative thefts from folks of color, Led Zeppelin were heavy metal giants who influenced and inspired many young Black fans who'd go on to make their own music in multiple genres including hip-hop, Detroit Techno, and the ironically labeled "Black rock" of Prince, Fishbone, 24/7 Spyz, Lenny Kravitz, and Living Colour. Knowing the truth about Led Zeppelin's roots didn't make me any less of a fan either.

In September, 1980, Led Zeppelin announced a tour called "The 1980s, Part One," which would be bringing them to the Maryland/D.C. area in a month. Larry and I tried to figure out ways to get tickets and journey to the venue. "Maybe Robert knows how we can get them," I suggested, referring to his older brother. I even thought of asking J.T., who seemed like the kind of dude who knew how to get a scalper on the phone.

Having seen Led Zeppelin's concert film, I knew they put on a hell of a show, and got lost in my imagination envisioning a night of blaring music along with a lot of swagger, glitter, and booming pyrotechnics. Though I'd attended concerts since I was a kid (Ray Charles, The Jackson 5), this was to be my first rock concert, and I was excited. However, on the morning of Friday, September 26, 1980, as I was getting dressed for school, everything changed.

Outside the birds were chirping. Downstairs, mom was frying bacon. Inside my room, I was singing along to the Rolling Stones single "Emotional Rescue" when the DJ from 98 Rock interrupted the song and announced in a somber voice that "Led Zeppelin drummer John Bonham died yesterday at the age of 32." Afterward, I didn't hear anything else until the live version of "Stairway to Heaven" began to play. "Does anyone remember laughter?" Plant asked in the song as I sat on the side of the bed sadly shaking my head.

It was like a bad dream. Bonham's sudden death was not only his end but also the end of the tour and the band. It was near symbolic that a band that had dominated the 1970s was put to rest permanently nine months into the new decade. Ten minutes later, when the final note had played and the song faded away, I'd call Larry and tell him the news. But at that moment, I just leaned back on the bed, took a deep breath, closed my eyes, and waited for the blues to come over me.

More than four decades have passed since I was introduced to the music of Led Zeppelin, and I still go through periods when I rock out to their music, strumming the same electric air-guitar that I had played in high school. Many memories from those youthful days have faded like an old photograph, but I will always clearly remember Mrs. Sommer teaching me a musical history lesson that sent me on a mission to discovering the truth beyond the noise and spreading that wisdom to others.

CHAPTER 17

Auto-Ethnographical Notes on Whiteness

Kat Moore

I. My Nice White Family

THE INVISIBILITY OF WHITENESS

My great-great-great paternal grandmother wrote out, what she called, recollections from her life. Five short pages hold the 84 years of her life. Her name was Annie Elizabeth. She was born in 1851 in Franklin County, Alabama. My great-uncle, a physicist at NASA before he retired, preserved Annie Elizabeth's letter, typed it up just in case the ink were to fade or the paper crumbled, and emailed a copy to his nieces and nephews. My mother, knowing that I too write recollections from my life, forwarded it to me. Annie Elizabeth opens with her first memory of white snow and how she thought snow meant it was Christmas even when it wasn't. When I first read these pages, I wanted to feel connected to this woman. I rarely feel connected with my family beyond my mom and sister. My father used to tell me that he was the black sheep of the family and that I couldn't be the black sheep until he died. At his funeral in 2003, I whispered into his casket, "I'm the black sheep now." Black sheep. The Other. Black as Other. Whiteness is in our language and determines signification. The white snow that Grandma Annie Elizabeth saw falling from the sky. The assumption of white as pure and Annie Elizabeth's assumption of Christmas. The birth of Christ, who was not white except f in the paintings that hang in white churches. In the poem

"Summer, Somewhere," poet Danez Smith (2017) imagines an afterlife for Black boys murdered by the police or other organizations of white supremacy. The poem has a line that states, "If snow fell, it'd fall black" (p. 3). A reversal of language. An undoing of its whiteness. Snow as black, black as good, as heavenly. Annie Elizabeth liked the white snow, and it made her think it symbolized the birth of Jesus, of holiness, of God—white, the same color as her skin.

Only whiteness is present in Annie Elizabeth's five pages. She remembers Abraham Lincoln running for president and the talk of war. She writes that her father "joined the Southern Army" and that he died at the Battle of Murfreesboro. Her older brother also joined and fought until the war ended. First, this was a jolt to me, reading that I had relatives who fought for the confederacy. I wanted to believe that my Republican aunt and her husband were anomalies. My uncle displayed the Mississippi flag alongside the American flag on a pole in his front yard. Half of the Mississippi flag, until recently, was the confederate flag. My uncle could fly the confederate flag without flying the actual confederate flag. As a Mississippian, he could call it state pride. Again, the coded language of whiteness. Much like how, if asked, my uncle would've said the confederate war was over states' rights. A complete omission of slavery and all of its horrors.

Annie Elizabeth omits mention of it too. Her father was injured in the Battle of Shiloh and came home to recuperate before returning to the war. Annie Elizabeth claimed that the Battle of Shiloh was so close to their farm that she could hear the cannonballs being fired. Then her father returned to the war and died, died in the war over slavery. In 1860 in Franklin County, according to U.S. Census data, the population included 10,119 whites, 13 freed Black people, and 8,495 slaves (Blake, 2001). This means that enslaved people were 45.6% of the entire population, almost half. By 1870, the Black population, due to, I assume based on history, the freeing of enslaved people, had decreased by 84%. Yet Annie Elizabeth never mentions Black people. Between the Emancipation Proclamation and the death of her father, her life was surely affected by slavery and the presence of Black people. She even refers to Shiloh as "the famous Battle of Shiloh," which acknowledges that, when she wrote her recollections at the age of 79, she was aware of the narratives of history.

In a biography of William Apess, a Native American who fought in the Revolutionary War and became a Methodist minister and activist, Drew Lopenzina (2017) coins the term "unwitnessing." He calls it "an act . . . of rhetorically erasing the inconvenient truth of the persistence of Native Americans" (p. 3). Or, in other words, using the language of extinction in regards to Native people. As if Native people ceased to exist once the colonies flourished. In spite of the white man's cruelest efforts, Native people are still here. I also think "unwitnessing" can be used to discuss

Chapter 17: Auto-Ethnographical Notes on Whiteness 197

whiteness. Whiteness itself relies on an unwitnessing, like Annie Elizabeth's elision of slavery from her life's narrative. This type of unwitnessing keeps whiteness centered without ever having to reckon with the atrocities that white people committed. I have to admit here that I do not know if Annie Elizabeth or her family enslaved people. I do know, since she included it in her writing, that she lost siblings and children to typhoid fever. I do know that she lamented to the Lord to help her endure the "losses and the crosses." And though it is not written down, I do know that even if they didn't own enslaved people, they still participated in slavery with her father and brother fighting for the confederacy. But she never makes a claim about it either way. She completely unwitnesses slavery and therefore erases the sins of her kind, of my kin.

POLITENESS, AN ACT OF UNWITNESSING, IN THREE EVENTS

Event 1

At a coffee shop with a friend, likely in 2007, we sat outside on the patio; the sky was overcast, and I remember the wind blew through my hair. He was an older man who I knew from 12-step recovery. At the time, I only had two years of being clean/sober after a horrifying heroin addiction that rivaled parts of *Requiem for a Dream*. This man—I will call him Matt—knew my aunt and her family. Matt had grown up attending the same church and was mentored by my uncle, the one with the Mississippi flag, as a teenager. My uncle played music at the church, and Matt worked the sound board. Matt liked to hang out and drink coffee with the younger crowd and enter into lively debates with young men. He also liked to act as a guru, sharing sage wisdom from his time in 12-step recovery. He likened our talks at the coffee shop to "solving the problems of the world," which in itself is colonial thinking.

On that day, I was alone with Matt. He liked to meet with me alone, in public, to discuss Jesus. He knew I was open to it, whereas most 12 steppers were not. I don't remember what we were talking about on that patio. But I do remember that suddenly Matt's voice dipped as he said, "You know, with the Blacks." He did not mean a family with the last name Black. He meant Black people.

I immediately wanted to say, "No, I don't know what you mean"; but I didn't want a confrontation, so I just nodded. I instantly recognized his statement as racist. He had even lowered his voice so no one else would hear him. I felt a recoil inside myself, but I did not speak up. All these years later, I don't even remember what preceded his saying that, the context of the conversation; but I remember him saying it, and I remember being complicit. I was civil. I was polite. I nodded, even though I didn't agree. My politeness was an act of whiteness, a perpetuation of whiteness.

Politeness, including my own, keeps whiteness going. In the essay, "Know Your Whites," Dr. Cottom (2019) attends a 2016 pre-presidency Trump rally. She mentions people being polite to her—people nodding and smiling while holding babies in onesies that read, "Lock the bitch [Hillary Clinton] up" (p. 123). She also hears a white man shouting, "Crooked bitch," obviously referring to Hillary Clinton, and moments later being polite to Dr. Cottom, gesturing that he could move his wheelchair if she needed to get by him (p. 124). I've heard this described as cognitive dissonance. Dr. Cottom calls it the paradox of whiteness and states that "what is necessary for the paradox of whiteness to maintain the internal tension that defines it is for superiority to coexist with fragility" (p. 118). Fragility is a tool for whiteness. Don't upset the whites. According to whiteness, upsetting the whites is worse than any racist crime that has ever been enacted on Black people or Native people—this is one of the many false truths of whiteness. Civility is a tool for racism.

Event 2

In the summer of 2015, I went with my mother and a group from her church to Israel. She had recently left the Southern Baptist Church and begun attending a nondenominational church, one that is segregated, like most churches in Memphis, Tennessee. Her church was all white. In Bethlehem, the city where, according to biblical mythology, Jesus was born, we stayed at the St. Gabriel Hotel. We had a gorgeous view of the city and of the mountains rising up on the outer edges. From our balcony, I could watch the sun climb over the mountains and shine its glory onto the poverty down in the streets below. Inside a shoe store near the hotel, one my mother decided to check out, the shoes looked already worn. Bethlehem is in the Palestinian-controlled West Bank. A wall surrounds it. The wall on the Israeli side is white and clean, and the wall on the Palestinian side is covered with graffiti that protests the Israeli government. The owner as well as the workers of the hotel were Arab men. Women weren't allowed to the work in the public eye. During the day, we traveled to holy sites, we kneeled at the grotto of the birth, we drank water from Jacob's well, and my mother's preacher talked about the many miracles of Jesus and the love of God.

Every night, the hotel provided us with dinner, a feast of Middle Eastern cuisine with hummus, babaganoush, and falafel balls among other things. The hotel owner reminded me of Ellis from the first *Die Hard* movie. He always seemed to be working an angle. Schmoozing like a businessman. One night, he joined us for dinner. He told stories that made the group laugh. He laughed too at his own jokes and smacked the

Chapter 17: Auto-Ethnographical Notes on Whiteness   199

tables. I sat between my mom and another, older white woman. The preacher sat next to the hotel owner, completely entranced by the conversation. Suddenly and without a sequitur, the hotel owner said that it must be difficult to deal with Blacks. I remember being shocked that an Arab man would say this considering that Arab people were also stereotyped and targeted in America. Post 9/11, the police watch lists, which were usually filled with names of Black youth, were suddenly filled with names of Arab people (Chang, 2014, p. 243). It never occurred to me that this was precisely why he said this. He understood whiteness. He was appealing to our whiteness. He was distancing himself from whiteness's main racial Other. He was letting the good white Christians know that he was more like the good white Christians than he was like Black people.

At the dinner table, the woman next to me said, "I can never understand a word they say." So many of the group nodded and started agreeing out loud.

Unlike the time at the coffee shop patio, this time I said something. A quickly spoken "Wow. Christians being racist."

The conversation stopped. Everyone looked at me.

Finally, the hotel owner said, "Oh, it's not racist. Not at all."

Again, he understood whiteness. He knew this was what needed to be said to calm the dinner table, to keep his alliance with the white Christian Americans who came to the holy land every year and stayed in his hotel, and bought souvenirs and expensive gold Christian jewelry and ornaments from his adjoining shop. I got up and went to my room. My mom was embarrassed. Not by the racism, though she did agree that it was wrong, but by me pointing it out. This is also the fragility of whiteness, the way white people think their feelings should be more protected than Black people are from white people's racism.

Event 3

In 2016, on my way home from teaching sixth grade at a public school in Memphis, on the eve of Thanksgiving (a traditional celebration of the deadliness of whiteness[1]) break, a young white man rear-ended me with his car. It had only been a few weeks since Donald Trump had won the election. Only a few weeks since I consoled Black and Latinx children in my classroom. One Black boy student had expressed anger but said he wasn't surprised at all. One Mexican girl had cried, already worried that her dad would be deported soon by Trump. Her dad would be summoned within the year, and her parents would discuss moving back to Mexico before ICE (U.S. Immigration and Customs Enforcement) could arrest the father and separate the mother from her children. I stood with these children and wept with them and for them. Notice, I didn't weep for myself. I knew that my white skin would protect me from most of the dangers from Trump. I was a white teacher in a mostly Black city with, just like the churches, segregated schools. I had great instructional skills. I was "woke" enough to attempt culturally relevant pedagogy and assign books with characters who looked like my students, but I struggled with classroom management. My voice was trebly, and even statements sounded like questions with my valley girl inflections that I had picked up during my 1990's riot grrrl phase. A lot of the kids distrusted me because of my white skin. I understood this. I didn't blame the children. I blamed racism and whiteness, though I was just then becoming aware of whiteness as something inherent, especially how it manifested within me. Even now, as I write this, I'm still learning. But I understood that I needed to build a bridge with my students, and this bridge was in my encounters with both my students and the world outside the classroom.

Yet on the eve of Thanksgiving week, as I stood on the side of the road next to my car's dented bumper, the young white man who had hit me said, "With all that's going on in this country, I was so glad to see that you were white."

I glared at him, and my hands shook. I sent a text to my husband quoting what the guy had just said and calling him a racist asshole, and I tilted the phone so the young man could see it, but I said nothing. The heavy rush hour traffic crawled by as I stood on the sidewalk near the white man, and while I think he noticed my agitation, he didn't seem bothered by it. So much for building a bridge with my students. I had failed them in that moment. No, they wouldn't ever find out that the man said that and that I only passive aggressively tried to rebuke him, but in that moment, I had perpetuated whiteness. Whiteness is most deadly to children of color, especially Black children.

I am thinking back now on the young man and how he had said, "With all that's going on in this country," as if this hasn't always been going on, as if he and I, in that moment, didn't perpetuate its ongoingness. His overt racism. My complicity as a white woman. What would have been the point of saying anything to him? At the dinner in Israel, I disrupted a moment of racism, and it was not the first time I had embarrassed my mother by doing so. While it did not change the system or even the minds of most of those at the table, it did begin to change my mother. Over time, as I continued to cause these disruptions, my mother became aware of her own racism and of racist ideologies. My mother, now retired from the sheriff's office, where she had worked for 30-plus years, supports Black Lives Matter and defunding the police (I prefer abolishment). She did not vote for Trump in either election. This is one small, so very small, change. If I had said something to the guy who crashed into my car, it may have provoked him or he may have dismissed it. But what if I had said something, and then, as he continued to live his life of privilege, more and more people called out his statements of racism? Perhaps, he would change like my mother did. Perhaps, this method would be effective if it was many years ago. I know we need more than just white people confronting each other, but we don't even have that consistently and often. And on that night, I was complicit. I did not rupture the chain of whiteness, and I participated in its demands of complicity. Complicity allows the discourse to continue, to repeat itself, until it moves beyond language and into action. White women have been more than complicit. White women have access to power. Even if it is less power than that of white men, white women are protected by white men's power if they uphold whiteness, and they can unleash the violence of white men on their behalf. A white woman lies, and a Black boy dies. White men killed Emmet Till. But it was a white woman who first told the white men the lie about Emmet. It is white women who surveille the neighborhoods and supermarkets and call the police to enact violence on their behalf.

UNWITNESSING AS AMERICAN HISTORY

In Chapter 1 of *White Rage*, Dr. Carol Anderson (2016) reminds us that the late great emancipator President Lincoln wanted a mass migration of African Americans to "Chiriquí, a resource poor area in what is now Panama" (p. 6). Anderson explains that Lincoln wasn't attempting resettlement for the good of African Americans; instead, it was because Lincoln blamed African Americans for dividing the Union. Instead of recognizing that the notion of white supremacy and the horrific years of chattel slavery were what caused the divide, Lincoln blamed the formerly enslaved people who now wished to be full citizens of the Union. He wanted to expel Black people from the Union so he could *unwitness* slavery and therefore any responsibility for the abject damage slavery caused. Even Thomas Jefferson, who said, "I tremble for my country when I reflect that God is just: His justice cannot sleep forever," wanted to force the mass migration of African Americans in order to hide America from its sins. He also, in his *Notes on the State of Virginia*, Query 14 (1832), pled a scientific case for Black inferiority, including an attack against poet Phillis Peters (Wheatley), where he misspells her then last name (the surname of the family who purchased her) as Whately.

POLICE, THE BRUTES OF WHITENESS

My brother is a cop. I could list all the ways he was an excellent brother to me while growing up, but today there is a gap between us. Anytime there is a Black Lives Matter protest, he posts videos on Facebook that show Black people doing something violent. Usually, it is a video that only shows one moment from one angle and offers no context. These videos are unrelated to the protests, but he thinks these videos show that Black people need to be subdued. He posts these videos to justify police brutality. I remember back when I was 13 or 14, my brother, while on duty, once chased a man, a Black man, a suspect of a robbery, and followed the man over a fence. The other side dropped 30 feet into a concrete ditch. My brother shattered his elbow, and part of his bone poked out through his skin. The fleeing man was not injured. The fleeing man had a gun. My brother was able to disarm the man without shooting him and without causing any major harm to the man. All with a severely broken arm. This was when my brother had first joined the force. Perhaps, this was before the police force had time to indoctrinate him into becoming a racist brute cop. Fortunately, my brother, now much older, works inside the courts.

After Mike Brown was murdered by a white cop in Ferguson, Missouri, protests exploded. My brother, for some reason or other, decided to start messaging me about Ferguson. I can only assume it was because he saw me tagged on social media posts for the protests scheduled in Memphis. At first, it seemed as if my brother thought the police were wrong and that he saw how the police were instigating the violence and were themselves being the most violent. But then I realized that he wasn't calling the cops out for these things. Instead, he was asserting that the police had the legal right to act this way and therefore any act to stop the cops from enacting brutality was illegal. I messaged my brother back that he shouldn't be a cop if he feels that way. He stopped messaging me. Our relationship hasn't been the same since.

One of the protests in Memphis for Mike Brown occurred at the intersection of Poplar and Highland, a busy intersection on the main thoroughfare of Poplar. Some of the businesses had closed early for the night. Everyone chanted, "Hands up. Don't shoot," and a group of Black men carried a small casket through the crowd, and as they passed, we all knelt. When the protestors entered the streets, dropped to their knees, and raised their hands above their heads, the police followed with threats of arrests. You cannot disrupt the flow of traffic because it disrupts the flow of people's lives. This infers that the murder of Mike Brown did not disrupt the flow of people's lives and that the permanent disruption to his life was less important than the traffic disruption. Stopping traffic isn't a violent act. What the police do after the protest stops traffic is, more often than not, violent. Yet that isn't the narrative. The narrative calls any disruption violent. White people post on Facebook about how they would run over the protestors. This has happened. People have been injured and died. Heather Heyer, a white woman, was run over and killed at a protest in Charlottesville. The narrative of whiteness states that she shouldn't have been in the street (in the street for racial justice—had she been a white supremacist, then the narrative would change) and not that the man shouldn't have driven his car through a crowd of people. This is the same narrative used to benefit the police, the long arm of white civility, when they attack, shoot, maim, and kill protestors for standing in the street. Disrupting traffic disrupts the flow of society, the flow of whiteness. Protectors of whiteness see this as an act of aggression. Violence isn't the disruption of whiteness. Violence is birthed by whiteness's desperate desire to silence any and all opposition.

Additionally, at my first protest in Columbus, Ohio, in 1996, a protest against the brutal murders of two black men by the police, we all walked in pairs down the sidewalk in front of cafés and retail stores. The cops stood in the streets, jaws unhinged, spit flying, batons in one hand slamming into the other hand, while repeating, "You step into the street, your ass is mine." As long as we stayed on the sidewalk, they wouldn't beat us. But one step off, well, our ass, and more than likely our heads, was theirs.

GOD BECOMES WHITE, WHITENESS BECOMES GOD

Returning to the term "unwitness," it holds so much information. First, it contains the word "witness," which doesn't just mean to see; it also means to tell or testify. Witnessing is part of evangelical white Christianity. Even today, white missionaries go off to other countries to witness Jesus to the Black people who live there, who already have their own beliefs and cultures. Evangelist witnessing infuses a white god into the narrative.

When my mom and aunt talk about their childhoods in the late 1940s and 1950s in the American South, they have two different memories. Twenty years ago, my mother's memories were different, but over time, she has slowly become aware of, at least, a few components of whiteness. My mother now tries to get her sister to be aware too, but my aunt refuses. My mom remembers segregation. She remembers playing with the Black children of the Black woman who, on occasion, babysat her and her sisters (Black women as caretakers of white children is another problematic trope rooted in racism). Yet when she would see them out in public, she knew she couldn't play with them in front of everyone else. She knew that the woman and her children rode in the back of the bus, while she and her sisters rode toward the front. She knew that she and her sisters sat on the ground floor in the movie theater, while the woman and her children had to sit in the balcony. My mom remembers not understanding why this was so and then how one day it no longer mattered to her. Segregation became an accepted part of her life. This horrifies my mother. How as a child she knew segregation was wrong but then she eventually accepted it as fact. My aunt remembers segregation as fact, as a part of her life. She also remembers Black children throwing jujubes on her head at the movie theater. My mom remembers this too.

But my mother feels shame that she got to sit in the good seats, and my aunt feels anger at the children for not staying in their proper social and legislated roles. Audre Lorde (2007) understood the complicity of white women when she said, "Mainstream communication does not want women, particularly white women, responding to racism. It wants racism to be accepted as an immutable given in the fabric of your existence, like evening-time or the common cold" (p. 3). It is partly ingrained civility but also an ingrained passivity to accept the racism of whiteness. Both my mom and my aunt, both Christian women, accepted segregation. Only my mom, with reflection and self-examination, sees it differently now. My mother saw the Black children as people, as human. My aunt didn't see them at all until they threw movie snacks down at her white head, and even then, she didn't truly see.

This is where white Christianity comes in. This is where Adam naming the stars becomes white men controlling everything and everyone else. Who needs science if you have the Lord on your side? Puritan preacher John Winthrop (1630) was the first to call what would become America "the city upon the hill." This, of course, comes from the Bible, Matthew 5:14–16, which begins with "You are the light of the world. A city set on a hill cannot be hidden." Winthrop claimed that the Puritans "entered into covenant with Him [God]." This belief persisted, as can be seen when, on November 3, 1980, Ronald Reagan referred to America as "the city upon the hill." If one truly believes that America is the city on the hill and that America was constructed by white men, this means that the white man is "the light of the world." Thus, whiteness becomes divine.

In 2018, my aunt posted on Facebook a quote attributed to the late Southern Baptist preacher Dr. Adrian Rogers. As a child, I attended his church every Sunday. His voice shook the rafters—the saved nodded, and the sinners silently wept—as he threatened that the fires of hell would be waiting. His voice hurt my ears, and one time I threw a tantrum about it until my father finally carried me out of the sanctuary. My aunt respected this man. My mother, at one time, did so too. My mother taught Sunday school at his church, Bellevue Baptist, when it was still in mid-town Memphis, before white flight caused the church to build an even larger complex near the newly sprung up and ever-expanding suburbs outside the city limits. Dr. Rogers was a leader, a beloved man of God. His booming voice was a performance, man acting as God's thunder to shake awake the backsliding souls. In 2005, Dr. Rogers died. Then, years later, amid media coverage of families being separated, of children being kept in dog pens, the then president shouting about terrorists in caravans, and so many white people screaming about free-loading immigrants, my aunt posted the quote. It was a picture, a meme, I guess, of the quote; it ended with an em dash and Dr. Rogers' name and the year 1931. However, there was no way that Dr. Rogers had said this in 1931, or anything except the coos of a baby, because 1931 was the year he was born. The quote was the erroneous belief about those who have and those who have not and how if we give to the have-nots then that promotes laziness.

According to a quick Google search, Dr. Rogers said it in a sermon in the 1980s, but he was quoting someone. The person who originally said it was Gerald L. K. Smith. Smith came from three generations of preachers, and he too became one. Smith was also a Nazi sympathizer. Though I think "sympathizer" is too polite a term. He was a Nazi. He may not have lived in Germany and been an SS man, but he did form The America First Party, which sought alliance with Hitler's Nazi Party. Aligning with Nazis makes him a Nazi. How do Christians slide into Nazism? Essayist Elisa Gabbert mentions in her essay "Witches and Whiplash" (2020) that the infamous Salem Witch Trials were due in part to the rising poverty and the presence of beggars and that to alleviate personal guilt for not following the dictates of Christ, a new narrative formed, one that said that the poor were bad, evil, demonic, even witches. The quote posted by my aunt contains the effect of the new narrative, a subversion of the gospel. It makes a person no longer have to care about other people and their well-being. It promotes a hoarding of wealth under the auspice of poor people being lazy freeloaders. To continue to believe they are the light of the world, these white Christians must believe that their hatred aligns with the will of God and therefore it cannot be hatred. Though, it makes me wonder whether if white Christians are taking the narrative away from the actual gospel, then are they, in fact, dethroning their god?

When Trump lost the 2020 election, the narrative of election fraud emerged. A video of his personal evangelist Paula White went viral. In the video, she holds her Bible and repeats certain phrases and words, like "an abundance of rain" and "victory, victory, victory" over and over again. She also mentions "every enemy aligned against you," as if being against Trump is being against God. She then makes unintelligible noises before claiming that angels are being released from Africa (Now This News, 2020). If she knew history, she would know that angels from Africa would likely not be on her side or Trump's. Now, the narrative of election fraud is connected to God, to Christianity—that those who voted against Trump sinned against both America and God. There was no fraud. There was voter suppression as usual in Republican counties and states with large Black populations. Even the counties Trump's legal team went after were predominantly Black counties. He wanted to *unwitness* his loss (and particularly his crimes and abuse of power) by suppressing the Black vote, and he counted on whiteness to allow him to do so. And it very nearly did.

My Nazi-quoting aunt voted for Trump twice and yet considers herself a devout Christian. When she posted the Nazi quote, I responded with

"Here's what Jesus said," and I copy/pasted from the gospel of Matthew. Within an hour of posting my comment, my cousin, my aunt's eldest daughter was messaging me to not ever correct her mother in public. She also added that I was going to give her mother a stroke. My cousin obsessively posts about pedophilia (she is very into Qanon and the conspiracy theory that Democrats are devil-worshipping sex traffickers). My cousin attends church weekly and has done so her whole life. She is also an English teacher at a public school in Memphis, a majority-Black city, and her students are mostly Black students. Yet she determines the validity of a source based on whether or not it aligns with her beliefs.

I met one of my cousin's students once. A young Black girl in middle school. I was in line at Walgreens, and the young girl in front of me wore a T-shirt with a middle school's name on it, the middle school where my cousin taught. I was exhausted from a day of teaching. My eyes hurt from daylong exposure to fluorescent lights. A bright red jacket hung around the child's waist, and she shifted from one foot to the other. Occasionally, she said something to her mother. As the line lagged, she noticed my ID card hanging from my neck and asked if I was a teacher. I told her that I was, and then I asked if she went to the school named on her shirt. It turned out that my cousin was her English teacher. She raved about my cousin. She said she was the kindest teacher she ever had. That she never raised her voice or yelled at the kids. Yet, unbeknownst to this child, her beloved teacher had voted for Trump twice. The paradox of whiteness. The cognitive dissonance of being kind and loving to her students while posting memes that degraded other people's humanity, while voting for a man who degraded her students' lives.

CODA

In 11th grade, a Black classmate who had aligned with me to report a problematic racist and sexist teacher said to me, "You've changed. The stuff you said in 9th grade made me not like you." I didn't ask her what I had said, but I remember that I felt bad for ever having said something that could have hurt her. I have many other moments and thoughts that I could confess. I'm not cured of racism or of the whiteness that keeps it going. I have to keep trying. I have to keep studying, both myself and the work that has already been done, and follow through with action. In this essay, I quote from Black women—Dr. Tressie McMillan Cotton, Dr. Carol Anderson, Audre Lorde. I also quote from the queer Black poet Danez Smith. If you are white, pause reading this essay and buy their books.

My family is divided, like the country is and has always been. But the problem isn't the division itself. There's already a narrative forming that now, with Joe Biden winning the election, the left must reach out to

Chapter 17: Auto-Ethnographical Notes on Whiteness 207

Trumpers. A call to reconcile with whiteness and not to reckon with and offer reparation for the horrors caused by whiteness. My cousin once messaged me that the problem with this country was the way everyone yelled at each other. Everyone being impolite. Remember, for whiteness to thrive, since Lincoln didn't get his great migration that would make the violence of whiteness vanish, we must be polite and pretend not to notice. The problem, of course, is whiteness, and it has always been whiteness. The schism cannot be mended as long as whiteness persists, and, paradoxically, eradication can only come through the schism.

Perhaps, division is the first step in the right direction. White people must continuously look for ways to disrupt the ideology of whiteness, to stop the subtle and not so subtle ways in which it corrodes and oppresses, and this cannot begin and end within only family units. White readers, as white people, must attempt to stop the consciousness of this ideology in the body of the polis. To change a system, there has to be a shift in consciousness. I believe this shift is happening, and that is why there is such a schism, why violence in the name of white supremacy (i.e., mass shootings, hate crimes) seems to be rising—it is the desperate roil of whiteness to save itself. But it is also why there has been more of a turnout for the Black Lives Matter protests, such as the ones against the murders of George Floyd and Ahmaud Arbery. More people are confronting whiteness and its violence.

During the time of these protests, I saw tweets from Black activists and Black writers who were shocked at the way white people at the protests called the cops "fuckin' pigs" to their faces. I have been guilty of this too. I thought yelling at the police was radical. But it was whiteness. As a white person, I have the privilege of yelling explicit insults at cops without worry of being shot. There is an unsettling connection between the privilege of white protestors and how white shooters are arrested alive and how some are given Burger King by the police. My relationship to the police, to any enforcers of the state is privileged because of my skin. I should use my whiteness for direct action but without putting BIPOC (Blacks, Indigenous people, and people of color) at risk of retaliation. If I am linked arm-in-arm in a confrontation with the police at a protest and yell inflammatory words at them, I am putting the people in my immediate surroundings at risk. I need to use my privilege to shield and community I am protesting with (and for) instead of opening them up to potential harm because I wanted to yell at the police.

In 2015 in Memphis, I attended a protest against the murder of Darrius Stewart by a Memphis police officer. I ran into a friend, a fellow writer, at this protest. When I took his photo, he held up his protest sign in front of his face. My friend is a Black man. This act of covering his face with the sign does two things: It protects him from my white desire to virtue signal by posting photos from a protest on social media, where he could be identified and targeted by the local police. It also centers the message of the protest and not himself—it puts him as part of a whole, as part of a community who is protesting. This is how white people should protest too. I learned from him that day that protest must be done collaboratively, as one of among many attempting as living bodies together to create a shift in the power paradigm of whiteness, and that I should only use my whiteness to protect others and never to center myself. This is why I am intentionally not citing the tweets to protect the tweeters.

I hope that through individual (within our families) and collaborative (with communities) direct action just and equitable change can come. I want to be optimistic: I want to believe that whiteness has an end.

NOTE

1. Most Americans celebrate Thanksgiving in commemoration of some mythical feast among the Pilgrims and Native people. However, it was Abraham Lincoln who, in 1863, declared the last Thursday of December a national holiday for Thanksgiving. He did this to remember the "lamentable civil strife" among citizens of the Union during the Civil War and to celebrate recent victories of the Union in the soon to be won war (Abrahamlincolnonline.org).

REFERENCES

Anderson, C. (2016). *White rage: The unspoken truth of our racial divide*. Bloomsbury.

Blake, T. (2001, May). *Franklin County, Alabama: Largest slaveholders from 1860 slave census schedules*. https://freepages.rootsweb.com/~ajac/genealogy/alfranklin.htm

Chang, J. (2014). *Who we be: The colorization of America*. St. Martin's Press.

Cottom, T. M. (2019). Know your whites. In *Thick: And other essays*. New Press.

Gabbert, E. (2020). Witches and whiplash. In *The unreality of memory: And other essays*. Farrar, Straus & Giroux.

Jefferson, T. (1832). *Notes on the state of Virginia*. https://www.loc.gov/item/03004902/

Lopenzina, D. (2017). *Through an Indian's looking glass: A cultural biography of William Apess, Pequot*. University of Massachusetts Press.

Lorde, A. (2007). The uses of anger: Women responding to racism. In *Sister outsider: Essays and speeches*. Crossing Press.

Now This News. (2020, November 5). *Donald Trump's faith advisor leads viral sermon day after election* [Video]. YouTube. https://youtu.be/I4daeEacIVI

Smith, D. (2017). *Don't call us dead*. Graywolf Press.

Winthrop, J. (1630). *A modell of Christian charity*. https://history.hanover.edu/texts/winthmod.html

II. Until the Wolf River Howls

Violence is decoupled from its original causes by the workings of time.

Nixon (2011, p. 15)

I grew up among rivers filled with snakes and rats, rivers that stank of progress, churned history, and spoke the secrets of my hometown, Memphis, a large city snug in the corner of West Tennessee. A majority-Black city with a white mayor. Memphis has two rivers, the well-known one, the mighty Mississippi, and the lesser-known one, the Wolf River. The Wolf ends when it merges with the Mississippi along the banks of downtown. Next to where the two rivers meet looms a bridge for cars, and then further down where the rivers have become one, there is another bridge for pedestrians and cyclists, and lights that reflect neon rainbows onto the dark surface of the river at night. The two rivers are forever connected in a seemingly disconnected city.

> I ask the Wolf River to speak to me.
> There is no answer. Just a babble of water, a jump of fish, and the stink from the chemicals that the men poured in. The men who sang, *Open up, river. Open up, and swallow.*

The Chickasaw people traveled from Central America, building civilizations along the way, complex dwellings and infrastructure; and they built again when they stopped at the Wolf River in what is now known as the city of Memphis. The Chickasaw people then lived along the Wolf River, rode its currents on canoes, traversed the waves as an aquatic highway for travel, trade, water, and food. Woodland bison lived along the river too.

Then the European settlers came—first the Spanish, and then the French. A Chickasaw man guided the French along the Wolf River. He told them his name was Loup, and the confused Frenchmen began calling the river "Loup." The white man always messes up names. Always assigns new ones. Always thinks he has the power to name. When the English settlers came, they heard the word "Loup" and assumed it was French—in French, *loup* means "wolf." A mistaken translation, an appropriation. This is how the Wolf River was named. The English settlers drained the water, broke apart the flow, wiped out the swamp beds, and built plantations.

In *A Billion Black Anthropocenes or None*, Kathryn Yusoff (2018) writes, "The Anthropocene might seem to offer a dystopic future that laments the end of the world, but imperialism and ongoing (settler) colonialisms have been ending worlds for as long as they have been in existence" (p. xiii). Other worlds existed before now. Not other earths—at least not to my knowledge—but other civilizations and cultures that the arrival of the British ended or at least splintered. In 1838, the Indian Removal Act forced the Chickasaw people off the wetlands and onto the Trail of Tears, which is now called Poplar Avenue and is the main thoroughfare in Memphis. The Chickasaw reservation closest to Memphis is now in Oklahoma. This is where the ancestors stopped along their forced removal and created a place for themselves. For Memphis's 200-year birthday, a few tribe members returned to honor their people who were here first, before the white man came, before the river was drained. I don't mean to imply extinction. Chickasaw people, and other Native people, live in both rural and urban areas (including Memphis) all over the world, and despite the continued violence, despite the past genocide, they persist. But the world that was here prior to the white man's arrival is gone.

*

In my ignorance, I claimed to have Native American inheritance. White girl. White bread. As a child, I learned the Thanksgiving story. The nice one. The one where Natives willingly gave their food to white people. I went to church. We outlined our hands on construction papers, turned them into turkeys, and wore feathers in our hair; we placed hands over mouths and mimicked a "warrior" cry.

In my ignorance, I claimed that pictures of my maternal great-grandmother proved I was part Chickasaw. *Her cheekbones*, I said. *It's so obvious that she was part Indian.* Though I don't think I ever saw a photo of her. Lies. Indoctrination. I was imitating what had been modeled for me.

> When I say, *in my ignorance*, what I mean is *in my whiteness*—racism, my inheritance.

*

The cypress-tupelo trees grow alongside the Wolf River—a tree made for water, for swamplands, wetlands. Drive down Covington Pike past the car dealerships, over the bridge that crosses one of the disconnected tributaries, and see the branches rising up out of the dark water, twisting limbs toward the blue of the sky. The car dealerships, capitalism, progress, are where the river used to be when it was one wide flow from Northeast Mississippi up into Tennessee and then west to the mouth of the mighty Mississippi River. When it rains, the drained land floods; the water seeks its home.

*

I stand on the banks of the river—the smell of sulfur, the sludge of mud. I dip a hand in and pull out a film-like oil—like if I threw a match in the water, it would burn. I think of burning. A force so huge and large, overcoming nature. Since I am white, I was taught that nature doesn't need me, nature held no secrets, and nature was the cross that the crucified white Jesus was hanged from. Or it was the storm he calmed and the water he walked upon. Imagine if the calming had been interpreted as taking care, as soothing an ailment. Instead, it is often interpreted as domination. Jesus commanded nature to His will—isn't it all about the will? The Baptist church in Memphis that now sits out east (white flight) over multiple acres, larger than a plantation, taught me that environmentalism is secular and sinful because we are like Jesus and it/nature must adhere to our will. Even Jesus' death was His will, in spite of him crying out with nails in his flesh, thorns ripping the skin, asking God why he was forsaken. How do Christians identify with Jesus if they think God is always with them? Maybe to be Christ-like is to be forsaken instead of being the one that forsakes.

Perhaps, this destruction of land and water, of animals, and of people isn't of God or Jesus. I believe it is the trajectory of whiteness. A trajectory I have witnessed.

*

In the 1950s in Memphis, autograph books were popular. My mother, a child in middle school, passed hers around at school like a yearbook. Most of the children, all white—pre-integration because Memphis did not fully integrate until the 1970s, when it was forced by a federal judge—signed their names inside the autograph books, and some added sentimental phrases. The most popular phrase, according to my mother, was "Yours 'til the Wolf River howls."

Howl: "The prolonged and mournful cry of a dog, wolf, etc., which dwells upon the vowel u/u:/ or some kindred sound; the similar sound of the wind or other inanimate agent (OED Online, n.d.). The river named Wolf. Mournful. Grief. Pain. Inanimate. Not real. A thing. An *it*. I've heard people referred to as *it*. Humans that weren't things. Were flesh. Blood. Heart beating.

*

Today in East Memphis, on the Wolf River wetlands, there is Shelby Farms Park, but in 1825, Francis Wright started The Nashoba Community,

Nashoba being Chickasaw for "wolf." Franny was a white woman. The project claimed to educate and free enslaved people. Franny would purchase the enslaved people from their owners and then set them to work in the wetlands tending to crops. Once she had made enough money from the harvest, she planned to send them to the free colonies of Haiti or Liberia. Franny bought people, made them farm her land, made a profit off their labor, and then planned to send them to free colonies in other countries. Franny's profit margin was not as high as it needed to be to complete her plan. She ended up turning the project into a free-love commune, much to the disappointment of the enslaved people. Interracial dating and even marriages occurred on the wetlands, but how free could free love be when 30 of the people there were still chained to the owner of the land, chained like the land? Eventually, Franny sailed to Haiti with the 30 people, and in Haiti, there were more chains—two years of agricultural work until the 30 people could have their freedom (Bederman, 2005).

> Freedom, something conditional given to someone by someone else.
>
> Freedom, a construct like everything else.

*

In *In the Wake*, Christina Sharpe (2016) centers her experiences and the collective experiences of Black people while focusing on the term "wake" to show the continued violence on Black people and how the violent deaths of Black people is an intrinsic thread in the fiber that wove America. Sharpe wrote,

> Wakes are processes; through them we think about the dead and about our relations to them. . . . Wakes allow those among the living to mourn the passing of the dead through ritual . . . the accompanying drinking, feasting, and other observances, a watching practiced as a religious observance. (p. 21)

Sharpe is discussing the deaths of her own brother, her sister, and her nephew and the customs of mourning. Wakes, across many American cultures, are a part of funerals. Sometimes, they are potlucks postfuneral, usually at the house of the bereaved. In my white family, we call it "visitation," and it usually occurs inside the funeral home the night before the actual funeral. It is often catered or potluck. When my grandmother died in 2014, my mom and aunt had it catered, with finger sandwiches, cookies, and tea. People stood in line to shake hands with and hug the family. In 1992, when my eldest brother died of AIDS, there was no food. Yet the room in the funeral home overflowed with the beautiful bodies of queer men and women. The procession to the cemetery stretched for miles and looked more like a parade. A celebration of queer love. A celebration of my brother's life. A life cut short by the politics of the heteronormative patriarchy and the rise of Moral Majority, a group of bigoted evangelist white men. Evangelism has its roots in colonialism. And while it eschews the rituals of Catholicism, Evangelism, a type of white Christianity, has other rituals for the dead.

In 1994, at Thanksgiving, my sister and I sat at the table in my aunt's dining room. The ritual sacrifices were spread out along the table, steam rising, and everyone cooed about how great it all tasted. This was about a wake, but my people were not the mourners and were instead celebrating death, genocide, under the auspice of thankfulness to God for their country. Cousins, elbow to elbow, munched on deviled eggs, cornbread dressing, green bean casserole, and the flesh of birds. I was 16, and my sister was 21 and home from college. Our parents did not attend college; they worked in factories and grocery stores, and even sold cemetery lots. My aunt had a master's in education from the local college. Her two daughters also got their degrees there. My sister worked constantly and got little to zero financial support from our parents.

My uncle tore into my sister and picked a fight with her. He loved God and country, he flew the American flag and the confederate flag, and he was a good Christian man. He felt it was his duty to make sure my sister didn't think she was better than the rest of our family, and he had to make sure she was kept in her proper place. He needed to root out all the radical intellectual, empathetic ideologies that those *East Coast liberals* were putting into her head. Then he yelled, fork in hand, the turkey spraying out of his mouth. He shouted about people on welfare with clenched fists and gritted teeth. No one at the table was on welfare. He likely didn't know anyone on welfare. My mother was on welfare briefly, between her first and second marriages, when she was a single mom with my sister. But he didn't know that. My aunt, red-faced, turned to my sister and ordered her to obey, to respect this man, my aunt's husband, the patriarch.

My sister stood up and calmly stated that she would go wait in the car. The light above the dining table cast a bright light across our white skin. My mother's hand covered her mouth. She liked to keep the peace, and pushing back was not peaceful. I rose from my chair. My two older cousins, a blond and a brunette, both married to men, both mothers, stared at me, waiting to see what I was going to do. My aunt pushed her curly hair away from her face and said, "Y'all are going to give me a stroke," and by "y'all," she meant me and my sister.

I screamed, "Fuck you," and walked out to join my sister in the car.

That was the year I was waking up. That was the year I became aware of my whiteness.

*

The Wolf River moves, a seen presence, movement, animacy. It has entire ecosystems inside it and beside it, catfish and jumpseed, carrion and sedges in its understory, and then on its surface the humans of Memphis, canoeing, yoga-ing on paddleboards, fishing in boats. The people of Memphis also drink its water.

Water is said by the failed biologist Jacque Benveniste to hold memory, to retain a recollection of substances once dissolved. However, when other biologists attempted to reproduce Benveniste's experiment, no evidence of a soluble substance was found in the water ("Memory of Water," Ball, 2004). I think water does have memory, not exactly in Benveniste's way or like a memory in the human brain—well, at least not to our finite knowledge. Bodies of water, like oceans and rivers, perhaps hold traces of the lives, animal and human, they have both sheltered and taken. When a life is taken in the water, if not retrieved, it will become part of the ecosystem. Since matter can be neither created nor destroyed, the water must hold the matter of a body after it dissolves in it. Sharpe (2016) describes more types of wakes when she says, "But wakes are also the track left on the water's surface by a ship; the disturbance caused by a body swimming, or one that is moved, in water . . . a region of disturbed flow" (p. 21).

In the 1950s, my aunt's middle school boyfriend drowned in the Wolf River. In the 1970s, a distant cousin, out drinking with my older brother, the brother who would die from AIDS in 1992, jumped into the water but never made it back up. In the late 1990s, musician Jeff Buckley waded out into the Wolf River near the mouth of the Mississippi, and his body washed ashore a few days later. But Sharpe's water wakes go back further to ships full of enslaved people, people being forced across the water and often times into the water by people who believed they could control water like their Jesus did. The people who created the wakes caused the water to swallow the rest.

*

In 1925, the Shelby County Penal Farm was built on the wetlands, the same area as that of the ill-fated Nashoba Project. The inmates labored in the soil, growing vegetables for the kitchen to feed them and for the county to sell in order to turn a profit.

The 13th Amendment: Section 1. Neither slavery nor involuntary servitude, except as a punishment for crime whereof the party shall have been duly convicted, shall exist within the United States, or any place subject to their jurisdiction.

Now, the wetlands are Shelby Farms, a 4,500-acre recreational park with a small lake and pedal boats, and paved-over trails for cycling, jogs, and dog walks. A movie screen for outdoor films in the summer. Every Christmas, it has winter lights all aglow, and the cars clog the entrances and back up to all the surrounding roads.

Chapter 17: Auto-Ethnographical Notes on Whiteness

But on the outer west edge sits a new penal farm for convicted male felons, now called the Mark Luttrell Division of Corrections, and the jail for women, known as Jail East, cradles the park too. Jail East is divided into pods: A-pod. B-pod, and C-pod. While Jail East is called the women's jail, C-pod holds male juveniles charged with violent felonies. From 2014 to 2016, I volunteered in C-pod. I brought in poems and stories. The boys were between 14 and 17; all had grown up in poverty, been kicked out of run-down schools, and been affiliated with certain groups that promised them the luxury that comes with money, a fleeting, momentary luxury, but it was the only access to a sort of capitalism, the American dream, that these boys had. During my time volunteering, all the boys were Black. One teenage boy was arrested when he was 16, still a child. He remained at Jail East unable to make bail. When he turned 18, he was moved to the downtown jail, called 201 for its 201, Poplar address, to be among charged adult men still awaiting trial. His trial happened after his 18th birthday, once he was larger than a child, heavier from jail food, and bulky from having not much to do. The jury convicted him for life with an option for parole—the parole option only because he was a minor at the time of the offense. I would like to tell more about him. He was kind. He wrote an amazing analysis of *Macbeth*, made an A in his online honors English class, and earned his high school diploma. He often said he would like to be a writer. But beyond that, his story is not mine to tell. I hope he one day gets to tell it, but the system is not in his favor.

To be clear,
I walked into C-Pod a free woman.
I walked out of C-Pod a free woman.
What I'm saying is that I'm not innocent.

My whiteness implicates me. I have benefited from a system that preferences white skin and offers more opportunities to white people. I do not go to C-Pod to save but to share. I share my love of words, my love of the power of words. We, me and the teenagers, we write together. We share our stories. We applaud one another. We laugh. A collaboration of words, of pen on paper. We sometimes cry—a ripple in the best way, a connection instead of a severing. A small act of humanity. To share without expectation of a return is in direct opposition to white settler colonialism, which took and destroyed.

To be clear, Jail East sits on the cleared-out wetlands of Wolf River, and 201 is on Poplar, which is a paved-over portion of the Trail of Tears. This isn't a coincidence. This is the wake.

*

Returning to Yusoff (2018), she explains,

> If the Anthropocene proclaims a sudden concern with the exposures of environmental harm to white liberal communities, it does so in the wake of histories in which these harms have been knowingly exported to black and brown communities under the rubric of civilization, progress, modernization, and capitalism. (p. xiii)

Another murder. Another wake. Where will the water ripple? Will there be more drownings?

In the 1980s, *Veliscol* dumped chemicals into Cypress Creek, a runoff of the Wolf River, and poisoned the soil in a historically Black, low-income North Memphis neighborhood near Jackson Avenue. Pesticides lingered in the runoff, dieldrin and aldrin. Dieldrin is linked to cancer, to Parkinson's, to birth defects. The chemicals were dumped in the late 1980s, but the soil wasn't tested until 2004. In March 2004, the residents were notified of the presence of dieldrin in the soil. In 2006, a local Black pastor filed a lawsuit against *Veliscol* for their dumping of chemicals and its connection to the high infant mortality rate in the neighborhood. Yes, dead babies. But that is the language of the right wing: Think of the children, but no not these children, only the ones in the womb, the white ones inside the white wombs. But in this neighborhood, a lot of living babies died. The pressure from the lawsuit finally resulted in the release of the health department's findings: Eight of the 11 persons who consented to blood testing had measurable amounts of dieldrin in their serum (U.S. Department of Health and Human Services, 2008).

In 2010, *Escherichia coli* was in the creek. Yet all the reports concluded that the soil and water were safe.

*

Memphis is known for its drinking water. At my mom's house, she can drink water straight from the tap. No need for Brita or Pure. No need for store bought or boiled. Memphis has underground aquifers, which are replenished by the Wolf River.

In *Animacies: Biopolitics, Racial Mattering, and Queer Affect*, Mel Chen (2012) theorizes how seemingly inanimate things have intrinsic relations to our lives and how language can delineate but also blur the separation between life (animate) and thing (inanimate). Water is obviously intrinsic to our lives. We need water to live, yet not everyone has access to clean water for drinking. See Flint, Michigan. See both Texas and Memphis in the winter of 2021. See numerous countries whose soils are tilled for resources to make iPhones or for diamonds or oil while their own citizens lack clean water. See numerous counties in the United States that allow fracking. Since 2021, water is being traded and sold on the stock market. Sometimes water is undrinkable because it contains lead. Chen points out how the English language likens lead to murder. "In some sense it is an old story," Chen writes. " To pump someone full of lead is to kill them" (p. 183).

In November 2019, the local newspaper reported that 10 Memphis public schools had lead in the water. The lead was actually in the fountains that the children drank from, fountains that had been in the schools for half a century. "One fountain near the library at Gardenview Elementary School tested more than seven times above the state's threshold for unsafe water, which is 20 parts of lead per billion parts of water" (Aldrick & Kebede, 2019). The water fountain turned gun—turned by who? My hometown, Memphis, the city where Martin Luther King Jr. was shot and killed, where children are pumped full of lead—the ongoing destruction from settler colonialism, the violence of whiteness.

In early 2021, there were plans for a crude oil pipeline to be built over the Memphis aquifers, where a leak would destroy the city's water supply. The Byhalia pipeline would run through the poorest zip codes in the city. On February 20, 2021, actress Jane Fonda tweeted, "A resilient predominately Black community in Memphis is fighting the multi-billion-dollar crude oil Byhalia Pipeline. The company seeks to profit $7B in yearly revenue while risking the drinking water." The tweet ended with an urging to sign a petition, followed by a link to the petition. Fonda was using her privilege both as a white woman and as a celebrity to bring attention to the pipeline. Notice how her tweet begins. She centers the people of Memphis who are Black, she highlights that Memphis is a majority-Black city, and she compliments the community for being resilient. The word "resilient" denotes that other issues have been trudged through and overcome by this Black community. This is a small example of what white people can do. To the white reader, the able-bodied white reader: Use your social media platforms to bring awareness. However, don't just virtual signal (tweet to show you are woke but without ever doing anything). Find ways to take direct action, but don't center yourself. Find the activists and organizations that are already building a movement and organizing. Join them. Collaborate. Make direct action communal. Think of power as horizontal, a shared act. The way this essay is not written solely by me—there is research, intertextuality, influence, editors. The way water moves across the earth, the influence of the moon on the tides, the need for rain to keep our wells from running dry, the way we all share the water from the earth. Learn from those already doing the work. Show up at the protests. By the end of 2021, the pipeline was halted because of the direct action of people through petitions and protests.

In Memphis and elsewhere, in countless cities, follow the water, and you will find the trajectory of white supremacy disguised as progress. But if you ask the white men who published the reports (U.S. Department of Health and Human Services, 2008), they will answer,

Nothing to see here.
No correlations found between dust, soil, and blood.

If you ask the river, you will see the evidence is there, in the rush of tides, in the wakes caused by the bodies we drank, in the grief of its howl. Water remembers even when we forget.

REFERENCES

Aldrick, M., & Kebede, L. (2019, November 7). High lead levels found in the water at 10 Memphis schools. *Commercial Appeal.* https://www.commercialappeal.com/story/news/2019/11/07/lead-10-memphis-schools-water-testing-found-high-lead-levels/2519778001/

Ball, P. (2004, October 8). Memory of water. *Nature.* https://www.nature.com/news/2004/041004/full/news041004-19.html

Bederman, G. (2005). Revisiting Nashoba: Slavery, utopia, and Frances Wright in America, 1818–1826. *American Literary History, 17*(3), 438–459. https://www.muse.jhu.edu/article/185372

Chen, M. (2012). *Animacies: Biopolitics, racial mattering, and queer affect.* Duke University Press.

Fonda, J. [@janefonda]. (2021, February 20). *A resilient predominately Black community in Memphis is fighting the multi-billion-dollar crude oil Byhalia Pipeline. The company seeks to profit* [Thumbnail with link attached] [Tweet]. Twitter. https://twitter.com/Janefonda/status/1363206404451008514

Nixon, R. (2011). *Slow violence and the environmentalism of the poor.* Harvard University Press.

OED Online. (n.d.). Howl. In *Oxford English dictionary.* Oxford University Press. https://www.oed.com/view/Entry/89030?rskey=3peAPG&result=1&is Advanced=false

Sharpe, C. (2016). *In the wake: On blackness and being.* University of Duke Press.

Smith, D. (2017). Summer, somewhere. *Poetry Magazine.* https://www.poetryfoundation.org/poetrymagazine/poems/58645/from-summer-somewhere

U.S. Department of Health and Human Services. (2008, September 26). Health consultation (Exposure Investigation Report). https://www.atsdr.cdc.gov/HAC/pha/CypressCreekSub-AreaIII/Cypress_Creek%20HC-EI%209-25-2008.pdf

Yusoff, K. (2018). *A billion Black Anthropocenes or none.* University of Minnesota Press.

INTERLUDE
White Solidarity: A Dangerous Idea
Robert Baird

Political appeals to white solidarity diminished slowly but certainly. In 1955, for example, Winston Churchill could still imagine that "Keep England White" was a winning general election theme, and even as late as 1964, Peter Griffiths, a Conservative candidate for Parliament, would score a surprise victory after endorsing a nakedly racist slogan. By 1968, however, when Enoch Powell delivered his "Rivers of Blood" speech—in which he approvingly quoted a constituent who lamented that "in 15 or 20 years' time, the Black man will have the whip hand over the white man"—he would be greeted by outrage in the *Times*, which called it an "evil speech," and expelled from the Conservative shadow cabinet. In the United States, too, where a century of racial apartheid had followed a century of slavery, open expressions of racism met with increasing public censure. Throughout the 1960s and into the 1970s, Congress passed a series of statutes that rendered explicit racial discrimination illegal in many areas of public life (https://www.theguardian.com/news/2021/apr/20/the-invention-of-whiteness-long-history-dangerous-idea).

SECTION III
The Consequences

The Black Speculative Arts Movement (BSAM) has transformed global society over the past decade. Led by scholars like Reynaldo Anderson and artists like Nettrice Gaskins, BSAM opens new doors for leadership and diplomacy in ways that advance decolonization in the twenty-first century. More commonly called "Afrofuturism," these cultures of the African diaspora emerged from the literature of Black science fiction in the last decades of the previous century. Nothing, however, captured the world's attention more than Marvel Studios' Wakanda—a fictional African nation based on the ideas of speculative science. Combining the literary and animated works of Dwayne McDuffie, Christopher Priest, Reginald Hudlin, and Walter Greason, Wakanda became a vision of a world without enslavement, segregation, or injustice. It offers the reality that white nationalists cannot permit the world to create.

As Rasheedah Phillips presented in New York City in 2022, chronomorphism—the ability to reshape the experience of time—uses the example of Wakanda to undo the damage caused by industrial segregation and colonization over the past two centuries. Allen Chukwuhdi, Dory Lerner, Kurt Wagner, Asha Criner, C. N. E. Corbin, Danielle Littlefield, and Odell Hall present a range of solutions that combine hip-hop and Afrofuturism to reshape both culture and landscape to promote equity and inclusion. These breakthroughs in humanities and social science research offer new frontiers in the interdisciplinary fields of African diaspora studies, ethnic studies, media studies, and American studies around the world. In defining new (and evolving) parameters for visual and auditory landscapes, these voices offer a new approach to advanced study that places indigenous experiences at the center of the archive. The consequences of critical race theory, and the clapback in its defense, entail the wholesale reconstruction of knowledge over the next century.

CHAPTER 18

Storming the Capitol: An Exercise in the Patriotic Right to Violence

Allen Chukwuhdi

On January 6, 2021, a mob of violent extremists raided the U.S. Capitol in a rebellion that was coordinated online. This is significant because the influence of the internet in the construction of "Self" has increased. Along these lines, Bloch (2016) emphasizes the importance of social media platforms in the formation of "modern group identity." She illustrates, for example, how Twitter and Fox News were central to the construction of a "False Self" (Winnicott, 1960) within the "Trump Crusade." Moreover, she asserts that thinking and feeling are not a dichotomy but are mutually intertwined. From a psychological perspective, she accentuates the fact that the development of both individual and group identities of "exclusive citizenship" are predicated on feelings of disdain for the "Other."

This is important because notions of benevolent citizenship and patriotism have historically been used to shape narratives of violence. However, even though individual and group identity may share some similarities, there is an analytical distinction between them. I suggest that group identity inevitably develops a character of its own that cannot be associated with any member of the group. That is, it absorbs distinctiveness and, by the same token, personal responsibility in empowering individuals to "act out" in ways that they otherwise may not. In other words, individuals tend to dissociate themselves from the behaviors of a group, and a potent example of this is the "insurrection" or attack on the 117th U.S. Congress on January 6, 2020.

On the other hand, the "insurrection" and its aftermath, specifically law enforcement's reluctance to prosecute the insurgents on any serious charges, reveals that white Americans are perceived as true citizens and therefore not subjected to the same emotional constraints, feeling rules, or reprisals as "Others." In fact, notions of "affective citizenship" (Jones, 2005) are embedded in the construct of "whiteness." To put it another way, those who had whiteness conferred upon them were

> deemed worthy of citizenship [because] White people were understood to be upstanding, law-abiding, moral, and intelligent. Conversely, non-White people, from whom citizenship was withheld, were thought to be base, criminal, untrustworthy, and of lesser intelligence. (Desmond & Emirbayer, p. 342)

Consequently "patriotic citizens" have, by and large, been able to act out in ways that Others have not, and moreover, violence is regarded as a component of their effectiveness. This is evidenced by the fact that while white insurrectionists were released on their own recognizance, 20-year-old Emmanuel Jackson, a Black male who turned himself in, was deemed too dangerous to let out into the community. Moreover, law enforcement's response to the rebellion was inconsistent with its reaction to Black Lives Matter protests following the murder of George Floyd. To be precise, white Americans have benefited from "collective anger," feeling rules, and disparity in the notions of "emotional complementarity." That is to say, in Western society, some displays of emotions are considered "white only." However, feelings of superiority resulting in exclusivity of embodied emotions have created a "societal psychosis."

In fact, the United States was founded on that psychosis—specifically, the pillars of African enslavement and the violent conquest of native lands. Therefore, I submit that the definition of a "good citizen" in American culture is a violent citizen who proves himself/herself by actively excluding Others. For example, notions of good citizenship were used to justify lynching, maintain segregation in the South, as well as engage in immigrant bias. Yet for a good citizen, this is not a matter of intolerance, aggression, or the denial of outgroup meanings; it is "an exercise in community building" (Gourevitch, 1999).

However, as previously stated, the influence of the internet in the construction of Self-identity and collective identity has increased. Consequently, cyberspace has allowed

> right-wing terror groups [to become] increasingly global in their reach. For example, . . . a French computer programmer committed suicide after giving hundreds of thousands of dollars to U.S extremist causes. The recipients included a neo-Nazi news website. (Rotella, 2021)

On the other hand, Parler.com has a significant domestic user base comprising Trump supporters, conservatives, conspiracy theorists, and right-wing extremists. As a result, their online platform was instrumental in the planning and execution of the raid on the Capitol, which draws attention to the importance of social media in the formation and maintenance of intemperate group identity.

Notwithstanding, "affective citizenship" in the United States has been driven by feelings of resentment since the Civil War, and these emotions are often located at the intersection of race and class. In one classic study, Hovland and Sears (1940) found that the total number of lynchings in the 14 southern states was negatively correlated with economic conditions ($r = -.67$). Thus, the less money farmers could get for their cotton, the more frustrated they were presumed to be, and so the more violent they became in terms of extralegal aggression (Baumeister & Bushman, 2003). Likewise, studies have shown that feelings of victimization and resentment are crucial to the development and sustenance of white supremacist ideologies. I suggest that those feelings are both conscious and unconscious, which again underscores Bloch's (2016) assertion that thinking and feeling are not a dichotomy but are mutually intertwined. Therefore, we must consider "the importance of emotion in social processes . . . [and likewise] . . . the significance of resentment in class formation . . . because it is essential to what took place in Washington D.C. on January 6th" (Barbalet, 1998, p. 63).

According to Scheler (1912/1994), "ressentiment" (resentment) is the "condemnation of what one secretly craves but cannot achieve" (Barbalet, 1998, p. 63). Scheler's definition speaks volumes when we consider the images of "nooses" outside the Capitol building, "Camp Auschwitz" T-shirts, medieval shamans dressed in animal skins, and men brandishing confederate flags as they ran amok in the halls of Congress. This is worth noting because it illustrates how the insurrectionists' feelings of resentment moved them from the "plane of consciousness" into the realm of psychotic fantasy. To be precise, those obscenities show that the in-group dynamic focused its resentments (feeling) on "racial fantasy" (thinking) and how their violent thoughts and feelings were used for "group glory." However, like violence, *fantasy* is embedded with emotion. Moreover, "we sow . . . emotions as well as fantasies, object representations as well as superego anxieties in our . . . *common relations*" (Azzone, 2018, p. 260). Therefore, the question that we are confronted with is in what ways are *fantasy*, emotion, and (im)moral identities linked? Furthermore, is the solution to "exclusive affective citizenship" rooted in the ability to feel?

This is substantial when we consider Freud's idea that unconscious fantasies about objects may, under certain circumstances, take the place of actual relationships with people. This idea was later built on by

Abrahams, Klein, Winnicott, and Fairbairn. Melanie Klein, for example, believed that "object relations" exist from the beginning of life. The primary object is the mother's breast, which is split into the good breast and the bad breast. Moreover, she felt that the "splitting" is accompanied by jealousy, envy, and the object of our internal desires. This is noteworthy when we consider that "in groups, splitting enables members to protect the idealized group image and to experience hostility, aggression, and envy stemming from external objects" (Azzone, 2018, p. 263).

By contrast, Bion viewed "projective identification" as both an interpersonal and an intrapersonal process, wherein we are manipulated to play a part in others' fantasies—as in the relationship between Trump and his supporters, between "exclusive citizens" and Others or, in the alternative, when we see images of patriots burning or vandalizing Black Lives Matter paraphernalia because they are attempting to force the Other into accepting a narrative they have constructed.

On the other hand, Winnicott (1960) thought that fantasy is associated with the interplay between inner and outer reality. In addition, he felt that there were multiple "self-organizations" that were functioning in relation to each other within a "personality system." According to Winnicott, there is a "true-self personality system" and a "false-self personality system," which seem to work in opposition to each other. Nevertheless, from an "object relations" point of view, "transference" can be thought of as taking one of two forms depending on whether it is the role of the "object" or that of the Self in the "internal object relation." This is important when we consider that the insurrection of January 6 demonstrated how

> meanings, in which cognitive and cultural factors are realized, attach to objects ... *for example, Donald Trump as the President, the Confederate Flag, or a noose* ... only ... *because of* [italics added] ... how [the] actor's expectations and understandings lead those objects to be used. (Barbalet, 1998, p. 66)

I submit that both meaning, and identity are strengthened by such actions and, along these lines, the seditionists' feelings of patriotic citizenship were strengthened by group aggression.

Despite this, resentment motivates feelings of revenge, and revenge is a potent indicator of violence. Nevertheless, a noose, Auschwitz, the confederate flag, and MAGA hats all carry incessant meanings related to dominance and, likewise, notions of *citizenship*, as well as the emotion of anger, which involves prized male attributes. However, as previously stated, the development of both individual and group identities of exclusive citizenship are predicated on feelings of disdain for the Other. That is to say that in-group meanings are shaped by the outgroup. To put it

Chapter 18: Storming the Capitol

another way, the aggressor is in a relationship with his victims, and therefore the question that we are confronted with is "Who or what would the insurrectionists be without those they hold in contempt?" This is the dilemma for those who oppose "critical race theory," or rather teaching the truth about American history.

> All the same, . . . resentment is crucial in influencing the processes of class systems . . . *and by the same token*, [italics added] . . . class resentment [and] . . . the feeling of indignation against inequality . . . is necessary for class . . . *or Race* [italics added] . . . antagonism to occur. (Barbalet, 1998, p. 68)

However, "receiving and attempting to interpret a cultural message is . . . a transferential event" (Stack, 2005, p. 72).

Emotions are associated with both racial and political violence. And although "affective polarization," which includes feelings of self-importance and aggression, is integral to party politics, it does not always result in violence. However, "the combination of the emotions of anger, contempt, and disgust (ANCODI) produces a more volatile mix than any one of these emotions alone" (Matsumoto et al., 2015, p. 369). David Matsumoto and colleagues (2015) found that anger, contempt, and disgust function as a unit and that together they are essential in the escalation of political violence. Therefore, it is reasonable to assume that this emotional mélange is, to some extent, vital to feelings of patriotic exclusivity and also to the insurrection on January 6. In addition, the researchers found that "these emotions function through the ability of anger to motivate action, of contempt to motivate devaluation of others, and disgust to motivate the elimination of others" (p. 369). Furthermore, their leader's countenance and verbal cues embedded within their communications were crucial to the development of violent behaviors.

This is significant when we consider President Trump's refusal to denounce the Ku Klux Klan when he said, "There were fine people on both sides" following the violent protest by white extremists at the Robert E. Lee monument in Charlottesville, Virginia, in August 2017. During the presidential debate in September 2020, he told the white nationalist group Proud Boys (considered a terrorist group in Canada) to "stand down and stand by." In addition, prior to the certification of Joe Biden as the president elect in January 2021, he told those who would go on to siege the Capitol, "If you don't fight like hell, you're not going to have a country any more. . . . They're not taking this White House. We're going to fight like hell." Likewise, the then secretary of state Mike Pompeo, who is rumored to have presidential ambitions, said, "Multiculturalism is not who America is" on his last day as the top U.S. diplomat, a day after Martin Luther King Day (January 18, 2021).

What is more, according to recent news reports, many of the insurrectionists did not vote in the 2020 election—an election they believed to be stolen? Arie Perliger, a University of Massachusetts Lowell professor specializing in right-wing domestic terrorism, told CNN, "When we see that significant ideological groups are stopping participating in the Democratic process, that may mean they are looking for other ways to participate, and those other ways could be more violent" (Lahut, 2021).

However, as previously stated, Freud posited that under certain circumstances unconscious fantasies about objects may take the place of relationships with people. Moreover, meanings in which cognitive and cultural factors are realized attach to objects or symbols like the Confederate flag or Donald Trump as president. On the other hand, change signals temporality, and "patients who experience difficulties with differentiation from the objects are especially sensitive to this and it provokes their hostility" (Lemma, 2014, p. 227). I propose this as a fractional explanation for the attack on the 117th U.S. Congress.

However, as previously stated, cyberspace has allowed right-wing terror groups to become global in their reach, and this draws attention to the importance of social media in the formation and maintenance of an "intemperate group identity." In fact, having "all the great minds of the patriotic Christian movement linked together and joined into one computer" and having the ability "to call up and access those minds" was an idea that Louis Beam, the "Grand Dragon of the Texas Knights of the Ku Klux Klan," had as early as 1982, after he acquired a Commodore 64, one of the earliest computers (Smith, 2021). Consequently, he presented that idea to a group of white nationalists calling themselves the "Covenant, the Sword, and the Arm of the Lord" (CSA), who were stockpiling weapons and training for an imminent race war at a remote 250-acre commune called "The Farm" (Smith, 2021).

Assertively, the CSA provides us with another illustration of how a group dynamic focused its resentment on an "embodied fantasy" and how the group's violent thoughts and feelings were used for "group glory." But, as previously stated, both *fantasy* and violence are embedded with emotion. Likewise, our perceptions are also entwined with emotion. Therefore, the question that we are confronted with is "In what ways are fantasy, emotion, and identity linked?" Nevertheless, this is alarming when we consider both the appeal of violence and that patriotic extremists feel they have the right to engage in it. For that reason, our ability to prevent any future insurrection is not predicated on "knowledge and cognition" but on "acknowledgment and recognition."

Notwithstanding, the literature on emotional information processing shows the existence of the "emotion congruency effect." According to the congruence principle, people are more sensitive to those types of emotions that are consistent with their own emotional traits (Lyusin, 2015). However, we must also take into consideration that "participation in the group experience is conditioned by variously motivated admission rules" (Azzone, 2018, p. 263).

As a result, the internet has given violent extremists a universal opportunity to engage with those who share their comportment and their *mis*perceptions call attention to what Horney (1950) describes as "neurotic claims." To be more precise, "they are neurotic needs which individuals have unwittingly turned into claims. And they are irrational because they assume a right, a title, which ... does not exist" (p. 42). In other words, they are excessive because they are made into claims instead of being recognized simply as neurotic needs.

On the other hand, an act of violence is also an "erotic transference." Moreover, a noose, Auschwitz, the confederate flag, and MAGA hats all carry incessant meanings related to dominance. This is interesting when we consider how Freud postulated that our sexual desires play a dominant role in our subconscious and that they are the impetus for our drives and desires.

In addition, he made a connection between "sex and aggression," and he hypothesized that we are each driven by a sexual prowess that is innate to the survival of our species. From a Freudian perspective, dominance also implies sexual dominance, just as hate implies love. What is more, if we bear in mind Scheler's (1912/1994) definition of resentment as the "condemnation of what one secretly craves but cannot achieve" (Barbalet, 1998, p. 63), then Freud's notion of *disavowal* is thought-provoking. It is the idea of a divided attitude toward loss, where "the attitude which fitted in with the wish, and the attitude which fitted in with reality exists side by side" (Freud, 1927, p. 156; Gutierrez, 2017, p. 1105).

Looking at it from this perspective, I would like to propose that like the opposition to "critical race theory," the insurrectionists' fantasy or "protest masculinity" is an irrational defense against reality. This is because "the neurotic feels entitled to special attention, consideration, [and] ... deference on the part of others. ... It is ... *not* ... up to him to do something about his problems; it is up to others to see that they don't disturb him" (Horney, 1950, p. 41).

CONCLUSION

The aim of this essay was to discuss emotions and their connection to the formation of racial and political violence. To be sure, "emotions constitute an important category of the psychological causes of aggression and violence" (Baumeister & Bushman, 2003, p. 479). They are responsible for intergroup behaviors used in the formation of the type of racial and political aggression that took place in the nation's capital on January 6, 2021. Furthermore, both racial and political vehemence contain fantasy and emotions, as well as notions of self-love, good citizenship, and group glory that, as a rule, have been used to shape narratives of violence. Future research should examine if the COVID-19 pandemic somehow played a part in the insurrectionists' ability to organize or willingness to storm the Capitol.

REFERENCES

Azzone, P. (2018). Understanding the crisis: Five core issues in contemporary psychoanalysis. *International Forum of Psychoanalysis*, 27(4), 255–265. https://doi.org/10.1080/0803706X.2016.1221134

Barbalet, J. M. (1998). Class and resentment. In *Emotion, social theory, and social structure: A macro-sociological approach* (pp. 62–81). Cambridge University Press. https://doi.org/10.1017/CBO9780511488740.005

Baumeister, R. F., & Bushman, B. J. (2003). Emotions and aggressiveness. In W. Heitmeyer & J. Hagan (Eds.), *International handbook of violence: Emotions and aggressiveness* (pp. 479–493). Springer. https://doi.org/10.1007/978-0-306-48039-3_25

Bloch, K. R. (2016). It is just SICKENING: Emotions and discourse in an anti-immigrant discussion forum. *Sociological Focus*, 49(4), 257–270. https://doi.org/10.1080/00380237.2016.1169901

Desmond, M., & Emirbayer, M. (2009). What is racial domination? *Du Bois Review: Social Science Research on Race*, 6(2), 335–355. https://doi.org/10.1017/S1742058X09990166

Freud, S. (1927). *The future of an illusion*. Broadview Press.

Gourevitch, P. (1999). *We wish to inform you that tomorrow we will be killed with our families: Stories from Rwanda*. Picador.

Gutierrez, L. (2017). Silicon in "pure gold"? Theoretical contributions and observations on tele-analysis by videoconference. *International Journal of Psychoanalysis*, 98(4), 1097–1120. https://doi.org/10.1111/1745-8315.12612

Horney, K. (1950). *Neurosis and human growth: The struggle toward self-realization*. W. W. Norton.

Hovland, C. I., & Sears, R. R. (1940). Minor studies of aggression: VI. Correlation of lynchings with economic indices. *Journal of Psychology: Interdisciplinary and Applied*, 9(2), 301–310. https://doi.org/10.1080/00223980.1940.9917696

Johnson, C. (2010). The politics of affective citizenship: From Blair to Obama. *Citizenship Studies*, 14(5), 95–509. https://doi.org/10.1080/13621025.2010.506702

Jones, R. J. B. (2005). The political economy of European citizenship. In R. Bellamy & A. Warleigh (Eds.), *Citizenship and governance in the European Union* (pp. 143–163). Continuum.

Lahut, J. (2021, February 2). Some Capitol insurrectionists didn't vote in the 2020 election that they tried to overturn by force: Report. *Business Insider*. https://www.businessinsider.com/capitol-siege-did-not-vote-in-2020-election-report-2021-2

Lemma, A. (2014). The body of the analysts and the analytic setting: Reflections on the embodied setting and the symbiotic transference. *International Journal of Psychoanalysis, 95*(2), 225–244. https://doi.org/10.1111/1745-8315.12147

Lyusin, D. (2015). *Biases in emotion perception: Emotion congruency and emotion complementarity effects*. International Society for Research on Emotion; Swiss Center for Affective Sciences. https://www.unige.ch/cisa/isre2015/sites/default/files/Lyusin.pdf

Matsumoto, D., Frank, M. G., & Hwang, H. C. (2015). The role of intergroup emotions in political violence. *Current Directions in Psychological Science, 24*(5), 369–373. https://doi.org/10.1177/0963721415595023

Rotella, S. (2021, January 22). *Global right-wing extremism networks*. Pro-Publica. https://www.propublica.org/article/global-right-wing-extremism-networks-are-growing-the-u-s-is-just-now-catching-up

Scheler, M. (1994). *Ressentiment* (L. B. Coser & W. W. Holdheim, Trans.). Marquette University Press. (Original work published 1912)

Smith, L. (2021, January 26). Lone wolves connected online: A history of white supremacy. *New York Times*. https://www.nytimes.com/2021/01/26/us/louis-beam-white-supremacy-internet.html

Stack, A. (2005). Culture, ion, and Jean Laplanche's enigmatic signifier. *Theory, Culture, and Society, 22*(3), 63–80. https://doi.org/10.1177/0263276405053720

Winnicott, D. W. (1960). Ego distortion in terms of true and false self. In *The maturational process and the facilitating environment: Studies in the theory of emotional development* (pp. 140–157). International Universities Press.

CHAPTER 19

From Visual Representation to Hip-Hop: Using Innovative Sources to Reconcile a Hard History and Inspire Young Activism

Dory Lerner

We are living in a time that is remarkable and promising, as well as discouraging and predictable. From 2015 to 2022, a consistent pattern in American history played out yet again—human rights activism took one step forward and many steps backward. People who bravely spoke out against injustice and fought for equal rights under the law met resistance even as they achieved progress. At the beginning of the Black Lives Matter (BLM) movement, people of all races were willing to stand up and put their bodies on the line in demonstrations for equality. Similar to previous social justice movements, that activism was met with brute force, fear mongering, and an overall attempt to stop people from standing up for diversity, equity, and inclusion.

In 2022, the moral panic and seemingly increased intolerance was a direct response to BLM and LGBTQ+ rights and inclusion gaining political ground. This clash of opposing forces is not new. Emanuele Berry, co-host of *This American Life*, shared stories of the backlash in Episode 758, "Talking While Black" (2002):

> The black squares are gone from Instagram. The random reparations money from friends, gone. We went from anti-racist books crowding the bestsellers list to banning kids' books about Rosa Parks.

This backlash, it's not surprising. This is what America does, Reconstruction, then Jim Crow, the Civil Rights movement, to the war on drugs, Obama to Trump.

After George Floyd was murdered, there was a moment that felt like progress was in sight. The BLM movement garnered international support. But that window of increased tolerance was swiftly closed with strong opposition from American conservatives directed at individuals and groups who were working toward a more just society. One specific space where that retribution played out was in American learning environments, which faced an onslaught of paranoia and bigotry from parents, school boards, and lawmakers. They all felt compelled to shape social studies and language arts curricula, and to control which books reside on school library shelves. Three words, "critical," "race," and "theory," were twisted into a refrain designed to sully the ideas and intentions of the social justice movements. Critical race theory (CRT) went from being a strictly academic term that addressed all the inequity, racial injustice, and systemic oppression of the past to becoming a scapegoat for it. In *Education Week*, Eesha Pendharkar (2022) wrote,

> The campaign against "critical race theory" started in September 2020 with an executive order signed by former President Donald Trump, which has since been revoked. Last spring, state lawmakers started introducing bills that banned "divisive concepts," and forbade teaching that people should feel guilt or anguish because of their race or sex, that all people of a certain race have unconscious bias, or that the United States is a fundamentally racist or sexist country. They deemed these concepts critical race theory.
>
> In reality, critical race theory is an academic framework that posits that racism is systemic as opposed to only individual acts of discrimination. It has now become a catchall term conservatives apply to any topics or lessons dealing with race and racism, gender identity, sexuality and sexism.

The term "critical race theory" previously referred to a graduate-level course in law school. It has been connected thematically to the ideals of diversity, equity, and inclusion (DE&I). Both associations have been vilified. Under its current, suddenly sinister iteration, CRT is now being used to describe any teaching of history that has a relationship to race. It is also being used to describe ideas about any connections between America's racist past and where we are today. These distortions of the original meaning of CRT originate with people who either do not see or do not want to see the links between the economic disparities that exist today and the advent of slavery in America. Furthermore, they refuse to consider the idea that, just possibly, the foundations of the U.S. economy were always heavily skewed in favor of white American wealth and white people's exclusive access to the "American dream." Opponents of CRT also express disdain for any curricula that could make their children feel ashamed of past or present treatment of Black citizens or members of the LGBTQ+ community. Learning the histories of marginalized groups of any kind also is thrown into discussions about the evils of CRT. The argument is that if we teach children history accurately and inclusively, and share all of the facts with them about the history of the United States, then students might actually fall apart on merely hearing of their racial connections to the injustice on which America was built. What does that say about this nation's past? And if we are not willing to acknowledge the mistakes of the past, then what does that say about the present moment?

Are the opponents of authentic teaching of CRT asking us to do more than just stop teaching the history of race in America? Are they trying to actually erase this history from the American narrative entirely? The provocative painting "Critical Race Theory" by Jonathan Harris invites us to consider what U.S. history would be without Harriet Tubman, Dr. Martin Luther King Jr., and Malcolm X (Misha, 2021). By censoring the curriculum, we are not only selectively making certain histories absent but are also treading on the dangerous path of erasing entire legacies altogether—the struggles and the triumphs of millions of freedom fighters who sought an equitable future for themselves and the generations that followed. This is the kind of slippery slope typically introduced in the early stages of fascism to control the narrative systematically for particular ends.

"Critical Race Theory" by Jonathan Harris (standing next to his painting).

When history is examined honestly and with the intent of truly understanding events of the past and their relationship to the present, there can be discomfort and even pain. But a vital part of learning often happens when we are pushed to these edges. The history of the United States, like that of many other colonial countries, is emotionally fraught with trauma. Chattel slavery displaced millions of Black people from their ancestral homelands and families for the economic and social benefit of white Americans and Europeans. Power, greed, and cruelty subjugated many for the benefit of a few in the United States for 250 years. It is the responsibility of both teachers and learners to delve into that history so that we can make connections between then and now, and not carry forward past misdeeds.

The most evocative tools teachers have for teaching history are stories, shared through primary and secondary sources. Authentic and masterful teaching requires that educators do not censor, whitewash, or sanitize history. We acknowledge any discomfort we may feel, and then we continue to teach based on rigorously researched historical facts. We realize the importance of not traumatizing students or glorifying the victimization of people who were oppressed. For example, we are careful not to share explicit photos that depict lynching or other atrocities without doing careful, contextual work with students beforehand. Teachers can open pathways of understanding between the distant past and the motivation to build a more equitable society today.

In this chapter, I reflect on object-based storytelling in my own experiences teaching about race in America. I tell stories and share history through museums and sites of memory, visual art, oral history, and music. I have shown fellow teachers how engaging and accessible pedagogy that uses these mediums can illuminate history and inspire learners to connect with and better understand the people, events, and cultures that constructed our present.

Every day, young people and learners of all ages see inequities or directly experience them. Understanding the origins of these inequities equips people to make useful connections between the challenges they face and the root causes of those obstacles and disparities. Every day, children see racist policies and systems at work in current events, social media, and their schools—particularly with the exaggerated disciplinary actions taken against African American students. No evidence supports the erroneous notion that if we don't teach the historical roots of inequality and racism, then students won't observe the inequalities in their daily lives. Teaching the difficult history that this country was built upon empowers students to cope with the injustices they face and want to change. If we give young citizens and community builders the tools to understand and process the hardships impoverished communities face, they can collaborate in finding solutions of reconciliation that balance out the scales of justice.

Racism exists all over the world. It is particularly poignant in the United States—a country that lives by the credo of freedom and equal rights for all people. Silencing 400 years of systematic disenfranchisement of people of color, which occurred both legally and extralegally, certainly doesn't erase or correct the errors of our ways. In Dr. King's famous "I Have a Dream" speech, given at the March on Washington on August 28, 1963, to 300,000 marchers, he not only spoke of his dream "that my four little children will one day live in a nation where they will not be judged by the color of their skin but by the content of their character," he also spoke of a bad check written by the founders of this country to Black Americans:

> When the architects of our republic wrote the magnificent words of the Constitution and the Declaration of Independence, they were signing a promissory note to which every American was to fall heir. This note was a promise that all men—yes, Black men as well as white men—would be guaranteed the unalienable rights of life, liberty and the pursuit of happiness.
>
> It is obvious today that America has defaulted on this promissory note insofar as her citizens of color are concerned. Instead of honoring this sacred obligation, America has given the Negro people a bad check, a check which has come back marked insufficient funds.

While undoubtedly this is the speech that is the most commonly quoted because of the joyous imagery in which children of all races could "hold hands as sisters and brothers," it simultaneously highlights both the great hopes of Black Americans and the contradictory realities of their experiences in the United States.

In other speeches, Dr. King told an even more complex story of frustration, strategy, and his willingness to sacrifice his life for racial equality and economic equity. In his final "Mountaintop" speech at the Mason Temple in Memphis, Tennessee, on April 3, 1968, the night before he was tragically assassinated, Dr. King told 1,300 sanitation workers who were standing up for their rights as men and human beings, "All we say to America is, 'Be true to what you said on paper'."

America is still not true to its founding tenets but, rather, has tried to brush the injustices of the past and present under the rug of denial. Dr. King (1968) also prophetically stated in that last speech, "I may not get there with you, but we as a people will get to the promised land." More than 50 years later, we certainly have not yet reached that promised land. We have a lot of work to do and many goals to achieve to get there together. Education will be vital in bridging the gaps between students from diverse socioeconomic backgrounds. Learning about our disturbing past builds empathy for groups who still face challenges.

Formerly the Lorraine Motel in Memphis, now the National Civil Rights Museum, the site where Dr. King was assassinated shares with visitors the power of "place." In my work as an educator there, I teach and interpret difficult history and learn about ways in which we can work collectively

(Left) National Civil Rights Museum at the Lorraine Motel. Courtesy of National Civil Rights Museum.

(Right) Balcony of Room 306 at the Lorraine Motel. Courtesy of National Civil Rights Museum.

toward a more just society. People of all ages, races, ethnicities, religions, and socioeconomic backgrounds travel from all over the world to this International Site of Conscience. While visiting the museum, people encounter and recognize the idea that Dr. King's legacy lives on through each one of us who is willing to stand up against inequality and fight for justice, equity, and freedom for all people. The museum's exhibitions, collections, programs, and staff serve to remind visitors, who come to pay tribute to the memory of Dr. King, that his legacy lives on. The outdoor space near the balcony of Room 306 is a place of mourning and tribute. The museum also shares stories of activists who used planning, organizing, and direct action to bring forth change. Some of these figures are familiar, such as Ruby Bridges, Rosa Parks, Fannie Lou Hamer, Malcolm X, and John Lewis. Many of their biographical books are currently banned from some school libraries due to the CRT debate. Also banned by those who vilify CRT are stories of groups such as the Student Nonviolent Coordinating Committee (SNCC), National Association for the Advancement of Colored People (NAACP), Congress of Racial Equality (CORE), and Freedom Riders. Each of these individuals and groups was instrumental in the success of the civil rights movement. Despite such bans, the museum continues to tell those stories, as well as those of less familiar heroes such as Bayard Rustin, who planned and orchestrated many of the movement's biggest demonstrations, including the March on Washington in 1963; Claudette Colvin and JoAnn Robinson, who were influential in sparking the Montgomery Bus Boycott in 1955; and the Memphis 13, a group of Black first graders who integrated Memphis's public school system in 1961. All of their stories deserve to be told because they bravely faced verbal assault, physical violence, and the threat of death simply for being upstanders. They stood up when they saw injustice and took action to change it. As we learn their stories, we gain wisdom from their successes and frustrations. In learning about their role in the civil rights movement, we realize that it is so much bigger than Dr. King alone and that it began long before 1955 in Montgomery, Alabama, with the bus boycott and in Money, Mississippi, with the lynching of Emmett Till.

Also, museum visitors learn that the civil rights movement did not end in 1965 with the passage of the Civil Rights Act or in 1968 with the assassination of Dr. King. The movement began when the oppression began, more than 400 years ago, when the first enslaved Africans were kidnapped from their homeland and brought to colonial lands by way of the inhuman Middle Passage. Once these individuals and families, whose lives had been stolen, made it to the Americas, they were forced to build this nation for no pay and with no rights, choices, or freedoms. African Americans resisted in every way they could. Resistance to injustice continues even today as inequality still pervades too many aspects of American life. One of the most effective ways for museums to bring history to life is through exhibitions of objects and artifacts. Many of these racist objects would be unfathomable today, particularly to people who didn't witness or experience segregation firsthand.

Cast iron sign from the era of Jim Crow segregation in the United States (ca. 1950s). Courtesy of National Civil Rights Museum. Photo credit Dory Lerner.

I have collected a range of teaching objects for students to handle and examine closely. The artifact that seems to have the biggest impact is a cast iron sign from the era of Jim Crow segregation directing Black people to use separate bathrooms from white people. This object is so powerful because while many students have seen pictures of a similar sign, they have not seen one in person. Students often notice when they touch the sign how cold and heavy it feels. We talk about the practice and the system of segregation being cold and heavy emotionally, and how the sign is symbolic not just for its words but for the heft and coldness it physically embodies. Many students feel sad or even angry when they touch the sign. The experience of this object makes the past feel visceral in a way that words in books, or even photos, often cannot do. It helps students to know that the tragically unjust era of segregation did in fact happen and the objects that museums have to share are incontrovertible evidence of that history.

(Left) Tear gas canister used by police officers during Black Lives Matter protest in Memphis, Tennessee, May 2020. Property of Dory Lerner. Photo credit Dory Lerner.

(Right) Replica of I AM A MAN and BLM signs. Property of Dory Lerner. Photo credit Dory Lerner.

Pictured on the left is an object that I often share with students to connect the brutality of the past with the present. While only 3.5 inches long and 1.5 inches in diameter, its impact was huge for the protestors who were being fired upon. I show this tear gas canister so learners can examine it closely and try to identify it. Typically, after a few tries, someone will guess what it is correctly. Once they know what it is, I ask if they think it was used in the distant or the recent past. Usually, they answer that it is from a long time ago. Then, I inform them that this particular tear gas canister was launched at BLM marchers in downtown Memphis in May 2020.

It shows students that the tools police officers use to try to control protests for civil rights have not changed too much from the "Bloody Sunday" in 1965 at Selma, Alabama, to today. This small metal cylinder is objective evidence of moments in history. Violent instruments of force that were used on people in the past who exercised their First Amendment rights of free speech and assembly are still employed against people today who stand up against police brutality and social injustice. Usually, I pair this object with protest signs and pictures of protests from 50 years ago and photos of protests that have taken place in recent years after the deaths of Trayvon Martin, Michael Brown, and George Floyd. The photos don't show the actual tear gas canisters that were launched. The photos show people standing up for their rights and the rights of fellow human beings. They show law enforcement officers using brute force against nonviolent protestors. But the canister itself is evidence of the ever-present tools of oppression, and it conveys the dangers faced by those who resisted racial injustice.

Each of us has the potential to stand up and amplify our voices when we see injustice, to appreciate diversity instead of merely tolerating it, and to support other people in any way we can. Racism and discrimination still pervade our society, not only because they were foundational to how the economic policies and social mores of the nation were constructed but also because there are not enough people who are willing to dismantle and rectify an unjust system. Practices such as racial profiling, housing discrimination, and mass incarceration of African American citizens, in addition to discriminatory laws like those that limit voter registration, are just a few ways in which racism persists today. To combat racism, individuals can speak out and vote for equitable legislation and create a ripple effect by encouraging others to vote for just laws. Allies can work to eradicate racism by marching on the front lines of protests and also by writing letters to decision makers, funding antiracist organizations, and spreading awareness on issues of injustice. One method for spreading awareness is to create art that helps shed light on racism and injustice. This combination of art and activism, which I call "artivism," can also be a method of visual storytelling.

The Quilts of Gee's Bend are an example of such powerful art. They connect back to citizens fighting for voting rights, fulfill a practical purpose, and have phenomenal visual impact. For more than a century, women have been quilting in the isolated community of Gee's Bend, using scraps of textiles including pieces of cotton sacks—the "work-clothes" that were worn while enslaved workers, and later sharecroppers, tended to farming in the fields. Now, people also send fabric to this community of quiltmakers, knowing that what they send will be quilted into remarkable works of art.

Gee's Bend, also known as Boykin, is a rural community in Alabama's Black Belt, an area renowned for its dark, fertile soil. Surrounded on three sides by water, it is isolated from businesses and hospitals. In this all-Black community, where citizens whose ancestors were enslaved live now, quiltmakers have been creating quilts that keep people warm and make powerful statements about the time and place in which they were made. In the 1960s, the majority of jobs held by African American women in the South were as domestic workers for white families. There were no white families in Gee's Bend though. The women there were artisans who produced quilts and pillow covers, which were sold in stores from Sears to Saks Fifth Avenue. Dr. Martin Luther King Jr. visited the Gee's Bend Freedom Quilting Bee in the 1960s and told the quiltmakers how empowering their work was. They were breaking the barriers of traditional, subservient roles for Black women, particularly in the segregated South.

As seen in museum exhibitions of the quilts and in the full-size color photos of the quilts featured in the book *The Quilts of Gee's Bend* (Beardsley et al., 2002), these hand-crafted works are usually very abstract visually and have geometric designs. While the mere act of making textiles that were marketable in mainstream America's department stores was an act of revolution in and of itself, rarely do the Gee's Bend quilts tell a pictorial story.

Instead, quilters like Irene Williams created a "vote quilt" as an artistic response to racially restricted voting rights in Jim Crow's America. It also addressed the typical methods of voter suppression she and others in Gee's Bend had experienced, such as literacy tests, poll taxes, and ridiculous trick questions. According to Theodore Johnson and Max Feldman (2020) at the Brennan Center for Justice, Georgia voter Clarence Gaskin recalled that he was informed that in order to vote, he first had to answer the following questions correctly: "How many kernels of corn are in the jar? How many bumps on the cucumber? How many seeds in the watermelon? And how many bubbles in the bar of soap?" Clarence didn't bother with guessing once the polling official admitted that there were no right answers. His vote was neither cast nor counted. In Gee's Bend there was another method that was even more apparent in its attempts to suppress the Black vote: removing the only method of public transportation that Gee's Benders could use to get to Selma or Camden, the nearest towns with voting places.

> At the height of the voting rights crusade, ferry access from Gee's Bend to the county seat was terminated. As Arlonzia Pettway recalls, "Lots of people from Gee's Bend were going over to register to vote. Must have been next week or the week after, the ferry was gone. Some of the white people said it had nothing to do with the marching. But it sure did. After that, we kept right on marching. One difference was that we had to load up in trucks and drive all the way around." Some Gee's Benders even remember the infamous county sheriff, P. C. "Lummie" Jenkins, saying, "We didn't close the ferry because they were black. We closed it because they forgot they were black." (Beardsley et al., 2002, p. 31)

The Gee's Bend ferry was cut off in 1962 and was not reinstated until 2006. Irene Williams's vote quilt was made to counter this act of white supremacy, which was intended to prevent Gee's Benders from registering to vote and from voting. The act of cutting off the ferry didn't go unnoticed, and yet it took 44 years to reverse this racist act. The removal or withholding of resources is not a new tactic of oppression. Creating art to express dissatisfaction with oppression is a commonly used method of resistance. These objects hold lessons based on both the ingenuity and innovation of the quiltmakers as well as their resolve to enjoy the freedoms for which the rest of Black America were fighting.

In addition to visual representations, oral histories are one of the best ways to understand history—hearing firsthand accounts from someone who has lived it. In Dr. Hassan Kwame Jeffries's must-read guide to pedagogy, *Understanding and Teaching the Civil Rights Movement*, Dr. Todd Moye (2019) defines an oral history as "an interview between someone who participated in or witnessed something historic and a prepared interviewer." He also writes that

> the act of sitting down with a participant in a civil rights movement, signaling that you think what the person did was important and that you were interested in hearing what they have to say about it, is a powerful action. (p. 198)

I wholeheartedly embrace this practice and consider it a true honor to hear stories of lived history. I recently interviewed Mrs Mary Lee Bendolph (b. 1935), who met Dr. King in Camden, where they drank water from the "white" water fountain together. She tried to get to Selma for the voting rights marches and to register to vote. Whenever she and I talk or I visit her in Gee's Bend, I spend time listening to her stories of hardship and of triumph over a system that isolated and impoverished Gee's Benders throughout her lifetime. During one of these conversations, Mary Lee told me,

> That ferry down here was cut off, so we had to find someone with a car to take us up to Camden to register. When we went in the car and got half way there on the highway, the police was there and they stopped us. But we kept going back. No matter how much they tried to stop us from going, and even if they threw that tear gas down on us, we said "that we was goin' to stand strong!" They didn't want us from Boykin to come there. But we stood strong, and we came. (Personal communication, January 21, 2022; oral history: voter suppression in Gee's Bend, Alabama)

Lauren Whitley (2020), senior curator of Textile and Fashion Arts at the Museum of Fine Arts Boston, Massachusetts, explains further why the quilts are so unique and how one particular quilt called "the vote quilt" is both a response to injustice and an artistic innovation made by an isolated artist:

> Over many generations, the women of Gee's Bend, Alabama, a rural, majority-Black community, have made quilts with remarkable innovation and creativity. Irene Williams's vote quilt is one powerful example. Williams pieced together strips of red, white, and blue fabric printed with the word "vote," arranging them in a novel variation of the log cabin pattern, called a Housetop, which was a favorite in Gee's Bend. Although she came from a community of exceptional quilters, Williams worked mostly alone as she lived in a remote neighborhood on the outskirts of Gee's Bend. Her solitary practice fueled her singular vision and unique approach. In this quilt, she deftly manipulated materials she had at hand, balancing the "vote" fabric with blocks of red, white, blue, and checked cloth. The strips meander in free-form lines that give movement and energy to the graphic print. The result is a complex collage, a visual feast of rhythm and color.

These images, courtesy of the Museum of Fine Arts Boston, visually reflect messaging about the Black freedom struggle and are proof of the resistance that Gee's Benders employed when the local government and lawmakers tried to suppress them.

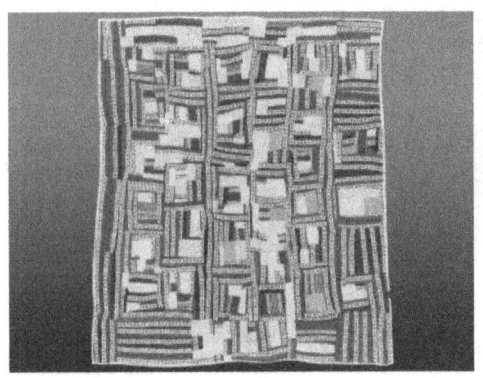 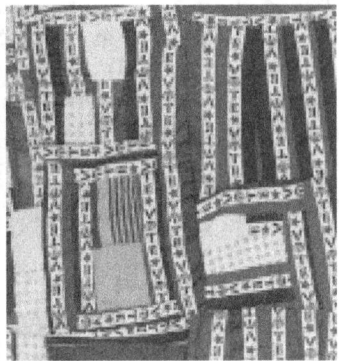

Irene Williams's 1975 "vote quilt": full quilt (left) and detailed swatch (right). Printed cotton plain weave, pieced. Gift of Souls Grown Deep Foundation from the collection of Vanessa Vadim. © 2020 Estate of Irene Williams/Artists Rights Society, New York. Photo from Museum of Fine Arts Boston: https://www.mfa.org/article/2020/vote-quilt.

In my four visits to Gee's Bend, I have had the honor of meeting and building friendships with several Gee's Bend quiltmakers. Mrs. Mary Lee has become my dearest friend there. I have known her since 2005, when

Chapter 19: From Visual Representation to Hip-Hop   245

we met in Memphis at the Brooks Museum of Art during the opening of a Gee's Bend Quilt exhibition there. Our friendship has been sustained through calls, letters, and visits for the past 17 years.

The Gee's Bends quilts speak volumes about the persistent socioeconomic disparities in this rural community. They reflect the lives of the artisans. They were first made to keep families warm and sometimes were even used as beds. Now these works hang on the walls of museums all over the world. They are genuine treasures of American history and art history.

The quiltmakers of Gee's Bend are only one example of how African American artists have confronted oppression and injustice. Black musicians have made powerful statements, inspired people to protest, and demanded equality and freedom through their art and through music—from spirituals, gospel, blues, jazz, and R & B to hip-hop. Teachers can highlight the power of Black music to speak truth to power, push communities forward, and even call people to action. I think of artists like Sam Cooke and Aretha Franklin, both of whom refused to play shows if the audiences were to be segregated. Dr. Charles Hughes (2019) reminds us of the power of Sam Cooke's "A Change Is Gonna Come" and Aretha Franklin's "Respect," both of which became anthems of the civil rights movement. Hughes also describes how the SNCC Freedom Singers, led by Bernice Johnson Reagon, went around the world performing "We Shall Overcome" and "Which Side Are You On?" to audiences of all races, nationalities, and ages with proximity to the movement. Any of these tracks are engaging primary sources to share with students. In his chapter, "Freedom Songs," Hughes observes,

> Music was more than just an accompaniment to this pivotal moment. Throughout the Civil Rights era, music was a site of struggle itself where musicians and audiences pressed for the same changes that motivated the larger campaign. Listeners sought to access African-American identified sounds and musicians, insisting that their ability to hear the uncontained energies of 1950s rock 'n' roll or the unmasked lyrical assertions of 1970s funk was connected to the larger push for racial justice. (pp. 209–210)

James Brown's "Say It Loud (I'm Black and I'm Proud)" and the Staples Singers' "When Will We Be Paid (for the Work We've Done)?" directly asserted Black pride and confidence. These songs and artists were influential to later forms of music that also made bold statements about the Black experience and the struggle for Black liberation. Hughes and Jeffries suggest the importance of sharing "Movement music" (the titles listed here are just a few) with students to bridge the past and the present. Hughes also recommends having students build a "Civil Rights playlist" as a practical way to remind them that their opinions matter. Incorporating their musical perspectives encourages them to be invested in the curriculum and engaged with both history and current affairs. It also illustrates the premise that songs produced by Black artists today continue the tradition of using music as a means of resistance, which includes the dawn of hip-hop music in the late twentieth century (Hughes, 2019).

Hip-hop is an accessible resource for teaching and learning about the socioeconomic divisions in American society, both past and present. Like the civil rights movement–era music, hip-hop speaks truth to power. This lyrical art form is in the classic oral tradition of storytelling. It is reminiscent of the many other innovations by Black artists that have been ignored, belittled, or even censored to silence their power. While some people hear it as a call to action, others may find it challenging to process some of the lyrics and take in the powerful messages that Black musicians have created through song and shared for the past 400 years. Hip-hop is the courageous and creative expression of artists who have knowledge, hopes, dreams, frustrations, pain, and triumphs to share with the world.

The spoken word and rhythmic beats of hip-hop, along with the use of turntables and mixers, combine elements of every genre from the long continuum of Black music. The use of call-and-response pays tribute to the tradition of old spirituals and to the foundational chants and percussions derived from West Africa. Hip-hop is protest music and an innovative form of artivism. The title of Jeff Chang and Dave Cook's (2021) book *Can't Stop Won't Stop* sums it up. In the book's introduction, DJ Kool Herc (known as the originator of hip-hop) wrote,

> It has given young people a way to understand their world, whether they are from the suburbs or whatever. . . . Hip-hop is the voice of this generation. Even if you didn't grow up in the Bronx in the '70's, hip-hop is there for you. It has become a powerful force. Hip-hop binds all of these people, all of these nationalities, all over the world together. (p. xii)

Hip-hop was my first love, starting in 1983. The beats and rhymes of Run DMC, Doug E. Fresh, the Fat Boys, and Kurtis Blow made it apparent to me that this music genre was groundbreaking and important. As a teenager, I listened to East Coast artists WuTang Clan, Nas, and Tribe Called Quest; West Coast artists Too Short, NWA, and 2Pac; and southern hip-hop artists OutKast, Triple 6 Mafia, UGK, and Geto Boys. Despite the music coming from all over the United States, it was easy to hear common threads in the stories. The sound—particularly the samples, the beats, and the tempo of lyricism—may have differed by region, but the messaging had commonalities, most of all honesty. One of the classic early hip-hop tracks out of the Bronx, "The Message" (1982) by Grandmaster Flash and the Furious Five famously rhymes about their daily circumstances and challenges:

Chapter 19: From Visual Representation to Hip-Hop

Broken glass everywhere
People pissing on the stairs, you know they just don't care
I can't take the smell, I can't take the noise
Got no money to move out, I guess I got no choice
Rats in the front room, roaches in the back
Junkies in the alley with the baseball bat
I tried to get away but I couldn't get far
'Cause the man with the tow truck repossessed my car
Don't push me 'cause I'm close to the edge
I'm tryin' not to lose my head
It's like a jungle sometimes
It makes me wonder how I keep from going under

This is a legendary example of the thousands of stories that intimately connect hip-hop artists to their listeners. For the listener, there is an opportunity to hear and know the artist's story. In her book *Prophets of the Hood: Politics and Poetics in Hip Hop*, Imani Perry (2004) posits the types of narratives we hear from hip-hop artists:

> The Real, or realism in hip hop as a movement, takes on two perspectives, "telling" narratives and "being" narratives, which, in terms of understanding hip hop as the production of a community and of individual artists, or mutually dependent. In "Cell Therapy," by Goodie Mob, we hear a "telling" narrative. "My family moved into our apartment complex / the gate with a serial code was put up next / they claim that this community is so drug-free / but it don't look that way to me." (p. 91)

CeeLo Green of Goodie MOb (1994) finishes his 16 bars with the line "I wonder if that gate was put up to keep crime out or keep us in." This is a very "telling" narrative if we are truly engaging with the lyrics by listening and considering their meaning in both practical and metaphorical senses. Perry (2004) says, "The speaker provides the sociological conditions and the prospects of social control through planned communities" (p. 91).

Regarding social control and moral panic being used to combat or stifle the power of hip-hop, they have always existed, even during the formative years of hip-hop. In the 1980s and 1990s, conservative lawmakers, parents, and believers in censorship started a moral panic that still persists, despite the court's ruling that this music is, in fact, art. There were campaigns of propaganda started and even police action taken to censor and ban certain albums and artists. According to the *First Amendment Encyclopedia*, in 1990, courts ordered the banning pof a rap album in Broward County, Florida. According to this source, "Police told stores selling 2 Live Crew album(s) would result in arrest." But two years later, "the appeals court based its decision on the fact that the state did not counter arguments that although graphic, the music had artistic value" (Fischer, 2009). Instead of thinking of hip-hop as a threat, listeners who are less familiar with this music genre could take the opportunity to look into the window it opens in order to have greater understanding and appreciation. If more people listened closely to artists around the country (and the world) truth telling through this powerful art form, there would be greater understanding of hip-hop as a method of resistance.

In 2021, on Nas's podcast *The Bridge: 50 Years of Hip-Hop*, the legendary rapper and motion picture mogul Ice Cube spoke about the power of hip-hop to connect people from inner-city neighborhoods and from all neighborhoods around the world:

> That's how I felt hearing "The Message," hearing records like *Hard Times*. These are records that spoke to me, and spoke the power of what the music can do. . . . I had no connection to the people until hip-hop made the connection and said, "Damn, they got broken glass everywhere, too!" . . . It was just a thing where it did validate what we were going through and what we were doing. Now with our music we wanted to be like the pros. And the pros was Biz Markie, Big Daddy Kane, KRS, Run DMC, Rakim. These are the pros to us, and we felt like we can't do what they do. We should just do what we do, and if we never get famous around the world, that's fine. We cool with just talking about what's going on around here . . . We had the homies in the neighborhood bumpin' our little tape. That was good enough. And coming from that pure point of view, everybody accepted it. . . . People all across the world are going through similar things, and we all connected through our experiences, and now . . . it's the first time our thoughts are with each other, . . . and we have spent 20–30 years telling our stories. We all are kind of on a mission to change the paradigm, how to change what is going on, how to change who we are, and to be better, and to understand our obstacles. And they're real, they're not imaginary. (Jones & Oh, 2021)

Hip-hop offers a unique firsthand perspective into the inequities that still pervade our communities today, as well as the ways by which people rise above adversity and change their communities for the better. For educators, it is important to remember that learners possess and use multiple intelligences (Gardner, 1983), or learn in a wide variety of ways. If we hope to reach the broadest range of students, we should employ a diverse set of tools and tactics to teach the hard but important history of race in America. We can use primary and secondary sources such as speeches, historic artifacts and sites, oral histories, visual arts, and music. These sources tell stories in ways that should broaden students' understanding of the arc from where we have been, as a nation, to where we are now. Teachers who want to empower their students can take an ethical stand by teaching history truthfully.

We must move beyond the current moral panic and recenter our focus on progress for equity and social justice. History matters, and it shouldn't be sanitized. Instead, it should be illuminated to inspire our students to take an interest in learning and to remind them of their potential as civically engaged citizens. By approaching history honestly, we can work to reconcile the past, create a more equitable society, and foster justice for future generations.

REFERENCES

Beardsley, J., Arnett, W., Beardsley, J., Livingston, J., & Arnett, P. (2002). River Island. In *The Quilts of Gee's Bend*. Tinwood Books in association with the Museum of Fine Arts, Houston.

Berry, E. (2022, January 7). 758: Talking while Black [Transcript]. *This American Life*. https://www.thisamericanlife.org/758/transcript

Chang, J., & Cook, D. D. D. (2021). Introduction (D. J. K. Herc). In *Can't stop won't stop: A hip-hop history* (pp. xi–xii). Wednesday Books.

Fischer, P. (2009). *The First Amendment encyclopedia*. 2 Live Crew. https://www.mtsu.edu/first-amendment/article/1447/2-live-crew

Gardner, H. (1983). *Frames of mind: The theory of multiple intelligences*. Basic Books.

Goodie Mob. (1994). Cell therapy [Song]. On *Soul food*. Organized Noize.

Grandmaster Flash & the Furious Five. (1982, July 1). The message [Song]. Sugar Hill Records.

Hughes, C. L. (2019). Freedom songs: Building a playlist. In H. K. Jeffries (Ed.), *Understanding and teaching the civil rights movement* (pp. 209–211). University of Wisconsin Press. https://doi.org/10.2307/j.ctvvsqcd0.21

Johnson, T. R., & Feldman, M. (2020, January 16). *The new voter suppression*. Brennan Center for Justice. https://www.brennancenter.org/our-work/research-reports/new-voter-suppression

Jones, N., & Oh, M. (Hosts). (2021, November 16). Ice Cube (No. 3) [Audio podcast episode]. In *The Bridge: 50 Years of Hip Hop*. Spotify. https://www.podchaser.com/podcasts/the-bridge-50-years-of-Hip-Hop-2175636/episodes/recent

King, M. L. (1963, August 28). *I have a dream* [Transcript]. American Rhetoric. https://www.americanrhetoric.com/speeches/mlkihaveadream.htm

King, M. L. (1968, April 3). *I've been to the mountaintop* [Transcript]. American Rhetoric. https://www.americanrhetoric.com/speeches/mlkivebeentothemountaintop.htm

Misha, O. (2021, December 12). Detroit artist Jonathan Harris strikes a nerve around the world with "Critical Race Theory" painting. *Detroit Metro Times*. https://www.metrotimes.com/detroit/detroit-artist-jonathan-harris-strikes-a-nerve-around-the-world-with-critical-race-theory-painting/Content?oid=28718822

Moye, J. T. (2019). Everybody say freedom: Using oral history to construct and teach new civil rights narratives. In H. K. Jeffries (Ed.), *Understanding and teaching the civil rights movement* (pp. 197–208). University of Wisconsin Press. https://doi.org/10.2307/j.ctvvsqcd0.20

Pendharkar, E. (2022, January 27). Efforts to ban critical race theory now restrict teaching for a third of America's kids. *Education Week.* https://www.edweek.org/leadership/efforts-to-ban-critical-race-theory-now-restrict-teaching-for-a-third-of-americas-kids/2022/01

Perry, I. (2004). *Prophets of the hood: Politics and poetics in hip hop.* Duke University Press. https://doi.org/10.2307/j.ctv31jm90p

Too Short. (1990, October 8). The ghetto [Song]. On *Short dog's in the house.* Jive Records.

Whitley, L. (2020, June 30). *Vote quilt.* Museum of Fine Arts Boston. https://www.mfa.org/article/2020/vote-quilt

CHAPTER 20

Integrity and Responsible Journalism: Fact Checking False Narratives

An Interview With Jesse J. Holland

Danian Jerry

Jesse J. Holland: Good morning. No, I'm sorry, good afternoon.

Danian Darrell Jerry: Good afternoon, Jesse. How are you?

Jesse J. Holland: I'm doing good. How are you today?

Danian Darrell Jerry: I'm well, thanks. Before we start the interview, I wrote a short bio I want to read.

Jessie J. Holland, accomplished writer, award-winning journalist, and distinguished professor, hosts the Saturday edition of C-SPAN *Washington Journal*. His first nonfiction book, *Black Men Built the Capital: Discovering African American History in and Around Washington, D.C.*, published in 2007, is described as the first of its kind and a fascinating outlook on the history of Washington, D.C., as well as the African Americans who helped construct the capital city. In 2017, his second nonfiction book, *The Invisibles: The Untold Story of African American Slavery in the White House*, won the silver medal for U.S. history at the Independent Publisher Book Awards.

Holland has won numerous awards and accolades, earning the rare credentials to report on all three branches of government in Washington, D.C. He served as the race and ethnic writer for the Associated Press. He served as an assistant professor of media and public affairs at George

Washington University and was a former distinguished visiting scholar in residence at the John W. Kluge Center of the Library of Congress. A critically acclaimed fiction writer, Holland is the author of *Star Wars: The Force Awakens: Finn's Story*, the "Heritage" issue of the *Represent* series from DC Comics, and the first prose novel to feature Marvel Comics's most popular black hero, *Who Is the Black Panther?*

I think I left out the title of the series, but the title of your book is called "Heritage."

Jesse J. Holland: Everything's good with the intro.

Danian Darrell Jerry: Let's get started. We understand that critical race theory is a branch of civil rights law, created by a cohort of lawyers that included Derrick Bell, Kimberlé Crenshaw, Richard Delgado, and others. We also understand that critical race theory recognizes the importance and the relevance of everyday lives and experiences to scholarship. In your opinion, why is this so?

Jesse J. Holland: I think critical race theory is important because it encourages. More thought on exactly how we as Americans have gotten to where we are today. Historically, history is not only written by the victors. History is written by the majority. As we look over our past, we find many stories that were never told because the perspectives and the consequences of history on the minority population were never considered. History is only told for the people who are in power. Now that America is becoming a minority–majority country, we are taking the time to go back and look at history with a critical and modern eye and figure out how the structures we live under actually came into being. Telling the story the way that it was in reality, rather than just from the perspective of the people who are in power, who tell stories to justify the way they got into power. For the first time, we're going back, and we're looking at how the current power structures in the United States came to be, rather than only telling the stories that justify how the current power structure came to be.

We can look back on many of the processes that exist today and find the racial background behind the existence of these processes. Policing in the United States exists in part to keep slaves under control. Housing in the United States exists in part post–World War II due to redlining. Public education in the United States exists in part because after the civil rights movement white Americans pulled their children out and started a private school system. A lot of the things we look at around the country and ascribe to benign origins come back to race in some shape, form, or fashion. If we want to present ourselves as an example to other countries around the world, we first have to be realistic about who we are. And critical race theory begins to teach us who we are, as opposed to the mythology of who we are.

Danian Darrell Jerry: Your nonfiction engages these ideas of honest and truthful accounts of our origins as a country. Your first book, *Black Men Built the Capital: Discovering African American History in and Around Washington, D.C.*, for example. What inspired you to write that book? What were you attempting to accomplish? What ideas did you attempt to explore?

Jesse J. Holland: The secret origin behind *Black Men Built the Capital* was simple. I'm a Mississippian, and if you know anything about southerners, we're obsessed with history. When I first left Mississippi, I moved to South Carolina, then New York and Washington, D.C. One thing I always did when I moved to a new city was try to learn the history of that place, so when I moved to Washington, D.C., in 2000, I did the tourist thing. I went to the White House, the National Mall, the Capitol, the Supreme Court, the Library of Congress; I went to all the places. But I noticed there were few or no representations of African Americans in any of these national symbols, and I began to wonder. Washington, D.C., is a southern city. There have been African Americans in every southern city since they were founded. There must be some African American history here, and I began to ask around Washington, D.C. To my surprise, there were a bunch of people who knew about the African American history of Washington, D.C. The thing was, they didn't tell anybody. All of these professors and historians and doctors and frankly even people on the street would say, "Benjamin Banneker did this" and "Frederick Douglass lived here."

I learned over my career that if you don't write a story down, it has the potential of being lost. Because as our storytellers die, their stories either get changed or forgotten. So I took it upon myself to start writing these stories down about all of the contributions that African Americans made to not only Washington, D.C., but to the Pentagon, to College Park in Maryland, to Prince George's County. But after I started writing them down, I said to myself, "Well, here's the problem. If you just write down the story the way it's being told, somebody else will come along and say, 'Well, that's not true. That's not the way it happened.' So why don't you go research and separate the fact from the fiction?" And that's how *Black Men Built the Capital* got its start. I was collecting these stories, trying to figure out what was historically accurate versus what was urban legend. I wanted to be sure that all of these true stories about Washington, D.C., were preserved for future historians, future African Americans, future Americans.

Knowing the history that we have with Washington, D.C., the U.S. Capitol, the White House, the Lincoln Memorial gives us ownership in the structures of this country's history. The more we're involved, the more we as a people should care about what's happening to them. Part of my reason for writing this book was to ensure that these stories didn't get lost, to ensure that we knew what was fact and what was fiction, and to give us ownership not only in Washington, D.C., but of the U.S. government, which would not exist without us.

Danian Darrell Jerry: Your second nonfiction book, *The Invisibles: The Untold Story of African American Slavery in the White House*, deals with a different aspect of D.C. history. What was the inspiration behind that book? What made you sort of tell that part of the story?

Jesse J. Holland: *Black Men Built the Capital* is the macro, the 50,000-foot view of Washington, D.C. *The Invisibles* is the micro, the seat of power in Washington, D.C., and what African Americans suffered through for it to exist today. I actually tell part of that story of African American slaves in the White House in *Black Men Built the Capital*, but I wasn't able to devote enough time to it in a book that's talking about the entire capital region. So I wanted to go back to that story and tell that story properly. Because slavery and the White House doesn't begin in Washington, D.C. It begins in New York.

George Washington took his slaves from Mount Vernon up to New York to work in what was then the seat of the U.S. government; so even from the beginning of the U.S. government as we know it today, slavery was a part. The president purposefully took his slaves from Mount Vernon, Virginia, to New York to work for him as president, enslaved, working in his household. He took them from New York to Philadelphia, from Philadelphia to Washington, D.C. Knowing that African Americans were there from the beginning gives us ownership in what happens to the White House and what comes out of the White House.

I wrote *The Invisibles* after doing *Black Men Built the Capital* because of all the stories being told about the U.S. presidency; by the way, I wrote *The Invisibles* around the same time Barack Obama ran for president—the historic run of Barack Obama for president, how he would be the first Black man in the White House. That just offended me as a quasi historian because Black people had been there from day one. They had been ignored, which is how I got the title *The Invisibles*, because they were there from day one, even before the White House was built. They helped build the White House, but history is written for the majority. The people who wrote the history of the White House, the history of the presidency, ignored the African Americans who made those things come about.

I decided that it was time for the story of the people who were there to be told. And that's what *The Invisibles* does. Most of the time when we read about the U.S. presidencies and the U.S. presidents who were slave masters, the story is told from the master about the slaves. With *The Invisibles*, I tell the story of the master from the slave's point of view. In that way, you get a more realistic image of who the masters were, rather than them telling the story of who they thought they were. That was the idea behind *The Invisibles*, to once again give us ownership of the White

Chapter 20: Integrity and Responsible Journalism

House by revealing our contributions to it and the fact that we've been there since day one—not to rewrite American history but to include us in it, the way it should have been from the beginning. The first time, it was written by the majority, about the majority, and for the majority. *The Invisibles* updates that story by including everyone. Not saying that their history didn't happen; we're just saying it wasn't the whole story.

Danian Darrell Jerry: I'm intrigued by the ideas of ownership, true reporting, and setting the bar straight, countering the idea of African American history as opposition to American history, telling the story as it occurs without changing or removing elements for ulterior motives.

Jesse J. Holland: Well, a lot of time we separate African American history from American history. You'll have African American history here, and we'll have American history there. No, the two are actually the same thing. It's just that one side has been left out. And part of the intention of those two books was to weave our story into the greater fabric of American history. I'm not saying George Washington wasn't the first president. I am saying that George Washington as the first president brought along slaves from Mount Vernon, who made sure he was able to do the things that we know him from in history. Yes, I am saying that when Thomas Jefferson was president in the White House, he brought slaves from Monticello, and they were the ones who brought some of the fine cuisine that the White House is known for.

They were the ones who brought those recipes to the White House, not Thomas Jefferson. When Andrew Jackson came to Washington, D.C., he brought slaves from the Hermitage with him to Washington, D.C., and their part of his story in Washington. We're not saying that the U.S. presidents don't deserve their places in history. We're saying that the people that they brought with them deserve their places too. They're not people who should be ignored. Their story completes the story of Washington, D.C. It doesn't exceed it. It completes. Without knowing their stories, we're only finding out part of the history.

Danian Darrell Jerry: What kinds of challenges come along with reporting and recording the histories and life experiences of African Americans? What sorts of challenges arise from covering these issues inside the nation's capital?

Jesse J. Holland: The greatest challenge is the responsibility of getting it right. A lot of times, especially as a journalist, I know this to be true. A lot of times, the first thing people hear is the thing that they will believe. If you're writing historical nonfiction, you have one shot to get it right because people remember whatever you say the first time. You can spend 20 years saying, "Oh no, I was wrong. It really was this." People will believe what they heard first.

Especially when you're talking about history, especially when you're talking about an ignored history such as African Americans share, you have an obligation to get it right the first time because it's going to be hard to change the story once it's known. Especially with *The Invisibles* and *Black Men Built the Capital*. A great deal of effort went into finding and proving the thing that someone said was true: not going by urban legend, not going by your grandfather told my grandfather and he told me, or hearsay; pointing to documents, receipts, peer-reviewed study that said this is how it happened. I knew from the moment I started working on these books there would be people who would challenge the idea of including African Americans into the story of the most beloved U.S. symbols like the National Mall and the White House. When that challenge came, I wanted to be able to say, you can look at this, this, this, and this. If you can find fault in that, you can find fault in what I'm doing.

The greatest challenge is ensuring that what you're doing is correct, knowing that there will be people out there who will not want to believe that the myths they grew up with have a reality behind them that may not be as pretty as the myth.

One of the other challenges, especially when dealing with African American history, especially as a journalist and not a historian, is the challenges you will get from people who are historians but never bothered to look at anything outside of the actual myths. For example, I was challenged by several historians and several Washingtonians who said, "Hey, you're from Mississippi. What gives you the right to come to Washington, D.C., looking around and telling these stories? Why aren't you telling the stories of Mississippi instead of Washington, D.C.?" My answer was "Because *you* didn't."

You wouldn't believe how many times I heard when those books came out, "Why is this outsider coming in, nosing around our history as if Washington, D.C., belonged to them? And telling these stories?" Once again, my reasoning was if I don't do it, who will? And if it's not done now, when? We've already been here 400 years, and nobody else has bothered to do it. Why should I sit back and wait for somebody else to do something that needs to be done?

For the historical part, I'm first and foremost a journalist. I write the first draft of history. I am more than willing to consider both *Black Men Built the Capital* and *The Invisibles* to be the first draft of that history. If someone thinks they can write a more complete version or a better version, I would love to read it.

I would have loved to see Henry Louis Gates write this book. I would love to see Cornel West write this book. I would love to see any of our prominent African American historians come and tell the story; but they didn't, and I would rather preserve what I can rather than wait and hope someone with greater credentials comes in one day and decides that this is worth it.

Danian Darrell Jerry: Let's discuss another issue challenging journalists in today's media. As a journalist, can you give us a little background on the news stories surrounding "critical race theory"? How did all the uproar and controversy originate?

Jesse J. Holland: I'm probably not qualified to tell you officially about the beginnings of critical race theory. From my understanding, it began as a legal theory; but I can tell you that I had never heard of critical race theory until Republicans began complaining about it. I have been in the news business for a while. Before becoming a political reporter in Washington, D.C., I was an education reporter in New York. I would be utterly flabbergasted to find out critical race theory was being taught anywhere in the United States in K through 12 any time in the 2000s, because I have done enough work covering schools from elementary, high school, to college to know that until the last two to three years, the words "critical race theory" had never been uttered anywhere below college level.

I won't say it didn't happen, having not set foot in every school in the United States; perhaps there was some lawyer who decided to begin teaching in a high school or an elementary school who brought elements of critical race theory with them. But I guarantee you, most of the United States had heard absolutely nothing about "critical race theory" until it became a media issue with Republicans and conservatives.

Critical race theory is the current boogeyman that's being used for political purposes. There have been similar words in the past: "welfare queens," "The Wall," "Shariah Allah."

My suspicion is that if you ask the common American what Shariah Allah was, they'd have no idea, but they would tell you it's bad. If you ask the common American what "critical race theory" was, they'd have no idea, but they would tell you people say it's bad. It's being used in a way to scare certain voters into voting in ways that the people who are in power want them to vote. There's no debate around critical race theory, like there's no real debate going around about vaccinations or climate change. For there to be a debate, you need two informed sides. In none of those situations do you have two informed sides. You have one side that is informed, and you have one side that's operating on what they were told.

While I would suggest there's probably only a few thousand people in the United States who actually have seen paperwork describing what critical race theory is and how it's being used. Everyone else is operating on what someone told them. Many of those people have been told that critical race theory is bad. Today it's critical race theory. Tomorrow it's climate change. The day after that it's Shariah Allah. After that the boogey man could be tacos or green beans or electric cars. It's all media and political manipulation, and I wish we could just ignore it, but unfortunately it's being used to keep certain interests in power. Therefore, it's incumbent upon the people who know to explain to the people who don't.

Danian Darrell Jerry: What advice would you give to up-and-coming journalists who want to report on issues of race or race relations, who want to uncover hidden truths and investigate marginalized topics?

Jesse J. Holland: Be brave and be persistent. Be brave because there are always going to be people who are going to ask, "Why should you care?" But you have more important things to do. When someone says, "Nobody wants to read this," ignore all of that. If your organization won't run it, find an organization that will; and be persistent because there will be several roadblocks—whether it's inside your organization, whether it's the people around the issue that you are wanting to write about, or whether it's actually getting your work out in front of people. *Black Men Built the Capital* took about 5 years to get published. *The Invisibles* took 10.

I was told repeatedly with *Black Men Built the Capital* that nobody cared about African American history in Washington, D.C. I was told with *The Invisibles* that writing about slavery was not something people want to read. It sounds weird today now that we have shows like *Underground Railroad* and *Harriet* and *Lovecraft Country* that depict African Americans. Less than 20 years ago, nobody wanted to hear this, but if you think it's worth reading, then it's worth writing. You have to be persistent. You have to be brave because there may be people who don't want you to tell those stories and not just people who are opposed to the stories. There may be people involved that you want to write about who don't want those stories told. But you have to be persistent if you think the story is worth telling.

Danian Darrell Jerry: Speaking of stories, you write fiction in addition to your historical books and your journalism pieces. You worked with DC Comics on a graphic memoir detailing your childhood in Holly Springs, Mississippi, on farmland owned by your family. In the light of the troubles that Black farmers are experiencing with discrimination from the USDA and biased federal loan practices, what challenges has your family faced while keeping your farm successfully? How did those experiences inspire you to write your graphic memoir?

Jesse J. Holland: Let me start by going back to one of your previous questions, when I said, don't let anything get in your way. While I was writing *The Invisibles*, I was in an MFA graduate program. Several professional writers said to me, "Why are you writing about these slaves you're not related to? You could be writing about your own family, your own story from Mississippi." I said, "My story wasn't going anywhere. I know my story. It wasn't going to get lost. This was more important." But as years have gone by, I have thought more and more about what my family went through in Mississippi. We were able to trace our family all the way back to the first slave that was freed in Holly Springs after the Civil War and the first acre of land he bought in the 1800s in what is now a near-dead town called Hudsonville, Mississippi. Technically, I'm not from Holly Springs. I'm from a farm about 15 miles outside of Holly Springs.

My people have lived there since the Civil War, and they've been able to build up a homestead from that first acre that was bought after the war, and we've been on that land since the Civil War. My father, my mother, my two sisters, and my brother still live on that land in Mississippi. There have been challenges over the years in keeping that land from the USDA, tax collectors, people who want the timber from the land, and a family that's gotten so large, there are so many cousins who own this acre and that acre and want to sell it to people who are not family members.

One thing that we have all agreed to, at least amongst my family, is that only blood relatives will ever own part of this land because this land is our history. This is where we've been. This is where we'll always be. Even if we don't live on the land, we will own it, and the land will be passed down to the next generation. When DC came to me and said, "We want you to write a story that means a lot to you," this was the one. The only idea I had was to write about our land and our connection to it. There are so many different stories I could tell about that one acre of land that we started and how it's expanded, but when it came time to tell the story, my perspective of that land was the story I decided to tell. There's going to be more along those same lines. I just have to figure out the best way to present them.

Danian Darrell Jerry: That's just amazing. Your family held on to that land over the years. While there are so many instances of families losing their land or parting with the property piece by piece. Or they took out loans they couldn't pay.

Jesse J. Holland: Let me be exact. In theory, we should have more land because of my mother's people. This entire story is told by my father's side of my family. My mother's side of the family lost all of their land, thousands of acres, around the Great Depression because they couldn't keep it because of taxes and because part of their land was swindled from them. Theoretically, we should have even more than what we have now. My mom's family was able to save the part of the land that they lived on, but they should have thousands and thousands of acres where they grew up. I don't want it to sound like what happened to everyone else didn't happen to us. My dad's side was able to hold on to its land, while my mom's side of the family land has been reduced significantly over the last 100 years. I haven't gotten to that story yet. Believe me, I'll get around to writing that side of it too.

INTERLUDE
Afrofuturist Design
Kurt Wagner and Walter D. Greason

Theory

Reynaldo Anderson argues that the Black Speculative Arts counter the hegemonic theoretical assertions of the Frankfurt school of critical theory. His assertion is correct in that the framework for Afrofuturism places the intellectual accomplishments of the African diaspora at the start of any conversation regarding creativity and civilization. Maghan Keita does similar work in advancing this foundation in his book *Race and Historiography*, where he destabilizes assumptions about the historic "whiteness" of Europe (both modern and ancient/medieval) while showing the global presence of African intellectual influences in Europe and Asia throughout antiquity. The core concept of Keita's argument is plausibility. It replaces the European notion of objectivity in the construction of history, allowing for multiple evidentiary narratives to coexist in tension with one another. Instead of reifying modern simplicity, Keita's assertion of plausibility opens the door to creativity in historical writing and the emergence of Black Speculative Arts in the twenty-first century.

Nell Irvin Painter develops an entire world history of the idea of whiteness to dismantle it as a construct in the modern world—no easy task. She recognizes multiple reinventions of whiteness after the eighteenth century. The confluence of whiteness as rationality and productivity helped structure the systems of global capitalism. In this paradigm, people defined as "Black" have no subjectivity, no authority to exist as intellectuals, no capacity to accumulate capital. At the start of the twentieth century, it was these structures that W. E. B. DuBois described as "the problem of the color line." The battle for the next four generations was the creation of histories of the African continent and diaspora that would demand that the world abandon its irrational antiblackness. The success of these cultural projects opened the door to the gospel blues, the evolution of jazz, and the explosion of rhythm and blues alongside hip-hop.

In the shifting terrain that defined the emergence of rap music, break dancing, and graffiti art, Afrofuturism began to take shape. The triumph of Black history as a civilizational project enabled larger movements like the one to end South African apartheid to advance the standards established by the Black Freedom Struggle over the previous two centuries. Samuel Delany and Octavia Butler broke through the doors of science fiction literature, building on generations of journalism, history, graphic art, and literature to imagine new possibilities for Black identity and community. Their work illustrated the vision of Jesse Jackson's presidential campaigns in 1984 and 1988, energizing the creation of comic visions like Milestone Media and lyrical revolutionaries from Public Enemy to Immortal Technique. In the last decade of the twentieth century, digital platforms and listservers emerged that allowed a new generation of writers and artists to develop an endless array of these possibilities, anticipating a world that would reject the boundaries of objective categories.

Anderson is one of the leaders of that moment in the early twenty-first century, alongside Ytasha Womack, John Jennings, and hundreds of young Black scholars and artists. Beyond the work of defending civil and human rights, this generation manifested the demand to build a civilization that affirmed humanity in comprehensive and systematic ways. Ta-Nehisi Coates took a first step with his essay on reparations. Nikole Hannah-Jones amplified these challenges with the 1619 Project. Ibram Kendi organized millions of educators to adopt the platform of antiracism. These initiatives might appear discrete, but they are part of a multidimensional, rhizomatic structure that reorganizes systems of exploitation to enable new forms of human freedom. The core institutions of a free society have begun to evolve because the Black Speculative Arts have gained strength and acclaim since the election of Obama and the release of Marvel Studios' film *Black Panther*. The confluence of media, education, and history relies on Anderson's challenge of critical theory and Keita's suggestion of historical plausibility. As a result, humanity no longer relies on Platonic forms or Euclidean proofs; science and art combine to shape Afrofuturist ambagesques that produce new understandings of Indigenous paradigms.

Ambagesque, George Hart, 2016

From the Latin word for 'tangle,' *Ambagesque* is a five-foot diameter wooden sculpture made of 60 identical flat pieces with the shape below.

The structure has icosahedral symmetry, with 2-fold, 3-fold, and 5-fold rotational axes. All together, there are 60 distinct symmetries! To a chemist, the point group of the sculpture is the purely rotational subgroup I of the icosahedral group I_h. To an algebraist, the symmetry group is the alternating group A_5 of even permutations on 5 elements.

Commissioned by the Department of Mathematics, Statistics, and Computer Science, the pieces were cut by students in the Department of Art and Art History, and the sculpture was assembled by students at a 'sculpture barn raising' on March 22, 2016.

This work was funded in part by Kurt and Janine Winkelmann, as part of the Macalester College Math and Society Lecture Series.

Practice

The practice of Afrofuturist analysis requires familiarity with multiple disciplines. In this arena, it is not enough to think; the analyst must also do. From the foundation laid by Antonio Gramsci or Paolo Friere, action defines the power of critical analysis. In the case of the Afrofuturist design exhibits in New Jersey in 2019, the collaboration between Monmouth University's Guggenheim Library, the T. Thomas Fortune Cultural Center, and the Main Street Art Gallery in Freehold showcased how theory and praxis combine to produce social change through institutional action.

Rupa DasGupta created a series of promotional images about Walter Greason's academic work that attracted global attention to his "Worldprofessor" platforms on Facebook and Twitter, 2012-2017. These projects showed how digital media created new audiences for intellectual content.

John Jennings and **Stacey Robinson** produced new content with a style and grace that derived from the urgency of the historic moment with the furious pace of a hip hop freestyle. Their images tapped into the power of black history in ways that inspired a new generation of scholars, activists, and artists around the world.

HOAHOA TAKETAKE

Institutional action requires years of quiet sacrifice, especially in service to a mission to protect and preserve Black history. The exhibit at the Main Street Art Gallery challenged centuries of antiblack racism in central New Jersey. Freehold literally was a synonym for the plantation owners who enslaved Africans starting in the seventeenth century. Those enslavers' names still litter the landscape, and their practices of wealth accumulation endure in places named Holmdel and Colts Neck. The irony of the Black Brain Belt—a series of communities where thousands of Black scientists built their homes—and the military strength of the Cold War United States notwithstanding, the traditions of exploiting and destroying people of African and Indigenous descent prevail daily in that region.

Thus, the decade-long campaign to restore the Fortune Center is a unique occurrence. The global patterns of destroying Black and Indigenous communities is a central feature of the colonial process. Whether called gentrification, displacement, or erasure, it is all dedicated to the derogation of cultures considered foreign to white Europeans and their descendants. When Gilda Rogers and Roger Mumford formed a partnership to restore Fortune's national landmark, they challenged both the genocidal systems of empire as well as the range of tools available in service to liberation. Instead of systems of capital dedicated to destroying maroon communities, the Fortune Center inverted the relationship, showing that capital could serve the preservation of Black history. As a result, millions of dollars of new investment flowed into community action under the authority of local activists. The model inspired dozens of initiatives to protect Black communities nationwide.

To confront the damage wrought by Woodrow Wilson required more action. In 2016, Monmouth University unanimously affirmed the legacy of segregation by preserving his name as the symbol of the campus's main administrative building. Two years later, the Board of Trustees made a symbolic gesture by creating a monument to Dr. Martin Luther King Jr. and his visit to the campus in 1966. The murder of George Floyd in 2020 changed the campus dynamic, and the new president Patrick Leahy removed Wilson's name from the building in response to massive student outcry. All of this momentum gathered through the 2019 exhibit about Afrofuturism. The confluence of the work in the Main Street Gallery and the Fortune Center attracted international attention to the university. Junior faculty like Hettie Williams and Anwar Uhuru learned the lessons well, expanding both campus programming and curricula. Most powerfully, education faculty like Tina Paone, Nicole Pulliam, and Vernon Smith expanded this mission through the graduate curriculum in antiracist counseling. They won a multimillion-dollar grant in 2021 to transform regional education by emphasizing social justice teaching and professional development.

Implications

In these ways, institutional action in a deeply racist region has countered the rising tide of white nationalism. Praxis, in conjunction with theory, endures. It safeguards the work of democracy, based on the principles of Afrofuturist design. Maulana Karenga suggested that the Swahili principles of *Umoja*, *Ujaama*, *Ujima*, *Kujichagulia*, *Nia*, *Kuumba*, and *Imani* form the core of the annual Kwanzaa celebration, defining a pan-African heritage and cultural commitment. The Black Speculative Arts movement, which has animated global engagement with Afrofuturism over the past 30 years, complicates this formulation by examining the contradictions within these systems of value and knowledge. Critical analysis and creative asymmetry are two fundamental aspects of the speculative intellect. In addition, the path requires an interdisciplinary orientation that combines multiple methodologies to connect the emergent epistemologies. Most often, these techniques involve combinations of art, literature, music, and history. New paths continue to emerge that combine mathematics, computer science, physics, and biochemistry. Where hip hop culture relied on the fusion of break dancing, sampling, rap lyrics, and graffiti art, Afrofuturism allows a freedom of creative, intellectual expression that reinvents both perspective and methodology. The layers of reinforcing feeling and knowing with a balanced approach to both intuition and understanding opens the door to something beyond postmodern surrealism. One essential terrain are the contemplative terrains of indigenous design.

Indigenous Design

Hoahoa Taketake. The Maori phrase describes a fundamental orientation toward conscientious synthesis moving toward an unconscious synergy. For both Rene Descartes and Immanuel Kant as rational philosophers, the understanding of consciousness was first and foremost. As "things that think," reasoning emerged as the core of European Enlightenment philosophy. The range of binary categories that emerged from this basis multiplied exponentially through the nineteenth and twentieth centuries. With the emergence of evidentiary science after 1910, European science began to distinguish between problems of simplicity that occupied their interest for four centuries and the problems of 'disorganized complexity' that could be studied in the decades ahead. The frustration with resolving this second category of problems forced a resignation to understanding problems of "organized complexity" at the start of the twenty-first century. Manuel Lima's lecture for the Royal Society of the Arts in London presents these discussions succinctly. Simplicity can be illustrated by natural objects (like trees for Charles Darwin), implying hierarchies and resilient structure. Organized complexity allows for the perception of fractals and rhizomes, enabling a conceptual architecture that permits contradiction and multi-faceted relationships. Still, beyond the reach of both, disorganized complexity remains. Indigenous design provides a humility that reinforces Keita's historical sense of plausibility. People can ask innumerable questions, suggesting infinite answers. Among those answers will be a majority of wrong conclusions, but a significant plurality of correct ones, too. Indigenous design promotes the synergy of both simple and complex answers, while also promoting the plausibility of wonder at mysticism, intuition, and those answers not yet discovered. There is a chance to reconcile the disparate traditions of human exploration and discovery in the centuries ahead, if humanity can break its tradition of subordinating indigenous design.

CHAPTER 21

Innovating Racism in Digital Detroit

Asha E. Criner

Ruha Benjamin (2020) and Safiya Umoja Noble (2018), in their books *Race After Technology* and *Algorithms of Oppression*, respectively, make powerful critiques on our technological systems. Considering that technological engineering and design is one of the fields that is most dominated by white men, their insight as Black women studying the field is both wholly necessary and valuable as we enter an era that will be fully influenced by technology in ways that it never has been before. The formal definition of technology has always hinged on the consideration of what makes life more practical. One of the first applications of new technology known to man was the creation of fire, which allowed for the consumption of a more diverse array of meal options and consequently worked to improve the life spans of humans altogether. Another ancient application of technology was the creation of the wheel, which made the ostentatious designs of ancient tribes and kingdoms possible. Technology makes the impractical practical. After all, who would reject an invention that can make a lifetime's work take only seconds to complete instead? Today, technological advancements attempt to continue their ancient role, although modern forms of technology promote more complicated benefits than a flame or wheel. Phones brought us ways to communicate with people far away, transportation allowed us to travel to areas and learn new ways of life that were previously off-limits, and computers gave us a way to replace the shelves and shelves of phonebooks and documents that could not be stored any other way. At face value, it is convincing that technology has had overwhelmingly positive effects on the quality of life for many people. Technology is not, however, without its flaws.

Laced within this facade of practicality is the misconception that technology is entirely objective and innately unflawed. All too often, people applaud and exhalt the minds that create the technologies that improve the practicality and efficiency of life. This tendency relies on the belief that creating new technologies that have positive impacts makes that technological advancement entirely positive, with no negative effects associated with it. While it may be true that the creation of new technology depends on some advanced knowledge, becoming overly dependent on those who create these new technologies stands to do more harm than good.

Concepts like Afrofuturism help to bring this awareness into focus. Afrofuturism emphasizes how the occurrence of techno music in Detroit developed through the extreme, almost dystopian, conditions of life in Detroit. Initially, the connection between Afrofuturism, Noble, and Benjamin might be unclear, but the true connection reveals that techno music represents the solution that Noble and Benjamin pursue in technological systems. One cannot expect that the technological failures exposed by the two authors can be rectified through musical expression; rather, techno music represents the proposed solutions shown in Noble and Benjamin's analyses.

Black people persist through the failures imposed on them by demanding to be allowed to define themselves on their own terms. Techno music had a unique birthplace in Detroit, particularly because industrial segregation and deindustrialization sabotaged civil rights activity so deeply there. Harkening back to Noble's claims about mainstream culture, one conclusion is that the riots and uprisings that took place in the city represent Noble's discourse; accordingly, as a result of this discourse, Detroit itself became cast out of the mainstream. But rather than assuming its outcast title as a label of shame, artistic expression was allowed to flourish, facilitating a space for Detroit artists to redefine who they were for themselves.

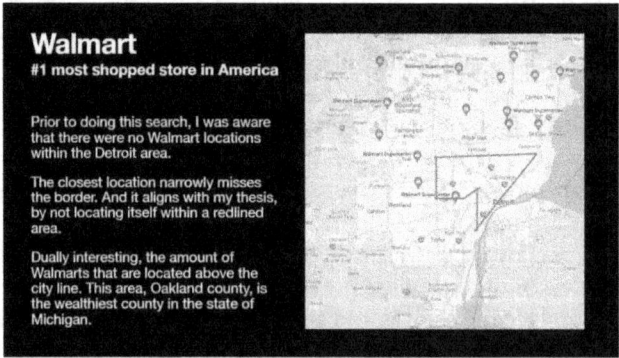

Figure 21.1 Walmart is one indicator of the persistent segregation in the Detroit metropolitan regional economy.

Chapter 21: Innovating Racism in Digital Detroit 273

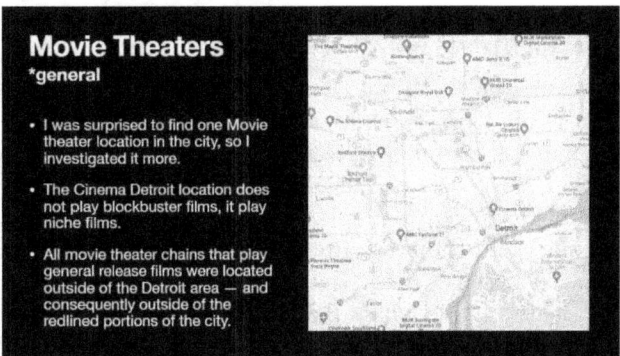

Figure 21.2 The distribution of movie theaters demonstrates gentrification as part of the regional economy.

In *Race After Technology*, Benjamin (2020) reveals to her readers just how flawed today's mediums of technology can really be. From something as simple as getting a professional photograph taken to artificial intelligence (AI), Benjamin seeks to prove that technology is what will determine social definitions of race and gender in the future. If this is true, Benjamin also proposes that technology consequently can have a direct role in perpetuating forms of racism in today's society. Noble's (2018) book *Algorithims of Oppression* points to issues that do not stray too far from the claims that Benjamin makes in her book. By comparison, Noble's book takes a central focus on how search engines and databases of knowledge for public use have a direct role in defining marginalized groups. When placed in juxtaposition with each other, these two texts assert that technology is not isolated from the racial dynamics that direct public behavior. They argue that because technology can be subjective and biased, it is entirely capable of facilitating and sustaining false narratives and definitions that consequently harm marginalized groups.

Benjamin begins by providing examples of how racist narratives can be sustained in technological environments. In the first chapter of *Race After Technology*, titled "Engineered Inequality," Benjamin (2020) poses a seemingly simple question: Can robots be racist? The irony in this question is that robots are not human. They do not have their own thoughts; in fact, their actions and capabilities are a pure product of their design. For Benjamin, that detail alone is the reason why the answer to her question is resoundingly, yes. "Robots, designed in a world drenched in racism, will find it nearly impossible to stay dry. To a certain extent, they learn to speak the coded language of their human parents—not only programmers but all of us who contribute to 'natural occurring' datasets on which AI learn" (p. 62). Benjamin's statement not only asserts that robots can be racist, but it argues further that their actions are complete reflections of the societal issues that already exist among humans. This is significant because it exposes that coding and programming alone do not permanently shield robots from contributing to the social biases that affect marginalized groups.

Stating that a robot can be racist does not imply that AI will be found doing something as jarring as directing obscenities at marginalized individuals; rather, the forms of racism that Benjamin points to are much more inconspicuous. For example, Benjamin (2020) notes how something as simple as autocorrect can have implications that go on to affect class and racial designations: "Consider the simple corrections of our computer systems, where words that signal undue privilege are not legible. The red lines tell us that only one of these phenomena, underserved and overserved, is legitimate while the other is a mistake, a myth" (p. 65). Here, Benjamin is questioning why "underserved" is considered a word while "overserved" is not. Her observation showcases what happens when a dominating group has unequal power over how subdominant groups are defined. Dominating groups determine the classifications, and that is evident in the deficit of definitions that are created for the dominating group.

By comparison, Noble's (2018) early claims in *Algorithms of Oppression* clearly point to the negative effects of these subtle lapses of sensitivity in the classification of groups of people. In the novel, her focus is primarily on the search engine, Google. One of her first major issues with search engines that she acknowledges concerns how search results often reflect the sentiments of the majority. If this is true, what is acting against the fact that the minority will always be underrepresented? Noble's answer would likely be that the sentiments and desires of minority groups are often neglected, leaving these groups to depend on the classifications made by the majority. Noble addresses these issues early on. "Marginalized and oppressed people are linked to the status of their group and are less likely to be afforded individual status and insulation from the experiences of the groups with which they are identified" (p. 26). What is important about this statement is that it reveals what results when definitions are made by a dominant majority.

Noble (2018) expands on these thoughts as she contends with the implications of Google's flawed search engine, more specifically how it fails Black girls and other marginalized groups. When studying one day, she was encouraged to google the term "Black girls" by one of her colleagues who correctly postulated that the results would be shocking to Noble. What Noble found was a list of pornographic websites that had the keywords "Black girls" in them. Rather than images of young Black girls playing games and enjoying themselves, she found something that was not only violating for Black women themselves but also dangerous because it promoted a stereotypical and inaccurate portrayal of Black women based on racist characterizations of them on the

Chapter 21: Innovating Racism in Digital Detroit 275

whole. Benjamin's above quote is substantiated by Noble's finding. Not only are Black women being categorized by a majority, but they are being categorized and defined by the false and explicitly racist depictions that a specific group may believe to be an accurate representation of "Black girls."

Noble's experience may come as a surprise to some, but it exposes a troubling pattern of misrepresentation, especially of Black women, that has been occurring for years. Black studies classes sometimes offer the opportunity to listen to the song "Four Women" by Nina Simone. It is a song that ambiguously tells the story of four women, each one with different life experiences and sentiments that make each of their stories unique. What is significant here is the fact that each woman is named not particularly of her own accord but by what people would label her based on her appearance and temperament (more specifically, a stereotype). These characteristics are not entirely within the women's control. This approach implies that the song actually tells the story of how Black women, historically, have had to struggle to define themselves. In this historical context, the failure to adequately define Black girls on a digital search page becomes more than just a happenstance technological flaw; instead, it represents a societal failure that is manifesting itself in our digital mediums of existence without being called out and changed.

In class, we were also able to consider how labeling can be used as a source of power. Black studies courses also sometimes introduce the story of Jean Grey, a comic character who was one of the few women in the *X-men* comic book series. Many viewed her character as a representation of resilience and power. Because of this, the appropriation of the name Jean Grae and its association with the song titled "Phoenix" allowed the musical artist who took up the *X-men* hero's identity to take on this new label in order to associate with its meaning. This process is the complete opposite of the case of the women in "Four Women" because the musician, Jean Grae, was able to take on a name of her own. Within the song, she has no reservations. She is entirely herself and has no regard for anyone who seeks to question her. The case of hip-hop artist Jean Grae is important because, when thinking about the effects of false representation in the media, many analysts conclude that these systems essentially limit the ability of young girls to define themselves in ways like Jean Grae created. Instead, these girls will be permanently affected by the false representations of black femininity sold as facts on digital search engines.

Toward the end of Benjamin's (2020) book, she discusses how a company called Diversity Inc. uses different algorithms to determine the ethnic background of potential customers. The purpose of doing so was to hopefully improve profit by targeting specific ethnic groups. Not only is this practice particularly concerning, but it furthers the idea that was conveyed in the "Four Women" song. Creating algorithms that seek to predefine individuals before they can actually define themselves is a direct assault on one's individuality. Additionally, it aligns with an earlier point made by Noble (2018) that marginalized groups will always be defined by the majority. Noble also asks the question of who determines what behaviors are characteristic of a particular ethnic group and, more specifically, whether these definitions are backed and defended by those particular ethnic groups or by scientists who may not have any true connection to their ethnic background at all.

Suppose in a digital setting, your entire identity were studied and observed—without knowledge of your appearance—and an AI were instructed to make a representation of who you are based solely on your search habits, would the result be accurate? My answer is no because individuals are much more multifaceted than what one solid definition or characterization can ever communicate. To that end, seeking to inspect future consumers to assess their potential for purchasing a specific product is incredibly harmful because it exploits stereotypical assumptions just to make money. Benjamin (2020) relates this to historical patterns when she writes,

> Today companies are more interested in curating a range of markets to bolster their profit margin. And, whereas the purpose of identifying an individual's race during the Jim Crow era was to discriminate effectively, now the stated aim is to "better serve" or "include" different groups. (p. 147)

Although the intention may be to counter the racist past, this practice continues to depend on the promise of stereotyping to produce a product for potential consumers. Ethically and morally, this is alarming.

The central question is what are the real consequences of false representations of minorities in technological environments. Additionally, it is important to ask how the less explicit forms of false representations also affect racial experiences. One form of these false representations that is not covered in Noble's 2018 book deals with the hypervisibility that occurs due to the inability to accurately identify Black people. More often than not, software that was designed by a majority of white people experienced a higher rate of accuracy in its identification of white facial features than of Black facial features. Benjamin (2020) describes how these inaccuracies pose significant concerns: "Now consider that these software programs are used by police departments all over the country; in those departments 'digital eyes watch the public,' comparing individual faces in real time to 'hot lists' that are filled disproportionately with Black people" (p. 113). Essentially, Benjamin is saying that the inability to accurately identify Black people can result in yet another factor that has the potential to feed into the issue of racial profiling—which is prevalent enough without the presence of technological aid. This is

Chapter 21: Innovating Racism in Digital Detroit   277

dangerous because many people fail to understand that technology is capable of being inconsistent in such ways. Through the assumption that these technologies, like the surveillance technologies that Benjamin discusses, are more accurate than humans are, we not only fail to challenge bias but we make an entire community more vulnerable because more people are willing to accept a technological system without fact checking it.

Throughout both texts, the authors seem to agree that there are ways in which these issues could be addressed. Benjamin (2020) points out early on in her book that "coded inequity . . . can be met with collective defiance, with resisting the allure of (depersonalized) personalization and asserting, in this case, the sociality of learning" (p. 17). Similarly, Noble (2018) articulates that there should be much greater pressure put on large technological companies that continue to fail to employ professionals who can adequately navigate the racial dynamics that if improperly dealt with can create real damage to vulnerable communities. A lot of what Benjamin and Noble discuss in their books can be applied to the texts with additional research in critical media studies. Stuart Hall's essay "What Is This 'Black' in Black Pop Culture?" (Morley & Chen, 2005) sought to directly consider how blackness is defined in relation to whiteness. It is a question that directly considers the problematic consequences that Noble addresses as she questions how searching for Black girls on the internet can have such a disappointing result. From Stuart's perspective, the solution aligns with considering a more diverse representation of these definitions. He explains this by stating, "Each [positionality/micro-identity] has for us its own point of profound subjective identifications. And that is the most difficult thing about this proliferation of the field of identities and antagonisms: they are often dislocating in relation to one another" (Morley & Chen, 2005, p. 470). This concept from Stuart supports Benjamin and Noble's assertion that many of the false or missing representations in technological systems can be dealt with by including a wider range of perspectives in the process of creating and monitoring these systems. Noble (2018) also highlights how search results can prioritize beliefs by differentiating between mainstream beliefs and alternative perspectives. Toward the end of the book, she points out that the ordering of information provided in classification schemes "tends to reflect the most mainstream version of these relationships" because "classificatory structures are developed by the most powerful discourses in a society. The result is the marginalization of concepts outside of the mainstream" (p. 240). At face value, this can mean the difference between assuming a scholar can be male, female, or nonbinary.

However, Noble's perspective can also be applied to how social media forms can popularize specific beliefs and practices online. In many ways, social media can facilitate more direct discourse, and the result tends to be what Noble is speaking about in the above quote—the marginalization of concepts that are outside the mainstream. A good example of this is simply what would be considered cool versus uncool: A teenager would be considered cool if they liked or had similar traits to a well-known Tik Tokker but uncool if they didn't know what Tik Tok was to begin with. This example may veer away from how Noble initially explains it, but it highlights how the identification of what is mainstream ultimately defines everything outside the mainstream. Most chillingly, it outlines how conformity of thought can threaten our ability to question or challenge what we see online—this translates comprehensively across scale to how race, among other identifying traits, is categorized in a digital world.

Benjamin does not explicitly point to this in her own book, but the discussion on how companies use AI to identify desirable employees and customers can be related to Noble's point here as well. In this case, it is the companies that are dictating who falls into the desirable categories and who doesn't. Once again, we see how a powerful majority plays a direct role in defining marginalized groups. This is directly comparable to Noble's point because the powerful group is continuing to determine what ultimately matters.

Noble and Benjamin, in their books, contend with issues that are facing our world today. As technology continues to incorporate itself into every facet of our daily lives, the two authors' claims prove that the roles that technology plays in our lives are not minor. In fact, they dictate so much about how society thinks and acts. The authors show readers that without appropriate monitoring of how technology is incorporated into people's everyday lives, specific minority groups will be left defenseless against the social issues that have always been present. Benjamin and Noble's claims reveal an urgent need to address the true causations of these social issues so that they are not reproduced and coded into the technological systems that society intends to rely on so heavily in the future. Overall, these two authors prove that without a formal way of accounting for the regurgitations of racial bias and social issues in the technology we incorporate into our daily lives, the danger of perpetuating our social problems becomes all too possible.

REFERENCES

Benjamin, R. (2020). *Race after technology: Abolitionist tools for the New Jim Code*. Polity. https://doi.org/10.1093/sf/soz162

Hines, A. H., Nelson, A., & Nguyen T. T. H. (Eds.). (2001). *TechniColor: Race, technology, and everyday life*. New York University Press.

Morley, D., & Chen, K.-H. (Eds.). (2005). *Stuart Hall: Critical dialogues in cultural studies*. Routledge.

Noble, S. U. (2018). *Algorithms of oppression: How search engines reinforce racism*. New York University Press. https://doi.org/10.2307/j.ctt1pwt9w5

CHAPTER 22

The Dark Green City: The Liminal-Space of the In-Between

C. N. E. Corbin

The double entendre "dark city" has often been conveyed and conceptualized as a blighted urban landscape while also connecting to the racialized populations that inhabit them, more specifically inner cities. Although historically represented as impoverished, racialized, high-crime urbanities, inner cities are transitioning into green city centers with a vastly different demographic. White and wealthier people populate these urban oases, who now occupy a landscape with far greener pastures (Gould & Lewis, 2016). Globally, cities have been implementing environmental policies and practices that have led to the proliferation of green spaces (parks, gardens, and urban agriculture), which gave rise to the concept of the "green city," an urban area designed to advance sustainability goals, address climate change, and improve quality of life (Lehman, 2010). The dark city and the green city can be understood as two competing realities simultaneously unfolding within the urban landscape as cities negotiate with their pasts and their futures in the present. The "dark green city" marks the fault line where these two tectonic realities, the dark city and the green city, are shifting and creating catastrophic friction and massive societal change while re-creating both the urban landscape and its inhabitants. Within the dark green city, one's economic and racial status determines whether one's urban experience is utopian or dystopian.

To understand these divergent and warring urban concepts of race and space, we must deconstruct them and anchor them within their histories. Within the U.S. context, the lineage of the dark city goes back to the turn of the nineteenth century at the rise of the industrial era. The urban landscape was a perilous place to live in the late 1800s; foods of European immigrants overwhelmed the inadequate urban infrastructure (Zimring, 2016). Overcrowded housing was the standard, and health conditions were dire. Neighborhood streets flowed with open sewage, and those fortunate enough to have windows would have to cope with panes blackened by soot from coal-burning stoves. Industrial factories spewed noxious smoke and gases onto the surrounding communities, causing severe health crises. Cholera and typhoid decimated neighborhoods due to the unsanitary conditions. The hordes of questionable, non–Anglo-Saxon immigrants with their starkly strange cultural differences coupled with desperate urban conditions were implicated as both the cause and the product of the dark and dirty city.

It was during this period that the ideological underpinnings of modern environmental thought emerged. Affectionately known as the father of national parks and the founder of the Sierra Club, John Muir was pivotal in constructing the concept of nature. He was an environmental philosopher, scholar of the natural sciences, and praised as a botanist. Muir's legacy and his perception of "the wilderness" ultimately created the chasm between the natural environment, the wilderness, and the built environment, the city. For Muir, the wilderness was the epitome of what nature was in its most pristine form, untouched by man (DeLuca & Demo, 2001). This construction of nature also created the ideological schism between nature and man, resulting in the understanding that human beings are outside of and separate from nature and, even more crucially, that nature must be protected from man, who will destroy nature for its resources and to create more cities. Thus configured, nature was a place to travel to and a landscape to escape from the dirty urban landscape, the human habitat. Cities were hopelessly unable to ever hold or grow nature in any authentic or meaningful way.

What often gets overlooked, if not outright ignored, in the narratives around the creation of the national parks, and Yosemite in particular, is the violent removal of Native Americans from their ancestral lands (Spence, 1996). This policy was influenced by Muir himself, accomplished through the intervention of the federal government, carried out through the use of military force, and implemented with genocidal intentions; these "protected lands" did not protect the non-white populations who called them home. They became and continue to be a refuge and retreat for the city's elite, carved into a white middle-class cultural practice of camping and hiking from the 1950s to the present (Spence, 1996).

New York's Central Park, created only years before Yosemite National Park, has a similar story. Frederick Law Olmstead and his company were epic in urban park creation. A British garden aesthetic intended to mimic a natural landscape defined Central Park's design (Spence, 1996). This

Chapter 22: The Dark Green City

built nature was only simulacra, a simulation, to the sublime wildness of Muir's landscapes. While Olmsted had an anthropocentric or human-centered view when considering nature, he believed that the working class and not just the elite should have access to nature. His company and his sons also upheld segregationist beliefs, which were implemented within city laws and practices and in park systems. So, as with the national park systems, they too supported the displacement of the residents of these lands (Rothstein, 2017). The construction of Central Park dismantled and destroyed Seneca Village, a thriving, predominantly African American community of homeowners who were displaced using eminent domain (Fordero, 2011). Today, lining the perimeter of Central Park are some of the most expensive private homes on the globe.

The suburbanization process of the 1940s to 1960s that welcomed whites into middle-class status and homeownership also funneled African American populations into atrophying urban centers, re-creating a new concept of the dark city, the ghetto. Kenneth Clark's seminal work *Dark Ghetto: Dilemmas of Social Power* (1967) contextualizes the racialized urban space as ugly, dirty, and filthy, with crowded streets and seedy parks that show lack of care, where "the only constant characteristic is a sense of inadequacy" (p. 27). By contrast, the emergence of the green city holds to both an environmental ideology and an ethic, standing in direct contrast to, and in contempt of, the dark city and its residents.

The green city concept is revealing its sordid environmental roots and reproducing the ongoing violent removal of local *undesirable* populations to protect "the environment," only this time embedded in the rhetoric of sustainability and climate change mitigation. This disturbing and emerging trend of gentrification that touts an environmental ethic, green gentrification, has come to bear on the most vulnerable residents, people of color and low-income individuals, forcing them to the bottom of their city's concerns (Checker, 2011). The green city concept is perpetuating environmental injustices in which vulnerable communities are not only subjected to environmental disadvantages but also prevented from benefiting from environmental amenities. Now people of color have to contend with the other side of environmental racism—displacement from areas with green space creation, restoration, and beautification projects.

Through city planning and the implementation of urban environmental policy and practices, green gentrification has become not only the tool but also the outcome of a new urban renewal strategy. This green urban renewal process is displacing the very populations who need healthy urban environments the most. It is also creating an environmental justice crisis as not only are those who are displaced being forced out of their neighborhoods but in places like Oakland and San Francisco, California, they are being displaced from their city and in many cases from their state altogether. They are most likely to move to another environmentally unhealthy area. Although green gentrification does not always come at the expense of displacement, it always transpires as a form of exclusion. For example, newer signature parks like Railroad Park in Birmingham, Alabama, are lined with condos and market-rate housing, allowing only the wealthy the opportunity to live next to this newly created and charismatic urban nature.

As dark cities transition to green cities, municipal master plans, policies, and practices work together to displace and erase low-income neighborhoods and communities of color. Ultimately, cities are envisioning a greener future without them. But we stand in the liminal space of an in-between in which neither the dark city nor the green city has fully taken place. The truth is that dark cities were never fully dark. Despite the lackluster landscape, dark cities have always had bursts of light that emanated from the diverse communities that found ways to celebrate their life and culture in beautiful ways, in the streets, in parks, and among neighbors. And green cities will never be perfect urban utopian landscapes if they are made to sanitize and exclude the diversity of humanity solely for economic and environmental ends.

REFERENCES

Checker, M. (2011). Wiped out by the "greenwave": Environmental gentrification and the paradoxical politics of urban sustainability. *City & Society*, 23(2), 210–229. https://doi.org/10.1111/j.1548-744X.2011.01063.x

Clark, K. B. (1967). *Dark ghetto: Dilemmas of social power*. Harper & Row.

DeLuca, K., & Demo, A. (2001). Imagining nature and erasing class and race: Carleton Watkins, John Muir, and the construction of wilderness. *Environmental History*, 6(4), 541–560. https://doi.org/10.2307/3985254

Fordero, L. W. (2011, July 27). Unearthing traces of African-American village displaced by Central Park. *New York Times*. https://www.nytimes.com/2011/07/28/nyregion/unearthing-an-african-american-village-displaced-by-central-park.html

Gould, K. A., & Lewis, T. L. (2016). *Green gentrification: Urban sustainability and the struggle for environmental justice*. Routledge.

Lehmann, S. (2010, September 9). Green urbanism: Formulating a series of holistic principles. *S.A.P.I.EN.S. Surveys and Perspectives Integrating Environment and Society*, No. 3.

Rothstein, R. (2017). *The color of law: A forgotten history of how our government segregated America*. Liveright.

Spence, M. (1996). Dispossessing the wilderness: Yosemite Indians and the national park ideal, 1864–1930. *Pacific Historical Review*, 65(1), 27–59. https://doi.org/10.2307/3640826

Whiston, S. A. (1996). Constructing nature: The legacy of Fredrick Law Olmsted. In W. Cronon (Ed.), *Uncommon ground: Rethinking the human place in nature* (pp. 91–113). W. W. Norton.

Zimring, C. A. (2016). *Clean and white: A history of environmental racism in the United States*. New York University Press.

CHAPTER 23

Into the Ether: The Rap Battle as a Parable for the Slow Burn of Critical Race Theory

Elle L. Littlefield

"Critical race theory"—in the past year, these three words congealed to cross the lips of every local and syndicated newscaster in the country. Somehow burrowed into the minds of southern Republicans, they spewed forth and leapt onto the pages of congressional bills—sprawled themselves onto poster boards, climbed above the heads of cheer moms and t-ball coaches, and stormed emphatically into school board meetings across the United States of Suburbia. To date, bills banning critical race theory (CRT) or restricting speech, teaching, or training related to race, diversity, or gender equality have been introduced in more than 40 states and passed in more than 15. Such bills, which—make no mistake—*do not* address CRT, serve the dual purpose of simply red-flagging those three words, said in that particular order, while effectively banning fact-based history or any other truths inconvenient for an increasingly uncomfortable white America.

Prior to the present time, CRT had moved with limited motion, primarily handled by legal and academic scholars, Black and POC (people of color) intellectual artists, and activists. Scarcely did it circulate throughout the Black community at large. Now, mishandled by the ill intentioned, it has been fashioned into a weapon—high-powered, automatic, indiscriminate. Designed to take out those it was meant to empower and protect. This short discussion aims to respond to that weapon—in a perhaps unconventional way.

THE BATTLE OF GOD'S SON AND JAY HOVA: A PARABLE

It was the day of Jay Hova's birth—an unholy, warm fourth of December in 2001—when Nas dropped "Ether" on the world of hip-hop and the soul of his artistic rival. The opening gun spray split the air and summoned a voice from the lower realm who spoke forth, "Fuck Jay-Z." "I was told a long time ago," said Nas, "ghosts and spirits don't like the fumes from ether, and I just wanted to affect him with my weapon and get to his soul." This is a telling remark, as their battle could parallel one between spiritual forces.

Jay-Z's moniker, Jay Hova, proclaims him as the Supreme Being, a god among men. His discography employs a theme of organized crime and a survival-of-the-fittest, started-from-the-bottom narrative synonymous with the stereotype of the urban Black male. This narrative is inherently based in the capitalist American dream, grounded in and morally justified, at least theoretically, by the historical suffering and present-day plight of the Black man, and subsequently the larger Black community. Album titles like *Reasonable Doubt*, *Hard Knock Life*, and *The Dynasty: Roc La Familia*, his fifth album, clearly exhibit this narrative, an idea that his music, style, and demeanor further emphasized. Even the song that initiated the battle is called "Takeover," with an obvious correlation to criminal turf war and ideas of colonialism and manifest destiny.

As his fifth album signifies, the name of his label, Roc-a-Fella, references the American financial empire—a salute to the wealth-making potential of hip-hop capitalism—while the vernacularization of the phonetics of the Rockefeller name changes its meaning. He employs the slang term "to rock," which in one context means to hit, punch, knock out, or even shoot, as in to "rock one to sleep" or even "rock one's world" in a negative way. This phrase is one Nas will re-vernacularize, further signifying the term in "Ether" when he says, "I rock hoes, y'all rock fellas"—"rock" in this sense meaning to wear, use, hang out with, or be seen with.

Correlative to his opponent, Nas's moniker, God's Son—inked across his abdomen and the cover of his sixth album—proclaims him as a Jesus figure, a human incarnation of the spirit of God. It speaks to an overarching theme of biblical and philosophical consciousness present throughout his discography. This theme plays out explicitly over the spectrum of his first seven albums. Nas's debut album, *Illmatic* (1994), announced the barely 20-year-old as a prodigy, a bright and morning star. *It Was Written* (1996), *I Am* (1999), and *Nastradamus* (1999) weaved the conceptual thread of divine prophecy. *Stillmatic* (2001), the album that contains "Ether," signified his epic debut and proclaimed that the prodigy was not dead, that in fact he was risen. *God's Son* (2002) and *Street's Disciple* (2004) completed the seven.

This narrative, Nas's aesthetic, and his body of work intellectualized the otherwise playboy/gully gangsta narrative of the mid 1990s and early 2000s. The title *God's Son* is a representation of hip-hop consciousness. Nas delivers a visual representation of himself as the crucified Christ in the "Hate Me Now" video. Simultaneously, his alternate moniker, Nasty Nas, de-glorified the idea of the conscious rapper of the same era and proved that he was no martyr to be sacrificed. Together, the dual faces of the rapper etched an image of Nas that is nearly indistinguishable from his on-screen character Sincere (*Belly*, 1998). The loyal, justified gangster standing atop a moral high ground. The prophet with a pen, peering thoughtfully through gold-rimmed glasses. More than 20 years later, Nas remains seen by many as the quintessential, conscientious rapper, an intellectual poet smoldering behind a book.

At the height of his early stardom, Jay-Z seemed to most a Goliath-sized opponent, yet Nas proved to be no weak, meek David, releasing "Ether" on Jay-Z's birthday. This hardly publicized fact reveals the raw nature of their presently resolved conflict. The track came as a deafening, calculated response to Jay-Z's escalation of warfare six months earlier, when after years of cold word subliminals, Jay-Z launched Takeover before a crowd of 10,000-plus at the infamous Hot 97 Summer Jam. The performance was undeniably epic, featuring an appearance from none other than Michael Jackson. When faced with what may have seemed to others an unbeatable force, Nas struck with venom and precision. The venom of the tongue and the precision of the pen. He struck at the soul, lyrically dissecting the core of his opponent's reputation, and in listening, we all heard that which we can never un-hear. We saw images we could never clean from our minds' eyes. Images conveyed in the lyrics "Tae-Bo ho," "getting chased through your building," with whiskers like a rat," and "scared to smile, they called you ugly" are unforgettable. Even more, Nas's attack goes beyond mere insults to critique his opponent's assimilation and perpetuation of capitalist greed. In his extension of the "Roc-A-Fella" wordplay, Nas speaks directly to this: "Rockafeller died of AIDS, that was the end of his chapter/And that's the guy y'all chose to name your company after? He feminizes and "sons" his rival:

> Y'all niggas deal with emotions like bitches
> What's sad is I love you 'cause you're my brother
> You traded your soul for riches
> My child, I've watched you grow up to be famous
> And now I smile like a proud dad, watching his only son that made it.

To witness a takedown of this nature changes the way we see his opponent forever. These words, these images, the information they carry, once released into the ether, may never be retrieved.

It is crucial to note that unlike the conflict between white Republican lawmakers and CRT or, in the greater historical conversation, between perpetrators of systemic racism and challengers from the Black resistance, the conflict between Jay-Z and Nas is not one of power, racial dominance, or oppression. Rather, their conflict derived from personal affairs and professional competition—in other words, beef. As rival members of an oppressed social group, their difference is one of artistic presentation and liberation strategy. While one chooses artistic and philosophical nationalism, the other chooses assimilation as a means to use the master's tools against him. Still, their artistic battle serves as a narrative through which we can envision victory against a formidable attack—a parable that illustrates the viability of conscientious criticism and impenitent truth in the face of illusionist fanfare and imperialist takeover. Like Nas's epic track, CRT also aims at the very spirit of American racism, breaking it down to its most fundamental particles.

IT WAS WRITTEN

What you call an infinite brawl, eternal souls clashing?
War gets deep; some beef is everlasting

—Nas ("One Mic," 2001)

Like our material world, CRT did not emerge fully formed. It was written. Its foundations were laid meticulously over time, structures formed by hand, and bodies of work constructed from the elements of the Black intellectual universe. Despite its sudden appearance in the media world, the truth is that CRT, like all other societal occurrences, was born out of a string of events over the course of centuries. The stars have aligned for its existence, and perhaps even the legal and sociopolitical attack it now faces.

CRT borrows philosophy from Jacques Derrida and other philosophers, as well as scholarship from prior movements, specifically critical legal studies and the women's rights movement. It builds on the work and ideas of past radical Black leaders and movements such as the Black Power and Chicano movements. It is hard to imagine that these past thinkers and authors had in mind the trajectory that their scholarship would take. This is indicative of the ethereal nature of powerful words, ideas, images, and narratives. Once introduced to the collective psyche, released into the ether so to say, such elements may not be retrieved or controlled, even by their own creators, and will move and grow in the way the universe determines. Likewise, CRT concepts like microaggression are baked into the ways we critique cultural content and read even our daily experiences.

Chapter 23: Into the Ether

In his infamous essay "Who's Afraid of Critical Race Theory?" Derrick Bell (1995) asserts the value of storytelling and experiential discussion in addressing the sensitive issue of racial oppression, emphasizing Daniel Farber's critique of CRT, which calls for racial problems to be viewed from the perspective of marginalized groups (LaPiana, 1998). Bell characterizes CRT as including, in addition to firsthand narrative and allegory, an interdisciplinary approach and unabashed creativity.

I, like many others, who have been aware of CRT for years, find myself now called to study and engage with its concepts and contributions in great depth. If its opponents and the laws they create aim to attack Black intellectuals, artists, and educators indiscriminately, then it seems we must all be armed with individual knowledge and the spirit of a collective, though not necessarily homogeneous, defense. Furthermore, if the greater Black community is to continue to receive and benefit from the invaluable ideas put forth by CRT scholars, then it may serve us well to convey those ideas in languages and terms that are accessible, relatable, and sustainable in the lives of those outside the elite professional sphere. Release them into the ether in forms that may not duplicate their original form or potency but retain the essence of their meaning.

Many fundamental concepts of CRT parallel common Black vernacular phrases, slang, and cultural beliefs; aligning these concepts may allow us to locate and reinforce the presence of CRT concepts in the Black collective mind so as to preserve their essence in other forms. For example, the requirement of action attached to knowledge and understanding, which fundamentally requires activism or resistance on the part of not only the oppressed but also the knowledgeable, can be gleaned in the common saying "When you know better, you do better." It is echoed in the protest phrase "White silence is violence." The principle of interest convergence and/or material determinism might be likened to the acronym coined by Wu-Tang, "CREAM"—"Cash rules everything around me." Though this acronym does not account for the psychic benefit of the social construction of whiteness, the core idea remains. Micro-aggression is essentially what would be referred to in hip-hop as "sneak dissing" or in Black popular culture as "throwing shade." Again, though not exact equivalents, both terms convey the action of insulting or targeting one in a way that is hard to address or prove to others. The tension between the call for nationalism and the tendency of assimilation can be conveyed through expressions like "Whatever's clever," "Get in where you fit in," or "Everything ain't for everybody."

The language of scholarship, in aiming for precision and unambiguous clarity, often further mystifies the meaning and practical application of the knowledge that it seeks to convey. Even the Republican lawmakers understood this. Take note that they knew not to task their suburban constituents with deciphering or even recognizing actual critical race theory. No, it seems this battle exists in the realm of the everyman, so we must respond as such. The power of Black myth, metaphor, and vernacular expression to sustain collective resistance in times of cultural and spiritual warfare is paramount to the survival of CRT and future movements to come.

REFERENCES

Bell, D. A. (1995). Who's afraid of critical race theory? *University of Illinois Law Review*, No. 4, 893–910.

LaPiana, W. P. (1998, July). The diversity of merit [Review of the book *Beyond all reason: The radical assault on truth in American law*, by D. A. Farber & S. Sherry]. *Humanities and Social Services Online.* https://networks.h-net.org/node/16794/reviews/16883/lapiana-farber-and-sherry-beyond-all-reason-radical-assault-truth

CHAPTER 24
Black Zombies
Odell Hall

One could argue that the entire chronicling of American history is an ongoing information war designed to remove the ability of African Americans to self-determine and to find their own place and acquire a piece of the American enterprise. The breaking of Black minds is essential in maintaining the position of the African as a near-permanent underclass on whose shoulders the system of capitalism rests. This positioning is accomplished through the fostering of a cultural cowardice by way of terror-driven capitulation.

America's relationship with Black people is an unending episode of persistent violent coercion, control of the food supply, and a consistent social isolation designed to remove hope and instill a nihilist, defeatist mentality. The societal mores of family, community, and love are systemically supplanted to prevent the congealing of blackness, thus leaving the Black diaspora, and Black Americans in particular, fragmented and in a perpetual *Hunger Games* state. Even if a few break the barriers of despair, they will feel imperiled by their proximity to their less fortunate brethren and conversely foster a jealousy and hunger from them, which makes it all but impossible to coexist. And so the best and brightest will only feel safe away from blackness, their guilt assuaged by proximity to whiteness.

This relationship leads to incredibly damaging side effects. Black people who succeed enough to be in corporate America or in spaces where they are few and far between are often subjected to constant micro-aggressions and held to higher standards, often living in constant fear that their time in the sun will be over and they will end up back in the underclass with the other shoe drops. The "gracious" whites allow themselves to believe that they cannot be racist because of the token Black presence, even while they remind Black people of their novelty.

The foundations of this dynamic are erected at the very beginning of socialization: the American school system. Black children are taught in classes overwhelmingly led by white teachers. According to Pew Research, 79% of teachers in the public school system identify as non-Hispanic white versus 7% who identify as African American (Schaeffer, 2021). No matter the race of their students, these teachers instruct from white-curated, state-sanctioned curricula. Black children in these classes, who are often grossly outnumbered, cannot escape the glaring lack of Black agency consistently presented throughout the telling of American history. American history and its ongoing framing play an extraordinary role as propaganda in a very real war against the advancement of Black people. You were savages when you got here. You did very little to free yourselves. Abraham Lincoln emancipated you. Lyndon Johnson made you citizens. Drugs. Broken homes. You brought this on yourselves. You could not bootstrap yourselves like the pioneers of this great nation did, and now you are complaining. The end. The advent of critical race theory (CRT) as an operative concept in the public consciousness comes as media and propaganda are increasingly repurposed and weaponized to color ideas to suit a political agenda.

In the midst of bombs bursting in air, manifest destiny, and frontier mythology, the history taught in American schools, regardless of the state, features Black people as blips of chains, whips, and proclamations. Harriets. Random rebellions, as if they were few and far between. Sally Hemmings exists solely to spice up Thomas Jefferson's story, with no consideration of her lack of agency to refuse a white man's advance. Blacks were freed by honest Abe, who is hailed by history as the great liberator and savior of America. However, Booth's bullet may have been the only thing that prevented Lincoln from implementing his long-held ideas of recolonizing Black Americans to Central America or the Caribbean once the Union prevailed after the war. Although most of his public thoughts on this issue ended with the Emancipation Proclamation in 1863, we can only guess what a Lincoln unencumbered by war and empowered by a newly unified United States would have been able to enact.

John Brown and his futile freedom fracas are elevated, while Nat Turner, whose freshly hung body was boiled to grease, has only recently been accorded his proper revolutionary stature (Cromwell, 1920). What is not told is that Brown's Harper's Ferry plan was so doomed to fail that Frederick Douglass referred to the raid as "the perfect steel trap." None of the raiding party members survived, and Brown himself was ultimately hanged.

Chapter 24: Black Zombies

Rosa Parks is pictured in history books peering out of the bus window, often with no mention of her occupation as NAACP (National Association for the Advancement of Colored People) secretary or the planning that went into her selection as the figurehead in what would become *Browder v. Gayle* (1956; plaintiffs Claudette Colvin, Aurelia Browder, Susie McDonald, and Mary Louise Smith; W. A. Gayle was the mayor of Montgomery). Bo Bo Till. Medgar. Malcolm. Martin. Nooses, flames, and bullets segue to crack, crime, and contrition. Black people and their stolen labor were the foundation on which Western civilization was built. Yet when history is chronicled, we are forever the rescued. The freed. The inactive participants solely present to further the narrative of the greatness of whiteness.

The answers to these most primal quandaries of the Black American existence find their roots in the past, but these items are removed from school books and buried in history. When unarmed Black people are killed by the police and we hear the defense that the police feared for their lives, we are not taught that this defense was first used in *Rex v. Wemms*, the trial of the British soldiers arrested for the murder of Crispus Attucks during what became known as the Boston Massacre (Massachusetts Historical Society, n.d.; Rotunda, n.d.). Attucks, a Black man of Native American heritage who had escaped slavery, was working as a seaman and rope maker. He and other colonists engaged in the most American protest—foreigners taking their jobs (Friends of the Public Garden, 2021; Palliser, 2014)—when British soldiers, already unpopular because they were Britain's tax cops, came into a tavern to inquire about an advertised part-time job. Things escalated into the Boston Massacre, considered the tipping point to the Revolutionary War. Attucks and four other protesters were shot dead in the ensuing conflict. Future president John Adams defended the British soldiers in court and employed the same race-driven fear-mongering used in the twenty-first century to make teenager Michael Brown seem like a rampaging supernigger. Adams described the scene with Attucks as the lead in the following narrative as part of his summation:

> Now to have this reinforcement coming down under the command of a stout Molatto fellow, whose very looks, was enough to terrify any person, what had not the soldiers then to fear? He had hardiness enough to fall in upon them, and with one hand took hold of a bayonet, and with the other knocked the man down: This was the behaviour of Attucks;- to whose mad behaviour, in all probability, the dreadful carnage of that night, is chiefly to be ascribed.

> And it is in this manner, this town has been often treated; a Carr from Ireland, and an Attucks from Framingham, happening to be here, shall sally out upon their thoughtless enterprises, at the head of such a rabble

of Negroes, &c. as they can collect together, and then there are not wanting, persons to ascribe all their doings to the good people of the town. (Virtual Americana, n.d.)

Ignore the fact that the very first bullets for the sake of this country were caught by Crispus Attucks. And that the defense of the British soldiers who fired the shots, proffered by a future president nonetheless, would form the precedent for the present-day idea of qualified immunity, which protects so many police personnel from being punished for ending the lives of so many unarmed Black men on the basis of fear for their lives.

These incidents, and so many more, are hidden from Black children during their formative years, thus robbing them of the ability to see themselves as history makers with the capacity for self-determination. That they have a claim to the spoils of the empire. That their experience on these shores was absolutely necessary for the survival of the republic that hates them. And so we are here now, well into the twenty-first century, and Black people are still pressed to defend their humanity and their American citizenship. Our dehumanization is at the heart of how America treats us and how we treat each other. Black people have been conditioned to hate themselves. And even when that chain is broken, the process necessary to break through erodes our compassion for our brothers and sisters who did not make it. Giving Black children ammunition in this war would fortify them in the earliest stages of the systemic assault on their self-esteem.

CRT is an attempt to challenge or disrupt the idea that racism emanates from people. The true power of racism and its ability to disrupt the lives of Black people is not in a pickup truck–driving, Confederate flag–waving old white man. Rather, it is the laws, the systems, and the societal mores that reproduce, reinforce, and empower racism. Its value is in the recognition that race is the central element of American infrastructure. The underpinnings of capitalism have always been centered on the exploitation of those at the bottom of society, and chattel slavery essentially created and maintained that lower tier with the bodies of enslaved Africans.

The native population had the lay of the land and an initial population advantage. They would not be enslaved; they would have to be removed and reduced. Through bullets, bribery, the breaking of treaties, and germ warfare, along with the destruction of the food supply (the buffalo), the soon-to-be Americans treated the native population with extreme prejudice. The question of labor still remained, particularly because of the brutal temperate weather of southeastern North America. American history is designed to draw as little attention as possible to the murderous violence that shaped the American landscape. But in doing so, its structure reduces the accomplishments of Black people, minimizes the opposition to a free Black people, and discourages the nurturing of self-determination in Black children through the lens of blackness. From the very beginning of our time in this country, the illegality of Black literacy cast chains on our children and a ceiling on Black minds, limiting their aspiration for the high ideals of liberty and justice. The ruling class has always been keenly aware of the power of ideas and stood firm in their reluctance to enable the capacity for free thinking in Black minds.

Present-day white Americans hide behind the fact that they "owned no slaves" and "don't see color," because their ignorance of what actually happened is a particularly snug blanket inside which they sleep comfortably. Present-day Black people have to exist in a world where they seemingly did not exist before they were chained and in which Black people created nothing. They have been severed from their own greatness and have had their history already shaped by omission. As if there was only one slave rebellion. You see the youth saying that the slaves were not their ancestors as they stayed enslaved and did not resist. However, Maroon societies of perpetual resistance to enslavement exist in almost every country where slavery was the preeminent way. The old colonial powers gave up chattel slavery earlier than the United States because they could no longer afford the military costs of suppressing constant insurrections and micro-guerilla wars in their foreign colonies.

The movement against CRT is primarily driven by the idea that the framing of history through a lens that identifies the force that systemic racism has exerted on the course of American history would make white Americans undeservedly the scapegoats for the ills that plague Black people. It presents the idea that some sort of reverse racism would occur that would demonize white people. This idea runs counter to the aim of CRT, which is to emphasize laws, systems, and mores. CRT remains vulnerable because its application is open to discourse from a decidedly racist opposition that can frame it as a theory that can be disputed. It transfers the immutable truth of events that have actually transpired into the realm of theory, which can be disproven. Opposing ideas are given equal footing in any discussion irrespective of how baseless and unsupported they may be. Hip-hop's decentralized nature, despite the concentration of control in the music business, allows for ideas to be spread without a filter.

The power of hip-hop's enduring and consistent narrative is its capacity to allow those at the bottom, Black people in particular, to have equity in telling their stories. Its practitioners provide a view into their realities to relay what happened through the lens of an active participant. Whether or not those stories align with some overarching moral sensibility or collective truth is immaterial. The opportunity to relay what happened is at all times present, with no preference for the meek or the mighty.

Couched in these stories is the ongoing Black struggle to survive, which was presented in every genre of Black music that came before. How to get over before we go under. Instead of survivor's guilt, we find joy in survival and give thanks. We take pride in perseverance and draw lessons from defeat. But as Black people living in the wealthiest country, built by our free labor, too often we find that there is no place for us. What hip-hop has done is provide a specific agency to Black people by allowing the world at large to see things through the Black lens. Once the culture moved toward storytelling and the continuance of the oral tradition, we began to see how powerful a tool it could be in presenting the authentic Black urban experience to the masses.

Melle Mel, widely regarded as the first hip-hop lyricist, gave us a glimpse in his seminal hip-hop work "The Message," but it is his less heralded song "Beat Street Breakdown" that truly cemented the power of hip-hop to use the dark present as a tool to erect an Afrofuturist lens on world affairs, as seen in the following explosive lyrics:

> A newspaper burns in the sand
>
> And the headlines say "Man Destroys Man"
>
> Extra extra, read all the bad news
>
> On the war for peace that everybody would lose
>
> The rise and fall, the last great empire
>
> The sound of the whole world caught on fire
>
> The ruthless struggle, the desperate gamble
>
> The game that left the whole world in shambles
>
> The cheats, the lies, the alibies
>
> And the foolish attempts to conquer the sky
>
> Lost in space, and what is it worth?
>
> Huh, the President just forgot about Earth
>
> Spendin' multi-billions and maybe even trillions
>
> The cost of weapons ran in the zillions
>
> There's gold in the street and there's diamond under feet
>
> And the children in Africa don't even eat
>
> Flies on their faces, they're livin' like mice
>
> And their houses even make the ghetto look nice
>
> Huh, the water tastes funny, it's forever too sunny
>
> And they work all month and don't make no money
>
> A fight for power, a nuclear shower
>
> A people shout out in the darkest hour
>
> Sights unseen and voices unheard
>
> And finally the bomb gets the last word

Christians killed Muslims and Germans killed Jews
And everybody's bodies are used and abused
Huh, minds are poisoned and souls are polluted
Superiority complex is deep rooted
Leeches and lices, and people got prices
Egomaniacs control the self-righteous
Nothin' is sacred and nothin' is pure
So the revelation of death is our cure
Hitler and Caesar, Custer and Reagan
Napoleon, Castro, Mussolini, and Begin
Genghis Khan and the Shah of Iran
Men spill the blood of the weaker man
The peoples in terror, the leaders made a error
And now they can't even look in the mirror
'Cause we gotta suffer while things get rougher
And that's the reason why we got to get tougher
So learn from the past and work for the future
And don't be a slave to no computer
'Cause the children of Man inherit the land
And the future of the world is in your hands

Melle Mel spoke of nuclear proliferation, the Arab–Israeli conflict and geopolitics, as well as a future driven by computers and technology overtaking man as the dominant force under the auspices of a humanity bent on self-destruction. On a more personal level, hip-hop, which rose from the fires of urban decay became the ultimate vehicle to tell the stories of Black people in the modern era.

Nasir Jones (Nas) makes a particularly compelling case to observe because of his personal history. At age 14, with his father Olu Dara's decision to leave their home, Nasir, along with his brother Jabari and with Olu Dara's support, dropped out of the New York public school system. Such a decision on face value would seem like a recipe for disaster, but Olu Dara, with his Mississippi roots, recognized the innate anti-blackness of the New York school system and its penchant for destroying the self-esteem of Black male children. It was certainly a gamble that could have ended in tragedy as, to paraphrase Baldwin, if you turn your back on society as a Black man, you could very well die. And if Nas wanted to be anything other than an artist or someone who operated on the fringes of society, it almost certainly would have been a suboptimal outcome. Nas chronicled this journey in "Breathe"

(2008) from his *Untitled* album, a tour de force of pro-Black exposition. He notes,

> I'm fresh out of city housing, ain't have too many options
> Pennies on a pension or penitentiary bounded
> Plenty Henny in me, envy was simply they trend, see
> My enemy was every hater that was bigger than me

Even in a metropolitan, northern and supposedly progressive "melting pot" city as New York, its Black citizens who are forced to make daily choices such as this one: to consider removing their Black male children from an overtly hostile learning environment designed to minimize their contribution to society at large. A cursory examination of Nas's catalog unearths a rich, consistent legacy of introducing concepts and ideas that act in the manner of a CRT approach, challenging the prevailing American zeitgeist and overarching power structure in the name of Black survival and progress.

Nas is an artist whose project-based milieu enables him to reach the underclass with a sincerity that isn't off-putting, and his approach has endeared him to millions of listeners, allowing him to coexist as a multi-platinum commercial artist and a believable griot of street tales and blackness. From the very first recorded verse, Nas placed himself on the opposite side of the mainstream. In his universally lauded seminal verse from Main Source's "Live at the BBQ," Nas hurls himself headlong into our consciousness with the line "Nasty Nas is a rebel to America, police murderer, I'm causing hysteria," which placed him squarely in opposition to the prevailing societal order.

Nas was clearly devoted to giving a voice to the ghetto, even to the detriment of his career, often making song choices that eschewed pop ambition and, until very recently, barred him from Grammy accolades. A central theme is the effect of poverty on intra-Black relationships and how the allowance of a few elite Black people in the face of such mass paucity generates jealousy and envy and the conditions for urban warfare, which is really a scarcity-driven conflict for resources.

While conservative pundits and news organizations deliver notions of "Black-on-Black crime" in an attempt to reduce the humanity of Black people and ignore the idea that starving people make bad decisions to keep living, Nas goes deeper, with a far more intimate examination and allegorical references to multiple conflicts that exist in places with high Black populations and low opportunity. The 2001 "Every Ghetto," from the much-lauded *Stillmatic*, expounds on this idea with striking efficiency. Nas notes regretfully,

Chapter 24: Black Zombies

> Was once a young gangsta hangin' with youth offenders
> But since I tasted paper it started losin' the friendships
> Watchin' kids freeze in winters, they still poor
> How could I tease them with Benzes and feel no remorse?
> Drivin' past them in the lively fashion, diamond colors clashin'
> Red stones, blue stones, red bones and black ones
> Fuck did I expect with bucket seats in a Lex
> And spendin' time in Chuckie Cheese with Little Des?
> Got guns when I'm with my daughter
> Hate to bring a violent aura in her presence
> She know what daddy taught her, it's lessons
> Black princess, it's a ugly world
> I put my life up for yours, see I love that girl

Nas acknowledges that his ascension meant separation from his old environment; for his own safety and that of his family, he was forced to separate himself from the criminal element in which he was once immersed. He does not forget that while fortune smiles on him, the ones he left behind are still starving, and while he can still visit, it would be cruel to flash the ostentatious trappings of wealth to a people regularly forced to consider crime in order to survive. Tragically, he notes that even when out with his child, to introduce her to the place where he came up, he cannot be unarmed and must always be on his guard because he inhabits a place of envy and jealousy for those for whom the ghetto is inescapable. He is forced to shorten the childhood of his seeds with knowledge of the cold world, as many Black parents do when their children arrive at a still-too-young age when society begins to identify them as threats to the prevailing order.

Nas alludes to the survivor's guilt that so many athletes and entertainers from these areas feel when they make it out of poverty but leave behind lifelong friends or, more dangerous, bring some of those friends along who are ill suited for the new lifestyle. He artfully introduces the conflicts of colorism and warfare between the Bloods and Crip gangs through allegorical reference to his jewelry (red bones and black ones, red stones and blue stones, respectively). The leverage of any advantage, whether physical or territorial, to escape the trappings of urban decay does not exist in a vacuum, and Nas ties these things together with a succinct efficiency.

In this, we witness truly powerful social realities from a personal, intimate, anecdotal vantage point that goes deeper than clinical observation. The absence of the arm's length observation reduces the opportunity to observe truly human relationships and interactions as some sort of a statistical relationship. It is at once informative and incredibly humane to present these situations as stories of people and not as observations of data points in a survey, where you can create a social distance from the horrors that real-life people face. Nas effectively disarms our expectation of simple, flippant statements by forcing listeners to deal with people in real-life situations and reducing the proximity between the ghetto and the mainstream without the romanticism of dangerous situations that is rampant in American popular music.

To further this, Nas goes elsewhere to introduce the idea that no matter what ghetto you inhabit, the same forces exist to create the same tension and stresses for Black people. While Nas is decidedly New York, down to his trademark blue-and-orange Mets and Knicks hats and apparel, he is painfully aware that across the country in cities large and small, places urban and rural, poverty is the root of evil. In his classic "No Ideas Original," Nas raps over Barry White's 1977 classic "Playing Your Game, Baby." Nas expounds,

> We coincide, we in the same light, maybe a time difference
> On a different coast, but we share the same sunlight
> Your part of the world might be like colors and gangs
> While on my side, brothers'll murder for different things
> But it all revolve around drugs, fame and shorties
> Stuck for your bling, stripped for your chain, the same story
> From, Czechoslovakia to Texas metropolis
> The treacherous rastas and the Mexican mafias
> Be scrappin' with tats on they back, violent wars
> Nothin' less than a lethal injection if ever caught
> Courtrooms, eagles and flags, American style
> While in our world, the ghetto stays incredibly foul
> Watchin' for paint chips, don't want no lead in yo' child
> But them gangstas put lead in yo' child, the bezzy be out

From New York to California and ultimately on a global scale, the pressures of poverty and the war for resources and recognition follow the same destructive paths. The paradigms may be different, and the manner in which those wars are waged, and the nature of the combatants and even their races and nationalities may vary, but the results are all too familiar. The need to exist gives rise to the necessity of consumption. Curtail the capacity to consume, and even the lowliest blade of grass will battle with the mightiest redwood for soil, water, and nutrients. This is a universal truth, which is somehow always lost when it relates to consideration of the condition of Black people in America, whether in textbooks or in mass media. It is as if Black people just dropped out of the sky impoverished and belligerent, never with a cause-and-effect rationale assigned to explain why things are what they are. This leads to the conclusion that Black people *must* be inhuman. Because everything else operates by the aforementioned necessity for resources for survival. In just a few lines of verse, Nas encapsulates this principle with dexterity and clarity, in a manner that cannot be legislated or debated.

The role of Black people in the construction of American culture and art is also not lost on Nas. While in 2023, we are still hearing of Black firsts, the rich accounts of Black contributions to this country are still being overlooked and are lost to history. In his controversial album *Untitled*, for which he posed with his logo formed on his back with scars from a whiplash, similar to what the enslaved endured, Nas immersed himself in Black themes and culture, embracing ideologies from scholars such as Ivan Van Sertima and featuring artists such as the Lost Poets (Abiodune Oyewole). The album is a rich exposition and noncommercial, with a scathing commentary against the conservative news outlet Fox News, an indictment of fried foods and their detrimental effects on Black health, and wondering whether the then president-elect Barack Obama would actually bring about the change he espoused. One song, in particular, "You Can't Stop Us," is a triumphant march through history, bringing Black moments from the periphery to the center in celebration of our place in America. Nas raps,

> From Willie Lynch to Willie Hutch, right on, we Superfly
> Made Gucci the shit, Louie too, suits and ties
> Player trophies, pray to Goldie
> Picture wax museums full of Black Panth's and triple OGs
> Aunt Jemina hoes, historic horse shit
> Girls from long time ago, stagecoach with the horse, kid
> Witchdoctors, good ol' pickpockets
> Sip moonshine, so-called coons, shines, and darkies
> I love y'all, pyramids to cotton fields
> To Wrigley Fields, forgotten men who did get killed
> Crispus Attucks, the first blasted
> Peace to the rich lady purse snatcher shot in the back
> I know your hunger kid, I know they hung your dad
> Burnt ya mama crib, I know that hurt you bad
> Minstrel shows, from gold to shackles and back to gold

> We act like we home, matter of fact, we are home
> Bad attitudes, octoroon skin tones
> Slave food turned to soul food, collards to neck bones
> Betsy Ross sewed the first American flag
> Bet she had a nigga with her to help her old ass!

Nas shouts out to Stagecoach Mary, made popular again with the 2021 Netflix Black Western, *The Harder They Fall*, as well as the aforementioned Attucks and his status as the "first blasted." He notes how Black swagger has elevated even luxury brands such as Gucci, which were not intended for the poor but were advanced by urban designers to the point where they eventually copied designs from the Harlem legend Dapper Dan, whom they once sued for trademark infringement. Nas notes the advance of Black civilization from "gold to shackles back to gold" and from "pyramids to cotton fields to Wrigley Field," while noting the propensity of Black people to make the best of what was given ("slave food to soul food"). A short string of words able to encapsulate hundreds of years of the Black experience.

And so while we acknowledge the necessity of the idea of CRT, we must also recognize its vulnerability with regard to media manipulation and its weaponization by the right as a form of anti-white ideology. Ironically, white Americans, too are victims of the truncation of history and the myth making involved in crafting the American dream. They are unaware that the American system benefits them over Black Americans even as they lose their homes to economic calamities and have been made the villain as the mores of the zeitgeist shift toward diversity and inclusion. They often wonder about this supposed privilege when they too are damaged by economic stratification. Unfortunately for them, CRT has been poisoned to the point where white fragility cannot be amenable to the idea of it.

Hip-hop, and the music of Nas in particular, has proven capable of maneuvering through the obstacles of politics and media criticism. The ideas presented in the music often run counter to what is proposed in schools and even in studies with regard to the Black experience in America and around the world. Regardless of whether that cultural diffusion actually would improve race relations, the music itself has provided jobs and resources not only to the artists but also to the people providing their support systems and infrastructure. The promotion of ignorance and the celebration of anti-Black violence is an unfortunate side effect of the commerce associated with the art. But culture's role in conveying the Black story from an unflinchingly Black vantage point places it squarely in a position to operate where CRT cannot. Hip-hop is a reflection of life and not a theory to be disproven or debated. That

Chapter 24: Black Zombies

proximity to truth is critical to building a true understanding of the role of race in America and illuminating our path forward.

To close, we take a look at Nas's immaculate "Black Zombies." In one song, the rapper totally encapsulates the Black condition in an America that has fractured its collective mentality so completely that it no longer has to actively suppress or chain Black people in order to keep them in line and in a constant state of a *Hunger Games* mentality. If anything ever illustrated the need for CRT or a reasonable facsimile of such, it is "Black Zombies." Peace.

> Uhh, yo, you believe when they say we ain't shit, we can't grow?
> All we are is dope dealers, and gangstas and hoes?
> And you believe when they be telling you lie, all on the media?
> They make the world look crazy to keep you inside?
> Why you listen when the teachers at school
> Know you a young single parent out struggling, they think you a fool
> Give your kids bad grades and put 'em in dumber classes
> Killing shorty future, I wonder how do we last it?
> Underground in they casket, ancestors turning
> I'm learning something every day, there is no Lazarus
> Words like God is Greek or Latin
> So if you study Egypt, you'll see the truth written by the masters
> My niggas is chilling, getting high, relaxing
> Envisioning ownership, yo it can happen
> What do we own? Not enough land, not enough homes
> Not enough banks, to give my brother a loan
> What do we own? The skin on our backs, we rent and we ask
> For reparations, then they hit us with tax
> And insurance if we live to be old, what about now?
> So stop being controlled, we black zombies
>
> [Chorus]
> Walking talking dead, though we think we're living (black zombies)
> We just copy-cat, following the system (black zombies)
> Walking talking dead, though we think we're living (black zombies)
> We just copy-cat, following the system (black zombies)
> Ayo, we trapped in our own brain, fucked behind bars
> We've already gone insane

We've already gave up, cut our own heads offs
Stab our own backs and dream too much
Without fulfilling reality; too greedy and
Can't have one or two chains, we need three of them
Can't have one or two guns without squeezing 'em
On our own people and, fuck black leaders
'Cause whites ain't got none leading them, the rhythm is cosmic
Nas is divinity, the deity's prophet
Let's all get down and get up
Victims walking 'round with Down's Syndrome, all stuck
Fainting, shouting, catching Holy Ghost in church
Scared to do it for ourselves 'less we see somebody doing it first
We begged, we prayed, petitioned and demonstrated
Just to make another generation—black zombies
You scared to be yourself, 'cause you in a trance
Feel free, hear the music and dance
If you cared what they think, why wear what they wear, just for you
Dumb niggas with long beards like they Arabs or Jews
Or from Israel, Bismillah al rahman al rahim
Islam's a beautiful thing
And Christian and Rastafari, helps us to bring
Peace against the darkness, which is ungodly
So what's the black man's true religion, who should we follow?
Use your own intuition, you are tomorrow
{*roaring*} . . . That's the sound of the beast
I'm a Columbia record slave, so get paid
Control your own destiny, you are a genius
Don't let it happen to you like it did to me, I was a black zombie

REFERENCES

Browder v. Gayle, 142 F. Supp. 707 (1956).
Cromwell, J. W. (1920). The aftermath of Nat Turner's insurrection. *Journal of Negro History*, 5(2). https://www.journals.uchicago.edu/doi/10.2307/2713592
Friends of the Public Garden. (2021, February 12). *Crispus Attucks: First martyr for liberty*. https://friendsofthepublicgarden.org/2021/02/16/crispus-attucks-first-martyr-for-liberty-february-12-2021/

Massachusetts Historical Society. (n.d.). *Perspectives on the Boston massacre.* https://www.masshist.org/features/massacre/trials

Palliser, J. J. (2014, March 5). The hidden life of Crispus Attucks. *Journal of the American Revolution.* https://allthingsliberty.com/2014/03/the-hidden-life-of-crispus-attucks/

Rotunda. (n.d.). *The Adams papers.* https://rotunda.upress.virginia.edu/founders/default.xqy?keys=ADMS-print-05-03-02-0001-0004&mode=TOC

Schaeffer, K. (2021, December 10). *America's public school teachers are far less racially and ethnically diverse than their students.* Pew Research Center. https://www.pewresearch.org/fact-tank/2021/12/10/americas-public-school-teachers-are-far-less-racially-and-ethnically-diverse-than-their-students/

Virtual Americana. (n.d.). *Boston massacre.* https://virtualamericana.org/massachusetts/boston-massacre/

CONCLUSION

Afraid Not of None of You, Cowards, but of My Own Strength

Walter D. Greason

Anyone who understood and taught critical race theory knew that the backlash was always ongoing. The use of this language was an explicit concession that the conservative right could not convincingly argue against the Black Lives Matter movement. Instead, they attempted to reject critical race theory as a paradigm to break the shackles of white supremacy, not on African Americans and immigrants, but on white Americans. Nothing illustrates the potency of this power more than Nas's first album, *Illmatic*. Hip-hop started as an art form to allow the truly disadvantaged, in William Julius Wilson's jargon, to express themselves and feel free. By the time Nasir Jones (Nas) entered the booth, the movement had already begun to redefine the social and economic conditions that young Black people faced. Over the next 20 years, hip-hop created a new sense of purpose and consensus that questioned, if not outright rejected, the core principles of traditional conservatism. It forced white Americans to listen, to learn, and to accept new voices and perspectives under the banner of American democracy. As the authors in this collection demonstrate, hip-hop was not simply an aesthetic, it was an epistemology—a fundamental transformation of the ways people know themselves and their world. In this way, the clapback—the consequences—that followed the divisive and manipulative condemnation of critical race theory was truly illmatic. Deception may travel with great speed, but truth will inevitably overcome it as people pursue their own ideals of freedom.

The collected authors in this text offer a multidisciplinary range of evidence and methods to counter the rhetoric that defined the latest moment of white backlash. The first five chapters present theoretical interventions in legal analysis and education. The combination of these two approaches reflects the legacy of the *Brown v. Board of Education* (1954) decision, where the rationale that "separate was inherently unequal" prevailed because the disparities between white schools and Black schools were so obvious and crippling. This definitive experience for generations of Americans then provokes the second section of the text, where testimonies and speculative art become the platforms to move readers beyond the limitations of past versions of systemic racism. The third section provides a crucial approach to understanding white identities through the lens of hip-hop and Afrofuturism, breaking the psychological hold on Europeans worldwide and convincing them of their common humanity with Indigenous, African, and Asian people. The final chapters examine the structural creation of justice and equity through the emerging trends in urban design and architecture, providing a new inspiration for the next generation of emcees to build the communities they always imagined.

When Nas crafted the lyric "Afraid not of none of you cowards but of my own strength," he captured a psychological advantage that stretched back to the legends of Stagolee and John Henry—defiant Africans whose strength overcame whatever obstacles they faced. The power of Black folklore kept these legends alive until the reality of African American excellence met and exceeded the standard set by these heroic men. Paul Robeson transformed every facet of the world's politics and entertainment to make peace the standard of international diplomacy. W. E. B. DuBois reshaped the entire structure of critical inquiry in the Western world to make true science and knowledge production possible. Ella Fitzgerald and Aretha Franklin made music the fundamental magic of spiritual and emotional intelligence to articulate countless legacies of freedom dreams. Malcolm X, Martin Luther King Jr., Fannie Lou Hamer, Ella Baker, and Angela Davis crafted concepts as weapons to dismantle systems of exploitation. Steve Biko, Miriam Makeba, and Nelson Mandela marshaled these weapons to dismantle the remnants of African enslavement and European imperialism. These traditions are the strength that Nas describes. Aime Cesaire and Franz Fanon debated the power of this force as negritude. It is the ability to face violence, terrorism, and oppression with a resilience that defies belief. The strength of blues, jazz, hip-hop, and the entire range of the Black Speculative Arts Movement exceeds anything a conservative pundit and his corporate media sponsors might design. Everyone who understands critical race theory knows that the reactionary racists are the cowards, and the only real barrier to our success as African revolutionaries is our ignorance of the strength we carry in our families and communities.

Let these chapters offer a step forward in understanding our power and abolishing our fears.

About the Authors

Lee E. Ross is Professor of Criminal Justice at the University of Central Florida. A graduate of Rutgers University, his research spans a variety of areas, from his seminal work on religion and social control theory to more recent publications in the areas of critical race theory and criminal justice systems' responses to domestic violence. As the author of *Domestic Violence and Criminal Justice* (2018), his scholarship can be found in a variety of academic journals, including *Justice Quarterly*, *Journal of Criminal Justice*, *Journal of Crime and Justice*, and *Journal of Criminal Justice Education*.

Christel N. Temple is Professor of Africana Studies at the University of Pittsburgh, where she specializes in Africana cultural memory, the intersections of history and literature, comparative Black literature, and cultural theory. She is the author of *Muhammad Ali in Africana Cultural Memory*, *Black Cultural Mythology*, *Transcendence and the Africana Literary Enterprise*, *Literary Spaces: Introduction to Comparative Black Literature*, and *Literary Pan-Africanism: History, Contexts, and Criticism*. Additionally, her essays, commentary, and reviews have appeared in the *Journal of Black Studies*, *Western Journal of Black Studies*, *International Journal of Africana Studies*, *Journal of Pan African Studies*, *CLA Journal*, and more. She is a native of Richmond, Virginia, and earned her PhD from Temple University's Department of Africology and African American Studies.

LaTanya White is the recipient of the North Star and Innovative New Scholar awards for entrepreneurship in education and research. She is an expert in belonging, racial equity, and entrepreneurship. As a result of her leadership and contributions to the education and business administration sectors, Dr. White was recognized by the U.S. Department of State as a Fulbright Specialist. She leverages her research and expertise on Black entrepreneurship and the racial wealth gap to help entrepreneurs and the inclusive organizations that support them develop racial equity in their policies, practices, and programming. Dr. White is a 2x author, TEDx speaker, and founder of Concept Creative Group, a professional and management development training firm focused on empowering Black entrepreneurs, their families, and their communities.

Andre L. Smith writes widely on issues relating to race and administrative law, taxation, sports and entertainment, as well as jurisprudence, including critical race theory, and law and economics. He is the author of numerous articles, book chapters, and manuscripts, including *Tax Law and Racial Economic Justice: Black Tax* (2015). Professor Smith also wrote "Other People's Property: Hip-Hop's Inherent Clashes With U.S. Property Laws and Its Rise as Global Counter Culture" in *The Virginia Journal of Sports and Entertainment Law* (2007) and "If Hip-Hop Is Dead, Did the Law Kill It: How Overzealous Interpretations of Copyright Law Promote Sex and Violence in Hip Hop Music" in *Hip Hop and the Law* (2015).

Ronda Racha Penrice is the editor of *Cracking the Wire During Black Lives Matter* and the author of *African American History for Dummies* and its update, *Black American History for Dummies*. Her work as a cultural critic, entertainment reporter, lifestyle journalist, and Black history enthusiast has appeared in numerous publications, including *theGrio, Essence, The Root, Upscale, Uptown, Medium, The Wrap,* and *Ebony*.

Benjamin Perry Levy (they/them and he/him) is an undergraduate student, educator, and leader at Macalester College in St. Paul, Minnesota, majoring in American studies with an emphasis on Black studies and expecting to graduate in May 2023. Reminded by their mother and maternal grandmother growing up to "never forget their people" and where they come from, Levy's upbringing in Kingston, Georgia; Tulsa, Oklahoma; and Beloit, Wisconsin, has fundamentally shaped how they engage with the community and academic life—with interests ranging from the relationship between memory, new media, and Afrofuturism; to spatial justice and architectural theory; to Black aesthetics and politics. Their interests have led them to conduct qualitative research with Research in Action in Minneapolis, Minnesota, and at the University of Cape Town in South Africa.

R-Son the Voice of Reason is an old dude with a Philly attitude, rhyme skills, and a true school flavor adds two degrees in criminal justice and forty years of comic book nerdery. He takes a mic in his hands, links up with some of the dopest cats around, and becomes R-Son the Voice of Reason! An MC's MC, he delivers extraordinary wordplay and freestyle fire alone, with Mental Advisory, and with the world's greatest bluegrass hip-hop band, Gangstagrass.

Dwayne Matthews began to appreciate hip-hop when he first heard "I Refuse Limitations" by Goodie Mob. While serving as a U.S. Peace Corps community health advisor in Malawi, Africa, he created and launched Malawian Empowerment Through Hip Hop & Organizational Development (METHOD), a program that used hip-hop to reduce youth recidivism. His experience also includes leading a 12-month hip-hop course in a Malawian prison, instructing a "Hip Hop Africa" course at Howard University, and serving as a board member of Words Beats and Life, a D.C.-based nonprofit that serves as an advocate of hip-hop culture. More recently, he was accepted into Howard University's Social Justice Consortium. Originally from Little Rock, Arkansas, Dwayne is currently a sociology Ph.D. student with a focus on criminalization in hip-hop at Howard University.

Bijoun Eric Jordan is a high school English teacher in his 19th year. His greatest professional pleasure is stoking enjoyment of words and ideas and, after school, making students world travelers. Bijoun studied education at New York University, followed by a gap of a year abroad, then a master's in English literature at Hunter College. A self-professed nerd and staunch advocate of the Oxford comma, Jordan is also a consummate hip-hop head and a recovering lyricism addict whose other passions include politics, pop culture, gaming, and creativity. He lives in Brooklyn with his wife, daughter, and son.

Ryan J. Petteway is a public health professor and social epidemiologist—meaning that his research, writing, and teaching focus on the structural factors that shape health opportunities/inequities (e.g., structural racism, sexism, heterosexism). His scholarship integrates critical theory, participatory research, and decolonizing methods to engage notions of epistemic, procedural, and distributive justice within public health knowledge production processes. Before doing all of this, he listened to Nas, Mobb Deep, and Nina and drank orange drinks while conducting observational studies of project life. He reads Langston and Dunbar, Audre and Baldwin, Fanon and hooks while running real-time PCRs in an infectious disease lab. He drops bars and closes open mics for repair. Some bars, never caught, still roam free in the wild as he types this . . . in Portland, Oregon, sippin' dark roast and trying to keep his Griffey Max 1 Freshwaters dry.

Michael B. Dando, English professor at Saint Cloud University, holds a PhD from the University of Wisconsin–Madison. An author who specializes in science fiction and fantasy novels, his research explores how students engage youth culture and sense making during academic endeavors in ways they find personally meaningful. In particular, he studies how students and teachers use elements of hip-hop to interpret and assimilate central representations of self, community, and a prosocial worldview, and how educators might enhance these environments to provide rich learning experiences that students will see as highly connected to formal tools and ideas. This work involves closely attending to the design of representations and tools within these academic spaces as well as the artifacts (both tangible and intangible) constructed by teachers and students. His writing appears, or is forthcoming, in SAGE publications, *African American Intellectual History*, and *Race, Gender, and Class*.

John Jennings is Professor of Media and Cultural Studies at the University of California at Riverside. Jennings is co-editor of the Eisner Award–winning collection *The Blacker the Ink: Constructions of the Black Identity in Comics and Sequential Art*. Jennings is also a 2016 Nasir Jones Hip Hop Studies Fellow with the Hutchins Center at Harvard University. Jennings's current projects include the horror anthology *Box of Bones*, the coffee table book *Black Comix Returns* (with Damian Duffy), and the Eisner Award–winning, Bram Stoker Award–winning, *New York Times* best-selling graphic novel adaptation of Octavia E. Butler's classic dark fantasy novel *Kindred*. Duffy and Jennings recently released their Bram Stoker Award–nominated graphic novelization of Butler's prescient dystopian novel *Parable of the Sower* (Abrams ComicArts). Jennings is also the founder and curator of the Abrams Megascope line of graphic novels.

David Brame is blackity Black and an Afrofuturist, and refuses to comb his hair. He'd rather spend that time making comics. He's worked on titles such as *Is'Nana the Werespider*, *Medisin*, *Baaaad Muthaz*, *Box of Bones*, and *Necromancer Bill*. He lives in Mexico. You can follow him on graphicpoetics.biz or on Instagram @amazingdavidbrame.

Zebulon Vance Miletsky is Associate Professor of Africana Studies at Stony Brook University, New York. His new book, *Before Busing: A History of Boston's Long Black Freedom Struggle*, was published in December 2022. Dr. Miletsky is a historian specializing in recent African American history, civil rights and black power, urban history, mixed race and biracial identity, and hip-hop studies. His research interests include African Americans in Boston, Massachusetts; northern freedom movements outside the South; mixed-race history in the United States and passing; and the Afro-Latin diaspora. He is the author of numerous articles, reviews, essays, and book chapters and is currently working on an edited volume on new directions in Boston African American history and school desegregation. He is also at work on his second monograph, a history of interracial marriage and racial passing in Boston and in Massachusetts. He earned his PhD in African American studies with a concentration in history from the University of Massachusetts at Amherst in 2008.

Stacey Robinson is an artist from Albany, New York, who creates graphic novels, art exhibits, and other multimedia works of art that explore the idea of "Black utopias" through an Afrofuturist lens. Robinson graduated from Fayetteville State University with a Bachelor of Arts and went on to complete his Master of Fine Arts as an Arthur Schomburg Fellow at the University of Buffalo. He is part of the collaborative artist duo Black Kirby alongside John Jennings, which explores Afro speculative existence through the aesthetic of Jack Kirby. Robinson's artwork explores the idea of futures where Black people are free from the harmful impacts of colonialism. His work can be seen around the world at

Modern Graphics in Berlin, Bucknell University, and the Schomburg Center for Research in Black Culture.

Matthew Teustch is currently the director of the Lillian E. Smith Center at Piedmont University. He's published articles and book reviews in various venues, including *LEAR*, *MELUS*, *Mississippi Quarterly*, *African American Review*, and *Callaloo*. Matthew's research focuses on African American, southern, and American literature. He is the editor of *Rediscovering Frank Yerby: Critical Essays* (2020), and his current project examines Christopher Priest's run on *Black Panther*.

Michael A. Gonzales is the coauthor of the seminal music text *Bring the Noise: A Guide to Rap Music and Hip-Hop Culture*. A former writer-at-large for Vibe, The Source, and Ebony, he has written essays for *Essence*, *The Paris Review*, *The Village Voice*, *Wax Poetics*, *CrimeReads*, *Longreads*, and Soulhead.com. His Black book series The Blacklist appeared in Catapult. Gonzales's short fiction has appeared in *The Oxford American*, *The Magazine of Fantasy & Science Fiction*, TaintTaintTaint.com, *Under the Thumb: Stories of Police Oppression* (edited by S. A. Cosby), *Black Pulp*, *The Book of Extraordinary Femme Fatale Stories* (edited by Maxim Jakubowski), and *Get Up Offa That Thing: Crime Fiction Inspired by James Brown* (edited by Gary Phillips).

Kat Moore is a PhD candidate in English/creative nonfiction at the University of North Texas. Her essays have been published in *Brevity*, *Creative Nonfiction*, *Image*, *Hotel Amerika*, *Passages North*, *Diagram*, *The Rumpus*, *Entropy*, *Hippocampus*, *Whiskey Island*, and *Salt Hill*, among others. An essay of hers appears in the anthology *Bodies of Truth: Personal Narratives on Illness, Disability, and Medicine*. She was a 2021 Bread Loaf Writers Conference Scholar. Her work has also been supported by the 2022 Tin House Winter Workshop and a 2017 SAFTA (South Asian Free Trade Area) residency.

Allen Chukwuhdi is a psycho-historian. He attended Fordham University, where he majored in both history and psychology. He is currently a PsyD candidate at the Boston Graduate School of Psychoanalysis. "It was my enthusiasm for history, and specifically Black history, colonialism, and the trans-Atlantic slave trade, that induced me to employ the psychological sciences. I believe that history and historical figures cannot be properly investigated without it." Chukwuhdi is interested in developing psychological interventions in Black communities that incorporate cultural solutions and use history to develop identity cohesion as well as to challenge constructed narratives.

Dory Lerner earned her BA in sociology from Willamette University in Oregon and her MA in museum education from Tufts University in Massachusetts. For more than 20 years, Dory has created engaging experiences in museums, schools, libraries, and community centers. As the

K–12 educator at the National Civil Rights Museum in Memphis, Tennessee, she develops programs and curricula to inspire learners of all ages and encourage activism. She served at the King Center in Atlanta, Georgia, the Field Museum, and the DuSable Museum of African American History in Chicago, Illinois. For Dory, growing up in Memphis instilled a strong moral conscience for racial and economic inequities both historically and in the modern context. Dory has volunteered and served on the board of Memphis Artists for Change and led a community vegetable garden with local youth for more than a decade.

Kurt Wagner is the university librarian of the Murry and Leonie Guggenheim Memorial Library at Monmouth University in West Long Branch, New Jersey, where he oversees the mission to cultivate an up-to-date collection that is excellent in breadth and depth across all resources and media types. Wagner works with the library staff as well as external stakeholders to identify, evaluate, and implement programs that improve services and facilities, enhancing the quality of resources and the operating efficiency of the library. Wagner has been a member of the Virtual Academic Library Environment of New Jersey since 2000 and is currently a member of its executive committee. Wagner is also a member of the American Library Association, the Library and Information Technology Association, the New Jersey Library Association, and the *Atlantic Journal of Communication*'s editorial advisory board. Wagner was awarded the New Jersey Library Association Technology Innovation Award in both 2009 and 2013 in part for his leadership and management of project teams.

Asha Criner is an undergraduate student studying neuroscience and urban studies at Macalester College in Saint Paul, Minnesota. In 2020, she guest-authored an op-ed for *Detroit Free Press*, a Pulitzer Prize–winning newspaper, discussing the consequences of insufficient Black representation in academic/high school curricula—a direct response to the social upheaval that arose after the murder of George Floyd. As a graduating high school senior, she was the recipient of the William Keane Award, which recognizes one student for exemplary achievements in writing.

C. N. E. Corbin studies the relationships between society and nature within the built environment by investigating the concept of the green city within the United States. As an environmentalist and political ecologist, her work focuses on public green spaces and how urban "sustainable development" initiatives and environmental policies and practices affect and shape land use and urban park access. Professor Corbin examines both sides of environmental (in)justice—the uneven distribution of environmental harms and the uneven development of environmental goods—in which low-income residents and Black, Indigenous, Latinx, and Asian communities are disproportionately exposed to environmental hazards while also being blocked from environmental amenities. She incorporates media studies and visual culture, often deploying speculative fiction and Afrofuturism, to understand how images represent and influence environmental, racial, and spatial understandings of urban spaces.

Elle L. Littlefield is an Afro-Mississippi writer, editor, and professor. A regular contributor to creative and literary projects in the "MemphiSippi" region, she works to document and preserve Black vernacular and culture from the American South. A two-time Callaloo Fellow, she holds an MFA from Sarah Lawrence College. She has served as editor and creative director of *BG Memphis Magazine* and as an assistant editor for *Hieroglyph*. In 2021, she co-curated the Afrofuturist virtual exhibition *Curating the End of the World: Red Spring*, the third installment of the series by the Black Speculative Arts Movement, hosted by Bill T. Jones's New York Live Arts and Google Cultural Institution. Currently, she serves as Assistant Professor of English and Department Chair of Humanities at HBCU Rust College in Mississippi and as a contributing editor at *Obsidian*.

Odell Hall is a Harlem-born, Charlotte, North Carolina–based writer, podcaster, and editor whose work has appeared in *SXSW Magazine*, AllHipHop.com, Planetill.com, *Love Peace and Slander*, *Cracking the Wire During Black Lives Matter*, and various other outlets. His cultural observations have run the gamut of music, politics, economics, society, and technology, across various media. In addition, he is cohost of the podcasts *Firing Squad Radio* and *Illside Radio* and a frequent guest on Volcalo Radio's *Weekend Gabe* show. His publishing company, Kagyai-Hall Publishing, is dedicated to chronicling the journeys and telling the stories of Black people across the diaspora.